DATE DUE

APR - 5 1995	
NOV 2 6 1996	
D·ec 11	
NOV 0 9 1998	
MAR - 1 1999	
MAR 2 2 1999	
MAR 2 0 2000	
APR - 5 2001	
APR - 3 2002	
DEC - 1 2003	

Contemporary China and the
Changing International Community

About the Editors

Dr. Bih-jaw Lin is Director of the Institute of International Relations and a Professor of International Relations at National Chengchi University. He is the author and editor of numerous articles and books, including *Kuo-chi cheng-chih yü wai-chiao cheng-ts'e* (International politics and foreign policy, 1990), *Education in Mainland China: Review and Evaluation* (1990), *Post-Mao Sociopolitical Changes in Mainland China: The Literary Perspective* (1991), *Forces for Change in Contemporary China* (1992), and *Asia and Europe: A Comparison of Developmental Experiences* (1993).

James T. Myers is Director of the Center for Asian Studies and Professor of Government and International Studies at the University of South Carolina. He is the author or editor of numerous works in the field of China studies including *Enemies Without Guns: The Catholic Church in the People's Republic of China* (1991) and *Forces for Change in Contemporary China* (with Bih-jaw Lin, 1993). He is co-editor of *Chinese Politics: Documents and Analysis*, vols. one (1983), two (1986), three and four (both forthcoming) from University of South Carolina Press

Contemporary China and the Changing International Community

Edited by
Bih-jaw Lin and James T. Myers

UNIVERSITY OF SOUTH CAROLINA PRESS

Contemporary China and the changing international community / edited
  by Bih-jaw Lin and James T. Myers.
    p.   cm.
    Selected papers presented at Sino-American-European Conference on
Contemporary China, held 1992.
    Includes bibliographical references and index.
    ISBN 1–57003–024–3 (alk. paper)
    1. Taiwan—Politics and Government—1988– 2. Taiwan—Economic
conditions—1975– 3. Taiwan—Foreign relations—1945– 4. China
Economic conditions—1976– 5. China—Foreign relations—1976–
6. Chinese reunification queston, 1949– I. Lin, Bih-jaw
II. Myers, James T.
DS799.847.C63   1994
951 . 05—dc20
                                        94–11684

CONTENTS

Tables

Figures

FOREWORD

In 1971 the Institute of International Relations (IIR) began to sponsor the annual Sino-American Conference on Mainland China, to be held in the Republic of China and the United States in alternate years. This conference soon became an important forum for Chinese and American scholars to exchange their views and insights on Chinese Communist affairs. Since the mid-1980s a similar conference of Chinese and European scholars has also been held annually.

With the gradual opening of Mainland China and the emergence of the Republic of China in the world community as a significant economic power with a democratic system of government and with increased contacts between Taiwan and Mainland China, many participants in these conferences suggested that these annual meetings also include affairs of the Republic of China. Therefore, the conference was renamed as the Sino-American Conference on Contemporary China. Moreover, many participants suggested that the organizers of the conferences try to bring Chinese, American, and European scholars together to consider problems of contemporary China. In response to this suggestion, the IIR decided that the 1992 conference should be a trilateral Sino-American-European Conference with special emphasis on the Republic of China, the impact of the collapse of the Communist world on Mainland China and related issues. Twenty papers presented at this conference were selected for publication in this volume. As this book is a systematic survey and analysis of both Taiwan and Mainland China in a global perspective in the post-Cold War period, it is believed that readers of this collection of papers may find this work useful in their study of contemporary China.

Hungdah Chiu, Chair
Advisory Committee
Institute of International Relations
National Chengchi University
Taipei, Taiwan
Republic of China

PREFACE

Developments on the Chinese mainland have always been a subject of great interest to intellectuals of the international community. To help both American and Chinese scholars in Taiwan better understand each other's perspectives on this topic, as well as to appreciate the structure and process of change in mainland China, the Institute of International Relations (IIR) at National Chengchi University in Taipei has organized an annual conference in cooperation with American research institutions since 1970. Each year, American and Chinese scholars have met together to share their insights, observations, and experiences. A similar conference series with European scholars began in 1984. The subjects of discussion were different, but they all centered on the study of China.

In view of recent developments in Taiwan and Hong Kong, and in relations across the Taiwan Strait, the IIR and its American and European counterparts decided to put together a trilateral conference in August 1992 to examine different aspects of contemporary China and its relations with the world. Political, economic, and constitutional developments in the Republic of China on Taiwan were the focal points of discussion. Taipei's recent diplomatic thrust was on the top of the agenda, and the participants also addressed relations between Taiwan and the mainland as well as mainland China's adaptation to global change. In particular, the conference provided a forum for exploring the prospects for regional integration from a trilateral perspective. In order that these topics may reach a wider audience, selected papers from the conference have been compiled into this book. A wide range of views are expressed, and it should be remembered that these are the views of the authors themselves and do not represent the opinions of the IIR.

To my colleagues, particularly Ming Lee, Yi-hua Francis Kan, Shen-chun Chang, and Judith Fletcher, who spent so much time and energy organizing the conference and editing the manuscripts, I am deeply grateful. Finally, the IIR wants to thank Dr. Hungdah Chiu for encouraging us to hold such a trilateral conference in Taipei. Without his support, the conference could never have taken place.

Bih-jaw Lin
Director, IIR
May 1993

INTRODUCTION

Two Paths to the Future

James T. Myers

The twenty-first conference on contemporary China focused more attention on the Republic of China than had been the case at any of the twenty pervious conferences. As a result, one cannot help but be struck by the divergent paths taken and the fundamentally different results achieved by the two Chinese revolutions of this century.

In the early 1920s, following the Bolshevik Revolution and the creation of the Soviet Union, at the time when Sun Yat-sen sought to reorganize the Kuomintang and to energize his revolution, there were essentially two models of modernization available in the world. One was the "bourgeois" model represented by the Western democracies; the other was the Marxist-Leninist model represented by the new Soviet Union.

The Soviet Union offered an attractive model for certain Chinese intellectuals. After all, the Bolshevik Revolution had overthrown an imperial system in a large, backward country which had been ruled for centuries by what even the early Russian Marxists considered a variant of "Asiatic despotism" perfected in China and brought to Russia by the Mongols.[1] The newly created Soviet Union seemed to many to be on its way to greatness and to have solved—or to have the potential to solve—many of the problems which afflicted China.

The Marxist developmental model which the Chinese Communists embraced rested upon a number of important assumptions about political and economic arrangements, about society, about the future, and about human nature. These basic assumptions included at least the following six items:

1. *A state stronger than society.* In the Marxist developmental scheme, the state exists for a specific purpose which is the building of socialism and communism, the state does not exist simply to serve the wishes of society, it has its own historic mission. Thus, the bourgeois democratic model is turned on its head as Mao Tse-tung (Mao Zedong) made clear in his essay "On New Democracy." Mao wrote that his revolution would not result in the creation of "old democracy" of the bourgeois type, but would be a "new Democracy" which was a part of the "proletarian-socialist world revolution."[2] The creation of a new democ-

---

1. Karl August Wittfogel, *Oriental Despotism: A Comparative Study of Total Power* (New Haven: Yale University Press, 1957). See chapter 9 for a full elaboration of this argument.
2. Mao Tse-tung, "On New Democracy," *Selected Works of Mao Tse-tung,* vol. 2 (Beijing: Foreign Languages Press, 1965), 343.

racy in China under the leadership of the Chinese proletariat would only be the first stage of the revolution. More important was the second stage; Mao wrote: "The revolution will then be carried forward to the second stage, in which a socialist society will be established in China."[3] There could be no discussion or debate about this future; it was the mission of the new Chinese state after 1949 to realize this Marxist historical destiny.

2. *Collective Ownership*. A second basic assumption of Mao's revolution was that collective or state ownership in the economy was superior to private ownership. Mao wrote: "In the new-democratic republic under the leadership of the proletariat, the state enterprises will be of a socialist character and will constitute the leading force in the whole national economy. . . . [W]e must never establish a capitalist society of the European-American type. . . ."[4]

3. *Central Planning*. The economy of People's China was to be operated according to a central plan. Taken together with the principle of collective ownership, this meant that market forces and private property would have no part to play in the eventual, hoped-for creation of socialism in China. Mao wrote in 1955 that the Party's "general line means the accomplishment step by step of the socialist industrialization of the country together with the socialist transformation of agriculture, handicrafts and capitalist industry and commerce in a period of roughly three five-year plans and thus the attainment of the goal of building a socialist society in China."[5]

4. *Class Struggle*. Central to the Maoist revolutionary vision was the idea that class struggle was the motive force of history. Without economic class struggle there could be no progress toward the communist millennium. Mao wrote: "Classes struggle, some classes triumph, others are eliminated. Such is history, such is the history of civilization for thousands of years."[6] This reliance on struggle caused the Maoists to reject the idea of conciliation and constantly to seek out new class enemies during the turbulent years up to the end of the Cultural Revolution. One by one, Mao turned against the non-Communist "united front" groups which had been his allies during the earlier phases of his movement. These groups included many of those who could have been most useful in the task of building a strong, prosperous, modern China.

5. *Revolutionary Transformation*. Mao's goal was more than merely modernizing China, however; he sought to transform China in a fundamental way according to his own particular vision of a Marxist Utopia. In his essay "On The People's Democratic Dictatorship," he wrote: "the road to the abolition of classes, to the abolition of state power and to the abolition of parties is the road all mankind must take; it is only a question of time and conditions."[7]

---

3. *Ibid.,* 347.

4. *Ibid.,* 353.

5. Mao Tse-tung, "Opening Speech at the National Conference of the Communist Party of China, March 21, 1955," *Selected Works of Mao Tse-tung,* vol. 5 (Beijing: Foreign Languages Press, 1977), 154.

6. Mao Tse-tung, "Cast Away Illusions, Prepare For Struggle, [August 14, 1949]," *Selected Works of Mao Tse-tung,* vol. 4 (Beijing: Foreign Languages Press, 1967), 428.

7. Mao Tse-tung, "On The People's Democratic Dictatorship, [June 30, 1949]," *Selected Works of Mao Tse-tung,* vol. 4 (Beijing: Foreign Languages Press, 1967), 411.

6. *Perfectibility of the Human Species.* None of the assumptions about achieving the Communist Millennium made any sense without the fundamental postulate that human beings are ultimately perfectible on this earth, in this life. Were this not possible, achieving utopia would be but an idle dream. The Party's task, wrote Mao, was to work hard "to create the conditions in which classes, state power and political parties will die out naturally and mankind will enter the Great Harmony."[8] Of course, pursuing perfection in human behavior meant that the Party would have to rely on a generous application of the ultimate sanctions of torture, deprivation and death to those who resisted the Maoist call to join the revolution and, finally, even to many of those who did answer the call.

The record of the policies which flowed from these assumptions is abundantly clear and well known: lack of flexibility in the economy, stifling of innovation, lack of incentives for farmers and workers, enormous waste of human talent, and a history of forty years of turbulence characterized by a succession of convulsive mass movements epitomized by the Great Leap Forward and the Cultural Revolution. It was the wreckage of the Maoist era that the reformers around Teng Hsiao-p'ing (Deng Xiaoping) sought to repair following the Third Plenum of the Eleventh Central Committee at the end of 1978.

All the while a different path was being followed by the "other" China across the water in Taiwan. Indeed, the different path taken by the Republic of China far predates its retreat to Taiwan. As Hungdah Chiu explains in his essay on constitutional development (chapter 1 in the present volume), Sun Yat-sen sought to create a representative system of government which combined both the traditional Chinese and Western systems. "Though he favored the Western separation of powers system of the executive, legislative, and judicial branches, he considered that the traditional Chinese independent civil service examination system and the independent censorate system should be added to the three-power Western system" (p. 7). Because China had no experience with democratic politics, Sun proposed that the Chinese people should undergo a period of Party tutelage under the leadership of the Kuomintang (KMT) in order to educate the people in the exercise of their four fundamental rights of election, recall, initiative, and referendum.

What is important to emphasize here, in contrast to the Marxist principles discussed above, is that these various Nationalist constitutions, beginning with the Provisional Constitution for the Period of Party Tutelage promulgated in 1931, were all based on the fundamental principle that the purpose of the state is to serve society, not to achieve a utopian result in some distant future.

The problems of constitutional change and development in Taiwan and of judicial review are discussed by Jaushieh Joseph Wu in chapter 2 of this volume and by Jyh-Pin Fa in chapter 3.

In the economic realm, as Gee San argues in chapter 4, "The economic development experience of the Republic of China (ROC) on Taiwan has attracted worldwide attention" (p. 69). San discusses the ROC economic development policies in detail and draws our attention especially to the manpower policies which focused on education and vocational training. He also cites the importance of the land reform program which

---

8. *Ibid.,* 412.

eventually gave "land to the tiller" and compensated landlords with commodity bonds and stock in public enterprises. This program stands in stark contrast to the land reform in the People's Republic of China (PRC) which fostered class struggle in the countryside and resulted in the "liquidation" of most of the landlords. In the Taiwan experience, that is, the wealthier class of land owners, rather than being eliminated, were given a stake in the success of the new economic order.

In the final analysis, as San writes, the ROC's development achievements "are no miracle but the result of careful planning and the observation of some basic economic development principles" (p. 84).

In a similar vein, Jan S. Prybyla, assessing the role of the ROC in building a global economy (chapter 5), writes: "Thus far, the ROC on Taiwan, unlike the China mainland and other socialist economies and polities, has been closely attuned to the movement of history and responsive to the rapidly changing requirements of modernization" (p. 103). Likewise, Chu-yuan Cheng (in chapter 6) notes that since the late 1970s, "the Taiwan success story has gained recognition among the world's top economists" (p. 126). Cheng cites the work of four Nobel laureates praising Taiwan and observes that even the leaders in Beijing "have admitted that in the contest of economic growth between the two parts of China, Taiwan appears to be the winner" (p. 126).

Writing (in chapter 20) about the possible relevance of the "East Asian Model" to the Baltic states, Walter C. Clemens, Jr., reaches a similar conclusion. He writes, "The big picture is clear: Those countries that bucked the First World trading system—much of the Third World as well as mainland China—did worse than those that joined it. Despite structural impediments, a late start, and other disadvantages, four low-income countries, Hong Kong, Singapore, South Korea, and the ROC, became medium- and even high-income countries within decades. Their growth benefitted from foreign aid and favorable circumstances, but depended ultimately on their own efforts" (p. 374).

One did not have to be a Nobel laureate, however, to recognize the significant differences which resulted from the different paths taken by the KMT and the CCP (Chinese Communist Party). As indicated above, even the leaders of the PRC had come to recognize the shortcomings of their economic system. And once the revolutionary goals of the Maoist era were put behind them, those leaders, too, sought to bring about an opening and limited marketization of their economy in an effort to achieve economic growth and increase in standards of living.

But this economic shift in direction was not to be entirely smooth and pain-free. Many of the serious problems faced by the Chinese Communist reformers are addressed in the essays in the previous volume in this series, *Forces for Change in Contemporary China.*[9] One significant set of problems concerns the nature of the political arrangements in the post-Communist era. Communism might have failed in the PRC, but what would replace it? What kind of political processes and structures would replace "democratic centralism" under the leadership of the Chinese Communist Party? In fact, the problem was not quite as simple as these questions might suggest.

While outside observers may have concluded that communism was dead in China, the CCP clung to a different notion. Outsiders may see China taking the capitalist road,

9. Bih-jaw Lin and James T. Myers, eds., *Forces for Change in Contemporary China* (Columbia, S.C.: University of South Carolina Press, 1993).

but the CCP has continued to insist that it was building "Socialism with Chinese Characteristics." Moreover, the CCP has insisted on the continued authority of the Four Cardinal Principles, perhaps the most important of which is the Leadership of the Communist Party. Indeed, the CCP seems to want to have it both ways: opening to the outside world and limited marketization of the economy, while at the same time maintaining the monolithic rule of the CCP, a situation which, in the end, may be impossible to maintain.

Despite the rhetoric of "Socialism with Chinese Characteristics," and the insistence of the CCP that they have not abandoned the principles of Marxism, academic discussion about future political arrangements in the PRC continues. In chapter 13 of this volume, Wen-hui Tsai confronts the issue of "Mainland China's resistance to political modernization." Gerrit W. Gong (chapter 14) examines the issue of "peaceful evolution" or "non-peaceful evolution" in the context of the requirements of the new information age.

The two Chinas have followed different paths in their international relations as well. The PRC became a part of the Soviet bloc while the ROC joined the Free World camp. The disintegration of the Soviet Union and the collapse of communism in Eastern Europe have confronted the leaders of the PRC with a world which is fundamentally different from that which existed when they made their revolution. The foreign relations of the PRC in the wake of the collapse of the Soviet Union are examined by Kenneth Lieberthal in chapter 15. Of course, as indicated above, the communist system has not collapsed in China. Despite evidence that China seems bent on pursuing a "capitalist" road in the era of modernization, the "Leadership of the Communist Party" remains one of the Four Cardinal Principles of communist rule in China. The "conundrum" which this state of affairs presents for Chinese foreign policy in the contemporary era is the subject of David Shambaugh's essay in chapter 16. In chapter 17, Tzong-Ho Bau also examines Beijing's diplomatic behavior in a rapidly changing world. He focuses special attention on the persistent problem of relations across the Taiwan Strait.

If the two Chinese revolutions of this century have followed fundamentally different paths up to the present, what might be the prospects for the future? Is some sort of reconciliation between the ROC and PRC in China's future and, if so, on what terms and on the basis of what social, economic, and political principles? If such a reconciliation were to take place, would it put the two Chinese revolutions on the same path to the future at last? Maria Hsia Chang (chapter 11) asserts that peaceful relations between the ROC and PRC are in their mutual interest. "More than that," she writes, "in important ways, Taiwan and the mainland complement each other. The CCP's professed goal is the economic modernization of China. The mainland is poor and backward, but rich in labor and natural resources. Taiwan is land and resource-poor but rich in capital and technology. In an ideal world, the two Chinese entities would cooperate with each other, each contributing its unique talents and assets, complementing the other for its deficiencies. Together, Taiwan and the mainland could rebuild China into a modern world power, restoring it to its historic prominence" (p. 215).

The future imagined by Chang is a beautiful vision. For it to be realized, however, the PRC will have to embrace a path to the future originally rejected many decades ago.

Contemporary China and the Changing International Community

Part One

Constitutional Reform and Political Development in the ROC

CHAPTER 1

Constitutional Development and Reform in the Republic of China on Taiwan

Hungdah Chiu

The Introduction of Western Constitutionalism to China

While China is the oldest living civilization in the world, it is, in comparison with Western countries such as the United States and the United Kingdom, far behind in developing a constitutional government for the Chinese people. The term *"hsien-fa,"* which is the Chinese term for constitutional law, does appear in ancient Chinese literature, but it does not connote the modern meaning of the Western term "constitutional law." In *Kuo-yu* (State chronology of events) written by Tso Ch'iu-ming sometime in the Spring and Autumn Period (eighth to fifth century B.C.), it is stated that "to reward good people and to punish evil people is the constitutional law of a state."[1] Thus, the use of the term constitutional law here does not imply that it is the highest legal order in a state. Therefore, it appears clear that modern constitutionalism, with its principles of separation of powers, checks and balances, and popularly-elected congress and officials, is unknown to traditional China.

In the early nineteenth century, Chinese officials had difficulty in comprehending the American constitutional government system. Thus, one finds the following interesting description of the American government in a memorial submitted by the Viceroy of Canton to the Chinese emperor, dated July 19, 1817:

> The commercial ships of America are . . . numerous and the Americans are most respectful and submissive to us. These barbarians do not have a king, but only a chief (*t'ou-jen* [i.e., headman]). It is their custom to elect several persons who draw lots to serve as chief for four years. Commercial business is managed by individuals; it is not controlled by their chief.[2]

---

[1] *Ta tz'u-tien* (Great dictionary), vol. 1 (Taipei: San-min shu-chü, 1985), 1688.
[2] Lo-shu Fu, *A Documentary Chronicle of Sino-Western Relations 1644-1820*, vol. 1 (Tucson: The University of Arizona Press, 1966), 411.

Although in traditional China the emperor possessed all legislative, executive, and judicial power, the imperial rule was not absolute, and there were some limitations on the emperor's authority in practice, usage, and the teachings of the ancients, particularly Confucius. Beyond that, the censors had the duty to watch and criticize any member of the entire official system, including the emperor.[3] Therefore, the Chinese tradition did embody a counterpart to the modern constitutional limitation on the power of the government, but this counterpart never developed into an effective check on the power of the emperor through an elected body such as a congress or parliament in Western countries.

With the gradual opening of China after the mid-nineteenth century, many Chinese went abroad as workers, students, or visiting scholars. As a result of this contact between China and the West, the Chinese came to know Western political systems and constitutionalism better. In 1889, Japan adopted a Western-style constitution (usually referred to as the Meiji constitution) and soon became an important power. This event also significantly influenced Chinese political and constitutional development.

On June 30, 1895, an intellectual named K'ang Yu-wei submitted a memorial to Emperor Kuang-hsu (1875-1908), urging him to take a series of reform measures. Among the proposed reforms were the creation of a parliament, the adoption of a constitution, and the division of power between the executive, the legislature, and the judiciary.[4] In other words, K'ang proposed a constitutional monarchy similar to that of Japan.ʹEmperor Kuang-hsu, K'ang, and his associates tried to implement part of the reform measures (but not the constitutional aspects) that K'ang had suggested between June 11 and September 20, 1898, but this ended only in K'ang's exile abroad and the "house arrest" of the Emperor himself by Empress Dowager Tz'u-hsi for the rest of his reign.[5]

On June 21, 1900, the Ch'ing government under Empress Dowager Tz'u-hsi, relying on the superstitious Boxers, declared war against the Western powers. The Western powers retaliated by sending an expeditionary force to invade China and soon occupied Peking, and on September 7, 1901, China was compelled to sign the most humiliating peace treaty it ever concluded.[6] The treaty not only required China to pay a heavy indemnity of 450 million

---

[3]Shao-chuan Leng, "Chinese Law," in *Sovereignty Within the Law*, ed. Arthur Larson and C. Wilfred Jenks (Dobbs Ferry, New York: Oceana, 1965), 245-46.

[4]Immanuel C. Y. Hsu, *The Rise of Modern China* (New York and London: Oxford University Press, 1970), 444.

[5]See ibid., 445-51.

[6]Final Protocol between Austria-Hungary, Belgium, Germany, Great Britain, Italy, Japan, the Netherlands, Russia, Spain, and the United States and China for the Resumption of Friendly Relations, signed at Peking, September 7, 1901, in *Consolidated Treaty Series*, vol. 190 (Dobbs Ferry, New York: Oceana, 1969), 61-78.

taels of silver, but also allowed foreign countries to station troops in the Chinese capital, Peking. However, this tragedy forced the Ch'ing government to institute some reforms leading toward constitutional government, in order to undercut the revolutionary movement to overthrow the Ch'ing Dynasty.

In 1905, the tiny constitutional monarchy of Japan defeated the colossal dictatorial Russian Empire. To many Chinese this was proof of the effectiveness of constitutionalism. They also discovered that nearly all leading Western powers were constitutional governments. The famous scholar-turned-industrialist, Chang Chien, commented that "the victory of Japan and the defeat of Russia are the victory of constitutionalism and the defeat of monarchism." He urged Yuan Shih-k'ai, then governor-general of Chihli, to assume vigorous leadership in promoting the cause of constitutionalism.[7]

At the same time, revolutionaries led by Dr. Sun Yat-sen opposed the idea of a constitutional monarchy and contended that it was essential for China to overthrow the Ch'ing Dynasty and establish a republican form of government, which of course would be based on a democratic constitution.

Finally, in July 1905, the Empress Dowager accepted Yuan Shih-k'ai's recommendation to send high officials abroad to investigate foreign political systems as a prelude to introducing a constitution. An inspection mission was soon sent to visit Japan, Great Britain, France, Belgium, the United States, Germany, the Austro-Hungarian Empire, and Italy. The mission returned in July 1906.

The mission reported favorable impressions of the British and German systems of government, but concluded that the Japanese constitution was more suitable to China because of greater similarity between the two countries. On August 27, 1908, the Ch'ing government issued an "Outline of Constitution," a parliamentary law, and prescribed a nine-year tutelage period (1908-17) before the constitution became effective.[8]

On October 10, 1911, revolution broke out in Wuchang, resulting in the abdication of the Ch'ing Dynasty on February 12, 1912. On November 2, 1911, in order to thwart the revolutionary movement, the Ch'ing government promulgated the "Nineteen Articles [on Constitutional Law]," which, however, never entered into force.[9] Therefore, no constitution was ever adopted before the downfall of the Ch'ing Dynasty.

Constitutional Development in the
Republican Period, 1912-46

The Republic of China (ROC) was established on January 1, 1912. A

---

[7]Hsu, *The Rise of Modern China*, 493.

[8]Ibid., 498.

[9]Text in Teaching and Research Office of Constitutional Law and Office of [Research] Materials

twenty-one article General Plan for Organization of the Provisional Government of the Republic of China had been adopted on December 2, 1911 by delegates from ten provinces, and after several revisions it was finalized on January 2, 1912 with the approval of delegates from seventeen provinces.[10] Article 21 provides that the General Plan would be effective until the adoption of the Constitution of the Republic of China. This is the first constitution adopted by China. This constitution bore some striking similarities to the original United States Constitution, as it made the provisional President the real chief-executive, and there was no mention of the basic rights and duties of the people.[11]

On March 11, 1912, a Provisional Constitution of the Republic of China was promulgated.[12] It contained fifty-six articles and changed the American-style presidential system established in the General Plan to the cabinet system based on the French model. A unicameral house, the Senate, was appointed by each province, Inner Mongolia, Outer Mongolia, Tibet, and Tsinghai and was to exercise the legislative power (Article 18). Within ten months, however, the Senate was required to enact laws for the organization of the Congress and its election method (Article 53). On August 10, 1912, the Organic Law for the Congress (House and Senate), the Election Law for the House, and the Election Law for the Senate were all enacted, and an election was soon held in early 1913. On April 8, 1913, the Congress was inaugurated.[13]

When formulating a draft for a permanent constitution on October 31, 1913, the Congress retained the cabinet system.[14] However, President Yuan Shih-k'ai opposed this draft constitution, and on November 4, 1913, he illegally dissolved the Congress. Yuan organized a Constitutional Conference to draft a new constitution, which was promulgated on May 1, 1914.[15] This constitution adopted a presidential system with widespread powers.

Yuan later attempted to restore the imperial system and make himself the emperor of China, but he failed and later died on June 6, 1916. For the next decade, the Chinese government was controlled by different factions of warlords. During this period a warlord, Ts'ao K'un, had himself elected president in June 1923 by the Congress through bribing its members.[16] He

---

of the Department of Law of Peking (Beijing) University, eds., *Hsien-fa tzu-liao hsüan-pien* (Selected materials on constitutional law), vol. 2 (Peking: Peking University Press, 1982), 251-52.

[10]Text in ibid., 253-55.

[11]Herbert H. P. Ma, "Republic of China," in *Constitutionalism in Asia: Asian Views of the American Influence*, ed. Lawrence W. Beer (Berkeley, Calif.: University of California Press, 1979), 40-41.

[12]Text in *Hsien-fa tzu-liao hsüan-pien* 2:256-61.

[13]Lo Chih-yuan, *Chung-kuo hsien-fa yü cheng-fu* (Chinese constitution and government), 3rd printing (Taipei: Cheng-chung shu-chü, 1979), 133.

[14]Text in *Hsien-fa tzu-liao hsüan-pien* 2:262-72.

[15]Text in ibid., 273-80.

[16]Hsu, *The Rise of Modern China*, 575.

promulgated a new constitution on October 10, 1923.[17] However, on November 2, 1924, Ts'ao was forced to resign by another warlord, Feng Yü-hsiang. General Tuan Ch'i-jui was invited by other warlords to be the executive of a provisional government, and Ts'ao K'un's constitution was abrogated.[18] Chief-Executive Tuan promulgated a six-article law on the organization of the provisional government,[19] and in December 1925 he put out a draft constitution.[20] But in April 1926, Tuan's government collapsed.

The Chinese Nationalist Party (Kuomintang, KMT) established a military government at Canton in southern China on August 25, 1917. In 1921, the parliament in Canton elected Dr. Sun Yat-sen as the president of the southern government. On July 1, 1925, the National Government was established at Canton. In June 1926, Chiang Kai-shek launched the Northern Expedition from Canton and on April 18, 1927 declared Nanking as the capital of China. In December 1928, the Nationalist Government unified China, and soon engaged in drafting a new constitution based on Dr. Sun Yat-sen's *Three Principles of the People*, that is, Nationalism, Democracy, and People's Livelihood.[21]

According to Dr. Sun, citizens should have the right of election, recall, initiative, and referendum to participate directly in the governing process. However, because of the extensive land area and large population of China, Dr. Sun proposed to create a National Assembly to represent the people at the central government in the exercise of these four rights.

With respect to governmental functions, he tried to combine the traditional Chinese and Western systems. Though he favored the Western separation of powers system of the executive, legislative, and judicial branches, he considered that the traditional Chinese independent civil service examination system and the independent censorate system should be added to the three-power Western system. Therefore, his ideal government system is a five-power system.

In view of the fact that the electoral system was unknown in traditional China and most Chinese people were illiterate or semiliterate, Dr. Sun proposed to have a period of political tutelage under the leadership of the Chinese Nationalist Party before full democracy was introduced to the whole Chinese nation. During the period of tutelage, the government was to expand education and teach people how to exercise four rights—election, recall, initiative, and referendum—at the local level.[22]

---

[17]Text in *Hsien-fa tzu-liao hsüan-pien* 2:283-98.

[18]Lo, *Chung-kuo hsien-fa yü cheng-fu*, 276.

[19]See ibid., 276-77.

[20]See ibid., 282-87.

[21]See Sun Yat-sen, *The Three Principles of the People*, abridged from the translation by Frank W. Price (Taipei: China Publishing Co., 1981).

[22]See Outline of National Reconstruction, promulgated by the National Government on April 12, 1924. Text in *Hsien-fa tzu-liao hsüan-pien* 2:299-302.

Based on Dr. Sun's theory, the Chinese Nationalist Party, which then controlled the National Government, announced on June 15, 1929 that it planned to end the Period of Political Tutelage by 1935. On June 1, 1931, it promulgated the Provisional Constitution for the Period of Political Tutelage.[23]

On May 5, 1936, the National Government promulgated the Draft Constitution of the Republic of China,[24] which was primarily based on Dr. Sun Yat-sen's five-power system and is unlike any system in the Western democracies. According to this draft,[25] the National Assembly elected by the people is the highest organ of the state. It elects or recalls the President, Vice President, Premier and Vice Premier of the Executive Yuan; the President, Vice President, and members of the Legislative Yuan; and the President, Vice President, and members of the Control (Censorate) Yuan. It may also initiate laws, exercise a referendum on a law passed by the Legislative Yuan, and amend the Constitution (Article 32). However, while the term of a delegate to the National Assembly is six years, the Assembly will meet for one month every three years. Only the President or 40 percent of the Assembly delegates may convene an extraordinary session of the Assembly (Article 31). Therefore, the legislative power, in fact, is delegated to the indirectly elected Legislative Yuan. Otherwise, the people would have great difficulties in supervising the government.

The executive power is vested with the President, who appoints or dismisses the Premier, Vice Premier, and all members of the Cabinet (Article 42). Each member of the Cabinet is individually responsible to the President (Article 59). The President can also veto a bill or other decisions passed by the Legislative Yuan, though the latter may override the President's veto by a two-thirds majority. After overriding the presidential veto, the President may still refer a law or a treaty to the National Assembly for referendum (Article 70).

In short, the Draft Constitution adopted a presidential system without an effective mechanism to check or balance the President's extensive power.

The National Government planned to convene the National Assembly to adopt the Constitution on November 12, 1936. Because of a delay in the election, the scheduled date for convening the National Assembly was postponed to November 12, 1937. However, the outbreak of the full-scale Sino-Japanese War on July 7, 1937 indefinitely postponed the convocation of the National Assembly.

---

[23]Text in ibid., 331-38.

[24]Text in ibid., 370-85.

[25]For a detailed analysis of this draft, see Chin Ming-sheng, *Kuo-min cheng-fu hsüan-pu Chung-hua min-kuo hsien-fa ts'ao-an shih-i* (An explanation of the draft constitution of the Republic of China announced by the National Government) (Shanghai: Shih-chieh shu-chü, 1936). For a summary comment on the draft, see Ch'ien Tuan-sheng, *The Government and Politics of China* (Cambridge, Mass.: Harvard University Press, 1950, reprinted in 1967), 303-6.

The Enactment of the 1946 Constitution

After the end of World War II in September 1945, the National Government convened a "Political Consultative Conference," composed of twenty-nine delegates representing different political parties and nonpartisan groups, from January 10 to 30, 1946. The May 5, 1936 Draft Constitution with its dominant presidential system was severely criticized, and the Conference adopted several radical changes to the May 5, 1936 draft as stated below:[26]

1. The National Assembly should be abolished.

2. The Executive Yuan should correspond to the Cabinet and the Legislative Yuan to the parliament, as in other democratic countries. Members of the Legislative Yuan should be elected by the people directly.

3. The Control Yuan (Censorate) should be transformed into an upper house with its members elected by provincial assemblies.

4. The President should be elected and recalled by representatives of county and provincial assemblies, before the popular election is held.

5. The President should be able to issue an emergency decree through the resolution of the Executive Yuan Council, but within one month the decree must be approved by the Legislative Yuan.

6. Each province should enjoy self-government and home rule.

The National Assembly was convened on November 5, 1946, and on December 25, 1946 it adopted the Constitution of the Republic of China, which entered into force on December 25, 1947. The main contents of this Constitution[27] are summarized below.

1. *Preamble.* It states that the Constitution is enacted in accordance with the teachings bequeathed by Dr. Sun Yat-sen.

2. *Chapter I. General Provisions.* The Republic of China shall be a democratic republic of the people, to be governed by the people and for the people (Article 1), the sovereignty shall reside in the whole body of citizens (Article 2), and there shall be equality among the various racial groups in the Republic of China (Article 5).

3. *Chapter II. Rights and Duties of the People.* All citizens are equal before the law (Article 7), and personal freedoms are guaranteed by a system

---

[26]For the complete text on the constitutional issue decided by the Conference, see Ch'in Hsiao-i, ed., *Chung-hua min-kuo chung-yao shih-liao ch'u-pien—Tui-Jih k'ang-chan shih-ch'i.* Ti-ch'i-p'ien, *Chan-hou Chung-kuo* (Preliminary compilation of important historical materials of the Republic of China—The period of the war resisting Japanese [aggression]. Part 7: Postwar China), vol. 2 (Taipei: Distributed by Chung-yang wen-wu kung-ying-she, 1981 [actual year of publication is 1984]), 240-42. For a summary of this issue, see Ch'ien, *The Government and Politics of China*, 317-18.

[27]English translation in *Republic of China Yearbook 1990-91* (Taipei: Kwang Hwa Publishing Co., 1990), 712-21. For an analysis of the structure of this constitution, see Tsao Wen-yen, *The Constitutional Structure of Modern China* (Melbourne: Melbourne University Press, 1947).

similar to habeas corpus (Article 8).[28] No person shall be subjected to trial by a military tribunal except for those in military service (Article 9). The people shall have freedoms of residence, change of residence (Article 10), speech, teaching, writing, publication (Article 11), privacy of correspondence (Article 12), religious belief (Article 13), assembly and association (Article 14). The people shall have the rights of existence, work, property (Article 15), presenting petitions, lodging complaints, instituting legal proceedings (Article 16), election, recall, initiative, referendum (Article 17), taking public examinations, and holding public offices (Article 18). With respect to duties, the people shall pay taxes (Article 19) and perform military service in accordance with law. In view of the Chinese tradition emphasizing education, the Constitution provides that the people have not only the right but also the duty to receive education (Article 21). There is also a provision guaranteeing those freedoms and rights not provided in the Constitution as long as they "are not detrimental to social order or public welfare" (Article 22). The freedoms and rights enumerated in the above articles "shall not be restricted by law except by such as may be necessary to prevent infringement upon the freedoms of other persons, to avert an imminent crisis, to maintain social order, or to advance public welfare" (Article 23). Article 24 establishes the state compensation system for damage done by a public functionary who, in violation of law, infringes upon the freedom or right of any person.

4. *Chapter III. The National Assembly.* The National Assembly is retained despite the fact that the 1946 Political Consultative Conference suggested its abolition, but the Assembly's power is now limited to the election

---

[28]Complete text of Article 8 is:

> Personal freedom shall be guaranteed to the people. Except in case of *flagrante delicto* as provided by law, no person shall be arrested or detained otherwise than by a judicial or a police organ in accordance with the procedure prescribed by law. No person shall be tried or punished otherwise than by a law court in accordance with the procedure prescribed by law. Any arrest, detention, trial, or punishment which is not in accordance with the procedure prescribed by law may be resisted.

> When a person is arrested or detained on suspicion of having committed a crime, the organ making the arrest or detention shall in writing inform the said person, and his designated relative or friend, of the grounds for his arrest or detention, and shall, within 24 hours, turn him over to a competent court for trial. The said person, or any other person, may petition the competent court that a writ be served within 24 hours on the organ making the arrest for the surrender of the said person for trial.

> The court shall not reject the petition mentioned in the preceding paragraph, nor shall it order the organ concerned to make an investigation and report first. The organ concerned shall not refuse to execute, or delay in executing, the writ of the court for the surrender of the said person for trial.

> When a person is unlawfully arrested or detained by any organ, he or any other person may petition the court for an investigation. The court shall not reject such a petition, and shall, within 24 hours, investigate the action of the organ concerned and deal with the matter in accordance with law.

and recall of the President and the Vice President, amending the Constitution, and voting on proposed constitutional amendments submitted by the Legislative Yuan by way of referendum (Article 27).

5. *Chapter IV. The President.* The President is the head of state (Article 35) and supreme commander of the land, sea, and air forces (Article 36). The President shall appoint and remove civil and military officials (Article 41) and exercise other powers; he shall promulgate laws and issue mandates only with the countersignature of the Premier of the Executive Yuan or ministers concerned (Article 37). This makes the President's position similar to that of Western democracies with a cabinet system where the real power is vested with the premier, a leader of the majority party or a coalition. However, the President still has some real powers under this Constitution. He may, in accordance with law, declare martial law with the approval of, or subject to confirmation by, the Legislative Yuan (Article 39). He can also exercise emergency powers. In case of a natural calamity, an epidemic, or a national financial or economic crisis that calls for emergency measures, the President, during the recess of the Legislative Yuan, may, by resolution of the Executive Yuan Council, and in accordance with the Law on Emergency Orders, issue emergency orders proclaiming such measures as may be necessary to cope with the situation. Such an order, however, shall, within one month after issuance, be presented to the Legislative Yuan for confirmation; in case the Legislative Yuan withholds confirmation, the said order shall forthwith cease to be valid (Article 43). Moreover, in case of disputes between two or more Yuans other than those for which there exist relevant provisions in the Constitution, the President may call a meeting of the Premier or Presidents of the Yuans concerned for consultation with a view to reaching a solution (Article 44). Finally, the President may approve the request of the Premier of the Executive Yuan to veto a bill passed by the Legislative Yuan, which the latter can override only by a two-thirds majority (Article 57, paragraph 2).

6. *Chapter V. Administration.* The Executive Yuan is the highest administrative organ of the state (Article 53). The Premier [President] of the Executive Yuan is appointed by the President with the approval of the Legislative Yuan (Article 55, paragraph 1) and is responsible to the latter (Article 57). The Legislative Yuan may by resolution request the Executive Yuan to change any important policy, but the latter may, with the approval of the President, petition the Legislative Yuan for reconsideration. If a two-thirds majority of the Legislative Yuan upholds the original resolution, the Premier shall either accept the resolution or resign from office (Article 57, paragraph 2). As stated earlier, the Premier may seek the approval of the President to veto a bill adopted by the Legislative Yuan, which can only be overridden by a two-thirds majority of the Legislative Yuan (Article 57, paragraph 3).

7. *Chapter VI. Legislation.* The Legislative Yuan is comprised of members directly elected by the people, occupational groups, and overseas Chinese and is the highest legislative organ of the state (Articles 62 and

64). Members of the Legislative Yuan may not concurrently hold any governmental post (Article 75) and this makes the Chinese system different from other cabinet systems. While the Legislative Yuan has extensive legislative and budgetary powers, it shall not make proposals for an increase in the expenditures in the budgetary bill presented by the Executive Yuan (Article 70). The Legislative Yuan may also propose constitutional amendments and submit the same to the National Assembly for referendum (Article 174, paragraph 2).

8. *Chapter VII. Judiciary.* The Judicial Yuan is in charge of civil, criminal, and administrative cases and disciplinary measures against public functionaries (Article 77). Its Grand Justices, who are appointed by the President of the Republic with the consent of the Control Yuan, are in charge of interpreting the Constitution and unifying the interpretation of laws and orders (Articles 78 and 79). Judges shall hold office for life (Article 81) and shall be above partisanship and shall, in accordance with law, hold trials independently, free from any interference (Article 80).

9. *Chapter VIII. Examination.* The Examination Yuan is in charge of matters relating to examination, employment, registration, service rating, scales of salaries, promotions and transfers, security of tenure, commendation, pecuniary aid in case of death, retirement, and old-age pensions of government employees (Article 83). Its President, Vice President, and members are appointed by the President of the Republic with the consent of the Control Yuan (Article 84).

10. *Chapter IX. Control Yuan.* The Control Yuan consists of members elected by Councils of Provinces or their equivalents (big cities) and overseas Chinese, and exercises powers of consent, impeachment, censure, and auditing (Articles 90 and 91).

11. *Chapter X. Power of the Central and Local Government.* The powers of the Central, Provincial, and City or County governments are specified in the Constitution (Articles 107 to 110). However, any matter not enumerated in the Constitution shall fall within the jurisdiction of the Central Government, if it is national in nature; of the province, if it is provincial in nature; and of the county or city, if it concerns the county or city. The Legislative Yuan shall settle any dispute (Article 111).

12. *Chapter XI. System of Local Government.* The self-government of provinces and counties or cities is assured in the Constitution, and the provincial governors, county magistrates, and city mayors shall be elected directly by the people (Articles 112-128).

13. *Chapter XII. Election, Recall, Initiative, and Referendum.* Except for those prescribed by the Constitution, all kinds of elections shall be held by universal, equal, and direct suffrage and by secret ballots (Article 129). All candidates are required to openly campaign for their election (Article 131). In various kinds of elections, the number of women to be elected shall be fixed by law (Article 134).

14. *Chapter XIII. Fundamental National Policies.* The land, sea, and

air forces shall be above personal, regional, or party affiliations, and they shall be loyal to the state and shall protect the people (Article 138). Neither political party nor any individual shall make use of the armed forces as an instrument in a struggle for political powers (Article 139), and no military man in active service may concurrently hold a civil office (Article 140). The national economy shall seek to effect equalization of land ownership and the restriction of private capital in order to attain a well-balanced sufficiency in national wealth and people's livelihood (Article 142); but private citizens' productive enterprises and foreign trade shall receive encouragement, guidance, and protection from the state (Article 145). Within the territory of the Republic, all goods shall be permitted to move freely from place to place (Article 148). In order to promote social welfare, the state shall establish a social insurance system (Article 155) and a system of public medical services (Article 157). All children of school age from six to twelve shall receive free primary education and all citizens above school age who have not received primary education shall receive supplementary education free of charge (Article 160).

15. *Chapter XIV. Enforcement and Amendment of the Constitution.* Laws that are in conflict with the Constitution shall be null and void, and the Judicial Yuan shall decide whether there is a conflict (Article 171). Ordinances that are in conflict with the Constitution or with the laws shall be null and void (Article 172). The Constitution may be amended upon the proposal of one-fourth of the members of the National Assembly and by a resolution of three-fourths of the delegates present at a meeting having a quorum of two-thirds of the entire Assembly (Article 174). As stated earlier, the Legislative Yuan may propose an amendment and submit the same to the Assembly for referendum.

* * *

General elections for delegates to the first National Assembly and members of the Legislative Yuan and the Control Yuan in areas under the control of the National Government were held in 1947 and 1948 in accordance with the Constitution. The president and vice president were elected by the National Assembly and they took office on May 20, 1948. A constitutional government had finally come into effect in China.

The defeat of the Republican forces by the Chinese Communist forces in the 1946-49 civil war and the removal of the Republican Government to Taiwan in late 1949 ended the operation of this Constitution on the mainland; but in Taiwan this Constitution has been in force since its entry into force on December 25, 1947.

Temporary Provisions of the Constitution and the President's Emergency Power

When the first National Assembly met at Nanking in March-April 1948, full-scale civil war between the government forces and the Chinese Communist forces had been continuing for some time; therefore, the National Assembly, through the constitutional amendment procedure, adopted "Temporary Provisions Effective During the Period of Mobilization for the Suppression of Communist Rebellion" on April 18, 1948 which became effective on May 10, 1948.[29]

According to these provisions, the President may, for the period in question, by resolution of the Executive Yuan (Cabinet) Council, take any emergency measure necessary to prevent the state or the people from facing immediate danger or to cope with serious financial or economic crises without being subject to the procedural restrictions of the Legislative Yuan, as prescribed in Articles 39 and 43 of the Constitution. These two articles provide the first of the President's emergency powers. Article 39 provides that the President may declare the institution of martial law (which in Taiwan is similar to a state of siege in other constitutions) but must secure prior or subsequent approval from the Legislative Yuan. Article 43 provides that during a natural calamity, epidemic, or a serious financial or economic crisis, when the Legislative Yuan is in recess, the President may issue emergency orders by resolution of the Executive Yuan Council and in accordance with the Law on Emergency Orders,[30] but that orders will lapse unless they are confirmed by the Legislative Yuan within one month. Under the Temporary Provisions, this procedural requirement of confirmation by the Legislative Yuan was removed, the term "orders" was replaced by the term "measures" and the situation authorizing the President to take such measures was changed to "immediate danger" rather than narrowly defined "natural calamity" or "epidemic." However, the Legislative Yuan, under Article 57 of the Constitution, can still modify or annul presidential emergency measures by a resolution. Such a resolution, however, is subject to presidential veto, which in turn can only be overridden by a two-thirds majority of the Legislative Yuan—an unlikely event.

Despite the extent of the President's emergency power, the experience of the last four decades has unequivocally demonstrated that the President has used maximum restraint in exercising this power. In fact, the President has invoked his emergency powers on only four occasions. In the first case, the power was invoked to declare the application of martial law in civil war areas in 1948-49, and in the second it was invoked to announce monetary reforms during the same critical stage of the civil war. The third case enabled the President to deal with serious floods that occurred in the central and southern parts of Taiwan in 1958. The last occasion was announced by

---

[29]See *Kuo-chia chien-she ts'ung-k'an*, ti-i-ts'e, *Tsung-lun* (National reconstruction series, vol. 1, General discussion) (Taipei: Cheng-chung shu-chü, 1971), 224-26.

[30]The law has not yet been enacted.

the President on December 16, 1978, to put the armed forces on full alert, to take necessary measures to maintain economic stability and development, and to suspend the pending election of national elective bodies when the United States abruptly announced its decision on December 16, 1978 to terminate diplomatic relations with the ROC on January 1, 1979, and to abrogate the U.S.-ROC mutual defense treaty a year later.

On March 19, 1966, the National Assembly amended the Temporary Provisions and gave the President additional powers.[31]

1. The President is authorized to establish, in accordance with the constitutional system, an organ for making major policy decisions concerned with the national mobilization and suppression of the Communist rebellion and for assuming administrative control in war zones; and
2. To meet the requirements of national mobilization and the suppression of the Communist rebellion, the President may make adjustments in the administrative and personnel organs of the Central Government, as well as their organizations.

Under these provisions, two agencies established by the "Temporary Provisions" have had considerable impact on the form of government. The National Security Council, which is chaired by the President, in several cases, decided major national policies and then instructed the Executive Yuan to implement or enforce them. The extension of compulsory education from six years to nine years, the extension of the territorial waters from three miles to twelve miles, and the establishment of a two hundred mile economic zone are well-known examples. Therefore, with the establishment of the National Security Council, the President, if he wants, can play a leading role in the national decision-making process. In addition, the Central Personnel Administration of the Executive Yuan, established by the President in accordance with the "Temporary Provisions," has assumed many functions previously held by the Ministry of Personnel of the Examination Yuan. It thus changes the relationship between these two Yuans.

On May 1, 1991, the Temporary Provisions were terminated, but the President's emergency power is retained in modified and more restricted form in Article 7 of the Additional Articles of the ROC Constitution[32] which entered into force on the same day. A President's emergency order shall be submitted to the Legislative Yuan for confirmation within ten days after its issuance. Should the Legislative Yuan withhold confirmation, the said emergency orders shall forthwith cease to be valid.

The National Security Council and the Central Personnel Administration of the Executive Yuan are also retained in Article 9 of the Additional Articles,

---

[31]*Kuo-chia chien-she ts'ung-k'an* 1:27.
[32]English translation in *Free China Journal* 8, no. 32 (May 2, 1991): 8.

but their organic laws are to be enacted by the Legislative Yuan by December 31, 1993.[33]

Martial Law and Military Trial of Civilians

Because of the Chinese Communists' threat to take over Taiwan by force, martial law (a state of siege) was declared on May 20, 1949.[34] The state of "martial law" in the ROC is, in fact, similar to a "state of siege" in civil law countries and is different from the concept of martial law in common law countries. This point needs further explanation.

The difference lies essentially in the divergent attitudes between the common and civil law systems toward the origin of this emergency measure. "Martial law" emphasizes the suspension of certain normal rules of law, whereas "state of siege" emphasizes the emergency as an effective threat against public safety and order. Thus, the prerequisite for martial rule in the United States is either that the civilian courts are closed or they can no longer perform their functions properly.[35] This condition does not apply to the civil law state of siege, under which the civilian courts may still function and only those crimes against national security, the Constitution, and the public safety and order are under the jurisdiction of military courts. The civil and military powers within the government work side by side in a spirit of cooperation and do not have to be substituted one for the other, as is the case in a common law country.[36] Another major difference should not be overlooked. The executive and/or the legislature in civil law countries has the final word as to whether an emergency situation has arisen; the courts assume this function under the common law.

All these features of the state of siege existed in the Republic of China between 1949 and 1987. The President had the power to initiate the application of martial law, that is, state of siege, although this power is subject to confirmation by the Legislative Yuan. Under Article 39 of the Constitution, the latter, by resolution, might have asked the President to terminate

---

[33]Ibid.

[34]Tuan Shao-yen, comp., *Liu-fa p'an-chüeh hui-pien* (Collection of precedents and interpretations on Six Codes) (Taipei: San-min shu-chü, 1963), 1788.

[35]Traditionally, the fact that civil courts are open has precluded the use of martial law. However, the doctrine has undergone a revision, because the nature of modern war has changed; it is still possible for the civil courts to be open even in the actual fighting zone. Therefore, whether the function of the courts is obstructed or not should not be the real criterion. See Charles Warren, "Spies, and the Power of Congress to Subject Certain Classes of Civilians to Trial by Military Tribunal," *American Law Review* 53 (1919): 201. Robert S. Rankin also cited a list of supporting articles on this point; see his *When Civil Law Falls* (Durham, N.C.: Duke University Press, 1939).

[36]For details, see Clinton L. Rossiter, *Constitutional Dictatorship* (Princeton, N.J.: Princeton University Press, 1948), 86-87.

the application of martial law. As a practical matter, the structure and functions of government and the way of life of the people in the ROC were virtually unaffected by the imposition of martial law between 1949 and 1987. Under martial law, nonmilitary personnel in the ROC were subject to a military trial if they had committed one of the four types of crimes: (1) sedition, (2) espionage, (3) theft, or (4) unauthorized sale or purchase of military equipment and supplies, or theft or damage of public communication equipment and facilities.[37]

In response to popular demand for swift and severe punishment against a rising trend of violent crime, in 1976 the government expanded the scope of military trials to include nine serious offenses such as homicide, robbery, intentionally killing the victim after a rape or robbery, and kidnapping. However, not all these types of cases were automatically placed under military jurisdiction; a decision by the Executive Yuan was required on a case-by-case basis before such crimes were referred to the military courts.[38] After imposition of military trials for these offenses, the number of robbery and snatching cases dropped from 833 in 1975 to 494 in 1976.[39] The deterrent effect no doubt has been realized and, consequently, between 1976 and 1980, there were almost no military trials for robbery or snatching.[40]

Trials in the military courts generally follow the model of the civilian courts. The most controversial aspect is that a judgment must be approved by a commanding officer before delivery.[41] However, this is not only a general practice of military trials in other countries, but, contrary to the American practice that no limitation be imposed,[42] the commanding officer in the ROC may express his disapproval only once.[43] Another problem related to military trials is that a defendant may be sent to reformatory education because of mitigating circumstances, or because he surrendered himself to the authorities.[44] The maximum period for reformatory education is three

---

[37]Measures of Dividing Cases to Be Tried by the Military Law Organs Themselves and Those to Be Tried by Courts During the Period of Martial Law in the Taiwan Area, promulgated by the Executive Yuan on May 10, 1952, in *Tsui-hsin Liu-fa ch'üan-shu* (Latest edition of Six Codes) (Taipei: San-min shu-chü, 1976), 350.

[38]*Chung-yang jih-pao* (Central Daily News) (Taipei), January 25, 1976.

[39]Research Center of Crime, Ministry of Justice [Legal Affairs], *Fan-tsui chuang-k'uang chi ch'i fen-hsi* (The condition and analysis of crimes) (Taipei: Ministry of Justice [Legal Affairs], 1979), 108-9.

[40]*Chung-yang jih-pao*, January 8, 1980.

[41]Article 133, paragraph 1 of the Military Trial Law, in *Tsui-hsin Liu-fa ch'üan-shu*, 557.

[42]See Edward M. Byrne, *Military Law*, 3rd ed. (Annapolis, Maryland: Naval Institute Press, 1981), 412-15.

[43]Article 133, paragraph 3 of the Military Trial Law, in *Tsui-hsin Liu-fa ch'üan-shu*, 557.

[44]Article 8 of the Statute for the Finding and Purging of Spies during the Period of Mobilization for the Suppression of Communist Rebellion, promulgated on June 13, 1950 and amended on December 28, 1954, in *Tsui-hsin Liu-fa ch'üan-shu*, 301.

years and it may not be extended. Upon the expiration of the term, he must be released immediately, although two guarantees may be required to assure his later behavior.[45]

How the military trial of civilians not in active service during the martial law period could be reconciled with Article 9 of the Constitution, which prohibits military trial of civilians, was a question which was never submitted to the Council of Grand Justices of the Judicial Yuan for an authoritative interpretation.

Another restriction on the people during the martial law period was the prohibition on organizing new political parties, though existing parties were allowed to continue to operate. This is contrary to Article 14 of the Constitution which guarantees people's freedom of assembly and association. A plausible justification might be based on Article 23 of the Constitution which authorizes the restriction of the freedoms and rights of the people by law if it is necessary "to avert an imminent crisis, to maintain social order, or to advance public welfare." This issue of prohibiting new political parties was also not submitted to the Council of Grand Justices for an authoritative interpretation.

On July 15, 1987, martial law in Taiwan was lifted by late President Chiang Ching-kuo,[46] and since then no civilians have been subject to a military trial, and the people's freedom to organize new political parties has also been restored.

Local Self-Government and the Question of the Election of National Elective Bodies

Local self-government began in Taiwan in 1951. All mayors, county magistrates, city or county councils, and the Taiwan Provincial Assembly have since then been periodically elected by the people. However, the governor of Taiwan and the mayors of Taipei and Kaohsiung, after the mid-1960s when both became special municipalities, have been appointed by the Central Government, and not elected by the people, despite the constitutional provisions to the contrary.

In 1951, the three-year term for members of the Legislative Yuan expired, and all members were due for reelection. However, at that time the Chinese Communists had already controlled the mainland, so no election

---

[45] Article 9 of the Statute for Punishment of Rebellion, promulgated on June 21, 1949 and last amended on July 26, 1958, in *Tsui-hsin Liu-fa ch'üan-shu*, 301.

[46] "Taiwan Ends 4 Decades of Martial Law," *New York Times*, July 15, 1987, 4. For an analysis of the martial law in Taiwan, see Tao-tai Hsia with Wendy Zeldin, "Laws on Emergency Powers in Taiwan," in *Coping with Crises: How Governments Deal with Emergencies*, ed. Shao-chuan Leng (Lanham, New York and London: University Press of America, 1990), 173-208.

could be held there. Therefore, by resolution of the Legislative Yuan, the members' terms were extended until a new election could be held. In 1954, the members of the Control Yuan were also due for a new election. Similarly, because the Chinese Communists controlled the mainland, no reelection was possible. Therefore, the question was submitted to the Council of Grand Justices of the Judicial Yuan for guidance. In its Interpretation (*Shih-tzu*) No. 31 rendered on January 29, 1954,[47] the Council of Grand Justices stated that pending a new election, members of the Legislative Yuan and Control Yuan elected in 1948 could continue to serve. In 1954, the delegates to the National Assembly also were due for an election, but it was not possible to hold an election because of the Communist control of the mainland. However, Article 28, paragraph 2 of the Constitution provides that "the term of office of the delegates to each National Assembly shall terminate on the day on which the next National Assembly convenes." Because it was not possible to hold an election calling for the next National Assembly, those delegates elected in 1948 continued to serve.

While through the above constitutional interpretations, the three elective bodies—the National Assembly, the Legislative Yuan, and the Control Yuan—could continue to function, this situation, in fact, prevented the people in Taiwan from moving to a leadership role in the national elective bodies, and it therefore came under increasing public criticism.

In 1966, a provision was added to the Temporary Provisions of the Constitution authorizing the President to "'initiate and promulgate for enforcement regulations providing for elections to fill, according to law, those elective offices at the Central Government level which have become vacant for legitimate reasons, or for which additional representation is called because of population increases, in areas that are free and/or newly recovered.''[48] In 1969, a supplementary national election was held to elect fifteen members to the National Assembly and eleven members to the Legislative Yuan. The Taiwan Provincial Assembly also elected two members to the Control Yuan. These new members were to serve "indefinitely"; that is, they enjoyed lifetime tenure.

The above measure was hardly a reasonable response to the popular demand for more democracy in Taiwan. Therefore, on March 17, 1972, the National Assembly again added another provision to the Temporary Provisions as follows:[49]

6. During the period of national mobilization and the suppression of Communist rebellion, the President may, in accordance with the following stipulations, initiate

---

[47]*Ssu-fa-yüan ta-fa-kuan hui-i chieh-shih hui-pien* (Collection of interpretations of the Council of Grand Justices of the Judicial Yuan) (Taipei: Secretariat of the Judicial Yuan, 1974), 53.
[48]*China Yearbook, 1970-71* (Taipei: China Publishing Co., n.d.), 720-21.
[49]*China Yearbook, 1972-73* (Taipei: China Publishing Co., n.d.), 747-48.

and promulgate for enforcement regulations providing for elections to strengthen elective offices at the Central Government level without being subject to the restrictions prescribed in Article 26, Article 64 or Article 91 of the Constitution.

(1) In free areas, additional members or representatives may be elected to all elective offices at the Central Government level by elections to be held at established times. The President may initiate regulations for the selection of members of the Legislative Yuan and the Control Yuan who were to have been elected from among Chinese nationals residing overseas but whose election could not be carried out because of the actual situation.

. . . .

(3) Representatives additionally elected to the elective offices at the Central Government level shall carry out the same functions as those elected previously. The new delegates to the National Assembly elected for additional representation shall stand for reelection every six years; those of the Legislative Yuan, every three years; and those of the Control Yuan, every six years.

In the same year, an election was held, and fifty-three delegates to the National Assembly, thirty-one members (plus fifteen appointed seats for overseas Chinese) of the Legislative Yuan, and ten members (plus five appointed members from overseas Chinese) of the Control Yuan were elected. They were subject to reelection every six years (National Assembly and Control Yuan) or every three years (Legislative Yuan). These elections came to be known as "supplementary elections." In 1986, eighty-four new delegates were elected to the National Assembly, and in 1989, seventy-two new members (plus twenty-nine appointed seats from overseas Chinese) were elected to the Legislative Yuan. In 1987, twenty-two new members (plus ten appointed seats from overseas Chinese) were elected to the Control Yuan by the Taiwan Provincial Assembly and Taipei and Kaohsiung City Councils.

On February 3, 1989, the President promulgated a law adopted by the Legislative Yuan for voluntary retirement of those members of the three elective bodies who were formerly elected on the Chinese mainland in 1948 and in Taiwan in 1969.[50] On June 21, 1990, the Council of Grand Justices rendered Interpretation (*Shih-tzu*) No. 261 which states that all members of the three elective bodies who were elected in 1948 and 1969 must resign from their offices by December 31, 1991 and that new elections should be held for these bodies.[51] Thus, from January 1, 1992, all members of the National Assembly, the Legislative Yuan, and the Control Yuan will be periodically elected in Taiwan.

---

[50]Text in *Fa-wu-pu kung-pao* (Gazette of the Ministry of Justice [Legal Affairs]), no. 104 (February 28, 1989): 15-17.

[51]Text in *Fa-ling yüeh-k'an* (The Law Monthly) 40, no. 9 (September 1, 1990): 21-24.

Reduction of Tension in the Taiwan Strait
and Constitutional Reform

Before early 1980, the policy of the Chinese Communist government toward Taiwan was to use force to "liberate Taiwan" at an appropriate time. This policy was even explicitly stated in the Preamble of the Constitution of the People's Republic of China (PRC) adopted on March 5, 1978.[52] Under such a constant military threat, the ROC government considered that it was necessary to restrict people's freedoms for national security reasons. However, since the early 1980s, mainland-Taiwan relations have significantly changed.

On January 1, 1979, when diplomatic relations were established between the United States and the PRC, the Standing Committee of the PRC's National People's Congress (NPC) sent a "Message to Compatriots in Taiwan"[53] calling for "unification" of Taiwan with the mainland. It said that the PRC leaders would take present realities in Taiwan into account in accomplishing the "great cause of reunifying the motherland," would respect the status quo on Taiwan and the opinions of the people in all walks of life there, and would adopt reasonable policies and measures in settling the question of reunification so as to avoid causing any losses to the people of Taiwan. It also called for establishing "three links"—mail, trade, and air and shipping services; and "four exchanges"—relatives and tourists, academic groups, cultural groups, and sports representatives—with Taiwan as a first step toward the ultimate goal of reunification.

On September 30, 1981, Marshal Yeh Chien-ying (Ye Jianying), then chairman of the NPC Standing Committee and de facto head of state of the PRC, made a specific nine-point proposal to Taiwan on unification. The proposal offered Taiwan "a high degree of autonomy as a special administrative region" after unification with the PRC. Taiwan could also retain its armed forces. The PRC also renewed its 1979 call for establishing "three links" and "four exchanges" with Taiwan.[54] This proposal set forth the basic principles of the Chinese Communists' unification policy toward Taiwan. While the PRC has not ruled out the use of force against Taiwan, the increased contacts through trade, investment, and travel have greatly reduced the tension in the Taiwan Strait. Under this more relaxed atmosphere, it was only natural for the general public in Taiwan to demand the full implementation of the Constitution of the Republic of China and further demand

---

[52]*Hsien-fa tzu-liao hsüan-pien* 1:305.
[53]"N.P.C. Standing Committee Message to Compatriots in Taiwan," *Beijing Review* 22, no. 1 (January 5, 1979): 16-17.
[54]"Chairman Ye Jianying's Elaboration on Policy Concerning Return of Taiwan to Motherland and Peaceful Reunification," *Beijing Review* 24, no. 40 (October 5, 1981): 10.

the ROC government make necessary amendments to the Constitution for its application to the Taiwan area.

On July 15, 1987, late President Chiang Ching-kuo lifted martial law, which also ended the ban on organizing new political parties. At the same time, the ROC also announced the relaxation of foreign exchange controls, so that anyone could remit up to a total of US$5 million abroad in a year. On December 25, 1987, President Chiang announced a plan to reform parliamentary bodies at the annual meeting of the National Assembly. Under that plan, all members of parliamentary bodies would be periodically elected in Taiwan within a few years.

Unfortunately, Chiang passed away on January 13, 1988 before he could implement this reform. Dr. Lee Teng-hui, who succeeded to the presidency on the same day, pledged to carry out Chiang's policy. Under Lee's leadership, the Central Standing Committee of the ruling Chinese Nationalist Party approved the reform plan on February 3, 1988. At the Thirteenth National Congress of the Party held in July 1988, Lee was elected the Party Chairman. The new Party Platform, which would serve as the government's policy guidelines for the next four years, stresses the continuation of the democratization and liberalization process in politics and the economy.

On January 23, 1989, the President promulgated the Civil Organizations Law adopted by the Legislative Yuan, which among others, sets rules for the formation of new political parties.[55] Thus, it marks a transition of the ROC's political system from an essentially authoritarian one-party state to a democratic, competitive, multiparty system. On February 3, 1989, the Election and Recall Law[56] was also revised to lift many restrictions on campaign activities.

On the question of reform of the Legislative Yuan, the Control Yuan, and the National Assembly, a voluntary retirement law was adopted for those members who were formerly elected on the Chinese mainland in 1948 and in Taiwan in 1969.

On March 21, 1990, after learning he was elected to a six-year term by the National Assembly, President Lee Teng-hui said that the government would hold a National Affairs Conference, and would invite legislators, scholars, experts, industrial and business leaders, and journalists to attend in order to develop a consensus on such major issues as constitutional reform and the policy toward the mainland.

In his inaugural address entitled "Opening a New Era for the Chinese People," delivered on May 20, 1990,[57] President Lee announced that, "with

---

[55]*Fa-wu-pu kung-pao*, no. 104 (February 28, 1989): 6-10.

[56]Text of the revised provisions in ibid., 10-15. The Law was revised again on August 2, 1991 to further liberalize restrictions on campaigning. For text, see *Fa-ling yüeh-k'an* 41, no. 10 (October 1, 1991): 18-23.

[57]Text in *Republic of China Yearbook, 1990-1991*, 722-24.

the changing domestic and international situation and the increasingly ardent desire of the people for democratic rule of law," he hoped that "a termination of the period of mobilization for the suppression of Communist rebellion" could be declared in the shortest possible period of time. In other words, he was willing to give up his extraordinary power granted to the President under the "Temporary Provisions" and return to normal constitutional rule.

Moreover, he also indicated his willingness to make necessary revisions of the Constitution to strengthen democracy in the ROC. He stated:

> Based on the many years of experience we have accumulated in implementing our Constitution and on the needs arising from the current national environment, forward-looking and necessary revisions will be made to portions of the Constitution concerning such matters as the parliamentary organs of the central government, the system of local government, and government organization to provide the Chinese people with a legal code that is in accord with the trends of our times, and to establish a great model of political democracy for all times.

In order to show his sincerity to carry out these reforms, he specifically stated that he hoped the reform could be completed within a period of two years.

The National Affairs Conference

The National Affairs Conference (NAC) was held from June 28 to July 4, 1990 in Taipei.[58] It was unprecedented in the political history of the ROC because its participants included people holding divergent political views, ranging from those who advocate Taiwan independence to those who are in favor of unification with the Communist-controlled mainland.

As only a limited number of people could have been invited to attend the NAC, the ROC government consulted a wide range of people to seek their opinions before the conference was held. A total of 119 discussion meetings were held in Taiwan and abroad with more than 13,000 people attending.[59] A National Affairs Box was set up at a Taipei post office and received 2,187 letters, and a National Affairs Hotline received 1,180 telephone calls.[60]

Two public opinion polls were conducted to identify the attitudes of social elites and the general public toward constitutional reform. The results were released on June 24, 1990, a few days before the conference.[61]

---

[58]For details, see *Kuo-shih hui-i shih-lu* (Faithful record of the National Affairs Conference), 3 vols. (Taipei: Secretariat of the National Affairs Conference, 1990).

[59]Ibid. 1:9-10.

[60]Ibid., 8.

[61]Ibid. 3:3007-62.

The social elites poll, conducted between May 17 and June 15, 1990, involved interviewing 284 college professors, 35 people's representatives, 156 entrepreneurs, 54 mass media workers, and 54 responsible officers of civic organizations relating to social movements. More than 86 percent of the elites polled considered that there is a constitutional crisis in Taiwan, while only 8.9 percent did not think so, with 2.6 percent expressing other opinions and 2.1 percent expressing no opinion. On the question of how to strengthen the constitutional system, 54 percent expressed the view that this should be done through amending the Constitution, 19 percent considered that full implementation of the Constitution should be sufficient, 12.2 percent were in favor of enacting a Basic Law to replace the present Constitution, 11.1 percent were in favor of enacting a new Constitution, 2.7 percent expressed other opinions, and 1 percent expressed no opinion. With respect to the question of who should exercise the power of amending the Constitution, 70.3 percent considered that it should be the National Assembly after the resignation of all life-tenure members who were elected in 1947 and after its other members were reelected in Taiwan, and only 9.6 percent considered that the National Assembly in its present composition (that is, at least 80 percent are life-tenure members elected in 1947) should exercise the power of amending the Constitution. On the question of possible Chinese Communist response to the constitutional reform, the interviewed elites considered that full implementation of the Constitution would raise the least suspicion of the Chinese Communists, followed by amending the Constitution or enacting a Basic Law, while enacting a new Constitution would cause high suspicion from the Chinese Communists. An interesting question relating to constitutional reform is the cost of social stability as a result of choosing different methods of constitutional reform. Interviewed social elites considered that amending the Constitution would have the least effect on social stability, followed by full implementation of the Constitution and enacting a Basic Law. Enacting a new Constitution would have a high cost on social stability. They also considered that amending the Constitution would be most appropriate in mitigating the dispute over unification and independence, while enacting a new Constitution would be the least appropriate one.

The poll of the general public was conducted through telephone interviews of 1,068 people. In sharp contrast to the social elites' opinion, 45 percent considered that there is no constitutional crisis in Taiwan, while 43.7 percent considered that there is such a crisis. On the question of which problems the government should pay special attention to in carrying out the constitutional reform, 93.1 percent designated the reform's impact on social stability as the most important one, followed by 83.1 percent on the timetable for reform, 67.2 percent on achieving a consensus and compromise with the Democratic Progressive Party (DPP), and 52.6 percent on taking into consideration the response of the Chinese Communists. Similar to the social elites' opinion, 57.8 percent of the people interviewed considered that constitutional reform should be carried out by amendment, followed by

15.6 percent who advocate full implementation of the Constitution, and 11.7 percent who would enact a new Constitution.

On June 21, 1990, a week before the opening of the NAC, the Council of Grand Justices of the Judicial Yuan rendered its Interpretation (*Shih-tzu*) No. 261, which states that all life-tenure representatives in the parliamentary bodies—the National Assembly, the Legislative Yuan, and the Control Yuan—should resign by December 31, 1991.[62] This view was accepted by the majority of the participants of the NAC, though some participants preferred an earlier resignation date. There was also a general consensus on favoring the direct election of the governor of Taiwan Province and the mayors of Taipei and Kaohsiung municipalities. As a matter of fact, the Constitution has already provided for such an election.

A high decree of consensus was reached on the ROC's policy toward the mainland and the need to enact a law to regulate relations between Taiwan and the mainland in such areas as trade, investment, travel, and culture. Most considered that the ROC government should clarify its present seemingly inconsistent mainland policy and liberalize functional exchanges with the mainland. The government should also consider beginning functional and nonpolitical negotiations with the Chinese Communists through an "intermediate body" with authority delegated by the government.

On the constitutional reform issue, all participants agreed that the "Temporary Provisions Effective During the Period of Mobilization for the Suppression of Communist Rebellion," which granted extraordinary power to the President and were annexed to the Constitution, should be terminated as soon as possible. They were divided, however, on the issue of how to achieve constitutional reform. The majority of the participants considered that reform should be carried out by amending the Constitution through the procedure provided in the Constitution. A minority would have liked to enact a new Constitution. The difficulty in accepting this view is that the President does not have the constitutional power to abrogate the present Constitution and enact a new one. Moreover, the ROC Constitution, enacted in 1947 when the ROC government was on the mainland, is the symbol of the "one-China" principle. To enact a new Constitution just applicable to Taiwan would undermine that principle and imply that Taiwan is independent. Because the Chinese Communists have repeatedly warned that they will not tolerate Taiwan independence and will use force to suppress independence, enacting a new Constitution will increase tensions in the Taiwan Strait.

The majority of participants considered that the present form of electing the President, that is, the National Assembly may elect anyone it likes to serve as the President without consulting the people's opinion, should be reformed. Almost all participants agreed that the President should be "elected

---

[62]See note 51 above.

by the people," but they were divided on whether the President should be directly elected by the people or by a system similar to that of the United States where voters cast ballots for electoral college delegates representing the electorate's views as proxies. Supporters of this view pointed out that the direct election of the President on Taiwan might give people the impression that the President is elected only by the people of Taiwan and thus imply Taiwan independence. An electoral college system may include some national and overseas Chinese seats apportioned according to the party preference of Taiwan voters.

The Process and Problems in Implementing Constitutional Reform

The participants of the NAC generally agreed that the Constitution should be amended by an organ with a basis in public opinion, that is, whose members are elected by the people for a fixed term. Therefore, the National Assembly under its composition at that time, with more than 80 percent life-tenure members elected in 1947, was inappropriate for exercising the function of amending the Constitution. Only when all members of the National Assembly had been elected in Taiwan for a fixed term should the Assembly begin to amend the Constitution. This, however, was not due to happen until late 1992 when the Assembly was scheduled for reelection. The complicated legal problems involved need explanation.

At that time, the National Assembly, in addition to life-tenure members, included eighty members elected for six-year terms in Taiwan and their terms were not due to expire until December 1992. However, according to Interpretation (*Shih-tzu*) No. 261 of the Council of Grand Justices of the Judicial Yuan, all life-tenure members of the Assembly should resign by December 31, 1991. If this decision was implemented, there would be only eighty members in the National Assembly in 1992. Legally, they would have authority to amend the Constitution, but politically, they would not be advised to do so because they were elected in 1986, and at that time the people did not give the members the mandate to amend the Constitution. In view of this, the government was considering holding an election in 1991 to elect 291 new members to the Assembly who would begin to serve on January 1, 1992. Under that arrangement, in 1992 a rejuvenated National Assembly would have 375 members[63] to amend the Constitution, all of them elected in Taiwan. This sounds like a logical solution, but the problem was whether the President had the legal authority to move the election date from December 1992 to December 1991 or even earlier, thus shortening the term of eighty members of the Assembly who were elected in 1986. A possible flimsy legal

---

[63]The ROC National Security Council proposed that in the future the total number of representatives of the National Assembly should be 375, all of them serving six-year terms.

basis for taking this action would be to invoke the emergency power under Article 1 of the "Temporary Provisions." However, the "Temporary Provisions" were abolished on May 1, 1991, so this approach was not possible.[64] Moreover, some of the members of the National Assembly, the Legislative Yuan, and the Control Yuan at that time had been elected for a fixed term under Article 6 of the "Temporary Provisions."[65] The termination of the "Temporary Provisions" on May 1, 1991, as announced by the President, undermined the legal basis for these members to continue to serve their terms until December 1992. If an election had been held according to the provisions of the ROC Constitution, and not on the "Temporary Provisions," only thirty-nine members would have been elected to the National Assembly[66] and twenty-seven to the Legislative Yuan.[67]

---

[64]Even if they were not abolished, both the Legislative Yuan and the National Assembly may rescind an emergency measure taken by the President.

[65]See note 49 above and accompanying text. Article 6 of the Temporary Provisions provides:

During the period of national mobilization for the suppression of Communist rebellion, the President may, in accordance with the following stipulations, initiate and promulgate for enforcement regulations providing for elections to strengthen elective offices at the Central Government level without being subject to the restrictions prescribed in Article 26, Article 64, or Article 91 of the Constitution:

(1) In free areas, additional members of the National Assembly, the Legislative Yuan, and the Control Yuan may be added through regular elections. Members of the Legislative Yuan and Control Yuan that must be elected by Chinese citizens living abroad who are unable to hold elections shall be chosen according to regulations established by the President of the Republic.

(2) Representatives elected to the National Assembly, Legislative Yuan, and Control Yuan in the first elections were chosen through popular vote by the people of the entire nation. These representatives exercise their powers of office in accordance with law; the same principle applies to the representatives elected to fill vacancies or provide additional representation.

Elections for the National Assembly, Legislative Yuan, and Control Yuan shall be held on the Chinese mainland one by one, as each area is recovered.

(3) Additional members elected to serve in the National Assembly, Legislative Yuan, and Control Yuan, shall exercise the same powers of office in accordance with law as the members elected in the first elections.

Additional members of the National Assembly shall stand for reelection every six years; members of the Legislative Yuan, every three years; and members of the Control Yuan, every six years.

[66]Article 26 of the Constitution provides:

The National Assembly shall be composed of the following delegates:

1. One delegate shall be elected from each *hsien* [county], municipality, or area of equivalent status. In case its population exceeds 500,000, one additional delegate shall be elected for each additional 500,000. Areas equivalent to *hsien* or municipalities shall be prescribed by law;

. . . .

[67]Article 64 of the Constitution provides:

Members of the Legislative Yuan shall be elected in accordance with the following provisions:

1. Those to be elected from the provinces and by the municipalities under the direct jurisdiction of the Executive Yuan shall be five for each province or

Another possibility was to adopt a two-stage constitutional reform, that is, to convene, immediately prior to the termination of the "Temporary Provisions," an extraordinary session of the National Assembly to amend only those provisions relating to elections in the Constitution and those Temporary Provisions relating to the President's emergency power and the National Security Council. Additional constitutional reform could be left for the next session of the National Assembly, which would be composed of members entirely elected in Taiwan. This was the approach later adopted by the ruling Nationalist Party and implemented in April 1991.

On April 23, 1991 the Extraordinary Session of the National Assembly adopted Additional Articles of the Constitution. On April 30, 1991, President Lee announced the entry into force of the above Additional Articles and the termination of the "Period of Mobilization for the Suppression of Communist Rebellion," beginning on May 1, 1991.

The Additional Articles of the
Constitution of the Republic of China

Additional Articles of the Constitution of the Republic of China[68] number only ten and their contents are summarized below:

1. *Membership in the National Assembly, the Legislative Yuan, and the Control Yuan:* According to Articles 1 to 3, the seats of the three elective bodies are allocated as follows:

(National Assembly)

(1) Two members shall be elected from each Special Municipality, each county or city in the free area. However, where the population exceeds 100,000 persons, one member shall be added for each additional 100,000 persons.
(2) Three members each shall be elected from lowland and highland aborigines in the free area.
(3) Twenty members shall be elected from Chinese citizens living abroad.
(4) Eighty members shall be elected from one nationwide constituency.

(Legislative Yuan)

(1) Two members shall be elected from each province and each Special Municipality in the free area. Where the population exceeds 200,000 persons, however, one member will be added for each additional 100,000 persons; and where the population exceeds one million persons, one member will be added for each additional 200,000 persons.
(2) Three members each shall be elected from lowland and highland aborigines in the free area.

---

municipality with a population of not more than 3,000,000; one additional member shall be elected for each additional 1,000,000 where the population exceeds 3,000,000;
. . . .
[68]English translation in source cited in note 32 above.

(3) Six members shall be elected from Chinese citizens living abroad.
(4) Thirty members shall be elected from one nationwide constituency.

(Control Yuan)

(1) Twenty-five members shall be elected from Taiwan Province of the free area.
(2) Ten members shall be elected from each Special Municipality in the free area.
(3) Two members shall be elected from Chinese citizens living abroad.
(4) Five members shall be elected from one nationwide constituency.

However, if an election district has between five and ten seats, one seat must be reserved for a woman. The same rule is applied to a party winning between five and ten seats representing overseas Chinese or one nationwide constituency. Where the number exceeds ten, one seat out of each additional ten must be reserved for a woman.

Elections for members of the National Assembly and Legislative Yuan shall be conducted by direct popular votes, but members representing Chinese citizens living abroad and one nationwide constituency shall be elected by party-list proportional representation (Article 4). Under the above stated amendment to the Constitution, there will be approximately 327 members of the National Assembly, 161 for the Legislative Yuan, and 52 of the Control Yuan.

2. *Transitional Arrangement.* Articles 5 and 6 set the date for new elections. The National Assembly election shall be held before December 31, 1991 and the elections for the Legislative Yuan and Control Yuan shall be held before January 31, 1993. The President should convene an extraordinary session of the newly elected National Assembly within three months after the election. Those members of the National Assembly who were elected in Taiwan for a six-year term in 1986 may continue to serve until January 31, 1993. If the revision of laws originally in effect solely during the Period of Mobilization for the Suppression of Communist Rebellion is not completed by the termination of the Period of Mobilization for the Suppression of Communist Rebellion, these laws shall remain in effect until July 31, 1992 (Article 8).

3. *The President's Emergency Power, the National Security Council, and the Central Personnel Administration.* These topics have been discussed in the earlier parts of this chapter.[69]

4. *Mainland-Taiwan Relations.* The relationship of rights and obligations between the people of the mainland China area and those of the free area, and the disposition of other affairs, shall be specially regulated by law (Article 10).

The December 21, 1991 Second National Assembly Election

On April 30, 1991, President Lee announced the termination of the "Period of Mobilization for the Suppression of Communist Rebellion" and the "Temporary Provisions" of the Constitution. At the same time, he announced the entry into force of the Additional Articles of the Constitution adopted by the extraordinary session of the National Assembly. According to Article 1 of the Additional Articles, 225 members are to be elected to the Assembly and an additional 80 nationwide members and 20 overseas members

---

[69]See notes 32 and 33 above and accompanying text.

are to be allocated according to the percentage of popular votes received by political parties which constitute at least 5 percent of all popular votes. Articles 5 and 6 set the date for the new election to the Assembly for not later than December 31, 1991, and the President is instructed to convene an extraordinary session of the newly elected National Assembly within three months after the election in order to revise the Constitution. The election date was later set for December 21, 1991.

During the campaign for the National Assembly election, the DPP advocated Taiwan independence while the KMT called for "reform, stability, and prosperity" and ultimate unification with the Chinese mainland. It also warned the public that supporting the DPP's cause can only lead Taiwan on a confrontation course with the Chinese Communists, which would only bring disaster to all the people of Taiwan.

The result of the election was a disaster for the DPP. A total of nearly 9 million voters went to the polls in 58 election districts, and the KMT received 71.17 percent of the popular votes and 179 seats, while the DPP received only 23.94 percent and 41 seats. With 60 nationwide and 15 overseas seats to be allocated according to the popular votes received, the KMT had a total of 254 seats, while the DPP had 20 nationwide and 5 overseas seats for a total of 66 seats. Because there were 78 members of the National Assembly (KMT had 64, DPP had 9, and other parties had 5) who were elected in 1986 and they were also permitted to join the Second National Assembly to amend the Constitution, the total members of the National Assembly were 403. The KMT had 318 members, that is, 78.91 percent of the total membership.[70] According to Article 174 of the Constitution, an amendment to the Constitution must be adopted by a resolution of three-fourths of the members of the National Assembly at a meeting having a quorum of two-thirds of the entire Assembly; the KMT thus had more than three-fourths of the votes in the National Assembly to amend the Constitution.

However, things did not go so well for the KMT in the Second National Assembly convened by the President on March 20, 1992, because of the KMT's internal dispute over the issue of how the President should be elected by the people—whether by direct election or by proxy vote.

The Issue of How to Elect the President

As stated earlier, during the 1990 National Affairs Conference, the participants were divided over the issue of how to elect the President. During the December 1991 election campaign, the majority of the KMT candidates campaigned on a platform supporting an electoral college system, where

---

[70]Susan Yu, "ROC Voters Give KMT Whopping Mandate," *Free China Journal* 8, no. 98 (December 24, 1991): 1.

voters cast ballots for electoral college delegates representing the electorate's view as proxies. On February 15, 1992, the KMT Constitutional Amendment Group, after several hundred consultative meetings, made a preliminary decision to propose the adoption of the electoral college system to the KMT Central Standing Committee, scheduled to meet in early March 1992. If approved, then the proposal would be submitted to the Third Plenum of the Central Committee scheduled for mid-March 1992.[71]

All appeared to go well up to this moment. However, at the KMT Central Standing Committee meeting held on March 9, 1992, instead of only the proposal for an electoral college system to elect the President, a proposal for the direct election of the President was also presented to the meeting, thus triggering a sharp debate among the participants.[72] The Central Standing Committee could not reach an absolute majority on this issue, so it decided to present both proposals to the Third Plenum of the Thirteenth Central Committee for a final decision.

At the Central Committee meetings held on March 14-16, 1992, marathon debates took place. Those in favor of an electoral college system, usually referred to as the "direct election by delegation" faction, argued that a President elected by a direct popular vote in Taiwan could give the impression of being a "President of Taiwan," thus implying Taiwan independence. Moreover, a system based on direct popular votes would exclude overseas Chinese participation in the election process. Some KMT members opposed this method of electing the President because the opposition DPP was on record as favoring such a constitutional change. Those in favor of direct election of the President pointed out that such a system would be in keeping with recent popular trends demonstrating the people's desire to have more participation in the government.[73]

The debate became so divisive, the Central Committee halted the debate and decided to adopt a compromise formula to defer the issue. The final proposal approved by the Central Committee provides that the President and Vice President will be elected by residents of free areas of the Republic of China in such a way as to reflect the public will.[74] In fact, it makes no decision on the method for electing the President.

The Adoption of Additional Amendments to the Constitution of the Republic of China

On March 20, 1992, the extraordinary session of the Second National

---

[71]*Chung-yang jih-pao* (International edition), February 17, 1992, 1.

[72]See *Shih-chieh jih-pao* (World Journal) (New York), March 10, 1992, 28.

[73]Susan Yu, "No Decision on Electing ROC President," *Free China Journal* 9, no. 18 (March 17, 1992): 1.

[74]Ibid.

Assembly was convened by President Lee Teng-hui. Because the question of how to elect the President was so divisive, President Lee Teng-hui, who is also Chairman of the KMT, decided to postpone the resolution of this issue. In a March 25, 1992 speech to 318 KMT members of the National Assembly, Lee said that he would call an extraordinary session of the National Assembly before May 20, 1995, for a final decision on this issue.[75]

On May 27, 1992, the extraordinary session of the Second National Assembly adopted eight additional articles (Articles 11 to 18) to the Constitution of the Republic of China which will be applicable to the Taiwan area before national unification. The contents of these articles are summarized below:[76]

1. *The President and the Vice President:* According to Article 12, both the President and the Vice President shall be elected by the entire electorate in the free area of the Republic of China; the method of election shall be decided by an extraordinary session of the National Assembly to be convoked by the President before May 20, 1995. Their terms in office are shortened to four years, and they may be reelected for a second term. With respect to the question of participation of overseas Chinese in the election of the President and the Vice President, Article 18, paragraph 7 vaguely provides that the state "shall accord to Chinese nationals residing overseas protection of their rights to political participation."

2. *The National Assembly:* According to Article 11, the terms of delegates to the National Assembly shall be shortened to four years. The President shall convoke an extraordinary session of the National Assembly annually. When the Assembly is in session, it shall hear a report on the state of the nation by the President, discuss national affairs, and offer counsel.

3. *The Control Yuan:* Members of the Control Yuan were formerly elected by the Taiwan Provincial Assembly and Taipei and Kaohsiung City Councils. There were strong criticisms of the bribery scandals surrounding those elections. Therefore, Article 15 abolished the election for members of the Control Yuan and converted this Yuan into a semi-judicial organ. From 1993 on, members will be appointed by the President with the consent of the National Assembly. Members of the Control Yuan must be beyond party affiliation and independently exercise their powers, discharging their responsibilities in accordance with the law.

4. *The Judicial Yuan and the Dissolution of Unconstitutional Parties:* Article 13 makes some minor revisions to the organization and function of the Judicial Yuan. The President, Vice President, and the Grand Justices of the Judicial Yuan shall be appointed by the ROC President with the consent of the National Assembly. Formerly, members of the Judicial Yuan were appointed with the consent of the Control Yuan, which was indirectly elected by the people through their Provincial Assemblies or Councils of Cities under direct administration of the Executive Yuan. Because the Control Yuan now is no longer a people's representative organ, but rather a semi-judicial organ, there is no reason for the Control Yuan to retain the power of consent to the appointment of judicial officials.

---

[75]Tammy C. Peng, "3-Year Delay in Vote on Electing President," *Free China Journal* 9, no. 21 (March 27, 1992): 1.

[76]For translation of the text of these articles, see *Free China Journal* 9, no. 44 (June 23, 1992): 7.

A new function is entrusted to the Grand Justices: the adjudication of issues involving unconstitutional political parties. Under the existing Civil Organizations Law, the Party Review Committee of the Executive Yuan may decide to dissolve a political party if said party advocates Communism or splitting national territory. This part of the law was criticized by some commentators as unconstitutional, because it appears to infringe without due process upon the people's right to association. Article 13, therefore, shifted this power to dissolve political parties to the Grand Justices of the Judicial Yuan. They will form a Constitutional Tribunal to adjudicate matters relating to the dissolution of unconstitutional political parties. A political party is defined as unconstitutional, "if its goals or activities jeopardize the existence of the Republic of China as a free, democratic constitutional order."

5. *The Examination Yuan:* Because the Control Yuan is no longer a people's representative organ, its power to give consent to the ROC President's appointment of the President, Vice President, and members of the Examination Yuan is shifted to the National Assembly, as provided in Article 14. Moreover, in the first stage of constitutional reform, Article 9, paragraph 2 of the Additional Articles authorized the Executive Yuan to establish the Personnel Administration, therefore, the Examination Yuan's function is now limited to "all legal matters relating to the employment, discharge, performance evaluation, scale of salaries, promotion, transfer, commendation and award for civil servants." In other words, the execution and implementation of these functions are now transferred to the Personnel Administration of the Executive Yuan.

6. *Local Self-Government:* Article 17 provides a legal basis for the Legislative Yuan to enact a law permitting the direct election of the governor of a province, that is, Taiwan Province. At present, the governor of Taiwan is appointed by the President with the consent of the Taiwan Provincial Assembly.

7. *Fundamental National Policy:* Article 18 adds certain items to fundamental national policy, which is the subject of Chapter XIII (Articles 137-169) of the Constitution. Among these items are environmental protection, the elimination of sexual discrimination, safeguarding personal safety for women, the right of handicapped and disabled persons to insurance, and legal protection for aborigines and other groups.

Future Prospects

The second stage of constitutional amendments has raised several important issues regarding the operation of the Republic of China's governmental system. The first issue is how the next President of the Republic will be elected if the extraordinary session of the National Assembly to be convoked by the President before May 20, 1995 cannot reach an agreement on the method of electing the President (either by electoral college or by direct election). This deadlock is possible because, according to Article 174 of the Constitution, any constitutional amendment can only be adopted by a resolution of three-fourths of the members of the National Assembly at a meeting having a quorum of two-thirds of the entire Assembly. If this happens, the logical solution to this issue is to refer the question to the Council of Grand Justices of the Judicial Yuan for an authoritative interpretation. However, the Council may also deadlock on this issue, because any constitutional interpretation from the Council is required to be adopted by a resolution of three-fourths of the members of the entire Council.[77]

Second, assuming that the 1995 extraordinary session adopts the method of direct election of the President, there remains the question of whether the President should be elected by absolute majority or by simple majority. In a report submitted to the KMT Central Standing Committee on the election of the President, the proposal for an electoral college and the proposal for direct election both adopt the simple majority rule. Therefore, in the future, there is a possibility that a minority President will be elected in the Republic of China, thus undermining the political stability of the country.

Third, according to Article 11 of the Additional Articles, the National Assembly is given the authority, at its annual meeting, to hear a report on the state of the nation by the President, discuss national affairs, and offer counsel. Since the Assembly has the power to amend the Constitution, whether it will use that power to expand its role in the future is a question that remains to be seen. If so, whether such an unprecedented bicameral parliamentary system will work is at least questionable.

In view of the above analysis, although the future of constitutionalism in the Republic of China appears largely positive, there exist some important questions and areas of potential conflict involving the implementation of the new constitutional amendments. Be that as it may, looking back at constitutional development in China, never before in China's history have the Chinese people paid so much attention to constitutional issues as the Chinese people in Taiwan do today. Constitutionalism, which was introduced to China early in this century, appears now to be an integral part of the political process in the Republic of China on Taiwan. If this trend continues, which is quite likely, it will have a significant impact on constitutional development on the Chinese mainland.

---

[77]See Article 13 of the Law Governing the Council of Grand Justices of the Republic of China, promulgated on July 21, 1958.

CHAPTER 2

The Politics of Constitutional Reform in the Republic of China: Problems, Process, and Prospects

Jaushieh Joseph Wu

After Spain, Portugal, and Greece all successfully transformed their political systems from authoritarianism to democracy, political scientists once again became interested in the phenomenon of democratization.[1] Some have looked at specific cases of democratic transition,[2] while others have tried to address the broader comparative and theoretical issues involved.[3] Now, in the final decade of the twentieth century, almost all of the authoritarian regimes of Eastern Europe have collapsed and given way to democratic governments. The Soviet Union, the founder and guardian of socialist Eastern Europe, has itself disintegrated into independent democratic republics. All of these changes occurred quite suddenly and were unthought of a few years ago. But these rapid transformations shed new light on the study of democratization, and show that every authoritarian country, no matter how

---

[1]Nancy Bermeo, "Redemocratization and Transition Elections: A Comparison of Spain and Portugal," *Comparative Politics* 19, no. 2 (January 1987): 213; also see Samuel P. Huntington, "How Countries Democratize," *Political Science Quarterly* 106, no. 4 (1991-92): 579-616.

[2]See, for example, Larry Diamond, "The Social Foundations of Democracy: The Case of Nigeria" (Ph.D. dissertation, Stanford University, 1980); Charles G. Gillespie, "Uruguay's Return to Democracy," *Bulletin of Latin American Research* 4, no. 2 (1985): 99-107; Richard Gunther, "Constitutional Change in Contemporary Spain," in *The Politics of Constitutional Change in Industrial Nations: Redesigning the State*, ed. Keith G. Banting and Richard Simeon (London: Macmillan, 1984); Sung-joo Han, "Democracy in South Korea, 1961-1985" (Paper delivered at the Conference on Democracy in Developing Nations, Stanford, Calif., 1985); Larry Diamond, Juan Linz, and Seymour Martin Lipset, eds., *Democracy in Developing Countries* (Boulder, Colo.: Lynne Rienner Publishers, 1988).

[3]See, for example, John H. Herz, ed., *From Dictatorship to Democracy: Coping with the Legacies of Authoritarianism and Totalitarianism* (Westport, Conn.: Greenwood Press, 1982); Samuel P. Huntington, "Will More Countries Become Democratic?" *Political Science Quarterly* 99, no. 2 (1984): 193-218; Juan J. Linz and Alfred Stepan, eds., *The Breakdown of Democratic Regimes* (Baltimore, Md.: Johns Hopkins University Press, 1978); Guillermo O'Donnell, Philippe C. Schmitter, and Laurence Whitehead, *Transitions from Authoritarian Rule: Prospects for Democracy* (Baltimore, Md.: Johns Hopkins University Press, 1986).

autocratic its regime may be, is subject to democratic challenges from within. The Republic of China (ROC) is a notable case of a Third World country that has made an attempt to democratize its polity through *reforma*.[4] Beginning in the mid-1980s, the ruling core of the Nationalist Party (or Kuomintang, KMT) has gradually relaxed its control over society. The subsequent formation of the first opposition party, the Democratic Progressive Party (DPP), forced the government to loosen its grip on society even further. Within a few years, martial law was abolished; bans on demonstrations, public rallies, opposition publications, and travel to mainland China were lifted; the Period of Mobilization for the Suppression of Communist Rebellion was called off; permanent members of the parliament were forced into retirement; and elections were held for the country's legislature and National Assembly. Undoubtedly, Taiwan's transformation during this seven-year period (1986-92) is quite impressive.

However, some factors still prevent Taiwan from qualifying as a full-fledged democracy. The most important among these is the need to revise the Constitution, to redesign the central governing system to allow the key government decision-makers, either the president or premier and cabinet ministers, to be elected through popular elections.[5] This is indeed a necessary step for all countries that have just gone through democratic change; political power needs to be reallocated to different democratic institutions and the rules of the game redefined.

Throughout contemporary history, constitutionalism has been one of the most important foundations of the democratic political system. Through democratic processes, such as electing constitutional representatives or holding plebiscites, people have decided the structure of their country's government and how it should be formed, how political power should be allocated among the different political institutions, and the rights and obligations of all citizens. As Duchacek puts it,

> No national system today therefore fails to establish and officially describe various central, regional, and local agencies in charge of legislation, administration, and adjudication. With a very few exceptions such a basic map of power organization is contained in a single written document, the national constitution, or, as it is sometimes called, the supreme law of the land.[6]

---

[4]As opposed to the *ruptura* in Portugal and Eastern Europe. See Bermeo, "Redemocratization and Transition Elections," 214; also see Juan J. Linz, "Transitions to Democracy," *The Washington Quarterly* 13, no. 3 (Summer 1990): 150-54.

[5]Under the current constitutional setup, the president is elected indirectly by the National Assembly, and the premier and his cabinet are appointed by the president. The president is the head of state and commands certain political powers, while the premier is the chief executive and separated from the legislative branch. The system is something of a mixture of the presidential and the parliamentary systems, but differs from both in that the top decision-makers are not elected.

[6]Ivo D. Duchacek, *Power Maps: Comparative Politics of Constitutions* (Santa Barbara, Calif.: American Bibliographical Center-Clio Press, 1973), 3.

The existence of a constitution is not a sufficient condition for the successful functioning of a democratic political system, but it is generally recognized that democracy will not succeed without a set of commonly accepted rules to regulate political processes and to, in Duchacek's terminology, map out political power.

Constitutions come in different forms. They can be a set of rules that a country has come to accept as a result of long years of political practice, as in the case of the United Kingdom, Israel, and New Zealand. Or they can be a new framework established from without, as in the case of most other functioning democracies. But no matter how a constitution is written or created, one thing is common to all successful democracies: the constitution is respected and observed by the government and the people. The government, through democratic processes, maintains its functions and operations by following the basic rules set out in its constitution.

However, the above argument does not imply that a constitution will lead a country to democracy. Almost without exception, all countries, even the most autocratic socialist regimes, have a constitution. These authoritarian regimes actually impose constitutions on their people as a means of political control.[7] These regimes also formulate sets of rules to guard against challenges by potential power-seekers. But these authoritarian governments cannot be termed democratic merely because they have constitutions.

Nevertheless, a constitution is such a prominent feature of democratic countries that people in authoritarian countries have learned that both constitution-writing and the political processes formulated by a constitution should be democratic in nature. When authoritarian regimes break down, people know what to accept and what not to accept in their new constitutions. In this indirect sense, a constitution can be seen as a factor conducive to the process of democratization.

This line of argument can be applied to the case of the ROC on Taiwan. The governmental structure prescribed by the 1947 Constitution was largely, although not entirely, based on the teachings of the founding father of the Republic, Dr. Sun Yat-sen. The system is unique in the sense that it is neither a presidential system like that of the United States nor a British-style parliamentary system, the two most widely followed models of democracy. Instead, it is headed by a president, who is elected by the National Assembly, and consists of five major government branches: the Executive, Legislative, Judicial, Control, and Examination Yuans. The first three of these are equivalent to the three major branches of government found in Western democracies. The Control Yuan was designed to oversee the entire government establishment and to guard against corruption. It has the power to

---

[7]William B. Simons, ed., *The Constitutions of the Communist World* (Germantown, Md.: Sijthoff & Noordhoff, 1980), xii.

investigate cases of suspected corruption involving government officials and to impeach them for impropriety or mismanagement of governmental affairs. Another distinctive feature of the ROC Constitution is the Examination Yuan, which was set up to conduct national examinations for recruiting civil servants. The original idea of this system was to make sure that the government bureaucracy only employed qualified persons and to prevent favoritism.

Even though some important provisions of the Constitution were frozen due to the prolonged state of war with the Communists, many of its important features have been implemented in Taiwan. For example, some elections specified in the Constitution have been held without interruption. In addition, people in Taiwan have also learned that the Constitution is, in essence, designed to establish a democratic government and to protect civil rights and political freedom. They were able to use the provisions protecting civil liberties to challenge government restrictions. In other words, the existing Constitution and the process of its revision are very important factors conducive to further democratization in Taiwan.

The purpose of this chapter is to explain the problems of the current ROC Constitution and the actors and politics involved in the process of revision. The conclusion, which may seem less optimistic than the government's own prediction, is that full revision of the Constitution according to established models of democracy will not become reality, and that Taiwan may expect more constitutional crises in the near future.

Problems of the Current Constitution

The ROC Constitution, though it directly or indirectly helped to bring about liberalization and democratization in Taiwan in recent years, contains important provisions that might hamper the future process of democratization. These provisions include the division between the presidency and the premiership, the need to retain the National Assembly and Control Yuan, and the need to appoint Mongolian, Tibetan, overseas Chinese, and minority representatives to the three chambers of the parliament. All these provisions were seriously debated during the constitutional revision process in the first half of 1992.

The ROC central government, as provided by the ROC Constitution, is neither presidential nor parliamentary, nor is it the mixed system found in France. Neither the president nor the premier is chosen according to the results of popular elections. Yet the president is the supreme commander of the military, has the power to declare a national emergency, and most important of all, must cosign all laws and orders issued by the premier.[8]

---

[8]ROC Constitution, Sections 35 to 43.

The Constitution also specifies that when there is a conflict between the different Yuans, the president has the power to mediate so that the government can continue to operate.[9] The constitutional provisions governing the presidency, therefore, provide the president with an enormous amount of power over government decision-making.[10]

At the same time, the premier is not a mere deputy of the president. The ROC Constitution clearly specifies that the Executive Yuan is the highest administrative organ of the nation, with the premier as the chief executive.[11] The Executive Yuan has the power to propose legislative bills and budget bills, treaties, and declarations of war and martial law to the Legislative Yuan.[12] According to the Constitution, the Executive Yuan should report to the Legislative Yuan about important government decisions and policies, and the members of the Legislative Yuan have the right to interpellate ministers, including the premier. Moreover, if the Legislative Yuan is dissatisfied with a particular bill, it can send it back to the Executive Yuan for revision, though the Executive Yuan may, with the approval of the president, refuse to rewrite the bill. In a similar way, the Executive Yuan may refuse to accept revisions made by the legislature to one of its bills. In both these cases, however, if a two-thirds majority of legislators supports the Yuan's original decision, the premier should either accept it or resign.[13] This provision is clearly similar to the no-confidence vote found under a parliamentary system. Yet one important factor distinguishes the ROC's five-power system from the parliamentary model: the premier and the ministers are not members of the Legislative Yuan. Rather, the president appoints the premier who in turn appoints the ministers subject to presidential approval. While the president is indirectly elected through the National Assembly, the premier is not held accountable to any public selection process, except that he has to be confirmed by the Legislative Yuan. In short, this is a very strange setup for a central government and the most important area that needs to be reformed if Taiwan is to make further progress with democratization. For Taiwan to be a true democracy, at least one of the two top executive offices *must* be open to a popular electoral contest.

Another area that has become a political problem is the existence of the National Assembly and the Control Yuan. Although these two institutions are very different in appearance and perform very different functions, they face the same challenge from the general public. An essential principle of the five-power system is that there should be a separation between ruling

---

[9]ROC Constitution, Section 44.
[10]Hui-yin Tu, "The Special Power of the President of the Republic of China," *Hsien-cheng shih-tai* (Constitutional Review) (Taipei) 11, no. 3 (January 1986): 16.
[11]ROC Constitution, Section 53.
[12]ROC Constitution, Sections 57, 58.
[13]ROC Constitution, Section 57 (2).

power (*chih-ch'üan*) and political power (*cheng-ch'üan*). While political power resides in the National Assembly, the ruling power is held by the five Yuans. And above these five Yuans, there is the office of president which is the highest political office in the country.

In the first four decades after 1949, the National Assembly was made up of deputies elected in mainland China whose only responsibility was to elect the president and the vice president. However, the chaotic presidential election of 1990 prompted thousands of college students to demonstrate in downtown Taipei, and they seriously challenged the Assembly's legitimacy.[14] The need for a National Assembly has since then been debated among the ruling KMT, the reform-minded liberals, and the opposition. The KMT's position is that if the National Assembly is abolished, the basic structure of the five-power Constitution will be destroyed, violating the principles of the founding father, Dr. Sun Yat-sen. But the opposition insists that the National Assembly is redundant, and that the people of Taiwan are intelligent enough to elect a president themselves.

The Control Yuan has faced similar challenges. Since the ruling party monopolizes the appointment of Control Yuan members, its effectiveness as an anti-corruption watchdog has been kept to a minimum. Moreover, the corruption allegations against recently elected Control Yuan deputies have increased people's distrust of this body. The KMT, however, is not eager to abolish this chamber, since it is an important part of Sun Yat-sen's unique five-power design. Nevertheless, as the opposition and the reformers argue, the function of the Control Yuan can easily be replaced by the Judiciary and the Legislative Yuan.

The ROC Constitution also specifies that the three chambers of the parliament, the National Assembly, the Legislative Yuan, and the Control Yuan, must contain overseas Chinese, Mongolian, Tibetan, and other minority representatives.[15] But since these minorities make up only a very small proportion of the population, and all of them have lived in Taiwan since 1948-49, there is really no need to reserve seats for them. In addition, the merits of selecting overseas Chinese representatives are challenged on the ground that the majority of overseas Chinese have given up their Chinese citizenship, putting their loyalty to the Republic of China into question.

These problems with the Constitution have become stumbling blocks to Taiwan's further political development. They need to be resolved so that the top decision-makers of Taiwan can be selected through democratic political process, and the parliament can avoid becoming systematically corrupted.

---

[14]*Chung-kuo shih-pao* (China Times) (Taipei), March 16, 1992, 1.
[15]ROC Constitution, Sections 26, 64, 91.

The Politics of Constitutional Reform

Constitutional Crisis and the
Preparatory Stage of Reform

As early as 1513, Niccolo Machiavelli observed:

> It must be realized that there is nothing more difficult to plan, more uncertain of
> success, or more dangerous to manage than the establishment of a new order of
> government; for he who introduces it makes enemies of all those who derived
> advantage from the old order and finds but lukewarm defenders among those who
> stand to gain from the new one.[16]

This statement was as true in Spain in the mid-1970s, or in Canada in the
early 1990s, or in Taiwan in 1992 as it was in medieval Italy.

Reform of the Constitution began to be discussed in Taiwan after the
authoritarian regime was forced by pressure from below to formally terminate
martial law in mid-1987. But in contrast to the Spanish experience, where
Franco's death brought down the existing political establishment and the
contending political groups met to create a new political system, the KMT
was able to maintain its ruling position after President Chiang Ching-kuo's
death in January 1988, and reaffirm its ruling position in the national elections of 1989 and 1991. In the 1989 Legislative Yuan election, the KMT
was able to win 63 percent of the popular vote and 71 percent of the con-
tested seats.[17] In the December 1991 National Assembly election, the per-
centages were 71 percent and 75 percent.[18] In other words, the political
establishment associated with authoritarian rule was not voted out after the
democratization process was set in motion.

Serious debates on reforming the Constitution surfaced in 1990 when
Lee Teng-hui was campaigning for the presidential election. Under the 1947
Constitution, the president of the Republic of China is elected by the Na-
tional Assembly. However, as the Assembly's delegates were convening in
March to discuss the election and possible constitutional revision, thousands
of students from all over the country staged a Tienanmen-style marathon
protest against the National Assembly in the Chiang Kai-shek Memorial
Park in downtown Taipei.[19] The protesting students, with the support of
opposition forces, issued several demands, including the dissolution of the
National Assembly, the ending of the Period of Mobilization, the convention
of a national affairs conference, and a definite schedule for political and

---

[16]Niccolo Machiavelli, *The Prince* (first published in 1513; Toronto: Bantam Classic Edition,
1981), 27.

[17]*Tzu-yu shih-pao* (Liberty Times) (Taipei), December 4, 1989, 2.

[18]Ibid., December 22, 1991, 1.

[19]The marathon protest, which lasted from March 16 to March 22, was widely reported in
Taipei's newspapers.

economic reform. In order to end the student protests, President-elect Lee
Teng-hui received student representatives in the Presidential Office on March
21, and promised to speed up political reforms.[20] A few days later, President
Lee held a historic meeting with the chairman of the opposition DPP, Huang
Hsin-chieh, in order to reduce tension between Taiwan's two major parties.
At the meeting, Lee put forward concrete suggestions concerning the national
affairs conference, a draft schedule for ending the Period of Mobilization,
and revising the Constitution.[21]

Amid the largest student demonstration in Taiwan's history, the KMT
fell into its fiercest internal power struggle over the issue of presidential
elections. Conservative KMT leaders, such as the then premier Lee Huan,
the then minister of defense Hau Pei-tsun, the head of the Judicial Yuan
Lin Yang-kang, and Wego Chiang, the second son of Chiang Kai-shek and
then secretary-general of the National Security Council, formed a power bloc
to challenge President Lee and his vice-presidential candidate Li Yuan-tzu.[22]
The power struggle created a deep division in the KMT between the "Mainstream" faction (*Chu-liu p'ai*), led by Lee Teng-hui, and the "Non-Mainstream"
(*Fei-chu-liu p'ai*) faction, led by Lee Huan. The bitter struggle was halted
temporarily only when Lin Yang-kang backed down from his bid for the
presidency and President Lee announced the nomination of General Hau
Pei-tsun as the new premier.[23]

The National Affairs Conference, the first high-profile forum for de-
bating constitutional issues, was held in June 1990 as scheduled. Even though
the conference provided an opportunity for Taiwan's social and political
leaders to exchange ideas on constitutional reform, it fell short of reaching
concrete agreements on constitutional issues, except for the direct election
of the Taipei and Kaohsiung city mayors and the provincial governor.[24]

In order to provide a legitimate basis for revising the Constitution,
the government requested the convention of the Council of Grand Justices
which passed a resolution requiring all senior deputies (those frozen in office
since 1947) in the three chambers of the parliament to retire by the end of

---

[20]*Tzu-yu shih-pao*, March 23, 1990, 3; *Washington Post*, March 22, 1990, A25 and March 27,
1990, A20.

[21]*South China Morning Post*, April 3, 1990, 14; *Lien-ho pao* (United Daily News) (Taipei),
April 2, 1990, 1.

[22]*China News* (Taipei), February 12, 1990, 1.

[23]Ibid., May 6, 1990, 3.

[24]Jaushieh Joseph Wu, "Debate on the Central Government System During the National Affairs
Conference," *Issues & Studies* (Japanese Edition) (Tokyo) 20, no. 1 (October 1990): 52. Even
though session chairman Wu Feng-shan, an independent, concluded the session on presidential
elections by declaring that the president should be popularly elected by the people of Taiwan,
this result was questioned by the KMT representatives at the conference on account of a
procedural error. See *China News*, July 5, 1990, 7.

1991. Moreover, the government also forced the National Assembly to adopt ten additional constitutional provisions in April 1991, the so-called first stage of constitutional revision, and to provide a legal basis for the election of a new Assembly with the sole function of revising the Constitution.[25] The KMT's intention was to use the existing National Assembly for one last time to legitimize the constitutional reform to be carried out by its successor. However, the ten additional provisions provided for more than the election of the new National Assembly; they also laid down specific conditions for electing the new parliamentary deputies, such as the allocation of at-large seats and seats reserved for overseas Chinese and Taiwan aborigines. The participation of senior National Assembly deputies in the first stage of constitutional revision caused a public uproar, but the new provisions did at least allow for the retirement of these veteran parliamentarians.

The Formal Process of Constitutional Revision

The formal process of constitutional revision in Taiwan differs from other known cases. In 1977, the Committee on Constitutional Affairs and Public Liberties of Spain's Congress of Deputies appointed a seven-member Ponencia (subcommittee), according to the relative strengths of the main political parties, to draw up a draft constitution which would later be elaborated and approved by the Congress.[26] In the case of the Philippines in 1986-87, President Corazon Aquino appointed a forty-seven-member constitutional committee, based on recommendations from different sectors of Philippine society, to draft a new constitution.[27] The draft was then formalized by a plebiscite in February 1987. In most established democracies, major constitutional changes brought about by a constitutional crisis take place either in the parliament, as in the case of Canada, or in a constitutional convention, as in Australia, or in a special committee of the parliament, as in India.[28] But the formal process of constitutional revision in Taiwan took an entirely different path: the Nationalist government in April 1990 decided to elect a new National Assembly, an existing institution with little political power, to modify the existing Constitution.

The election of the new 325-member National Assembly took place at the end of 1991 as scheduled. The KMT obtained 254 seats, while the opposition DPP got only 66 seats and the independents 5 seats.[29] But the

---

[25]*Lien-ho pao*, April 23, 1991, 2.

[26]Richard Gunther and Roger A. Blough, "Religious Conflict and Consensus in Spain: A Tale of Two Constitutions," *World Affairs* 144, no. 4 (Spring 1981): 397-98.

[27]Chen Hurng-yu, "A Comparative Study of Two Philippine Constitutions," *Wen-t'i yü yen-chiu* (Issues & Studies) (Taipei) 26, no. 6 (March 1987): 4-5.

[28]See Vernon Bogdanor, ed., *Constitutions in Democratic Politics* (Aldershot, UK: Gower Publishing, 1988).

[29]*Tzu-yu shih-pao*, December 22, 1991, 1.

Table 2.1
Party Composition of the Second National Assembly, ROC

Party	Const. seats	At-large seats	Overseas seats	1st N.A. members	Total seats	% total seats	% vote 1991
KMT	179	60	15	64	318	78.90	71.1
DPP	41	20	5	9	75	18.61	23.9
CSD[a]	0	0	0	0	0	0.00	2.2
IA[b]	3	0	0	1	4	0.99	2.1
YCP[c]	0	0	0	1	1	0.25	0.0
Ind.	2	0	0	3	5	1.24	0.4
Total	225	80	20	78	403	99.99	99.7

Sources: *Lien-ho pao* (United Daily News) (Taipei), December 22, 1991, 1; *Tzu-yu shih-pao* (Liberty Times) (Taipei), December 22, 1991, 1.
[a]CSD = Chinese Social Democratic Party.
[b]IA = Independents Alliance.
[c]YCP = Young China Party.

composition of the new National Assembly is complicated by the fact that, in line with the 1990 constitutional provisions,[30] the 78 deputies who won their seats in the 1986 election were also included in the second Assembly.[31] That put the total number of deputies in the new National Assembly at 403 (see table 2.1). This number is exceptionally large relative to Taiwan's population when compared to parliamentary bodies elsewhere.[32]

The KMT claimed that it had received a clear mandate from the people to direct the constitutional revision process. This claim is not surprising, since the KMT gained 71 percent of the popular vote and more than 78 percent of the total seats in the Assembly. This allowed the KMT to dominate the Assembly sessions, since the Constitution provides that a three-fourths

---

[30]Two KMT members of the first National Assembly, Chen Chuan and Hsieh Lung-sheng, were also chosen to fill at-large seats.
[31]*Lien-ho pao*, April 23, 1990, 2.
[32]The size of the major parliamentary bodies with constitutional revision powers can be found in Gabriel A. Almond and G. Bingham Powell, Jr., *Comparative Politics*, 2nd ed. (Boston: Little, Brown, 1978), 263. Even more detailed figures can be found in Gerhard Loewenberg and Samuel C. Patterson, *Comparing Legislatures* (Boston: Little, Brown, 1979), 305-10. For example, Canada's Parliament has 264 members, Mexico's Chamber of Deputies has 231, Argentina's Chamber of Deputies has 243, Brazil's National Congress has 364, Colombia's House of Representatives has 199, France's National Assembly has 490, Sweden's Riksdag has 350, Australia's House of Representatives has 127, and Israel's Knesset has 120. Taiwan's National Assembly is quite large in comparison.

majority is necessary to pass a constitutional reform proposal. But it was clear that this claim would only hold true if the KMT members in the National Assembly remained a united group and were willing to follow the orders of the party center, and if the party center in turn had a unified agenda for constitutional revision. However, KMT solidarity was put to a serious test when the National Assembly convened in March 1992.

Even though the legitimacy of the new National Assembly was recognized by the general public on account of it having been elected democratically, its exceptionally large size ensured that its sessions were chaotic. As noted by Gunther and Blough in their studies on Spain's experience in drafting a constitution in 1977-78:

> Numerous experiments in social psychology have shown that the number of participants [in negotiating a new constitution], per se, has a significant impact on the capacity of groups to make decisions; the optimum size for reaching collective decisions appears to be about six. Larger groups tend to dissolve into debating societies and reach decisions only with great difficulty.[33]

The above observation by social psychologists and experts on Spanish constitutional revision is confirmed by the experience of Taiwan's new National Assembly. Frequent disruptions caused by procedural problems, shouting matches, and pushing and shoving prevented the members from addressing key constitutional issues.[34] The tense atmosphere between the parties, and even between factions of the same party, did not allow issues and stands to be clearly represented.

The chaotic situation in the National Assembly could have been significantly improved had the ruling party itself reached a binding consensus on key issues, such as presidential elections and the selection of members of the Control Yuan. Group theory would have us believe that "the greater effectiveness of relatively small groups—the 'privileged' and 'intermediate' groups—is evident from observation and experience as well as from theory."[35] This is also emphasized in studies of the Spanish experience of constitution-making:

> Party elites . . . must have the capacity to obligate their followers to respect or support that compromise before it may be regarded as successfully resolving the conflict in question. In the parliamentary context, this requires the existence of party discipline. Outside of parliament, it requires that a party have the capacity to control the behavior of its supporters.[36]

---

[33]Gunther and Blough, "Religious Conflict and Consensus in Spain," 394.

[34]The most serious conflict came on April 16 when a fist-fight broke out between members of the two parties in which three members were injured. *Tzu-yu shih-pao*, April 17, 1992, 1, 2.

[35]Mancur Olson, *The Logic of Collective Action: Public Goods and the Theory of Groups*, 7th printing (Cambridge, Mass.: Harvard University Press, 1977), 53.

[36]Gunther and Blough, "Religious Conflict and Consensus in Spain," 395.

During the National Assembly election in late 1991, the KMT made it quite clear that the method of electing the president should be indirect, and done through the National Assembly. This stand was in very sharp contrast to that of the DPP, which argued all along that Taiwan should adopt a presidential system like that of the United States, and that the president should be popularly elected. But a few weeks before the National Assembly convened in March 1992, the issue of the presidential election suddenly became a topic of hot debate within the KMT's Central Standing Committee. Because of the KMT's absolute majority the new National Assembly became a battleground for an intensified power struggle between the two factions of the KMT that had formed during the 1990 presidential election campaign, and the debate with the DPP was set aside. This is an obvious example of how the ROC's experience of constitution-making differs from that of other democratic countries.

In view of its minority position, the DPP decided that its strategy in the National Assembly should be—in Albert O. Hirschman's words—to "voice" its discontent at the KMT's domination of the process and to threaten to "exit" the system.[37] Even though the DPP's long-standing position on the separation of powers between the three branches of government and the direct election of the president is clear and sound, as opposed to the KMT's unclear position on constitutional revision and unwillingness to depart sharply from the problematic five-power system, its minority position has prevented it from making a significant impact on the drafting of the new constitutional provisions. It could only engage in filibustering and raise procedural issues to attract public attention to its grievances. The opposition party also held rallies and demonstrations, those of April 19 through 24 being the most noticeable, to voice its discontent over the constitutional revision process. At times it also threatened to boycott the process, a quasi-exit option,[38] to make it clear that the KMT alone should be responsible for the constitutional mess.

In early May, the DPP deputies finally withdrew from the National Assembly. Three weeks later, eight members of the Independents Alliance also dropped out, leaving the constitutional revision process entirely in the hands of the KMT. The withdrawal of the opposition is understandable on account of its inability to affect the process. The DPP originally had high hopes of forming a temporary coalition with some KMT members to push for the direct election of the president. But this was forestalled when the ruling party, because of dissention within its ranks, decided to shelve this issue until a later session, possibly after 1995. Unable to influence the out-

---

[37]Albert O. Hirschman, *Exit, Voice, and Loyalty: Responses to Decline in Firms, Organizations, and States* (Cambridge, Mass.: Harvard University Press, 1970).
[38]Ibid., 86.

come, the opposition and its independent allies had no incentive to remain in the National Assembly and share the blame for not reaching a clear decision on this issue.

The opposition's withdrawal did not end the conflict in the National Assembly or improve the general atmosphere of the session. The KMT deputies were engaged in a tug-of-war on various issues, particularly on the proposal to increase the power of the Assembly and reduce that of the Legislative Yuan. The resulting chaos led to calls from the public for the abolition of the National Assembly altogether.

Actors and Conflicts of Interest

One of the most durable theories on political development has been brilliantly stated by that equally durable political scientist, Seymour Martin Lipset:

> Perhaps the most widespread generalization linking political systems to other aspects of society has been that democracy is related to the state of economic development. Concretely, this means that the more well-to-do a nation, the greater the chances that it will sustain democracy. From Aristotle down to the present, men have argued that only in a wealthy society in which relatively few citizens lived in real poverty could a situation exist in which the mass of the population could intelligently participate in politics and could develop the self-restraint necessary to avoid succumbing to the appeals of irresponsible demagogues.[39]

Taiwan's experience of democratization generally follows the pattern described by development theory. As the economy boomed in the 1970s and 1980s, Taiwan's society became increasingly pluralistic, and more and more people were willing to participate in politics and pursue political power through different channels.[40] At the time of the constitutional revision, the social and political conditions of Taiwan in general can be described as very open and competitive, and different political groups were eager to participate in the process.

However, because of this growing participation, conflicts of interest have become ever more complicated, making the consensus needed for a peaceful constitutional reform very difficult to attain. The Spanish experience in 1978 indicates that the ability of the top elites of major political groups to reach consensus on major issues is essential to constitution-making.[41]

---

[39]Seymour Martin Lipset, "Some Social Requisites of Democracy: Economic Development and Political Legitimacy," *American Political Science Review* 53, no. 1 (March 1959): 75. Numerous other authorities have expressed the same idea; for example, Huntington, "Will More Countries Become Democratic," 198-99; Larry Diamond, Seymour Martin Lipset, and Juan Linz, "Building and Sustaining Democratic Government in Developing Countries: Some Tentative Findings," *World Affairs* 150, no. 1 (Summer 1987): 10-11.

[40]Jaushieh Joseph Wu, "Toward Another Miracle? Impetuses and Obstacles in Taiwan's Democratization" (Ph.D. dissertation, The Ohio State University, 1989), 117-71.

[41]Gunther and Blough, "Religious Conflict and Consensus in Spain," 403.

But Taiwan's experience in 1992 is a different story. Some very complicated political groupings and crosscutting political interests were trying to inject their own ideas into constitutional revision without a proper mechanism to formulate a workable decision-making process.

Nevertheless, Taiwan's growing social and political pluralism is not the only reason for the intensifying conflicts of interests. One has to look at the general political system, particularly the electoral system, for further explanation of the growing factionalism and lack of party discipline. For a ruling party to function effectively in a parliamentary system, party discipline is essential. However, Taiwan's political system can hardly be described as being based on the parliamentary model. Many important decisions are made by the president or the premier or through the KMT Central Standing Committee, without any consultation of KMT members of the Legislative Yuan. Because the KMT is in process of breaking away from its authoritarian past, many of its legislators are eager to express their own ideas on the decision-making process and challenge the authority of the Central Standing Committee, many of whose members are not elected representatives. In other words, the weakening of the party center, which is due to the changing political environment, has coincided with the growing autonomy of Legislative Yuan members who correctly claim to represent a certain proportion of the population.

Moreover, the electoral system and the nomination process also contribute to the growing factionalism within the ruling party. For the party to maximize its gains in a multi-member district, the KMT often has to form coalitions of convenience with local factions and nominate candidates who have significant influence in local politics. But the interests of the local faction may not always correspond with the interests of the ruling party on the national level. As a result, the elected KMT parliamentarians, who have spent a tremendous amount of money and gone through great difficulties to win their seats, may well place their personal and factional interests ahead of the party's interests. They also form factions within the parliament to make sure their interests prevail. During the constitutional revision process, the party center might prefer direct presidential elections and wish to limit the power of the National Assembly. However, it would be inconceivable for the popularly elected members of the National Assembly to support the party's stands on these issues, as to do so would mean committing institutional suicide.

Because of the very pluralistic nature of Taiwan society and its conflicting political interests, it is difficult to divide the significant actors in the political arena into all-inclusive and mutually exclusive categories, although this is what has been attempted in figures 2.1 and 2.2.[42]

---

[42]The figures are the result of long and intense discussions with Dr. Szu-yin Ho, a colleague at the IIR and a specialist in Taiwan's elections. The author acknowledges Dr. Ho's comments and suggestions.

Figure 2.1
Important Actors in the Constitutional Revision Process, Legislative Yuan

Party Affiliation

		KMT	DPP
	Mainstream	Wisdom Coalition	Formosa
Faction			
	Non-Main-stream	New KMT Alliance Parl. Reform Assoc. Construction Research Assoc.	New Tide

Figure 2.2
Important Actors in the Constitutional Revision Process, National Assembly

Party Affiliation

		KMT	DPP
	Mainstream	Direct Election	Formosa
Faction			
	Non-Main-stream	Indirect Election	New Tide
		Military	

Both of Taiwan's major political parties are plagued with factional wrangling. As mentioned above, the KMT broke into "Mainstream" and "Non-Mainstream" factions in 1990, and since then the factional squabbles have continued and even spread to other political institutions.

In the Legislative Yuan, the Wisdom Coalition (*Chi-ssu hui*), a political group consisting of twenty-six legislators, became one of the most important blocs supporting the Mainstream Faction of the KMT. The Wisdom Coalition published its own ideas on constitutional revision as early as April 12, 1991, which advocated direct election of the president and the abolition of the National Assembly and the Control Yuan, making the Legislative Yuan the only chamber of the ROC's parliament.[43]

The New KMT Alliance (*Hsin Kuo-min-tang lien-hsien*), another group of eleven legislators, became a staunch supporter of the more conservative Non-Mainstream Faction, which has also gained the support of a dozen or so legislators with military backgrounds or military backing. The New KMT Alliance strongly opposes President Lee Teng-hui both as president and chairman of the KMT. However, the Alliance cannot decide whether the president should be directly elected and the National Assembly abolished, or whether the five-power system should be retained. The Alliance revealed its distaste for the National Assembly when its leader, Legislator Lee Sheng-feng, called Wang Ying-chieh, a leading KMT member of the Assembly, a piece of trash.[44] The subsequent attacks and rebuttals clearly showed that the New KMT Alliance did not want the government to retain the National Assembly. There are two additional groupings in the Legislative Yuan, namely, the Construction Research Association (*Chien-she yen-chiu hui*) and the Association for the Reform of the Parliament (*Kuo-hui kung-neng kai-ke hui*), which are loose organizations aimed at curbing the growing influence of the Wisdom Coalition.

In the National Assembly, the KMT is divided by the issue of presidential election, as the names of the two factions, the Direct Election Faction (*Chih-hsüan p'ai*) and Indirect Election Faction (*Wei-hsüan p'ai*) indicate. The two factions have had emotional confrontations on the floor of the Assembly over how the president should be elected and whether political power should be centered in the president or the premier, and have also tried to undercut the power of one or the other. However, on other issues, the two factions were not so clearly divided. Many members of both factions tried to increase the power of the National Assembly by proposing that it should institute a speaker (*i-chang*), the equivalent of the majority leader in the U.S. House of Representatives, and committees and subcommittees, which would make it a permanent institution instead of an electoral college on the

---

[43]Wisdom Coalition, "Draft of the Revised ROC Constitution" (April 12, 1991).
[44]*Chung-kuo shih-pao*, April 14, 1992, 2.

American model. They also wanted the Assembly to have the power to review legislation and confirm presidential nominations to the Control Yuan and the Council of Grand Justices. What makes the situation worse is that many National Assembly deputies want to restrict the power of the Legislative Yuan by overseeing its budget and shortening its term of office to two years. This latter proposal evoked violent reactions from the legislature which threatened to cut the National Assembly's budget.

On the DPP side, the traditional conflict is between the more moderate Formosa Faction (*Mei-li-tao*) and the more radical New Tide Faction (*Hsin-ch'ao-liu*). The two factions divide along the issue of whether Taiwan should pursue democratization from within its existing institutions or seek independence through mass movements.[45] The two factions of the DPP also differ in their emphasis on constitutional reform. The Formosa Faction stresses the need for direct election of the president, while the New Tide Faction wants to have a new constitution, a new political system based on the American model, and a new name for the country: the Republic of Taiwan. Nevertheless, the two DPP factions seemed to be able to contain their differences in the process of constitutional revision in 1992 and coordinated their activities both in the National Assembly and on the streets.

With great discrepancies in parties, in institutions, and in factions, and each trying to play a role in the constitutional revision process, it became very difficult to reach a consensus. Neither of the two political parties, particularly the ruling KMT, have been able to work out their internal differences and reach decisions binding on their members in the National Assembly. Even a temporary coalition between the KMT's Mainstream Faction and the Formosa Faction of the DPP would not have given supporters of a directly elected president the necessary three-fourths majority to pass a proposal in the Assembly. Moreover, for a KMT faction to ally with the DPP on one issue, some compromise would have had to be made with another KMT faction on other issues. The result of the compromise might not be what that coalition wanted. In addition, such coalition efforts would very likely antagonize other party members and cause the parties to split. Such a split would make the situation even more complicated and a consensus even harder to reach. This kind of political rivalry eventually made it impossible to revise the Constitution to suit Taiwan's needs.

A General Assessment of the New Provisions

The KMT's final plan for constitutional reform was approved by the Central Standing Committee on May 6, 1992, and sent to the National As-

---

[45]Wu, "Toward Another Miracle?" 192-203.

sembly for adoption.[46]   On May 27, the National Assembly adopted eight of the proposed provisions, but the article that would have lengthened the term of the Legislative Yuan from three to four years was purged.[47]   The most important feature of the new provisions is that they significantly increase the power of the president and the National Assembly at the expense of the premier and the Control Yuan.   The president, under the new design, has the power to nominate members of the Control Yuan, the Council of Grand Justices, and the Examination Yuan, and his nominations are subject to the approval of the National Assembly.   However, this reallocation of power lacks certain supporting features and makes the new constitutional setup look very strange.

First of all, the key issue of the method of electing the president is left undecided, leaving room for further factional conflict and political crisis. If it is decided at a later date that the president should be directly elected, there will have to be another round of revisions to delete those articles in the original Constitution relating to presidential election.   This would make the National Assembly virtually redundant.   Despite this possibility, the KMT's revision proposals give the Assembly new powers to confirm certain presidential nominations.   A fair explanation for this apparent contradiction is that the KMT center wanted to give the National Assembly additional powers to make up for possible future losses in other areas, and by doing so ensure the smooth adoption of its nine provisions.

Secondly, the distribution of power between the president and the premier, which sparked off the constitutional crisis of 1990-91, was not even touched upon in the KMT provisions.   The DPP and the nonpartisan National Assembly members had high expectations that the reform process would produce a presidential system of government with the premier as the president's chief administrator.   However, this idea was blocked by KMT members of the National Assembly, prompting the walkout of DPP members and independents.   The KMT, left to design its own revisions, had to shelve this issue on account of bitter factional rivalry.   This result may be seen as the institutionalization of the factional conflict within the KMT, and it means that the offices of president and premier will continue to be occupied by top leaders of the two opposing factions.   The new provisions thus failed to resolve the most important issue that had given rise to the original constitutional crisis.

Another strange feature of the provisions is the method for selecting members of the Control Yuan.   The Control Yuan has come under bitter criticism from the public for corruption, and the KMT Central Standing Committee decided to deal with this by having Yuan members appointed by

---

[46]*Tzu-yu shih-pao*, May 7, 1992, 2.
[47]*Chung-kuo shih-pao*, May 28, 1992, 4.

the president instead of elected either by the Provincial Assembly or municipal councils as at present or by the entire electorate. However, this change brings into question the Yuan's ability to oversee the operations of the government of which the president is part. In addition, one may reasonably suspect that the president will choose Control Yuan members on the basis of loyalty rather than merit.

In short, the great efforts put into the constitutional revision process did not result in a new government setup that would resolve the constitutional problems and prevent another constitutional crisis, and so the process may be judged a failure. Indeed, the new setup, far from resolving existing problems, also added new uncertainty to an already complicated system.

Conclusion: Problems and Prospects

As pointed out earlier, the need for constitutional revision stemmed firstly from the fact that Taiwan has undergone substantial sociopolitical change since the existing Constitution was drafted, and secondly from the constitutional crisis over allocation of power between the president and the premier. To solve this constitutional crisis rather than merely defusing it would require an entirely new design for the central government, one that would either draw a clear line between the powers of the two offices or, alternatively, establish a unified executive power. The National Assembly was unable to come up with such a design because it was riven with a power struggle. It may take a few more years and much more social and political upheaval before the constitutional setup can be redesigned to suit the needs of the rapidly changing political situation in Taiwan.

This analysis indicates that the 1992 revision of the ROC Constitution, which should have been the key event in the current stage of democratization in Taiwan, did not achieve any major breakthrough. The nine new provisions proposed by the KMT did not clearly reallocate power among the various institutions of the central government, and they will not prevent political conflicts from continuing outside of these institutions. Consequently, the process of democratization in Taiwan is still not complete, as key government officials are still not democratically elected. The prospects for Taiwan's quest for democracy are still uncertain. In contrast to many other countries that have successfully produced new democratic constitutions, Taiwan still lacks a constitution which meets with the expectations of its people.

CHAPTER 3

Constitutional Review in the Republic of China on Taiwan: The Changing Role of the Council of Grand Justices

Jyh-Pin Fa

In addition to the renowned series of political and constitutional reforms initiated by late President Chiang Ching-kuo during his later years, which culminated in the two recent amendments to the Constitution, a quieter, less-conspicuous constitutional evolution, sponsored by the Council of Grand Justices, has also taken place in the Republic of China (ROC) on Taiwan. This process has contributed to, and even accelerated, the unprecedented reforms. Furthermore, the Council has in recent years increasingly taken up other awkward constitutional problems in order to achieve, step by step, the goal of constitutionalism in Taiwan. It seems that the Council has shifted from the somewhat obscure and deferential role it assumed during its first twenty-nine years of the Constitution to become more assertive over the last sixteen years. This change is not an isolated one, nor is it an accident: the trend of political, economic, and social change during this period has been conducive to judicial transformation. Any extended discussion of this subject, however, is surely beyond the scope of this chapter. Instead, my focus here is on the Constitution as interpreted by the Council of Grand Justices, especially those interpretations rendered by the fourth term Council (1976-85) and the current fifth term Council (1985-94).

The Status of the Council of Grand Justices

According to the Principles for the Revision of the Draft Constitution of 1936,[1] drawn up by the Political Consultative Conference, a forum held

---

[1]Article 140 of the Draft Constitution of 1936 provided that "the question whether a law is in conflict with the Constitution shall be settled by the Control Yuan submitting the point to the

in 1946 in an attempt to achieve a political consensus in China, the judicial structure of the Republic was to be headed by the Judicial Yuan, which was also to act as the nation's supreme court. It was to be composed of a number of grand justices nominated by the president with the consent of the Control Yuan. This appears to follow the American model. Authority to interpret the Constitution was included alongside the other judicial function of deciding civil, criminal, and administrative cases not only in the draft constitution proposed by the Political Consultative Conference, but also in the final draft adopted by the government. Indeed, when Sun K'e, the president of the Legislative Yuan, which was responsible for the constitutional draft, reported on the draft to the constituent 1946 National Assembly, he did not hesitate to call the Judicial Yuan "equal to the Supreme Court of the United States."[2]

This simple arrangement for the judicial system was changed unexpectedly and confusedly by delegates to the National Assembly. The Assembly separated the function of constitutional interpretation from the regular judicial work of civil, criminal, and administrative litigation, and it assigned the grand justices the former task only. The underlying reason for the change has never been fully explained.[3] Since the 1947 Constitution still provides that the Judicial Yuan shall be in charge of civil, criminal, and administrative cases,[4] the Judicial Yuan itself exercises the functions of a supreme court and an administrative court. However, in the subsequent amendments to the Organic Law of the Courts and the Organic Law of the Administrative Court, pressure from members of the Supreme Court, especially those holding concurrent administrative positions who were afraid of any structural changes affecting their interests,[5] caused the status of the Supreme Court and Administrative Court to be kept intact.[6] The resulting

---

Judicial Yuan for interpretation within six months after its enforcement." However, it failed to specify whether the Supreme Court or another specialized court which it would create within the Judicial Yuan was to assume the task.

[2]See the Secretariat of the National Assembly, *Kuo-min-ta-hui shih-lu* (The faithful record of the National Assembly) (1946), 396.

[3]It has recently been suggested by a current grand justice, Mr. Chang Te-sheng, that this was in fact done by accident. See Chang Te-sheng, "Several Important Issues Concerning the Judicial System under Our Country's Constitutional Framework," in the Secretariat of the Judicial Yuan, *Ssu-fa-yuan ta-fa-kuan shih-hsien ssu-shih-chou-nien chi-nien lun-wen-chi* (Essays to commemorate forty years of constitutional interpretations by the grand justices of the Judicial Yuan) (Taipei: September 1988), 245.

[4]Article 77. For an English text, see *China Handbook 1953-54* (Taipei: 1953), 563.

[5]See Li Hsüeh-teng, "Highlights on the Interpretation of the Constitution," *Hsien-cheng shih-tai* (Constitutional Review) (Taipei) 14, no. 2 (1988): 4; Weng Yüeh-sheng, "The Guardian of the Constitution: Reflection and Prospects," in *Ssu-fa-yuan*, 145; and note 3 above. These authors are, respectively, a former grand justice (Li) and current grand justices (Weng since 1972 and Chang since 1985).

[6]Many considered this change to be in violation of the Constitution. For example, Lei Chen,

fragmentation of the judiciary makes the necessary coordination and supervision between courts and other judicial organs extremely difficult, if not impossible.

As a result of this arrangement, the Judicial Yuan, although it is the supreme organ of the judiciary as provided in the Constitution, does not in fact entertain litigation at all. Instead, the Supreme Court and various lower courts, the Administrative Court, and the Committee on the Discipline of Public Functionaries under the Judicial Yuan are responsible for this. Combined with the Council of Grand Justices, which is responsible for the interpretation of the Constitution and uniform interpretation of statutes and regulations, they constitute the major part of the Judicial Yuan. More specifically, the functions of the Judicial Yuan may be divided into two categories: the exercise of jurisdiction over civil, criminal, and administrative cases and over cases concerning disciplinary measures against public servants; and interpretation of the Constitution and unified interpretation of statutes and regulations. These functions are exercised by four distinct organs within the framework of the Judicial Yuan: the Council of Grand Justices, the Supreme Court, the Administrative Court, and the Committee on the Discipline of Public Functionaries.[7]

The Structure and Procedures
of the Council of Grand Justices

As the only organ which is explicitly empowered by the Constitution to interpret the Constitution and render a uniform interpretation of statutes or regulations (the latter function was exercised by the Judicial Yuan, the Supreme Court in practice, before the promulgation of the Constitution[8]), the Council of Grand Justices occupies a conspicuous position in the government structure. It is composed of seventeen members whose qualifications are specified.[9] Grand justices are appointed by the president of the Republic

---

Chih-hsien shu-yao (A concise history of constitution-making) (Taipei: 1957), 61-62; Lin Chi-tung, a retired three-term grand justice who served in the Council from 1958 to 1985 and who is also a leading scholar in constitutional law, concurred. See Lin Chi-tung, *Chung-hua-min-kuo hsien-fa chu-t'iao shih-i* (A detailed study of articles of the ROC Constitution) (Taipei: 1982), 39.

[7]Herbert Han-pao Ma, "The Council of Grand Justices of the Republic of China: Its Role in a Changing Society," in *Ssu-fa-yuan*, 478.

[8]See Lawrence Shao-liang Liu, "Judicial Review and Emerging Constitutionalism: The Uneasy Case for the Republic of China on Taiwan," *American Journal of Comparative Law* 39 (1991): 516.

[9]Article 4 of the Organic Law of the Judicial Yuan provides that only those persons who have one of the following qualifications shall be eligible to serve as a grand justice: "(1) not less than ten years' service as a judge of the Supreme Court with a distinguished record of service; (2) not less than nine years' service as a member of the Legislative Yuan and with a record of significant contribution to its activities; (3) not less than nine years' teaching experience in major courses at a university or college, and authorship of specialized writings in the field of law; (4)

after securing the approval of the National Assembly.[10] They serve a nine-year term and may be reappointed without restriction.[11] Therefore, through actual implementation and development, the Council of Grand Justices has been transformed into a "special court," somewhat similar to the constitutional courts established by West Germany and Italy after World War II.

From the establishment of the Council in 1948 up to 1991, there have been seventy-three grand justices. A superficial review will show that the Council has been comprised mainly of senior judges, law professors, and politicians. However, a more detailed analysis reveals that the number of politicians has been reduced substantially in recent times; the Council now recruits its members mainly from the bench and the universities.[12]

Having detailed the composition of the Council of Grand Justices, we can now proceed to the other side of the picture: the parties concerned. Who is best qualified to represent the interests involved in determining the validity or invalidity of a governmental act? The answer is not a simple one and, like other aspects of the judicial review system, the practice in civil law countries runs counter to that of America. The Constitution has no clause corresponding to Article 3, section 2, paragraph 1 of the United States Constitution, which limits the jurisdiction of the federal courts specifically to a "case or controversy." Thus, legislation regulating the jurisdiction of the Council of Grand Justices was drafted in 1957.

Article 3 of the Law Governing the Council of Grand Justices (hereafter "Governing Law") provides:

> As to the interpretation of the Constitution, the Council of Grand Justices is authorized to exercise the following: (1) to clear up doubts and problems arising from application of the Constitution; (2) to determine and explain whether a law or regulation is in conflict with the Constitution; (3) to determine and explain whether the statutes for self-government of provinces and counties and regulations issued by provincial and county governments are in conflict with the Constitution.

Except for laws relating to the self-government of provinces, which is the only type of statute that must be submitted by the province in question to the Judicial Yuan immediately after its enactment to determine its constitutionality,[13] the remaining functions have to be exercised upon the receipt

---

membership of the International Court or authorship of authoritative books in the field of public law or comparative law; and (5) erudition in jurisprudence and experience and renown in politics." Par. 2 of the same article further stipulates that the number of grand justices appointed by virtue of any one of the above qualifications shall not exceed one-third of the total number.

[10]Art. 79, par. 2 of the Constitution and Art. 13 of the Amendments to the Constitution.

[11]Art. 5, par. 1 of the Organic Law of the Judicial Yuan.

[12]For details, see Jyh-Pin Fa, *A Comparative Study of Judicial Review under Nationalist Chinese and American Constitutional Law* (1980), 75-76.

[13]Article 114 of the Constitution.

of an application for interpretation. Both governmental organs and individuals have the right to apply for constitutional adjudication if they meet the rather detailed conditions laid down by the Governing Law. In the case of the former, three conditions are provided:

1. When an organ encounters a question in applying a provision of the Constitution while performing its duties;
2. When a dispute arises between governmental agencies with regard to the application of a provision of the Constitution in conducting their official business; or
3. When a question is raised as to whether the application of a certain statute or administrative regulation is in conflict with the Constitution when it is applied.[14]

In short, any doubt concerning the Constitution, disputes between government organs, and the question of the constitutionality of legal norms are the three subjects open to the government applicant. As there is no "case or controversy" requirement, this direct—sometimes even abstract— review procedure has greatly expanded the scope of judicial review beyond that available in the United States. Interpretations in these cases are generally of an advisory nature. Although they conceivably link the Council closely with other government departments, they also embroil the Council in political whirlpools it would be wiser to avoid under the American doctrine of "political question." Interpretation No. 76, issued on May 3, 1957, may be cited as an example. In order to settle disputes among the National Assembly, the Legislative Yuan, and the Control Yuan, the Council held that they were all equivalent to a parliament or congress in the Western sense. This aroused strong opposition from the Legislative Yuan, which considered itself the only body qualified to be so identified. The legislature then enacted the Governing Law to clarify—in fact restrict—the functions of the Council.[15] We will deal with this point later. However, it is suggested that in view of the special status of the Council, whose function it is to clarify and resolve constitutional issues (if they are properly initiated according to prescribed procedure), and in the interests of constitutional clarity and certainty, the import of the political question doctrine may still be debatable.[16]

An individual may apply to the Council if he or she believes that his or her constitutional rights have been infringed, but only after regular legal remedies have been exhausted. However, the subject of review is limited to the constitutionality of the statute or regulation which was applied in the final decision on the case by the court of last resort.[17] Compared with the

---

[14]Art. 4, par. 1 of the Governing Law.

[15]For details, see Liu, "Judicial Review," 525.

[16]See generally, Mauro Cappelletti, *The Judicial Process in Comparative Perspective* (New York: Clarendon Press, 1989), 138; Donald P. Kommers, *The Constitutional Jurisprudence of the Federal Republic of Germany* (Durham, N.C.: Duke University Press, 1989), 163; "German Constitutionalism: A Prolegomenon," *Emory Law Journal* 40 (1991): 842. But see Liu, "Judicial Review," 554-55.

[17]Art. 4, par. 2. of the Governing Law.

above-mentioned government application case, it is easy to see that both the scope and procedure for individual applications are extremely restricted. This comparison is supported by empirical data. Between 1958, the year the door was opened to individual applications and also the beginning of the second Council, and 1976, the last year of the third Council, only one individual application succeeded in producing a constitutional interpretation.[18] The most common grounds for rejection were that the individual had either not exhausted legal remedies or had not indicated what specific constitutional rights had been violated. The significance of granting standing to individuals was thus seriously restricted by rigid procedural barriers. Moreover, it must be pointed out that even constitutional interpretations applied for by the government were not very numerous during this eighteen-year period. In all, there were only nine cases.[19]

However, a considerable number of interpretations (fifty-seven) on unifying the interpretation of statutes or regulations were rendered by the Council during this period. When the fifty-four uniform interpretations of the first term (1948-58) are included,[20] they constitute 76 percent of total interpretations up to 1976. It is clear that constitutional interpretation was given secondary importance as compared with the Council's other function. One major factor that contributed to this imbalance was the relatively loose procedural requirements in the case of uniform interpretation of statutes or regulations. Although only government agencies may apply to the Council for this procedure, a unified interpretation may be established by a simple majority of the grand justices present at a meeting with a quorum of not less than half the total number of grand justices. In the case of a tie, the president of the Judicial Yuan has the casting vote.[21] In contrast, a constitutional interpretation must be approved by three-quarters of the grand justices present at a meeting with a quorum of three-quarters of the total number of grand justices.[22]

Since September 1976, the beginning of the Council's fourth term, a few encouraging signs have been detected. First, the function of uniform interpretation has gradually declined from its peak during the third term (1967-76) when such interpretations comprised 91.67 percent of all the Council's interpretations. On the other hand, the Council's constitutional interpretation function, which had dwindled to the point that it could be totally

---

[18]Interpretation No. 117.

[19]*Ssu-fa-yuan*, 562, table 4.

[20]Ibid., 563, table 5.

[21]Art. 13, par. 2 of the Governing Law.

[22]Ibid., Art. 13, par. 1; Art. 6, par. 1 of the Organic Law of the Judicial Yuan. For the internal review procedure within the Council, see Ma, "The Council of Grand Justices," 481, and Liu, "Judicial Review," 520-23.

disregarded as a factor in Taiwan's constitutional development, began to pick up. Members of the fourth Council lost no time in doing everything possible to reverse the trend away from constitutional interpretation. Their efforts were rewarded, and over the fourth term 60.38 percent of their interpretations were constitutional interpretations. This trend continued when the fifth Council took office in September 1985. As of December 1990, 69 percent of the total interpretations have involved constitutional issues.[23]

Second, the number of successful individual applications for constitutional interpretation has increased substantially since 1976. Of all the constitutional interpretations rendered by the fourth Council, twenty-seven were applied for by individuals, comprising 84.37 percent of the total.[24] This contrasts sharply with the previous two terms, which accepted only one individual application in eighteen years, as mentioned above. This open-door policy has continued into the fifth term. Eighty-three percent of all constitutional interpretations originated from individuals as of December 1990.[25] A close analysis reveals that all twenty-three constitutional interpretations rendered by the fifth Council in the period from October 1985 to July 1988 were initiated by individuals,[26] with the government's backing. Perhaps the government realized that it was politically wiser to leave certain sensitive, even explosive, constitutional issues to the Council, rather than addressing them itself. One-third (seven) of the constitutional interpretation applications came from government organs in 1990.[27] Nevertheless, they may be construed as part of the expansion of individual applications because most of them were initiated by the legislatures: either the Legislative Yuan (No. 261), the provincial assembly (No. 260), or city councils (Nos. 250, 258, 259).

It is interesting to note here that there is a causal relationship between Interpretation No. 177 (see below) and this increase. Individual applications increased steadily each year to a total of fifty-eight in 1982. However, the number increased dramatically to 150 in 1984 and to 178 in 1987,[28] after the general public began to appreciate the significance of this interpretation. This increase in applications, of course, also increased the success rate, though actually only a very small number (about 2-3 percent) can survive the rigorous procedural scrutiny.[29]

---

[23]My own calculation from data in the Judicial Yuan, *Ssu-fa an-chien fen-hsi* (An analysis of judicial cases) (Taipei: October 1991), 82, table 13.

[24]*Ssu-fa-yuan.* 562, table 4.

[25]See note 23 above.

[26]*Ssu-fa-yuan,* 562, table 4.

[27]There were twenty-one interpretations (Nos. 251-271) in 1991.

[28]*Ssu-fa-yuan,* 557-58.

[29]Ibid., 560, table 2. This figure is comparable to that of the German Constitutional Court which grants full dress review to barely more than one percent of all constitutional complaints. See Kommers, *The Constitutional Jurisprudence,* 16-17.

The Effects of Unconstitutionality

Although Articles 171 and 172 of the Constitution expressly provide that unconstitutional acts (statutes as well as administrative regulations) shall be null and void, the effective nullification date of the unconstitutional statute, regulation, or judgment and the retroactive effect of the ruling on the case which generated the request for judicial review in the first place were two important problems which remained unanswered for many years. Legal uncertainties also cost the Council the necessary public confidence in its authority to implement or enforce its interpretations.[30]

These problems were largely solved by the Council's own efforts in recent years. In addition to the Council declaring solemnly that its interpretations shall be binding for all organs of government, including courts and citizens alike,[31] beginning from Interpretation No. 218 of August 1987, it has followed the Austrian model of fixing a target date for any verdict of unconstitutionality to become effective.[32] The Council declared that an administrative interpretation of the Ministry of Finance was to be made inapplicable within six months of the publication of the decision. Interpretation No. 224, rendered on April 22, 1988, went even further by pronouncing some provisions of the Law on Tax Collection unconstitutional and declaring them void not later than two years from the date of publication of the interpretation. This was because under these provisions only people who could afford half or one-third of the tax imposed were eligible to challenge a particular tax decision. The right of access to court and the principle of equality, both explicitly guaranteed by the Constitution, had thus been violated. The time limits for Interpretations Nos. 251, 289, and 300 are eighteen months, two years, and one year respectively, depending on the scope of unconstitutionality.

As for making applications by individuals retroactively effective, the major opposition came from the Supreme Court and the Administrative Court. A desire to maintain the final authority and integrity of the final judgment rendered by these courts of last resort was understandably the primary reason for their hardline position. But this attitude would make individual applications to the Council a mere symbolic appeal, because the individual would receive no benefit even if he or she secured a favorable

---

[30]The long delay in the implementation of Interpretations Nos. 86 and 166 is very illustrative here. See Jyh-Pin Fa, "Constitutional Developments in Taiwan: The Role of the Council of Grand Justices," *International and Comparative Law Quarterly* 40 (January 1991): 206, and Liu, "Judicial Review," 526-27, 531. The necessary amendments finally completed the legislative process in June 1991.

[31]Interpretation No. 185.

[32]Mauro Cappelletti, *Judicial Review in the Contemporary World* (Charlottesville, Va.: Michie-Bobbs, 1971), 89.

interpretation. This was another major factor that explains the past reluctance of individuals to apply for constitutional interpretations.

The Council finally decided to take the initiative. On November 5, 1982, the Council of Grand Justices, in Interpretation No. 177, recognized the necessity of limited retroactivity. This interpretation originated in a civil case. After deciding that a precedent was partly unconstitutional, the Council expressly declared at the end of the interpretation that "if the people are to benefit from the interpretation, its legal effect must be extended to the very case which generated the constitutional interpretation in accordance with the purpose of permitting individual application; and the applicant may thus seek legal remedies." That is, the individual may apply to the court of last resort, the Supreme Court or Administrative Court, for retrial. This position was confirmed again in Interpretation No. 185. This retroactive effect may only be extended to other pending applications on the same subject as that of the applicant, but no further.[33]

The Recent Performance
of the Council of Grand Justices

From the previous discussion, one may note that the Council of Grand Justices has adapted itself to the changing needs of society by following a more open and liberal policy since 1976. However, this policy has not been limited to procedural aspects only. The Council has also become more assertive in the substance of its constitutional interpretations. In addition to providing advisory opinions and legitimating government action, the checking function of the Council has been more apparent than ever before. The grand justices have more frequently been asserting their own opinions, not necessarily in accord with those of the government.

Compared with only one decision involving unconstitutional statutes before 1976 (Interpretation No. 86), as many as six statutes and one legislative resolution have been declared partially or wholly unconstitutional since then.[34] Eight interpretations have involved administrative regulations or interpretations which were found to be in conflict with the Constitution.[35] The objects of frequent attacks from the Council were pre-1947 judicial interpretations and numerous judgments rendered either by the Supreme Court or the Administrative Court.[36] Moreover, not only has the frequency of declarations of unconstitutionality increased substantially during the fifth term (beginning

---

[33]Interpretation No. 193.
[34]Interpretations Nos. 166, 224, 251, 264, 288, 289, 300.
[35]Interpretations Nos. 151, 167, 210, 218, 268, 273, 274, 280.
[36]Interpretations Nos. 156, 185, 187, 201, 213, 220, 242, 243, 256, 266, 271, 269, 275, 295.

from Interpretation No. 199), but the Council's attitude is now more straight-forward. The word "unconstitutional" or any close synonym was deliberately left out of Interpretations Nos. 86 and 166, both of which in fact declared some provisions unconstitutional.[37] This face-saving attitude is no longer considered necessary. However, in more than a few cases, the Council has also adopted a policy of lecturing and directing relevant departments to review and amend a statute, regulation, or specified measure while still holding it to be constitutional;[38] or else it has tolerated the present practice of rule by administrative regulations but required its prompt replacement by proper legislation.[39]

Among these interpretations, the exclusion of judicial review was clearly the primary concern of the Council on more than ten occasions;[40] the Council has confirmed time and again the absolute necessity of providing the individual with access to judicial review. The constitutional guarantee of the right of access to the court[41] has thus been firmly implemented. The emphasis is in fact in accordance with the approach adopted by Japan and Italy, both of which also explicitly guarantee the general right of access to courts in their present constitutions and which have adhered to this very strictly.[42]

The doctrine of requirement of law, which requires a legal base for administrative action when it concerns the fundamental rights of the individual or the government structure, is one of two wings of the rule of law in civil law jurisprudence.[43] Eight interpretations belong to this category, all of which required either a legislative bill to substitute the current administrative regulation,[44] or necessary legal authorization.[45]

Of the unconstitutional statutes mentioned above, half were related to personal freedoms. Two interpretations prescribed that petty offenses shall also be tried in court if a custodial sentence can be imposed.[46] A third interpretation further provided that the number of times a court can impose one-month sentences on one individual in a bankruptcy case shall be

---

[37]See Liu, "Judicial Review," 540-41.

[38]Interpretations Nos. 148, 153, 167, 195, 204, 205, 211, 214, 222, 247, 250, 263, 265, 270, 276, 277, 290, 294.

[39]Interpretations Nos. 222, 250, 259, 270, 289.

[40]Interpretations Nos. 156, 187, 201, 213, 220, 224, 243, 266, 269, 273, 288, 295, 298.

[41]Article 16 of the Constitution.

[42]See generally, Cappelletti, *Judicial Review*, 226-28.

[43]The other one is the supremacy of law. See Mahendra P. Singh, *German Administrative Law in Common Law Perspective* (New York: Springer-Verlag, 1985), 5.

[44]Interpretations Nos. 222, 250, 259, 270, 289.

[45]Interpretations Nos. 151, 167, 210.

[46]Interpretations Nos. 166, 251. See Ma, "The Council of Grand Justices," 493-95, and Liu, "Judicial Review," 531, 538-39, 541.

specifically restricted.[47] These cases evidently demonstrate that the personal freedoms guaranteed by the Constitution[48] are fully recognized by the Council of Grand Justices.

Besides cases concerning individual rights and the rule of law, which made up the bulk of the constitutional review workload, the Council also rendered decisions that directly contributed to the recently accomplished constitutional reforms. Adhering to the implementation procedure laid down by the Constitution (under which a unified statute, the General Principles of Provincial and County Self-Government, has to be passed by the Legislative Yuan before local self-government may be initiated in any province of the Republic),[49] the Council rejected categorically a limited legislative proposal applied specifically to Taiwan Province by either the Legislative Yuan or the Taiwan Provincial Assembly.[50] This meant that the only way to address Taiwan's special case was to amend the Constitution.[51] Interpretation No. 261 paved the way for representatives and legislators elected over forty years ago in mainland China to step down before December 31, 1991, and required the long-delayed second general election to be held in Taiwan. This most serious constitutional problem, which had haunted the government for many years, was accordingly rectified.

However, in spite of its active performance in recent years, the Council still faces some basic problems. Most of all, the status of both the grand justices and the Council as a whole remains unclear. Should grand justices be given the same status as judges are under the Constitution? According to the passages of the Constitution mentioned above, both constitutional interpretation and litigation are the business of the Judicial Yuan. But the Constitution provides that only judges shall have life tenure,[52] while the Organic Law of the Judicial Yuan provides a nine-year term for the grand justices. Whether a grand justice is also a judge with life tenure granted by the Constitution, and whether, accordingly, the related provision of the Organic Law is unconstitutional, has yet to be decided.[53] But this uncertainty has already undermined the authority of the Council as a whole.

Few countries with a special constitutional court provide life tenure for its members. Since 1967, Italian justices have held office for nine years, and since 1970, service on the Federal Constitutional Court of West Germany

---

[47]Interpretation No. 300.

[48]Article 8 of the Constitution.

[49]Article 112 of the Constitution.

[50]Interpretation No. 260.

[51]Article 17 of the Amendments to the Constitution.

[52]Article 81 of the Constitution.

[53]It is reported that this important constitutional issue has already been docketed in the Council for years, but for fear of a conflict of interests, the Council is reluctant to make a final decision. See Chang, "Several Important Issues," 250-51.

has been restricted to a single twelve-year term. Civil law countries have felt that life tenure might lead to carelessness in job performance or loss of contact with ordinary life. Therefore, in order to preserve the advantages of a limited term without jeopardizing the independence of the Council, restrictions on reappointment and a comfortable retirement plan for the grand justices seem desirable.

Whether the Council should be reorganized into a constitutional court is another question that is frequently raised. As it does not conduct trials, and rarely summons applicants for explanations or clarifications even under the present practice,[54] the work of transformation may not be easy. However, the process is beginning because, according to a recent constitutional amendment, a constitutional tribunal composed of all grand justices will rule on cases involving political parties suspected of "endangering the existence of the Republic of China or the nation's free liberal democratic constitutional order," and a dissolution order may then follow.[55]

Conclusion

Based originally on a vague perception of constitutional review and always constrained by a variety of unfavorable factors, such as martial law, one-party rule, the hostility of other branches of the government and other courts, public apathy, etc., the Council of Grand Justices struggled from the beginning to prove itself. Until 1976, its record was, at best, mediocre. Since then signs of change have been clearly identified. This is not, of course, a spontaneous development, but the result of political, social, and economic changes in Taiwan. The Council has not only introduced new vitality into the constitutional review system but stimulated and accelerated the recent constitutional reforms. Compared to the "judicial negativism"[56] of the Japanese Supreme Court, which has only declared a statute unconstitutional in five cases since World War II, the recent performance of the Council is indeed notable and deserves some credit. However, in view of the anti-majority nature of constitutional review, judicial activism should not be unduly encouraged. The Council of Grand Justices will be lucky if it can equip itself with sufficient intelligence and observation to strike a proper balance between judicial activism and passivity.

---

[54]Article 12 of the Governing Law.

[55]Article 13 of the Amendments to the Constitution.

[56]See generally, Yasuhiro Okudaira, "Forty Years of the Constitution and Its Various Influences: Japanese, American, and European," *Law and Contemporary Problems* 53, no. 1 (1990): 37-43.

Part Two

The ROC's Economic Development and International Economic Cooperation

CHAPTER 4

The ROC's Economic Development and Its International Cooperation Program

Gee San

The economic development experience of the Republic of China (ROC) on Taiwan has attracted worldwide attention. In the past four decades Taiwan has been able to achieve rapid economic growth combined with balanced income distribution; a successful transition from an agricultural to an industrial economy without serious labor conflict; a high degree of economic stability without serious inflation or unemployment; and financial solvency without foreign debt. The questions are, how did Taiwan accomplish this remarkable performance, and what policies and economic strategies were crucial to Taiwan's economic success? Apart from addressing these questions, this chapter will explore the relevance of Taiwan's experience to other countries and how it can be incorporated into the ROC's international cooperation program.

Taiwan's Economic Development Experience: 1950-79

In the 1950s, many less-developed countries which had just thrown off the shackles of colonialism were anxious to develop their economies in as short a time as possible. One of the most popular development strategies among these mainly agricultural countries was import substitution. Their basic argument was twofold. First, the terms of trade for imports of agricultural goods to industrial countries had deteriorated over the past century. In these circumstances, it was preferable that less-developed countries should not rely on agricultural exports to fuel economic development, but should develop their own industries which should be fostered by a policy of protectionism.[1]

---

[1]See Chi-ming Hou, "Strategy for Industrial Development," in *Proceedings of the Conference on Economic Development in the Republic of China on Taiwan*, CIER [Chung-Hua Institution for Economic Research] Conference Series no. 7 (Taipei: CIER, 1987), 245-74.

Second, in the light of U.S. experience during the Depression of the early 1930s and British experience after World War II, it was widely believed that public enterprises could, and should, play a significant role in economic stabilization and job creation. Clearly, there was a perfect match between the promotion of public enterprises and the implementation of an import-substitution policy which soon spawned a flourishing "infant" publicly owned industrial sector in many of the less-developed Asian and Latin American countries.

After the end of Japanese colonial rule in Taiwan in 1945, many of the enterprises set up by the Japanese were taken over by the ROC government. At that time, government economic policy was colored by Sun Yat-sen's principle of "enhancing the nation's capital and constraining the accumulation of private capital." So no effort was made to privatize all of these public concerns, although the development of the rather weak private sector was encouraged. Various import-substitution policies which were then in practice in other less-developed countries were introduced, and the primary goals of these policies were to protect the development of domestic enterprises and to conserve precious foreign exchange reserves.

Besides imposing high tariffs and various import restrictions to block the importation of foreign goods, the ROC also introduced a complex system whereby different exchange rates were applied to different types of imports. This was used to discourage the importation of consumer goods, especially luxuries, and to subsidize imports of basic raw materials and industrial products. Furthermore, to encourage investment in both the public and private sectors, interest rates were maintained at artificially low levels. It did not take long, however, for the government to recognize that the import-substitution policies described above were creating difficulties. For example, the artificially low interest rate policy not only created enormous inflationary pressure in the commodity market, but also failed to channel domestic savings into the capital market. As a result, savings in domestic institutions were discouraged and scarce investible capital was often wasted and misallocated. In addition, it was soon found that the limited domestic market was saturated and capital utilization rates in many important manufacturing industries were very low. Obviously, a more aggressive policy was needed in order to reallocate scarce resources and promote sustained economic development.

At the suggestion of S. C. Tsiang[2] in the mid-1950s, the government decided to drop its low interest rate policy and interest rates were subsequently adjusted several times in an effort to curb domestic inflation. As a result, the consumer price index fell from 18.8 percent in 1953 to 1.7 percent in 1954 (it was 9.9 percent in 1955, 10.5 percent in 1956, and 7.5 percent

---

[2]Now professor emeritus at Cornell University and chairman of the Board of Trustees of the Chung-Hua Institution for Economic Research.

in 1957). Scarce investible capital was then allocated in such a way as to ensure fair returns on investment. In 1958 the multiple exchange rate system was abolished. The importance of this move should never be overlooked, as the adoption of a single rate system represented a change on the part of the government from a passive policy of conserving foreign exchange reserves to one of actively creating them. Instead of overvaluing the currency to discourage imports, the currency was undervalued in order to promote exports. Taiwan was rapidly entering a new era of export expansion.

In tandem with the foreign exchange reform, many other important policies were introduced to ensure the success of the export promotion drive. These policies included the establishment of export processing zones (EPZs), customs rebates for imported materials, special low interest loans for export activities, and government-financed export promotion facilities and market research. These export promotion efforts proved to be extremely successful: the total export volume grew nearly ten times from 1960 to 1970, and the total volume of imports grew nearly six times during the same period. Furthermore, the export promotion drive transformed Taiwan from an agricultural to a more manufacturing-oriented economy. The agricultural sector's share of gross domestic product (GDP) declined from 28.7 percent in 1960 to 15.5 percent in 1970, while the share of the industrial sector increased from 29.5 percent to 41.3 percent. In addition, export promotion substantially improved the standard of living in Taiwan with per capita gross national product (GNP) more than doubling (from US$153 to US$387) during the period 1960-70.

It is important to note that an export expansion policy alone could not have achieved the economic success described above; it required the coordination of other policies to promote labor productivity and to better allocate scarce resources so that the overall competitiveness of the economy was sustained. Among the various policies implemented during the 1950s and 1960s, population control, the manpower policy, land reform, and the U.S. aid utilization policy were perhaps the most vital ones.

Population Policy

As the Taiwan economy recovered from World War II and both agricultural and industrial production gradually picked up in the 1950s, Taiwan inevitably encountered the challenge of whether it could break loose from the Malthusian low income trap. As living standards improved, the population growth rate naturally increased, and this could have adversely affected the growth of real per capita income and offset capital formation efforts.

The birth rate in the early to mid-1950s was as high as 4.5 percent in Taiwan. Obviously, some kind of birth control measures were needed in order to avoid this trap. Conversely, however, the idea of implementing birth control measures encountered strong resistance from various groups in the country. Many argued that in view of the threat of an invasion from Communist China, national security considerations should be placed above all economic considerations. Furthermore, it was argued that Sun Yat-sen's mandate in 1924 called for more people to fight against Western imperialism and birth control measures were certainly against Dr. Sun's teaching.[3] Despite these objections, a population control policy steadily gained the endorsement of key policymakers and won the support of the general public. Many realized that the quality of the population was more important than the quantity, and in the mid- to late 1960s prenatal examinations and contraceptive information and services were introduced. As a result of this birth control policy, Taiwan's birth rate gradually fell from 3.27 percent in 1965 to 2.34 percent in 1980 and 1.66 percent in 1990.

Manpower Policy

Efforts were also made to promote education and vocational training in order to fully utilize available manpower—one of Taiwan's most important and abundant resources. Some notable measures included extending compulsory education from six to nine years in 1968; diverting more junior high school graduates to senior vocational schools rather than senior high schools in order to meet the manpower needs of the rapidly growing manufacturing sector; establishing various public training programs and public training centers; and devoting efforts and resources to upgrading the skills of vocational instructors. As a result of these measures, public expenditure on education as a percentage of total government expenditure increased from 9.93 percent in 1951 to 16.51 percent in 1971 and to 17.77 percent in 1990, or as a percentage of GNP from 1.73 percent to 4.8 percent and 5.88 percent.

Land Reform

The agricultural land reform program of the late 1940s and early 1950s played a critical role in promoting the development of the agricultural sector and accelerating the transformation from an agricultural to an industrial economy. The first phase of the reform was a rent reduction program which capped the amount of rent that landlords could legally charge their tenants at 37.5 percent of the yield from the main crop. The program provided a strong incentive for farmers and eliminated possible exploitation by the landlords. Phase two involved the sale of public land to tenant cultivators at a price equivalent to 2.5 times the total annual yield of the main crop. Payments could be made in interest-free installments over a ten-year period. In the final phase of land reform, the "land to the tiller" program introduced in 1952, landlords were limited to slightly under three hectares of land and were obliged to sell the excess to the government. Landlords were then compensated with commodity bonds and stock in public enterprises. The land

---

[3]See K. T. Li, *The Evolution of Policy behind Taiwan's Development Success* (New Haven and London: Yale University Press, 1988).

was then resold to tenant farmers on the terms described above. It is reported that landlords' annual receipts from the commodity bonds were worth NT$538 million and the total value of the stocks in four public enterprises was NT$660 million. This huge amount of capital fostered capital formation in the private manufacturing sector and opened the door to further industrial development. This established a solid socioeconomic base for rapid economic development.[4]

U.S. Aid

One should not neglect the importance of the role of U.S. aid which from 1951 to 1965 comprised more than 30 percent (sometimes as high as 50 percent) of domestic investment each year in Taiwan. Of that, roughly 37.3 percent is said to have been devoted to improving the infrastructure, including electric power, transportation, and communications projects; 21.5 percent went to the agricultural sector in the form of help for irrigation and crop improvement schemes and low-interest loans to farmers; 25.9 percent was used for manpower training and training facilities; and only 15.3 percent served as low-interest loans to the manufacturing sector.[5] Clearly, the strategy in utilizing U.S. aid was to focus on overall improvement of the infrastructure rather than targeting certain narrow sectors of industry. This strategy proved to be effective in achieving balanced economic development in Taiwan.

* * *

The decade of the 1970s marked an important dividing line for economic development in the ROC. By the early 1970s, Taiwan was ready for an economic takeoff. Per capita GNP had grown from US$153 in 1960 to US$519 in 1972, which provided a solid base for capital accumulation. In fact, in 1972 the private sector already accounted for 67 percent of total national savings. In addition, the growth rate of industrial production had exceeded 15 percent (sometimes more than 20 percent) each year since 1964, which provided a solid platform for industrial development. In 1971, for the first time, the agricultural sector accounted for less than 14 percent of GDP, with industry accounting for more than 43 percent. Progress in economic development was also reflected in Taiwan's international trade activities: foreign trade accounted for as much as 60.3 percent of GNP in 1971 and Taiwan has enjoyed a commodity trade surplus ever since. Social factors

---

[4]See Yu-kang Mao, "The Role of Agriculture in Economic Development of Taiwan, ROC," in *Proceedings of the Conference on Economic Development in the Republic of China on Taiwan*, 363-420.

[5]See Neil H. Jacoby, *U.S. Aid to Taiwan*, Praeger Series on International Economics and Development (New York: Praeger, 1966).

such as the low unemployment rate (0.8 percent in 1972) and the suppression of the birth rate to under 2.5 percent also played their part.

Some notable policies aimed at promoting science and technology were adopted in the 1970s in an effort to maintain economic growth and cope with the first oil crisis in 1973. These included: (1) establishment of the Industrial Technology Research Institution (ITRI) in 1973 to assist the massive number of private enterprises to conduct research and development (R&D); (2) opening of the Hsinchu Science-Based Industrial Park in 1979 to attract both foreign and domestic investment in high-tech products; and (3) establishment of the Institute for Information Industry (III) to train information technicians and engineers and to promote automation and computerization in order to improve productivity. Obviously, the government's development strategy in the 1970s had gradually shifted away from labor-intensive manufacturing to the development of more technology-intensive industries. This change in development strategy was mainly the result of pressure from soaring labor costs in a situation of full employment since the mid-1960s, and of calls for better utilization of high quality manpower.

Other notable government policies in the 1970s included the "Ten Major Development Projects," the largest infrastructure construction effort since the suspension of U.S. aid in 1965. Embracing the construction of a north-south highway, nuclear power plants, railroad electrification, a large-scale steel mill, new harbors, and an international airport, the project provided Taiwan with a more efficient transportation and communications system, low-cost energy alternatives, and a more balanced industrial structure in preparation for further economic upgrading and development.[6]

Some More Specific Issues in
Taiwan's Economic Development Experience

In addition to the social and economic policies discussed above, there are other factors which played a crucial role in Taiwan's economic takeoff, such as government expenditure, public enterprises, savings, and foreign direct investment. We shall now address these relevant issues in turn.

The Structure of Government Expenditure

Besides adopting various policies to promote economic development,

---

[6]In 1991, the ROC government launched an ambitious Six-Year National Development Plan (1991-96), under which NT$8.2 trillion (approximately US$320 billion) will be spent on (1) major infrastructural projects including the expansion of port facilities, a high-speed railway, water-supply projects, highway expansion, and a fourth nuclear power plant; (2) the expansion of higher education and improvement of vocational education; (3) supporting projects for the development of key technologies such as opto-electronics, information software, industrial automation, biotechnology, etc.; and (4) other projects to promote social welfare and upgrade the quality of life.

Table 4.1
The ROC Government's Revenues and Expenditure (1963-90)

Unit: NT$ billion

Fiscal year	Total revenues	Surplus (+) or deficit (−)	Expenditure / GNP (%)	Foreign exchange rate (per US$) (buying)
1963	15.841	−0.616	19.9	40.00
1965	23.841	0.993	21.1	40.00
1970	51.215	2.062	23.4	40.00
1975	134.034	7.598	22.8	37.95
1980	368.922	23.526	25.9	35.96
1985	576.039	12.310	23.7	39.80
1990	1,198.602	43.059	26.5	27.13

Source: *Taiwan Statistical Data Book 1991* (Taipei: Council for Economic Planning and Development, 1991), 153.

the ROC government has always kept a tight curb on government expenditure, and with the exception of 1982, has enjoyed a budgetary surplus each year since 1964 (see table 4.1). Before 1987, ROC law stipulated that the total value of outstanding government debt should not exceed 40 percent of the central government's annual budget. As a result of this stipulation, the government has avoided having to compete with the private sector for the limited amount of credit available on the capital market. This has lubricated the development of the private sector, which in turn has generated more tax revenue for the government. This interaction between the public and private sectors is thus mutually beneficial.

A major source of government revenue in the 1950s was indirect taxes such as customs duties, commodity tax, land tax, etc. (see table 4.2). At that time, the import substitution policy meant that customs duties accounted for as much as 16.38 percent of government revenue. The second major source of government revenue at that time was the tobacco and wine monopoly, which in the 1950s through the 1970s was one of the major sources of income for salary payments to government employees. From table 4.2 we can see that the importance of this monopoly revenue has declined significantly from the early 1980s. In addition, due to the adoption of trade liberalization policies in the early 1980s, customs duties were drastically reduced, resulting in a sharp decline in the share of indirect taxes. In contrast, however, the share of direct taxes has been increasing over the years. One of the government's long-term goals is to increase the share of direct taxes in total government revenue in order to sustain Taiwan's relatively equitable income distribution. The ROC government has decided to privatize the

Table 4.2
The ROC Government's Revenue and Expenditure Structure

(%)

	1955	1965	1975	1985	1988	1990
Sources of Revenue						
Indirect taxes	44.9	40.0	45.2	38.1	31.5	28.6
Direct taxes	17.5	11.3	17.8	23.2	28.5	37.6
Monopoly revenue	13.8	14.0	9.8	7.2	5.3	4.4
Profits of public enterprises and utilities	3.8	13.3	10.6	13.3	13.1	10.1
Public bonds	—	5.1	0.3	4.2	9.0	1.3
Receipts from loans for economic construction	—	0.1	0.8	1.2	1.1	6.1
Others	20.0	16.3	15.5	12.8	11.5	11.8
Total	100.0	100.0	100.0	100.0	100.0	100.0
Structure of Expenditure						
General administration and defense	63.6	53.8	39.2	35.0	32.0	29.2
Education, science and culture	13.6	12.5	16.4	19.8	19.7	19.6
Economic development	10.0	19.1	29.7	24.5	25.6	25.3
Social security	6.7	7.6	10.0	15.7	17.5	17.3
Obligations	1.8	4.3	3.0	4.2	4.4	7.4
Others	3.7	2.7	1.7	0.8	0.8	1.2
Total	100.0	100.0	100.0	100.0	100.0	100.0

Source: *Taiwan Statistical Data Book 1991*, 157.

tobacco and wine monopoly in the next three years and replace it with a commodity tax on tobacco and liquor.

The ROC government's revenue from the sale of public bonds has always been very limited, therefore the share of its obligation payments is also very small (see table 4.2). One of the most significant items of expenditure for the ROC is undoubtedly defense which accounted for more than half of the government's total spending in the 1950s. However, as tension between Communist China and Taiwan has eased since the mid-1980s, the proportion of national expenditure devoted to defense has declined significantly. Most of these resources have been transferred to education,

Table 4.3
Distribution of Industrial Production by Ownership in Manufacturing Sector
(Based on Value Added at 1981 Prices)

%

Year	Distribution of industrial production		Annual growth rate	
	Private	Public	Private	Public
1955	51.3	48.7	14.9	1.9
1960	56.2	43.8	14.7	6.6
1965	63.2	36.8	19.7	10.3
1970	79.4	20.6	25.6	11.1
1975	85.8	14.2	9.0	1.5
1980	85.5	14.5	6.4	5.0
1985*	88.0	12.0	2.8	0.4
1990*	88.9	11.1	−1.4	−4.2

*Based on value added at 1986 prices.
Source: *Taiwan Statistical Data Book 1991*, 83.

scientific research, and social security payments which benefit the general public as a whole.

The Role of Public Enterprises

The role of public enterprises in Taiwan has always been very important both in terms of government revenue and the promotion of industrial development. Profits from public enterprises and utilities have accounted for more than 10 percent of the government's total revenue since the mid-1960s (see table 4.2). One should, however, interpret this figure carefully. Since most public enterprises in Taiwan are monopolies (such as Chinese Petroleum and Taipower) or oligopolies (such as China Steel) in their respective industries, the amount of revenue they generate may not reflect their performance or efficiency. Instead, a substantial proportion of their profits can be regarded as monopoly rent.

Most public utilities such as electricity, water, and telephones are publicly run, though public enterprises play a much less dominant role in the manufacturing sector (see table 4.3). It is important to note that the size of public enterprises in Taiwan has not been reduced at all, and the decline in their share of total production is really due to the rapid growth of the private sector since the late 1960s following the adoption of export expansion policies.

Although public enterprises have played a major role in manufacturing, the government never intended to monopolize industrial production. On the contrary, it has made every effort to promote the development of the private sector. From the 1950s through the 1970s, public enterprises served as important upstream suppliers of raw and intermediate industrial materials for private small and medium-sized enterprises (SMEs). As a result, private SMEs in Taiwan accounted for 60.0 percent of total export earnings in 1988 and 70.8 percent of total employment in 1989. They clearly constitute the backbone of the Taiwan economy.

The Incentive System for Private Enterprises

Various incentives have been introduced by the ROC government to encourage private investment. For instance, the Statute for Encouragement of Investment, introduced in 1960, allows firms in selected sectors either to enjoy exemption from enterprise income tax for a period of five consecutive years, or to opt for an accelerating depreciation rate for the servicing of their capital equipment. In addition, various government-sponsored institutions provide expertise in production, management, quality control, export promotion, and marketing information, dramatically reducing costs for private entrepreneurs.

Tax breaks or other incentive schemes alone cannot effectively encourage private investment. One of the most important factors encouraging private investment in Taiwan was the implementation of export promotion policies beginning in the late 1960s. Initiatives such as the establishment of EPZs, the undervalued local currency, and the introduction of an export tax rebate system are some of the main features of Taiwan's export expansion drive. Large numbers of highly export-oriented private companies were set up, which not only enabled Taiwan to establish complete industrial networks, but also helped Taiwan's entrepreneurs set up international marketing and technology transfer channels. It is fair to say that the export expansion policy was really the fundamental driving force behind the modernization of Taiwan's economy. Foreign trade now accounts for approximately 96 percent of Taiwan's GNP and the ROC was ranked as the world's fourteenth largest trading nation in 1991.

Again, the role of the government in terms of encouraging private investment is critical. Besides providing various tax incentives, the government has also placed a lot of emphasis on improving the infrastructure in Taiwan by, for example, building industrial zones or parks complete with electricity, water, and transportation services, and sometimes even with standard factory sites available for rent or for sale to private firms. These kinds of policies have fostered many talented new entrepreneurs who have production technology as well as connections to international markets.

The Role of Savings

There are several reasons why financial institutions have not played such an important role in promoting the development of the private sector in Taiwan. First, before 1991, most financial institutions were publicly owned, and they were widely criticized in business and academic circles for being

Table 4.4
Savings in Taiwan

Year	(1) Net savings / National income (%)	(2) Gross national savings / GNP (%)	(3) Average propensity to save
1955	11.2	14.6	0.04
1960	13.4	17.8	0.07
1965	17.5	20.7	0.11
1970	23.7	25.6	0.16
1975	24.7	26.7	0.16
1980	31.4	32.3	0.18
1985	30.5	33.6	0.25
1990	26.1	29.7	0.23

Source: *Taiwan Statistical Data Book 1991*, 57.

more like branches of the bureaucracy than commercial banks. The major complaint was that they frequently failed to provide financial services needed by the business community. Another reason is that many SMEs in Taiwan do not have regular systems of accounting, either because they lack the expertise or for tax evasion purposes or both. As a result, they find it difficult to obtain loans from formal financial institutions, and instead rely on informal channels or kinship ties to raise capital.

One of the most important sources of capital for the private sector is private savings. Taiwan has consistently enjoyed a high savings rate (see table 4.4),[7] and it is these savings, together with the close kinship ties in Chinese society, that provided the capital needed for many SMEs to start up their operations.

Perhaps one of the most important contributions made by the government in this respect during the past two decades is the maintenance of interest rates at sufficiently high levels to make saving worthwhile (see table 4.5). Other advantages of this high interest rate policy are that the inflation rate has been kept down and limited investible resources have been allocated to the most efficient projects. Since lending rates are generally two to three percentage points higher than the savings rates, it is obvious that Taiwan's rapid economic development was not founded on easy credit; it was based

---

[7]Taiwan's high savings rates have been variously explained as the result of the Confucian belief that one should prepare for a rainy day and as being due to the lack of a social security system. Savings do tend to be high in Confucian-influenced societies.

Table 4.5
Interest Rates, Wholesale and Consumer Price Increases (1961-90)

Year	(1) Banks' interest rate for one-year time deposits	(2) % change in wholesale price over the previous year	(3) Consumer price over the previous year	Real interest rates	
				(1) − (2)	(1) − (3)
1960	18.43	14.14	18.44	4.29	− 0.01
1965	10.80	− 4.66	− 0.08	15.46	10.88
1970	9.72	2.73	3.58	6.99	6.14
1975	12.00	− 5.07	5.24	17.08	6.76
1980	12.50	21.54	19.01	− 9.04	− 6.51
1985	7.75	− 2.60	− 0.17	10.35	7.92
1990	9.50	− 0.16	4.13	10.11	5.37

Sources: *Taiwan Statistical Data Book 1991*, 152, and *Financial Statistics Monthly* (Central Bank of China, ROC), various issues.

instead on a careful selection of investment projects by the mass of private entrepreneurs in Taiwan who had to make sure that the yields on their investment would justify their capital costs. SMEs that are unable to obtain loans through formal financial institutions have to pay even higher interest rates for loans through informal financial channels, such as friends or relatives or the curb market. The pressure on SMEs to make careful investment choices may thus be higher than that on well-established companies.

FDI in Taiwan

Besides providing various tax incentives to ease financial pressure on newly established local enterprises, the ROC government has also adopted an open door policy toward foreign direct investment (FDI). The Statute for Investment by Foreign Nations (SIFN), which was promulgated in 1954, guarantees foreign investors against government expropriation, allows them to convert their net profits or interest into foreign exchange, and offers investors in selected sectors (chiefly manufacturing) a five-year tax holiday or accelerated depreciation on their fixed assets. These preferential terms, combined with a favorable investment climate, caused FDI to expand very rapidly in Taiwan (see table 4.6).

The United States was Taiwan's largest source of FDI before the mid-1980s, when its position was taken over by Japan. During 1980-91, Japanese FDI accounted for 30.84 percent of the total, while the United States, Europe, and Hong Kong accounted for 27.29, 15.42, and 9.8 percent respectively. The top four industries attracting both foreign and overseas Chinese invest-

Table 4.6
Statistics on Approved Overseas Chinese and Foreign Investment

(Unit: US$ million)

Year	Overseas Chinese Case	Overseas Chinese Amount	Foreign Nationals Case	Foreign Nationals Amount	Total Case	Total Amount
1952-79	1,436	742.1	1,191	1,510.3	2,627	2,252.4
1980	39	222.5	71	243.3	110	465.9
1982	50	59.7	82	320.2	132	380.0
1984	74	39.7	100	518.9	174	558.7
1986	80	64.8	206	705.5	286	770.4
1988	89	121.3	438	1,061.1	527	1,182.5
1990	85	220.1	376	2,081.6	461	2,301.7
1991	65	219.4	324	1,558.9	389	1,778.4
1952-91 Total	2,253	2,173.2	3,909	12,856.7	6,162	15,030.0

Sources: *Statistics on Overseas Chinese and Foreign Investment in the Republic of China* (Investment Commission, ROC Ministry of Economic Affairs), various issues.

ment are electronics and electrical appliances, basic metals and metal products, chemicals, and plastic and rubber products.

In 1988, the government changed the approval system for FDI to a "negative list" system under which foreign investors may obtain automatic approval from the authorities for all investment items not on the government's prohibited list (these are chiefly the agricultural sector, transportation, and military-related manufacturing). This bold move has done much to encourage FDI in Taiwan.

FDI and Technology Diffusion

FDI has had a very positive effect on Taiwan's industrialization and economic development. One survey of 318 electronics firms in 1987 revealed that 71 domestic firms had high-level managers and engineers who had worked for foreign electronics firms in Taiwan. Of these, 42.50 percent felt that such experience had helped develop their management skills, 30.67 percent felt that it had helped their product design and development abilities, and 29.52 percent felt that it had enabled them to acquire market information.[8]

---

[8]Gee San, "The Status and an Evaluation of the Electronics Industry in Taiwan," *OECD Development Centre Technical Papers*, no. 29 (Paris: OECD, October 1990).

Clearly, technologies introduced through FDI can be transferred to the domestic sector through labor mobility. FDI not only directly contributes to the local economy through job creation, it also helps to diffuse technologies either indirectly, through job mobility, or directly, through technological cooperation, licensing, and joint ventures.

Taiwan has some regulations designed to enhance the formation of new technologies that capitalize on the technological capability of FDI. For example, there are various tax breaks available related to R&D expenditure and such expenditure is tax deductible for both domestic and foreign-invested companies. The government also stipulates a minimum ratio of R&D expenditure to total sales for both domestic and foreign companies. If enterprises fail to meet the prescribed level, they are required to contribute the difference to government-controlled R&D projects. In traditional sectors, such as the food and garment industries, the ratio is set at 0.5 percent, while for high-tech industries it is 1.5 percent.

Education and Training

Tax deductions or compulsory measures alone cannot effectively promote the formation of new technology. Neither is labor mobility sufficient in itself to ensure the diffusion of technology if the technology cannot be absorbed and mastered in the first place. The critical factor in promoting technological development and fully capitalizing on FDI is the quality of the labor force. In this regard, education is essential. Throughout Chinese history, great importance has always been given to education for all ranks in society. The ROC Constitution stipulates that at least 15 percent of the government's annual budget should be devoted to education spending, although this requirement has only been observed since the late 1980s due to the ROC's enormous defense budget.

In-service training has been another of the government's major concerns. Before 1972, hardly any in-service training was provided by employers, prompting the government to introduce the Vocational Training Fund Statute (VTFS) under which employers with forty or more employees were required to set aside funds equivalent to 1.5 percent of the company's total wage bill for in-service training. However, the VTFS was suspended indefinitely in late 1974 to ease the burden on businesses during the oil crisis. Regardless of the oil crisis, it has been argued that the VTFS was introduced too suddenly and with no proper preparation. Consequently, many companies were forced to organize training programs despite the fact that they did not have sufficient resources to provide proper instructors and materials. The minimum contribution rate of 1.5 percent of the total payroll was also criticized by local economists, who argued that the rate in each industry should depend on the size of the firm, the number of skilled workers employed, the future demand for skilled workers in that industry, the levels of skill involved, and other

Table 4.7
School Enrollment Statistics in Taiwan (1952-90)

Year	% of school-aged children enrolled in primary schools	% of primary school graduates enrolled in junior high school	% of junior high school graduates enrolled in senior high school	% of senior high school graduates enrolled in schools of higher education
1952-53	84.00	34.85	56.96	26.27
1955-56	92.33	43.94	63.13	44.27
1960-61	95.59	52.24	75.88	43.41
1965-66	97.15	58.23	78.52	38.30
1970-71	98.01	78.59	82.66	41.92
1975-76	99.29	89.47	65.82	39.80
1980-81	99.72	96.14	65.16	44.64
1985-86	99.85	98.73	71.31	40.19
1989-90	99.90	99.62	79.60	44.40

Source: *Taiwan Statistical Data Book 1991*, 259.
Note: The sharp increase in the percentage of primary school graduates enrolled in junior high school between 1965-66 and 1970-71 is due to the extension of compulsory education from six to nine years in 1968-69.

economic factors.[9] Today, the government encourages training through tax incentives, thereby reducing the cost of investing in human capital.

Industrial Relations

Good industrial relations have also been a crucial factor in Taiwan's economic development. Although some have attributed the absence of labor unrest to Taiwan's long period of martial law, the lifting of martial law did not trigger a significant increase in labor-management disputes.

There are, however, at least three major economic factors contributing to the inactivity of the labor movement in Taiwan. In terms of the economic structure, 99 percent of companies have fewer than 500 employees—or alternatively, over 70 percent of the work force is employed by SMEs—making it very difficult, if not impossible, to organize strong labor unions. Secondly, labor mobility is very high—the average accession rate in the manufacturing sector was 4.13 in 1983-85, while the corresponding separation rate was 3.83 percent. This high labor turnover also makes union activity very difficult. Thirdly, the government's labor-intensive industrial development policies of

---

[9] Gee San and Chao-nan Chen, *In-Service Training in Taiwan, ROC*, CIER Economic Monograph Series no. 20 (Taipei: CIER, April 1988).

the 1960s and 1970s have ensured almost full employment. Employers have therefore had to make every effort to attract and keep workers, and the level of real wages has soared, increasing by a factor of 1.69 in the manufacturing sector during 1976-86. This rapid improvement in worker compensation has not only amplified the spillover effect from unionized to nonunionized firms but has also reduced the need for collective bargaining, further limiting the role of unions.

The Relevance of the Taiwan Experience and International Cooperation

The Relevance of the Taiwan Experience

The main characteristics of Taiwan's economic development experience as described in the previous two sections are (1) an efficient utilization of scarce resources; (2) the provision of a stable socioeconomic base for rapid economic development—chiefly through the land reform program; (3) the improvement of manpower quality; (4) efficient population control measures; (5) the provision of infrastructure facilities; (6) tight controls on government expenditure; (7) the promotion of private sector development; and (8) a high interest rate policy which curbed inflation, gave people an incentive to save, and limited wastage of investible resources.

Indeed, the ROC's development achievements are no miracle but the result of careful planning and the observation of some basic economic development principles. The role of academics in fostering such major policy initiatives as the reform of the exchange rate system should not be underestimated.

It is not, however, the purpose of this chapter to propagandize the ROC's economic development experience. There are indeed a number of areas in which government policy has been lacking; for example, insufficient attention has been paid to environmental protection, the public infrastructure is inadequate, and the government has been unable to curb rampant land and real estate speculation. One lesson that may be drawn from Taiwan's experience is that there is a need for a better balance between the dual goals of economic growth and environmental protection, improved infrastructure, and a more appropriate land policy. Generally speaking, most aspects of the Taiwan experience are highly applicable to many developing countries and may be incorporated into the ROC's international assistance program.

The ROC's Technical Assistance Experience

The ROC's international assistance program dates back to 1961, when the Ministry of Foreign Affairs set up the Vanguard Project, the aim of which was to strengthen economic and political ties with the newly independent African countries, crucial potential allies for both Taipei and Peking (Beijing) in their battle for China's United Nations seat. The Vanguard

Table 4.8
Distribution of the ROC's Technical Assistance Missions (1959-92)

Area	1959	1960	1965	1970	1975	1980	1985	1991	1992
Africa			18	29	12	7	3	10	10
Central America				2	8	9	10	11	11
South America			1	5	3	7	4	3	3
Caribbean			1	1	3	2	6	9	9
Middle East			1	1	1	3	3	3	3
Asia & Pacific	1	1	1	3	4	7	8	8	9
Europe				1					
Total	1	1	22	42	31	35	34	44	45

Source: Provided by the Committee of International Technical Cooperation (CITC), Taipei.

Project focused on technical assistance rather than financial aid, firstly because the ROC did not at that time have the resources to offer substantial aid, and secondly because Chinese generally believe that "it is better to teach a person how to fish than to give him a fish."

The Project covers a wide range of technical assistance, including agriculture, irrigation, forestry, fisheries, farmer's organizations, public health, agriculture-related education, handicrafts, and food processing. As well as providing training programs in Taiwan for nationals of the recipient countries (165 technical training sessions were held for a total of 790 participants from 58 countries in the period 1967-91), the ROC also sends technical missions overseas. The first ROC agricultural mission was dispatched to Vietnam in 1959, and by June 1992, a total of 102 technical missions consisting of 1,867 technicians had been sent to 68 countries. The focus on Africa has shifted since the 1980s, however, and more missions have been dispatched to countries in Central and South America as well as the Asia-Pacific region (see tables 4.8 and 4.9).

The missions focus heavily on the production of staple food crops such as rice or sweet potatoes, adopt a hands-on approach with advisers working side-by-side with locals, tend to employ the most appropriate (not always the most advanced) technology and tools, and place a high premium on the participation of local farmers, workers, and village leaders. These characteristics have been crucial to the success of the program.[10]

---

[10]Hai-tu Tsai, *International Agricultural Cooperation: The Technical Cooperation Program of the Republic of China* (Taipei: Committee of International Technical Cooperation, February 1992).

Table 4.9
Distribution of ROC Technical Missions in June 1992

	Type of Mission					
Area	Agriculture	Fishery	Handicraft	Sugar	Medical	Total
Africa	6		1		3	10
Central America	7	3	1			11
South America	2	1				3
Caribbean	8	1				9
Middle East	2	1				3
Asia & Pacific	8			1		9
Total	33	6	2	1	3	45

Source: See table 4.8.

The IECDF and the Future Prospects
of the ODA Program in the ROC

Calls for the ROC to expand its overseas development assistance (ODA) program increased after the mid-1980s in view of the country's vast foreign exchange reserves and rapid growth of per capita income. In an effort to better organize future ODA programs and to allow for an increase in financial aid on top of the existing technical assistance program, an International Economic Cooperation and Development Fund (IECDF) was established in 1988 under the Ministry of Economic Affairs. This fund provides four kinds of assistance: (1) direct or indirect loans; (2) direct or indirect investment; (3) loan guarantees; and (4) technical assistance. The government is committed to setting aside NT$30 billion (US$1.2 billion) for the fund over the next five years. The IECDF has already approved applications for loans totaling over US$124 million, organized training seminars in Taiwan, and provided technical assistance grants for project feasibility studies in a number of developing countries.[11]

Political self-interest has been, is, and will remain the driving force in international development aid programs,[12] and the ROC is certainly no excep-

---

[11]Ti Liu, "The ODA Program of Taiwan, ROC and Prospective Relations with Multinational Development Organizations," in *Proceedings of the Seminar on the Economic Development of Taiwan, ROC: Past Experiences, Future Directions, and Overseas Development Assistance*, CIER Conference Series no. 20 (Taipei: CIER, October 1991), 71-80.

[12]Robert L. Downen, "The Politics of Development Aid: ROC Opportunities and Lessons from U.S. Experience" (Paper delivered at the International Conference on Development Aid: What Works, What Doesn't, Center of Area Studies, Tamkang University, Taipei, January 1990).

tion in this. Aside from humanitarian concerns, the ROC is also seeking to use the IECDF to gain reentry into the global community. The ROC needs the advice of the International Monetary Fund (IMF) and the World Bank in conducting its international assistance program, but protests from mainland China have blocked the ROC's participation in major international ODA programs run by these international organizations.

Restricted access to major international organizations means that the IECDF has had to establish its own cooperation and assistance policy. The main points of this are (1) recognition that a combination of economic growth and equitable income distribution is the only guarantee of growth, so the impact on income distribution will be taken into account in processing applications for loans and technical assistance; (2) balanced development of the public and private sectors, meaning assistance in developing SMEs as well as aid for government-sponsored projects; and (3) emphasis on the development of the light-manufacturing sector which will help conserve foreign exchange and have a significant impact on public welfare. In short, the IECDF will adopt a balanced economic development assistance strategy for the developing countries.[13]

The IECDF statute is currently under review in the ROC legislature. It is likely that a new organization under the Ministry of Foreign Affairs will take overall responsibility for the ROC's international cooperation and development programs, and the technical cooperation programs currently under the Committee of International Technical Cooperation (CITC) will be integrated with the IECDF. Such an arrangement would certainly enhance the efficiency of the ROC's international cooperation operations and produce more satisfactory results for the recipient countries.

Conclusion

Taiwan's economic development experience over the past four decades clearly demonstrates that coping with, not working against, the international environment is a key factor in economic success. The export expansion policy, combined with access to the U.S. and other international markets, has significantly contributed to the growth of the economy. Domestically, policies ensuring the efficient utilization of scarce resources and continuous improvement of the investment environment have also played a critical role in achieving enduring and stable economic growth.

Rapid economic growth, however, brings with it increased international responsibilities. The establishment of the IECDF, together with the existing technical assistance programs, will certainly strengthen the ROC's ability to conduct international cooperation. It is a common belief in the ROC that

---

[13]See note 11 above.

international cooperation programs should emphasize self-reliance in the recipient countries, as well as a good balance between the public and private sectors, and between economic growth and income distribution. In this regard, the ROC can provide not only capital and technical expertise, but also its own economic development experience.

Other References

Chen, Edward I-hsin. "The New Directives of ROC Foreign Aid Policy." Paper delivered at the International Conference on Development Aid: What Works, What Doesn't, Center of Area Studies, Tamkang University, Taipei, January 1990.

Fei, John C. H. "A Bird's Eye View of Policy Evolution on Taiwan: An Introductory Essay." In K. T. Li, *The Evolution of Policy behind Taiwan's Development Success*, 26-46. New Haven and London: Yale University Press, 1988.

Fei, John C. H., Gustav Ranis, and Shirley W. Y. Kuo. *Growth with Equity: The Taiwan Case*. Oxford: Oxford University Press, 1979.

Kuo, Shirley W. Y. "Economic Development in the Republic of China." In *Proceedings of the Conference on Economic Development in the Republic of China on Taiwan*, CIER [Chung-Hua Institution for Economic Research] Conference Series no. 7:21-62. Taipei: CIER, 1987.

Liang, Kuo-shu. "Financial Reform, Trade and Foreign Exchange Liberalization in the Republic of China." In *Proceedings of the Conference on Economic Development in the Republic of China on Taiwan*, 317-46.

San, Gee. "An Evaluation and International Comparison of Labor Laws and Regulations which Affect Labor Cost in Taiwan, ROC." In *Proceedings of the 1989 Joint Conference on the Industrial Policies of the ROC and the ROK*, 129-64. Taipei: CIER, February 1989.

_____. "Technology, Investment and Trade under Economic Globalisation: The Case of Taiwan." Chapter 4 of *Trade, Investment and Technology in the 1990s*. Paris: OECD, 1991.

_____. "The Economic Development of Taiwan, ROC: Experience and Challenges." *CIER Occasional Paper*, no. 9112. Taipei: CIER, December 1991.

Tsiang, S. C. "Keynote Speech: In Search of a Growth Theory That Would Fit Our Own Conditions." In *Proceedings of the Conference on the Economic Development Experience of Taiwan and Its New Role in an Emerging Asia-Pacific Region*, 11-28. Taipei: Institute of Economics, Academia Sinica, 1988.

_____. "Taiwan Economic Success Demystified." *Journal of Economic Growth* 3, no. 1 (1988): 21-36.

Yu, Tzong-shian. "The Role of the Government in Industrialization." In *Proceedings of the Conference on the Economic Development Experience of Taiwan and Its New Role in an Emerging Asia-Pacific Region*, 121-52.

CHAPTER 5

The ROC's Role in Building a Global Economy*

Jan S. Prybyla

The Global Economy

The World Techno-Economic Revolution

The dramatic changes in the political makeup of the world which surfaced suddenly in 1989 to the astonishment of nearly everyone—although they had been long in the making underground—are more than matched by, and indeed, have been caused in large measure by, revolutionary transformations in the world economy.[1] These, too, have a lengthy subterranean history, but now they also are surfacing at a heady, ever accelerating pace, radically and continually transfiguring the established economic structure's international and interpersonal relations, ways of life, markets, management and manufacturing structures, capital and labor mobility, assumptions, theories, beliefs—in short, everything.

It is not an exaggeration to say that the economic changes the world is undergoing today, while they issue from past quantitative accretions, are qualitatively different from anything that has gone before. They represent a historic discontinuity, as for instance, in the fields of information generation, storage, retrieval, processing, and transmission; transportation; biotechnology; and materials science. The changes are relentless and all-embracing: individuals (with a few monastic, hermit-inclined, or personal dropout exceptions) and societies cannot opt out of them without paying the heavy political, social, psychological, and material costs of standing still and last in a fast moving line.

So far, the emergence of extraordinary political and economic changes

---

*Very substantial portions of the first part of this chapter were first presented at an International Conference on the ROC and the New International Order, organized by the *China Times* in Taipei on August 21-23, 1991. They are used here, with thanks, by permission of the *China Times*.

[1]Uner Kirdar, ed., *Change: Threat or Opportunity?* (New York: United Nations Publications, 1992).

in the late 1980s and early 1990s has been marked, with some notable exceptions (e.g., Yugoslavia, Georgia, Armenia, Moldova), by benevolence, relative peacefulness (certainly compared to the slaughter attendant on the birth and development of socialism), and a low incidence of violence—a "velvet," civilized quality rare in the annals of revolution. In fact, the changes so far have had the net effect of reducing bipolar world tensions by quietly, and on the whole gently, removing one of the ideological and systemic poles. Over much of the world, including its original home, Communism has simply folded up as a sociopolitical and economic construct. This is not to suggest that new and ancient intractable troubles—ethnic, national, infranational, and regional ones—will not rise to replace the old divisions that dominated the world scene in the post-World War II decades. What matters is that the contemporary economic and political revolution has so far been in the right direction, in sharp contrast with the road to serfdom on which much of the world embarked under duress after the Petrograd putsch of October 1917. The revolution now unfolding is, on the whole, liberating and enriching, a spontaneous people's movement from below.

This revolution is driven by furious, apparently unstoppable, innovative advances in technology (defined as scientific and other systematized knowledge applied to the solution of practical tasks), realized by "the refusal of the innovators to accept reality as inevitable."[2] Technological progress, unprecedented in its rate, scope, and vitality, offers for the first time an achievable, not too distant prospect of real material betterment for the largest number of human beings ever. This prospect is not without its dangers and alarms, of course, but it is singularly devoid of utopian delusions and false promises.

Technological progress and its companion, the advancement of science, do not occur in an institutional void, nationally or worldwide, nor do they thrive in an environment shaped by restrictive, regulation-prone, prohibitionist, and know-all statist authorities or private monopolies. Intellectual, political, and economic freedom and competition are the necessary conditions for a healthy (that is, people-serving) growth of knowledge in its theoretical-scientific and applied-technological forms. The powerful and persuasive American presence in the post-World War II scene was an enormous force for good in this sense.

Components of the World Techno-Economic Revolution

The dramatic and profound changes in the world economy over the last forty years or so are, as has already been noted, largely the result of accelerated technological innovation, which has enabled giant strides to be

---

[2]Lewis M. Branscomb, "Technological Change and Its International Diffusion," in *Capital, Technology, and Labor in the New Global Economy*, ed. James H. Cassing and Steven L. Husted (Washington, D.C.: American Enterprise Institute, 1988), 105.

made in productivity. The technological revolution was made possible to a large extent by scientific progress based on judicious investment in education. Judiciousness in this context has meant concentration of capital and talent first and foremost on instruction, research, and development in what are known as the "hard" sciences (including mathematics) and engineering, as well as in the increasingly quantified "softer" disciplines of economics, business administration, and communications.[3] It has also meant fostering a spirit of uncensored inquiry, transparency, competitiveness, entrepreneurship, tolerance of and respect for dissenting views, individual responsibility, personal accountability, independent thought, and the disinterested pursuit of facts wherever they may lead; qualities natural to free societies, democracies, and the competitive market system. Education goes beyond the formal classroom into the workshop, where two-way incentive-enhancing linkages, as the Japanese have demonstrated, make a critical contribution to qualitative product improvement. The countries that made such judicious educational choices have reaped the economic dividends attendant on those decisions.

However, the sequence of judicious educational investment in the sciences, engineering, and "modern" attitudes, and the resultant accelerated pace, expanded coverage, and increased sophistication of technological innovation, growing productivity, and rising income, have been successfully realized in a comparatively small number of countries, the Republic of China (ROC) on Taiwan among them.

Of the many startling developments that call for rapid response and flexible adaptation and readaptation of human skills and economic structures, the following seem to be among the more important.

Compression of time: The word that best synthesizes the contemporary technologically driven economic revolution is speed. The compression of time is primarily the result of breakthroughs, subsequent refinements, and compounded discoveries in the technologies of information and transportation.

The almost instant availability of information worldwide at decreasing unit cost conveyed in an internationally comprehensible mathematical-symbolic language, combined with the technical ability to extend memory, store a rapidly expanding volume of past data in ever smaller physical spaces, instantly retrieve the ones needed, and combine them with present knowledge and models of simulated future events from a wide and expanding variety

---

[3]William Dietrich warns against oversimplifying the science-technology relationship. High technology, he argues, is not mainly the product of major scientific breakthroughs "but instead it evolves through thousands of small yet steady process and product improvements [on the factory floor]. . . . To speak of technology or 'high tech' as somewhat separate from manufacturing is to lose sight of what technology is all about: as products and processes improve, so does technology." See William S. Dietrich, *In the Shadow of the Rising Sun: The Political Roots of American Economic Decline* (University Park, Pa.: Pennsylvania State University Press, 1991), 31.

of separate and distinct knowledge sources are tantamount to synthesizing and fusing the past, present, and future into timelessness. The consequence is further acceleration of complex inventions and innovations; an unending enhancement of the intensity, dynamism, and pervasiveness of competition; an accelerating high-speed chase after cost reductions; unceasing transformations of manufacturing processes and locations, managerial methodologies (including just-in-time production) and institutional (including legal) structures; and constant, kaleidoscopic changes in the very way we look at, and interact with, our shrinking world.

Underlying the miniaturization of time is the widespread and growing applications of new technologies in photonics, fiber optics, semiconductors, digital electronics, integrated circuits, microprocessors, high-temperature engines, carbon fiber composites, fine ceramics, and so on.[4] But accelerated technical innovation and its rapid spread, while stimulating competition and driving down cost per unit function (at about 15 percent annually for computer systems in recent years), are themselves driven by pressure from all corners of the world to be at the cutting edge of competition not only in terms of cost, but above all, precise fit to customer requirements (customization of products and marketing strategies to meet specific needs and preferences in local markets), design, quality, timely delivery, and prompt, reliable after-delivery service.[5]

Compression of volume/expansion of conceptual values: The information revolution has been made possible in part by the miniaturization of space required for the generation, storage, conveyance, and processing of intelligence. The revolution in transportation is likewise due in part to the ability to compress the space needed to carry physical goods over long distances as well as the goods themselves, in volume as well as weight.

The downsizing of economic goods has been made possible by an increased substitution of ideas for physical volume: the progressive replacement of physical goods by conceptual values that now account for a significant (roughly half), and rapidly rising, share of an advanced economy's real output value. These conceptual values are "created by new scientific insights and knowledge," or in other words, by ideas or advanced cultural technologies.[6] They are comprised of high value-added ("up-market"), low-volume ("intangible"), specialized ("custom-made") services. Consumption services in the United States, for example, rose from 33 percent of gross na-

---

[4]Harald B. Malmgren, "Technology and the Economy," in *The Global Economy: America's Role in the Decade Ahead*, ed. William E. Brock and Robert Hormats (New York: W. W. Norton, 1990), 92-119.

[5]Yotaro Kobayashi, "Changes in International Marketing Techniques," in Cassing and Husted, *Capital, Technology, and Labor.*

[6]Alan Greenspan, "Goods Shrink and Trade Grows," *Wall Street Journal*, October 24, 1988, A9.

tional product (GNP) in 1950, to 55 percent in 1990. Between 1976 and 1986 Pittsburgh, Pennsylvania lost 40,200 steel workers, but added 66,000 high-tech service jobs.

Technically, the downsizing, strengthening, and lightening of goods has been made possible by quantum jumps in materials science and engineering. It should be noted that progress in this field goes beyond the miniaturization and other significant alterations of existing materials. More important for the future, it permits a qualitative shift from processing (changing the shape, composition, function) of natural resources in order to satisfy user needs, to creating from scratch completely new man-made materials (e.g., carbon fiber composites) to meet specific complex demands in dispersed markets. This has far-reaching implications for the future development of natural resource-poor economies, particularly where such new materials are created from renewable natural resources used by existing industries such as textiles.

One effect of the downsizing of physical goods is the transformation of the output structures and procedures of modern economies. Increasingly and insistently, supply is customized[7] to the precise and rapidly changing needs of buyers, through the application of specialized knowledge to production, market-segmented distribution (e.g., electronic shopping), and financing (e.g., home banking). Some see in this the emergence (or reemergence) of a personalized craftsmanship of the mind, a demassification that reduces the once important advantages of economies of scale derived from mass-produced standardized goods and long capital-intensive production runs, and mass markets born of the Industrial Revolution.[8]

Another effect is the transformation of the structure of international trade from a relatively leisurely exchange of physical bulk to the frenetic, almost instantaneous, electronic transmission of impalpable economic values: of data, designs, analyses, strategies, claims, and insights of all kinds.

A third effect is on labor costs, and hence on the cost advantages that producers can reasonably expect to derive from moving their plants to locations with comparatively low labor costs. In a world of rapid transfers of

---

[7]For example: according to Frank Bennack, president and chief executive officer of Hearst Corporation and chairman of the Newspaper Association of America, "down the road, we will be delivering highly customized newspapers. . . . Advertisers are telling us they like targeted audiences, not just mass audiences." The technology of such customization is available: "Huge, computerized inserting systems put papers together with advertising supplements and local news sections targeted for individual communities. And systems already in use by many newspapers offer readers information beyond the printed page—via telephone audio services and fax machines. . . . The Atlanta Journal-Constitution, for example, generated 15 million calls [in 1991] on its voice information service, which provides such things as sports scores, stock information, weather, and advertising." See Mark Rice, "Newspapers of the Future to Be Highly Customized," *Washington Times*, June 9, 1992, C3.

[8]Alvin Toffler, "Reordering Industry as the 'Era of the Masses' Passes," *Wall Street Journal*, June 16, 1983, 30.

high value impalpables, the share of labor expense diminishes as a component of total manufacturing cost. This can have perilous implications for the comparative advantage, as conventionally calculated, of developing economies with low labor costs. (Conventional calculations ignore "efficiency wages" that take into account the educational ability and motivation of the "low cost" workers to perform the tasks required of them.)

There are implications also for state protectionism. Because international trade is increasingly dominated by extremely rapid multilateral worldwide transfers of data, analyses, contracts, and money claims, intervention in this fluid international market by slow-moving national state bureaucracies reacting to often contradictory domestic special interests, would at first appearance seem to be more difficult to implement. In the spring of 1989, *daily* foreign exchange trading worldwide, which had doubled in just three years, came to more than US$500 billion. By comparison, the *annual* volume of world merchandise trade in 1987 was US$2.5 trillion; i.e., five-days' trade in fast-moving impalpables was equivalent to one-year's trade in more easily controlled physical goods.[9] The downside of this is the lucrative opportunities that unrestricted and rapid movement of information in its manifold forms across national borders provides for violations of privacy and intellectual property rights.[10] The International Anti-Counterfeiting Coalition says that pirated products represent 8 percent (US$80 billion) of annual world trade. Since 1988, they have cost the European Community (EC) 100,000 jobs a year and more than US$1 billion per year in lost tax revenues. More than 60 percent of the EC market for personal computer software consists of pirated products.

Globalization: Another revolutionary phenomenon, one that national governments have more trouble conceptualizing, accepting, and dealing with than do citizens in their roles as consumers, entrepreneurs, investors, and increasingly as workers (who migrate en masse, legally and illegally, permanently or temporarily, across national borders), is the institutional globalization of economic transactions. This reveals itself, albeit not always self-evidently, in the internationalization, multinationalization, or supranationalization of business firms in manufacturing, banking, insurance, investment, consulting services, and other occupations. In the simplest terms, money

---

[9]Penelope Hartland-Thunberg, *China, Hong Kong, Taiwan and the World Trading System* (New York: St. Martin's Press, 1990), 76; Richard B. McKenzie and Dwight R. Lee, *Quicksilver Capital: How the Rapid Movement of Wealth Has Changed the World* (New York: Macmillan/Free Press, 1991).

[10]The fact that data flows massively, quickly, and relatively freely across national borders and that some of a nation's data is located outside of nation-state borders makes governments concerned about the effect of this on (1) national security (inability to access one's own data when needed) and (2) "cultural heritage," (e.g., Communist China's recurring worry about imported cultural pathologies or "bourgeois pollution"). See Tony Carbo Bearman, "Comment," in Cassing and Husted, *Capital, Technology, and Labor*, 139-41.

moves quickly to where it expects to get the best rate of return, and the knowledge about comparative rates of return is readily available around the clock at the touch of a personal computer.

In a sense, this has always been so. At all times big money and monied people have had strong cosmopolitan inclinations and pliable political loyalties (indeed the money was big and the people were monied in large part because of such inclinations and negotiable loyalties), not being inhibited by political frontiers, whether of dukedoms, seigneuries, city states, or nations. When governments tried to make the extent of the market coequal with geographical spaces delineated by national boundaries, and the national interest identical with economically rational choice, the money simply sank underground, whence it seeped away abroad to nurture more receptive soils. In our own time the money has grown bigger, the loyalties more diffuse, migrations speedier, and goods and funds globe-hopping more commonplace, most often packaged in multinational corporate alliances, consortia, joint ventures, subsidiaries, and so on. The motivation behind this globalization of business structures is to spread financial risk, establish footholds in diverse, often protected or to be protected markets, and pool technological expertise.

The economic logic of internationalism and supranationalism has been cautiously embraced by some governments, albeit mostly on a regionally delimited scale. The trend toward globalization has been encouraged by international arrangements such as the General Agreement on Tariffs and Trade (GATT), and more formal organizations like the World Bank, the International Monetary Fund (IMF), and the Organization for Economic Cooperation and Development (OECD), while "tamed" globalization is promoted by regional bodies (e.g., the Asian Development Bank) and free trade area (FTA) pacts. It might be remarked that the globalization of markets · for goods, services, capital, and increasingly labor, while it has historical precedents, has been particularly dynamic since the end of World War II and reflects the confluence of two phenomena: the spontaneous workings of market forces and the deliberate establishment by governments (the U.S. government leading the way in the late 1940s and early 1950s) of international infrastructures such as Bretton Woods, GATT, the IMF, and others designed to facilitate the globalization of trade and finance.[11]

By discreetly altering the structure and distribution of world manufacturing and service activities, globalization has to a degree depoliticized the notion of what constitutes, say, a Japanese, a French, or an American product. The "nationality" of companies is becoming increasingly irrelevant from an economic standpoint, although concerns about the national security aspects of the question persist. Large multinationals "may be headquartered,

---

[11]Jagdish Bhagwati, *The World System at Risk* (Princeton, N.J.: Princeton University Press, 1991), 149-50.

or most of their shares owned in one country, but employ more people and pay more taxes somewhere else. What can their 'nationality' really count for?''[12] Today, more than half the value of U.S. exports and imports is attributable to transfers of components and services within the same global company. By conventional measurements, the U.S. balance of trade in 1986 was US$144 billion. By an ownership-based measurement, however, (one which takes account of the transactions of U.S.-owned firms abroad and foreign-owned firms in the United States), this US$144 billion deficit is transformed into a surplus of US$14 billion.[13] "A sports car is financed in Japan, designed in Italy, and assembled in Indiana, Mexico, and France, using advanced electronic components invented in New Jersey and fabricated in Japan."[14] What nationality is the car? Perhaps the answer is, in part at least, that it has the "nationality" of the country whose workers are responsible for most of the high value-added operations (Greenspan's "conceptual values"), because it is that nation that will benefit most from making the car in terms of high living standards. Of the US$10,000 paid by an American customer for a General Motors Pontiac LeMans, US$6,200 go to South Korea, Japan, Germany, Taiwan, Singapore, Britain, Ireland, and Barbados for a variety of operations ranging from routine labor and assembly (South Korea), through advanced components (Japan), styling and design engineering (Germany), small components (Taiwan, Singapore), advertising and marketing services (Britain), to data processing (Ireland, Barbados).[15] The balance of US$3,800 is paid to strategists and chief executive officers in Detroit, lawyers and bankers in New York, lobbyists in Washington, insurance and health care workers all over the United States, and to GM shareholders all over the world.[16] That is why some argue that "concern over the ownership of assets rather than their location is absurd."[17] The political notion of nationality is being redefined, they say, in economic terms to make economic sense. But such redefinition is resisted by adversely affected domestic special interests and often translates into protectionist legislation or executive regulatory action. For example, the EC has wrestled with the issue of whether Japanese cars made in European and American transplant plants in Europe are to be counted as European cars or not for purposes of voluntary export

---

[12]"The State of the Nation State," *Economist*, December 22, 1990, 44.

[13]Ibid.

[14]Robert Reich, "The Myth of 'Made in the USA'," *Wall Street Journal*, July 5, 1991, A6.

[15]New York Life processes its domestic insurance claims overnight in Ireland, employing for that purpose Irish university graduates who would otherwise probably be unemployed and are therefore cheaper than the American workers who would have to be hired to do the same job. To cut its labor costs, American Airlines uses a thousand data entry clerks in Barbados. See McKenzie and Lee, *Quicksilver Capital*.

[16]See note 14 above.

[17]"Of State and Industry," *Economist*, June 8, 1991, 15.

restraints, which the EC would like to see Japanese automobile makers observe. A negative ruling would tend to discourage Japanese firms from investing in Europe, which is pertinent for Europe in view of the fact that, on average, Japanese factories can assemble cars in less than half the man-hours it takes a European plant.[18] India's seemingly endless economic marasmus is not unconnected with the government's fear of dependence on foreign equity holdings, which until recent times were restricted to 40 percent (now 51 percent) and were tied up in red tape. As a result, such investment amounted to a minuscule US$200 million a year for a country of nearly 900 million people. (By comparison tiny, post-socialist, marketizing Czecho-slovakia with a population of under 16 million took in more than US$600 million in private investment in 1991.)

Global Multilateralism

The technological revolution is, as we have seen, exerting an influence in favor of worldwide economic fusion through the rapid proliferation of weightless, nationless economic transactions. Such global multilateralism—free trade in the widest sense—comprising goods, services, capital, and in-creasingly labor, can be sustained only by a workably competitive world market system aided, where necessary, by limited, albeit activist, market-friendly states.

A competitive market system is in essence the creation of merchants, a network of contracts voluntarily entered into by private buyers and sellers. But like any spontaneous complex social order, the system exhibits failings and insufficiencies which, from the outset, governments have tried (and as often as not, failed) to remedy and fill, frequently arrogating to themselves functions that properly belong to, and can be better—both more efficiently and equitably—performed by, the market itself. Although at times some governments (e.g., the U.S. government in the wake of World War II) eschewed mercantilist principles of trade management and industrial pro-tection on the behalf of politically defined national and/or special interests, the interventionist statist and, more broadly, the bureaucratic impulse is still very much alive today. It shows up, paradoxically, even in efforts aimed at transcending national economic divisions and constructing a regional eco-nomic community, as in contemporary Europe.

Despite the actions of private merchants and the exertions of GATT and other international (i.e., intergovernmental) forums and bodies to nurture multilateralism, more than half the world's trade today still falls into the "managed" or "preferential" (i.e., trade diverting) category, and only about one-third is free. Even the United States during the overtly pro-free market Reagan administration, under prodding from businesses, Congress, and 11

---

[18]"A Survey of Business in Europe," ibid., 23.

million displaced workers, became increasingly interventionist and protectionist, an evolution exemplified by the one thousand-page Omnibus Trade
Act of 1988 and its retaliatory section, "super" 301.
GATT itself has fallen on hard times.[19] It was originally designed as
a set of legal commitments by signatory countries to lower or remove tariff
barriers to commodity trade and to spread the benefits of this action to all
other signatory countries through most-favored-nation (MFN) treatment—
GATT's most important missionary weapon. In this task it has been remarkably successful: since 1947, tariffs have been reduced on the average
from 40 to 5 percent. However, the original pact left large areas open to
potential (and now actualized) poaching by protectionist neomercantilists,
statist unilateralists, and advocates of national industrial policies and managed
trade. These areas include services, agriculture, and intellectual property
rights. Although GATT is a rather loose and informal arrangement prone
to lengthy verbalizations (some call it the General Agreement to Talk and
Talk), arguments in favor of setting up a more formal, technocratic, intergovernmental—hence bureaucratized—International Trade Organization (ITO)
are unlikely to be realized.

Global Protectionism

At the opposite end from multilateral free trade lies nationally based
protectionism deriving from ancient parochial instincts of self-preservation
and rationalized by theories of national economic development. It was
dominant in the mercantilist era of Western imperial expansion of the late
fifteenth through the mid-eighteenth centuries, and survived in an extreme
anti-free market, socialist form until the collapse of the Marxist-Leninist
system late in our century—a system that had succeeded in reducing intra-
socialist trade to the status of primitive barter.
Among advanced market economies the practice of protectionism today
is sustained in large part by the demands of national macroeconomic fiscal
and monetary (especially stabilization and employment) policies, the growing
pressures and tensions of global economic competition (the national "competitiveness" issue), and the search for "fair" trade proceeding from the
suspicion that one's trading partners are not above cheating once in a while.
In the United States demands for protection have become directly correlated
with the size of the trade deficit. They also arise from concerns about the
decline, at times skirting elimination, of some defense-related domestic activities, such as automotive industries, branches of electronics, and precision
optics. Taiwan's post-1986 mainland trade and investment fever has caused
concern in some government quarters about the strategic implications for
the ROC of too much reliance on mainland trade and the migration to

---

[19]Bhagwati, *The World System at Risk.*

Fukien (Fujian) of sectors (not all of them labor-intensive) of Taiwan's manufacturing industry.

For Japan and the East Asian newly industrialized countries (the NICs— now just beginning to include parts of mainland China), there is also the issue of government support for private sector exports once seen as critical to the growth and development of their national economies. The close association of business and somewhat paternalistic, "enlightened," flexibly pragmatic, market-friendly governments has been vindicated in the eyes of the proponents of such partnership (and Western admirers) by those countries' phenomenal growth and modernization beginning in the 1960s, and by their joining—and increasingly dominating—the ranks of the world's leading traders and financiers.

In many less successful developing countries the causes of the protectionist impulse are more obscure. They seem to have a lot to do with the pursuit of private special interests linked to governing elites by bonds of blood, class, or caste.

Last but not least, the push toward economic integration is often matched by a virulent nationalistic (and infranationalist) counterpush. From 1945 to 1968, sixty-six new states were built from the wreckage of old colonial empires.[20] The process of nation-state building and rebuilding, and the putting-up of new impediments to the free flow of world commerce and finance, received a new impetus following the disintegration of the Soviet empire in 1990. Moreover, in addition to the 200 or so sovereign states today, there are at least 1,600 stateless quasi-nations (e.g., the Tamils, Sikhs, Ibos, Kurds, Shors, Tibetans, Baluchis, Pathans, Macedonians), striving for national liberation, often from cruel oppression, eager to experience the sense of political and social identity and prestige that goes with citizenship.[21]

With a few exceptions (e.g., the Organization of Petroleum Exporting Countries [OPEC]), modern protectionism, unlike the old medieval river and road tolls and nineteenth to mid-twentieth century tariffs and cartels, assumes the less blatant but not necessarily less trade-inhibiting, diverting, and distorting form of "managed trade": nontariff price and quantity-related barriers, such as voluntary export restraints, orderly marketing arrangements, structural impediments initiatives, multi-fiber arrangements, domestic export subsidies, exchange rate manipulations, turning a blind eye to intellectual property rights violations, combining advocacy of free trade for one's exports with regulation of one's imports, and so on. Roughly one-third of industrial production in the United States and France and one-fifth in Germany is

---

[20]Jean Bethke Elshtain, "As History Ends, Is Everything Getting Nicer? Nationalism Is as Deadly as Ever," *Wall Street Journal*, October 11, 1989, A18.

[21]Alexander Shtromas, "Grievances Around the World," *Wall Street Journal*, October 11, 1989, A18; "The State of the Nation State," 43.

sheltered by such means. When in 1991 the stock market scandal reached public ears in Japan, it became known that in a generous gesture the country's largest stock securities houses had spent in excess of US$1 billion to compensate more than 200 Japanese (not foreign) institutional (not individual) investors for losses suffered by the latter in the 1990 stock market crash.

National protectionism, while it may indeed temporarily increase a nation's share of the world market and for a time give the citizens a sense of national pride, smartness, dynamism, and well-being, derives from a narrow, producer-oriented, adversarial, and ultimately deconstructionist (that is, destructive) view of the world economy and trade. Protectionism restricts the consumer's right to choose—the essence of the free market system. It perpetuates and encourages productivity lags within the protected areas to the detriment of competitiveness in the world market, "the only market that can provide the necessary economies of scale for many industries."[22] Protectionism is highly contagious. If allowed to spread, it will rig and eventually paralyze the world market system. Given time, it will also help undermine the political democracy associated with the market system's most advanced form— something that Communism had failed to accomplish in more than seven decades by economic, political, police, and military means.

Free Trade Blocs

An intermediate response to the technological compression of time and volume, the spontaneous globalization of economic exchanges, and the accompanying intensification of worldwide competition, has been to create organizational infrastructures for regional economic and trade blocs. These range from loose cooperative understandings (e.g., Asia-Pacific Economic Cooperation [APEC] and the Association of Southeast Asian Nations [ASEAN]), through more formal geopolitically delimited free trade pacts (e.g., the U.S.-Canada, U.S.-Israel, and proposed U.S.-Mexico free trade areas, and the European Free Trade Area [EFTA]), to economic mergers aiming at supranational economic as well as political union (e.g., the European Community). At present there are, or are in the works, three such regional economic/trade groupings: the European Community, the North American free trade areas (with longer-range visions of extending them to the whole Western Hemisphere), and the eastern Pacific rim nations gravitating, sometimes reluctantly, around Japan. On the horizon, and at this stage rather hypothetical, is what some believe could be a "Greater China" economic cooperation or free trade area composed of a market-reformed and, I would argue, politically transformed mainland (or more likely perhaps, the southern parts of the mainland), Taiwan, Hong Kong, and Macao.[23]

---

[22]William E. Brock, "No, Let Us Praise Free Trade," *Washington Post*, June 13, 1983, A13.

[23]Jan S. Prybyla, "China's Revolution Without Borders . . . Will Founder Unless Party Walls Topple," *Asian Wall Street Journal*, March 16, 1992.

From the standpoint of a world system of workably competitive free markets, the proliferation of regional economic and economic-political blocs can be a force for good or for concern. It is a force for good insofar as it introduces competitive free trade within areas where formerly protectionism and bilateralism had been the rule. It is to be feared, however, that the MFN principle, especially in its unconditional form, could be discarded and regional blocs could become exclusive clubs barring outsiders, rich and poor alike, from joining; or to switch metaphors, medieval fortresses, moats, drawbridges and all, trumpeting their allegiance to global free trade especially with respect to their exports.

The motives for setting up regional economic or free trade blocs are often mixed, and sometimes downright suspicious, from the perspective of expanding, uninhibited world trade. Regional bonding, while on the surface compatible with the concept of multilateralism, carries with it dangers for multilateralist practice. These include what I would call the "five diversions": (1) trade diversion (e.g., favoring U.S. imports from Mexico instead of East Asia—read: Japan); (2) diversion of time and talent from pursuing GATT multilateralism (removal of barriers to world trade) toward bloc building and bloc adjunct membership (e.g., the EC's association with selected countries from newly liberated central Europe); (3) diversion of efforts from lowering and abolishing tariffs to multiplying special tariff schedules for regionally preferred partners (e.g., the United States is likely to have four tariff schedules in addition to the present standard two: one for MFN and another for non-favored nations, one to accommodate Canada and another to suit Mexico); (4) diversion of American, European, and Japanese funds from worldwide to regional financial institutions (e.g., to the Inter-American Development Bank, the European Bank for Reconstruction and Development, the Asian Development Bank); (5) diversion from spontaneous private flows of trade and capital to building regional technophiliac structures staffed with salaried, unelected administrators writing rules and codes of fairness and modeling ever more imaginative versions of trade management and industrial policy.[24]

A world economy comprised of blocs that are reasonably free inside but armor-plated on the outside would be at best a world of oligopolies, oligopolistic competition, and supranationally manipulated trade. Between the blocs, economic exchanges would be conducted on the basis of bilateral agreements, further fragmenting the world market and distorting world prices. (In 1987 the EC had eleven preferential arrangements with eleven separate categories of countries; the United States has preferential agreements with fourteen Latin American countries.) The politicization (using trade and

[24]Peter Truell, "Free Trade May Suffer from Regional Blocs," *Wall Street Journal*, July 1, 1991, A1.

investment as foreign policy tools), legislation, and bureaucratization of trade and finance would be enhanced by such a course.[25]

The argument can, of course, be made that regional multilateralism represents a movement in the right direction, toward a freer world economy; that forming regional free trade blocs and economic unions is simply the pragmatic and wise recognition of the facts of life, namely that you cannot have it all, all at once, without compromising, perhaps irreparably, the final objective of a worldwide competitive market system; and that regional trade and payments liberalizing commitments need not be exclusivist. But it is equally true that the path of regional blocs can be full of mercantilist potholes and statist traps. If taken, as indeed it appears to be by the world's major economic powers, it has to be followed with caution, in full awareness of its world market-inhibiting potential. In a 1992 survey of managers of multinational companies in sixty countries, 41 percent of the respondents expressed fears about growing EC protectionism, and 42 percent thought the economic and monetary union would not appreciably stimulate world trade.

Perils

The summary account of the contemporary techno-economic revolution has been upbeat on the whole, despite caveats and warnings introduced here and there to prevent optimism from sliding into utopian ecstasies. A fast-moving, miniaturized, monosystemic world of high technology and free markets has the unprecedented capacity to improve people's livelihood, and not just on the material level. However, as always, there are inescapable, but mostly manageable, trade-offs.

There are two broad categories of problems, emerging or already with us: cultural and technical.

Cultural problems: Speed and fixation on the future are not universally admired qualities. They are impatient with the contemplative life, irreverent, and indiscriminately dismissive of tradition. Cultural homogeneity—the standardization of attitudes, dress, and language—while it may reduce frictions and occasions for conflict and facilitate understanding, is purchased at a cost in diversity and some amiable idiosyncracies and eccentricities. Efficiency, productivity, competition, and economic valuation may raise living standards but also lower the tenor of life when they intrude, as they invariably do, into intimate nooks and crannies of interpersonal relations where they have no business to be. The positive correlation between rising affluence and civilized discourse is not as definitive as it is sometimes made out to be. Relative values are fine when they measure the terms of economic

---

[25]Lester C. Thurow, *Head to Head: The Coming Economic Battle Among Japan, Europe, and America* (New York: Morrow, 1992).

exchange, but not when they express moral relativism.

Technical problems: A world cyberspace of unobstructed information flow invites computer network vandals who spread virus infections through the system and steal what information they can. Soon the open door is slammed shut and access is to be had only by unlocking the electronic entrances with appropriate codes. Financial networks that span the globe can be used for constructive purposes or to engage in insider trading, launder drug money, and bankroll terrorists. Also, accelerated growth has been accompanied by frightful ecological degradation.

Yet, overall, the direction of the techno-economic revolution is liberating and meliorating, and its dynamic is well nigh irrepressible. The problems it creates or contributes to on its roller coaster course are susceptible to solution with the help of the very products of the transformatory tide.

ROC Development and the Global Economy

Under every conceivable indicator of performance, the ROC on Taiwan can be said to have actively participated in and, since the 1980s, has contributed to the world techno-economic revolution and global multilateralism. It has also begun to bring its political structures into line with its modern economic system of free market enterprise by embarking on the difficult process of real democratization.

Thus far, the ROC on Taiwan, unlike the China mainland and other socialist economies and polities, has been closely attuned to the movement of history and responsive to the rapidly changing requirements of modernization. Consequently, it has reaped many of the rewards and experienced relatively little of the turbulence attendant to modernization.

Judging simply by the record of the past four decades, there is not much reason to be concerned about the future course of the ROC's economy. But given the elemental changes currently unfolding in all spheres of society, outside the island no less than within, the outlook, while generally positive, remains uncertain. The emerging new world order and disorder present Taiwan with unprecedented challenges that a new and formally well trained generation of private and public decision-makers, now drawn from almost all political denominations, must judiciously respond to, at least as successfully as their now retired or retiring predecessors.

Historical Record

Taiwan's record of achievement in economic growth, development, trade, and modernization has been documented ad nauseam. It contains useful lessons, both positive and negative, for other NICs and aspiring NICs, particularly with respect to manpower—mainly brainpower—development, choice of systems, and what could be described as "fine-tuning the system." Rather than running again through the familiar statistical record of rapid-growth-with-stability-and-equity, I shall note a few points bearing directly on the essence of the techno-economic revolution and its expression in systemic choice and fine-tuning.

Techno-economic revolution: From the very beginning the ROC on Taiwan participated in the world techno-economic revolution by the emphasis and resources it gave to what has been earlier referred to as "judicious investment in education," or the training and effective utilization of its manpower. While vocational education was stressed early on, higher education in the hard and social sciences, both at home and through student migration abroad—mainly to American universities—received increased attention over time. Taiwan today has sixteen universities (some of them of very high caliber), twelve colleges, and seventy-seven junior colleges, and grants about 100,000 degrees a year. Nearly one-third of 18 to 21 year-olds (nearly half a million students) attend one of these schools, in addition to another half million who go to vocational schools. The return rate of Taiwan students from abroad has been rising over the years because of increased employment opportunities at home, salaries that are increasingly competitive with those in the West, a freer political climate, and what might be called cultural attraction. In the past few years, 2,250 high technology specialists returned from the United States to work at the Hsinchu Science Industrial Park founded in 1981, and 700 American trained technology (particularly semiconductor) specialists came back in 1990 alone.[26] In 1990-91, half of the university and college students were enrolled in agricultural science, natural science, medical science, and engineering programs (roughly in what Rustum Roy calls "real" science, the one that bears directly on the techno-economic revolution), and another 30 percent in increasingly ideologically unconstrained social and behavioral sciences programs (which bear on the choice, management, and fine-tuning of the sociopolitical and economic system). Taiwanese students abroad are also heavily concentrated in these areas. Typically, 30 percent of the returning students find employment in the private sector of industry and commerce, 10 percent are hired by government agencies, and most of the remainder work in educational and research institutions. Expenditure on research and development (R&D) rose from 0.95 percent of GNP in 1984 to 1.38 percent in 1989, still below the rates for Japan and Western advanced market economies, but catching up. Normally 35-40 percent of R&D money goes into applied research (on the Japanese model), 50 percent into product development, and the remainder to basic research.[27]

Participation in the world techno-economic revolution has until now not been synonymous with original contribution to the revolution. For

---

[26]Chu-yuan Cheng, "Taiwan's Economy in Transition: New Challenges and Prospects," *Asian Outlook* (Taipei) 26, no. 5 (July-August 1991): 10.

[27]*Taiwan Statistical Data Book 1991* (Taipei: Council for Economic Planning and Development, 1991).

example, in the area of computer hardware, Taiwan has taken giant steps in a very short time (early through late 1980s), raising its exports of micro-computers, disk drives, printers, terminals, and monitors from US$418 million in 1983 to more than US$5 billion in 1988 (ca. 95 percent of domestic production, most of it destined for the United States). However, a large (but declining) portion of the information industry's hardware products made in Taiwan for export or domestic consumption (ca. 70 percent in 1987, down from 84 percent in 1983) consisted of components and parts imported mostly from the United States (65 percent of imports in 1983; 33 percent in 1987) and Japan (22 percent of imports in 1983; 44 percent in 1987). "Most of the technologies new to the economy of Taiwan are incremental innovations adapted from the high-technology products of the industrially advanced countries."[28]

Choosing and fine-tuning a system: From the very beginning, the choice of economic systems for the ROC on Taiwan has been clear and, as it turns out, correct. Taiwan opted for the market system at home and the gradual integration of its domestic market economy with a global multilateral market system, the process of integration being paced in accordance with the domestic economy's gathering strength and ability to compete in the world league. "The emphasis on private initiative and the free market was important. Many less-developed countries failed in their development efforts because their governments assumed too many obligations for too long a time. Also, their economic development policies were more often guided by administrative controls than by market forces. Fortunately, this was not the case in Taiwan."[29]

However, the market system in both its domestic and global incarnations does not just happen by itself, and like a living organism it is subject to insufficiencies, failures, and breakdowns—as are, one must hasten to add, governments also. That is where the notion of fine-tuning the market comes in. Fine-tuning raises two closely related questions, which are starkly posed for Taiwan and other economies now that the basic question of systemic choice (market versus socialist planning) has been answered—except for the Communist hardliners in Peking (Beijing), Pyongyang, Hanoi, and Havana—by the collapse of socialist economics.[30]

The first question concerns the **balance between adherence to market principles and "flexible pragmatism."**[31] Adherence to market principles means

---

[28]Paul K. C. Liu, Ying-Chuan Liu, and Hui-Lin Wu, "New Technologies, Industry, and Trade—The Taiwan Experience," *Economic Review* (Taipei), no. 254 (March-April 1990): 22-23.

[29]K. T. Li, "Policy Formulation in a Dynamic Economy: The Experience of the ROC on Taiwan," *Economic Review*, no. 261 (May-June 1991): 6.

[30]Jan S. Prybyla, *Reform in China and Other Socialist Economies* (Washington, D.C.: American Enterprise Institute, 1990), 99-125.

[31]K. T. Li, "The Economic Transformation of the Republic of China: A Model of Success," *Economic Review*, no. 260 (March-April 1991): 5.

commitment to market choices and acceptance of market outcomes derived from the spontaneous and competitive exchange transactions of autonomous buyers and sellers in the market. "Flexible pragmatism" means fashioning, bending, and altering market rules through (1) the government's intervening in the domestic economy to encourage and/or modify market judgments when it believes conditions warrant, including aid and encouragement to sectors and industries the government considers to be the techno-economic wave of the future; and (2) the government's intervening in external trans- actions to help improve the country's international competitiveness and en- large its share of exports in the world (or in a targeted country's) market. In short, fine-tuning is another way of saying industrial policy and trade management. Industrial policy and trade management involve some degree of market planning by a government friendly to the market, to be sure, unlike socialist planning, which is market-hostile and designed to eliminate or confine to a cage individual free choice and private ownership. Never- theless, planning—market-friendly or not—always involves some substitution of government for individual preferences, and so raises the second question of **balance between individual and public initiatives and domains.** India, the Philippines, and many other countries demonstrate that you do not need market-phobic Communist governments to tie the market up in knots and tip the balance between individual and public initiatives to a point where, for all practical purposes, the market ceases to function as the vehicle par excellence of the techno-economic revolution. It is, as János Kornai has pointed out, a question of elusive but critical proportions of the components of the mix.

In the past Taiwan has avoided this mercantilistic trap by interpreting pragmatism "not [as] the government's power to predict which strategy would be successful but rather its ability to modify policies and strategies when changing [market] conditions so required."[32] It emphasized market principles and used flexible pragmatism as an adjunct to those principles. The world market identified the winners, and the government wet-nursed them at home. Similarly, the record reveals a principled commitment to the primacy of individual free initiative and private property, with public policy and state property playing an active and important indicative, but still sub- sidiary and supplementary, role in the economy's development.

The result has been an incremental transformation of the Taiwan economy's orientation and mode of operation, and an enlargement and re- finement of its systemic market and private property institutions. In 1952, 57 percent of industrial output came from state-owned enterprises; by 1962 the state's share had declined to 46 percent, 19 percent by 1972, 14 percent by 1982, and 10 percent by the end of the 1980s. However, the 10 percent

---

[32]Ibid.

included such "strategic-heights" goods as steel, electric power, a good part of petrochemicals, and shipbuilding.

In terms of value added, the changes in the economy's orientation have conformed closely to the early stages of the world techno-economic revolution: from labor-intensive to capital-intensive industry; from manufacturing to relatively low-end services, with the beginnings in each case of transition to high technology- and knowledge-intensive industrial and service pursuits.

In terms of longer range developmental direction, the movement has been away from autarkic temptations toward an open economy that can hold its own in fierce global market competition and which, at the same time, has a domestic base large and solid enough to absorb shocks to the home economy coming from disturbances and fluctuations in the world market. (Taiwan's foreign trade dependency ratio [the value of foreign trade divided by GNP] remains very high at 80 percent [down from 92 percent in 1988] compared to, say, Japan at 16 percent [1988].) The movement toward an open, globally integrated economy has gone through several stages: from economic colonialism to import substitution in light industry (late 1940s to early 1950s); to expansion of light industry exports (late 1950s to early 1960s); to import substitution in intermediate and capital goods (early to late 1970s); to economic liberalization and internationalization (more balanced, if not yet equal, emphasis on both exports and imports, beginning in 1984).[33]

It has often been pointed out that the market system can coexist with many brands of political authoritarianism, and even put up with advanced cultural pathologies, and still turn out goods more efficiently than any other tested (not academically or theologically imagined) economic system. Constitutional democracy, it is argued, is neither a necessary nor a sufficient condition for the development of a market system, an argument eagerly taken up these days by economic "reformists" in Peking and their claque in the West and some other places (e.g., Hong Kong millionaires who want social "stability" at all cost). I think this argument contains just enough truth to be superficially persuasive, but is otherwise seriously flawed.[34] A full rebuttal cannot be given here if only for reasons of space, but in the first part of this chapter I gave an inkling of the general argumentative line such a rebuttal would take. The techno-economic revolution requires freedom of thought and action to extend to all social and cultural spheres, not just to government-approved science, technology, and economics. At some point such freedom has to be formalized in constitutional democracy with all its many faults and irritants. (Many of Hong Kong's looming political troubles are traceable precisely to the failure, under British rule, to anchor economic

---

[33]Ibid., 2-5.
[34]Prybyla, *Reform in China*, 14-45.

and other freedoms in constitutional representative government.[35]) The ROC
on Taiwan has understood the relationship of an advanced market system to
political democracy, and since the mid-1980s, has taken concrete steps to
modernize, that is, democratize, its political order. Despite its many annoying
short-term inconveniences (e.g., fisticuffs in the Legislative Yuan), democracy
is best suited to absorb and creatively transform the social tensions generated
by the technology-driven global market revolution.

Future Challenges

To help overcome problems centering on quality—quality of products,
quality of the environment (both physical and investment), and quality of
life—brought about by rapid economic modernization, and to help make
possible Taiwan's transition to the status of a fully industrialized country
by the end of the century (when per capita GNP is projected at better than
US$17,000 per year, US$14,000 in 1996), the government put into effect a
US$300 billion Six-Year National Development Plan (1991-96) dependent in
large part on the private sector and foreign cooperation.[36]

In the theoretical schema presented here, during those years the following major challenges will be faced.

Techno-economic revolution: The economy is to make the important
qualitative transition from imitation, adaptation, and incremental improvement of foreign high technologies, to the creation of such technologies.

In order to help bring this about, several steps have been or are being
taken by the private sector-government partnership. These include (1) the
liberalization of inward and outward capital and know-how flows to (a)
attract packages of direct foreign investment (DFI) containing advanced
technology embodied in capital equipment, but also, and increasingly, in
the form of processes, designs, methods, and concepts in manufacturing,
business management, marketing, after-delivery service, banking, finance,
insurance, and other conceptual values, and (b) make it easier for private
Taiwanese ventures to invest in advanced market economies, thus not only
absorbing state-of-the-art technologies, but securing a foothold in lucrative
foreign markets, and promoting economic multilateralism to boot; (2) the
conclusion (with government assistance) of agreements between foreign telecommunications, electronics, avionics, and other high-tech firms (e.g., with
IBM, AT&T, HP, DEC, and McDonnell Douglas in the United States) and
Taiwan research institutes with the aim of setting up joint ventures; (3) improvement and better enforcement of laws regarding the protection of foreign

---

[35]William McGurn, *Perfidious Albion: The Abandonment of Hong Kong* (Washington, D.C.:
Ethics and Public Policy Center, 1992).
[36]"The Six-Year National Development Plan for Taiwan, Republic of China (1991-1996): Macroeconomic Development Targets," *Economic Review*, no. 261 (May-June 1991): 10-23.

intellectual property—a sore point with both the United States and the EC; (4) stepped-up government investment in technology—in fiscal 1992 alone, NT$11 billion to promote industrial R&D, automation, design, development of core-satellite manufacturing systems, pollution control, and manpower training; implementation of the Statute for Industrial Upgrading providing tax incentives to firms that engage in R&D, provide training to employees, establish their own brands and trademarks, conserve energy, and control pollution; (5) the use of massive government procurements in ways that stimulate the growth of domestic transportation, energy generation, tele-communications, and environmental protection;[37] and (6) taking steps to initiate exchanges of scientific personnel with the mainland. This last is less for knowledge acquisition than for long-term political purposes. All these measures aim at bringing Taiwan into the ranks of those advanced market democracies which power the techno-economic revolution by compressing time and volume, expanding conceptual values, and globalizing their economic structures.

The structure of the Taiwan economy in the next few years will undergo further qualitative transformations from being labor- to capital- and advanced technology-intensive, and from assembly and processing-type manufacturing and low-end services to high-tech manufacturing and high-end services such as industrial design, finance, banking, insurance, marketing, rapid low-volume high-value transportation, telecommunications, and information; that is, to the production and conveyance of high value impalpables. The aim is to make Taiwan into a first class transportation and transshipment hub and financial center in the western Pacific that would share those functions with Hong Kong, if the territory's present role in these areas is not destroyed by the 1997 reunification with mainland China, or, if so (as it may be unless between now and July 1, 1997, mainland China undergoes a dramatic economic and political transformation), to step into Hong Kong's shoes.

Systemic choice and fine-tuning: There is no question as to the commitment of Taiwan—of the great majority of its citizens and its present government—to market principles and the primacy of private initiative, and to the continued development of democracy. There is equally little doubt as to the country's present intention to enter the international economy and work for global multilateralism (viz. its pending application to join GATT) and, in the shorter term, to participate in regional economic associations of various kinds (e.g., APEC) and regional financial institutions (e.g., the Asian Development Bank) where it would presumably exercise its influence in favor of free trade and against bloc protection. There is also no question as to

---

[37]Vincent C. Siew, "The Six-Year National Development Plan and ROC's Future Economic Development" (Paper presented at the Conference on the ROC and the New International Order, Taipei, August 22, 1991), 6.

Taiwan's economic credentials, both as a successful model of development and in terms of the contents of its purse, for admission to such groupings and organizations. Taiwan in 1991 had a two-way trade of US$139 billion, the fourteenth largest in the world, the largest foreign exchange reserves in the world at US$83.2 billion (February 1991), and was from 1987 to 1991 the world's sixth largest supplier of capital, with overseas investments in that period totaling US$19 billion (including about US$3 billion on the mainland).

Taiwan has done everything that can be reasonably expected of a self-respecting country to gain readmission into the world community, now as a giver rather than supplicant. It has liberalized its trade and investment policies (its average tariff rate in 1992 is comparable to that of the OECD countries); facilitated foreign access to its expanding services market; significantly appreciated its currency; launched a program designed to reduce its long-term trade surplus (the bulk of it with the United States) by diversifying its export markets and expanding domestic demand for imports; it has established a Fund for International Economic Cooperation and Development to provide friendly (and the proviso is understandable) developing countries and the ASEAN NICs with concessionary loans and investments; improved the enforcement of its copyright, trademark, patent, and other intellectual property laws (although here much remains to be done); opened indirect trade and investment (as well as people-to-people) relations with the mainland; and put up with a heap of indignities to its official name, national flag, anthem, and other matters of symbolic importance to any sovereign nation.

Although on the basis of the ROC's past record and the strategies presently being implemented the future looks bright for Taiwan (so far as it can be predicted), there are some concerns about certain philosophical and policy trends in the richer and self-confident contemporary Taiwan that should be addressed.

Concerns

There is a troubling emphasis being placed on the "pragmatic" component of the principles-pragmatism mix today in Taiwan. Flexible pragmatism, of course, is a fine and essential quality when contrasted with inflexible dogma, but if not carefully weighed and restrained, it can become itself a principle which says that everything is negotiable and that there are always two sides to every question. Particularly troubling is the Taiwan business community's rush to the mainland, justified on the grounds of a pragmatic understanding of the inexorable demands of the world techno-economic revolution as it affects Taiwan these days. There is the possibility that what was intended as a rational weighing of feasible alternatives (relativity) may turn into moral and political relativism, where differences between theories and institutional systems are matters of degree, and *only* of degree.

A second concern is with the balance of private and public initiative and domain in the economy. Preservation and expansion of the private decision-making and ownership sphere (what Friedrich Hayek once called the individual's "sovereign domain") is as indispensable for a vigorous and properly functioning market system as it is for individual liberty. No matter how market-friendly and representative the government, government is bureaucratic and essentially coercive, prone to exponential expansion and ever-ready to substitute its preferences for those of individual citizens as buyers and sellers in the market. The process of privatizing public firms in Taiwan, while statistically impressive (see above), has been characterized by one observer as somewhat lagging.[38] The current Six-Year Plan, which laudably enough tries to supply the infrastructures needed to stimulate sluggish domestic private investment, nevertheless presents dangers of an additional presence of the public sector in Taiwan's future economy, with its large state enterprises and rule-happy bureaucrats.

The third concern has to do with the temptation to form regional blocs, particularly the rather loose talk about a Greater China Economic Sphere comprising the mainland, or parts of it (Kwangtung [Guangdong], Fukien, Hainan), Taiwan, Hong Kong, Macao, and perhaps even Singapore. While the possibility of such a construct cannot be dismissed offhand, its actualization presents at this stage extremely complex and delicate problems of very different economic and political systems that no amount of flexible pragmatism can bridge without abandoning some fundamental principles that have served Taiwan well in the past. In a broader context, "economic regionalization," according to ROC economic affairs minister, Vincent Siew, "may be the wave of the future." In the Asia-Pacific region the economies are highly complementary, he adds. "Japan excels in high technology, and managerial and marketing know-how; the 'four little dragons' are noted for their entrepreneurial vitality; and the China mainland and the ASEAN countries possess enormous reserves of manpower and natural resources."[39] Here, too, political problems (this time connected with Japan) abound. Even if such an association should materialize, however, Taiwan would still probably tend to exert within it an influence in favor of openness and multilateralism rather than bloc protection.

The last concern is about social harmony, which must be maintained if Taiwan's contributions to the world techno-economic revolution and global multilateralism are to be effective and its own standing among the advanced countries of the world assured. Economic policies henceforth demand not merely disciplined resolve, but broad political consensus freely arrived at among contending, often impatient, viewpoints that are ratified by the

---

[38]K. H. Yu, "Economic Prospects of the Republic of China on Taiwan at the Turn of the 21st Century," *Economic Review*, no. 253 (January-February 1990): 5.

[39]Vincent C. Siew, "Wider International Role for ROC," *Free China Journal* (Taipei) 9, no. 35 (May 19, 1992): 7.

ballot box. Although the concern is shared by many people on the island, the record has been reassuring so far, despite a few highly visible blemishes. All sides seem to agree that the democratic undertaking is not only valuable in an absolute sense, but indispensable for further modernization.

Opportunities

The economic challenges facing the ROC on Taiwan are minor compared to those that confront the formerly socialist countries of Eastern Europe and the ex-Soviet Union, and the still (but rapidly eroding) socialist mainland China. The challenge for Taiwan is to stay the course while upgrading its technology and further fine-tune (not fundamentally change) its economic system. The emergence and reemergence of market democracies in Eastern Europe and the Commonwealth of Independent States provides the ROC—both its entrepreneurial small and medium-sized private sector firms, and its government—with a historic opportunity to (1) gain an early foothold in a potentially large and lucrative consumer goods market through joint ventures, cooperative production agreements, wholly-owned enterprises, and other forms of direct private trade and investment; (2) further diversify its export markets; and (3) join in and give new impetus to the efforts of the advanced market democracies aimed at helping build a market system and encourage political democracy on the ashes of central misplanning and autocracy—a task for which Taiwan is eminently suited by reason of its exemplary record in both areas. The countries formerly enserfed by Communism will, I am sure, have fewer hang-ups about offending the totalitarian sensibilities of the remnant and obsolete Communist regimes, the mainland Chinese among them, than have the established Western democracies which have never experienced Communism (except occasionally on their campuses). These countries are likely to be more receptive than their Western counterparts to experimentation with novel forms of political cooperation with, and recognition of, the ROC.

In sum, and on balance, the future of the ROC on Taiwan is very promising provided investment in technological progress is not impeded, and the balance between principle and expediency, private and public initiative, global multilateralism and regionalism (with its protectionist tendencies) is at all times tilted toward the first component in all these pairs.

Other References

Kornai, János. "The Hungarian Reform Process: Vision, Hopes, and Reality." In *Remaking the Economic Institutions of Socialism: China and Eastern Europe*, ed. Victor Nee and David Stark. Stanford, Calif.: Stanford University Press, 1989.
Lee, Teng-hui [President of ROC]. "From Uncertainty to Pragmatism: The Shape of the Age to Come." Speech given to a group of professors attending the National Development Seminar, Taipei, August 8, 1991.

Reich, Robert. *The Work of Nations: Preparing Ourselves for 21st Century Capitalism.* New York: Alfred A. Knopf, 1991.

Roy, Rustum. "2 Kinds of 'Science' in Society: Real and Abstract." *Centre Daily Times* (State College, Pennsylvania), June 21, 1992.

Shieh, Samuel C. "Financial Liberalization and Internationalization in the ROC—Current Status and Future Directions." *Economic Review*, no. 254 (March-April 1990).

CHAPTER 6

The ROC's Role
in the World Economy

Chu-yuan Cheng

The Republic of China (ROC) on Taiwan has achieved an economic record rivaled by few other developing nations in the post-World War II period. As Taiwan has been transformed from a backward agrarian economy to a modern industrial society, its per capita income has risen sixty-fold in four decades. In 1952, the ROC's per capita gross national product (GNP) was only one-thirtieth that of the United States, but by 1990 it had advanced to one-third.[1] The ROC now ranks as the world's fourteenth largest trading country with the world's largest foreign exchange reserves,[2] and it plays an important role in the international economy. Over the past decade, the ROC has changed its financial position from a capital importer to a major capital exporter, investing extensively in mainland China and Southeast Asia. At the same time, it has promulgated a series of regulations to promote the liberalization and internationalization of the economy with the goal of building Taipei into a regional financial center by the end of this century.[3] The success story of the ROC has attracted worldwide attention. Many components of the Taiwan model are now being followed by other less-developed countries.

The purpose of this chapter is to assess the role played by the ROC in the world economy. The study focuses on three major aspects: the place of the ROC in the world's commodity and capital markets; the effects of Taiwan's experience on mainland China and other developing countries; and the ROC's potential influence in the world economy in the years ahead.

---

[1] Per capita income in Taiwan was US$50 in 1952. By 1990, it had reached US$8,000.

[2] By the end of 1991, Taiwan's foreign exchange reserves had reached US$82 billion, surpassing those of Japan and Germany.

[3] Samuel C. Shieh, "The Outlook for Taipei as a Regional Financial Center in Asia," *Industry of Free China* (Taipei) 76, no. 5 (November 1991): 31-41. (Shieh is governor of the Central Bank of China.)

Phenomenal Economic Growth

The initial conditions of the ROC on Taiwan were no better than those of other underdeveloped countries. In terms of natural endowments, Taiwan's land area of 36,000 square kilometers (13,885 square miles) is 7 percent of that of Thailand, 11 percent of that of Malaysia, and less than 2 percent of that of Indonesia. It is less than 0.004 percent of the area of mainland China. A mountainous island with very meager mineral resources, Taiwan's greatest natural resource is its arable land, which accounts for only one-fourth of the total land area.[4]

In 1949, when the Nationalist government retreated from the mainland to Taiwan, the island's economy faced two serious problems: the sudden increase in population and heavy military expenditures. Per capita GNP in 1952 was only US$50 (US$150 in 1980s terms) and inflation was rampant. These difficulties, however, did not deter the ROC government. Between 1950 and 1960, a host of reform and developmental policies were implemented. Notable among these policies were the establishment of a mixed economic system under which state and private enterprises coexisted, and an "indicative" national plan which operated together with the market mechanism. Other major measures included a peaceful land reform in rural areas, an export expansion development strategy, and an open-door policy to attract foreign capital and technology.

The pursuit of these policies has successfully transformed the island from an agriculture-based economy into a dynamic modern society. Taiwan's economic achievements are displayed in its growth, stability, equity, standards of living, and changes in the economic structure.

Taiwan's real GNP growth rate was 7.5 percent between 1952 and 1960, 9.7 percent between 1960 and 1970, 9.6 percent between 1970 and 1980, and 7.8 percent between 1980 and 1990. The long-term growth rate of 8.8 percent between 1952 and 1990 was one of the world's highest.[5]

Not only has the ROC achieved high rates of growth but it has also demonstrated a consistent and steady growth pattern. Throughout the entire forty years, Taiwan's per capita GNP rose every year with the exception of 1974 when the island suffered a brief recession caused by a worldwide energy crisis. But the short recession was soon followed by a rapid recovery in subsequent years.[6]

With a steady growth in per capita income, and the increasing abundance

---

[4]For details see Chu-yuan Cheng, "The Doctrine of People's Welfare: The Taiwan Experiment and Its Implications for the Third World," in *Sun Yat-sen's Doctrine in the Modern World*, ed. Chu-yuan Cheng (Boulder, Colo.: Westview Press, 1989), 244-71.

[5]*Taiwan Statistical Data Book 1991* (Taipei: Council for Economic Planning and Development, 1991), 2.

[6]Ibid.

of consumer goods, living standards in Taiwan have been the highest ever attained in Chinese history. Economic prosperity brought considerable changes in people's consumption patterns. In 1964, 59.7 percent of a family's consumption expenditures in Taiwan went toward food, beverages, and tobacco. The percentage dropped to 39.4 percent in 1981, and 33.7 percent in 1989. As people spent relatively less on food, they enjoyed better housing, education, and recreation. Consumption expenditures for housing rose from 17.2 percent in 1964 to 23.8 percent in 1989; and education and recreation spending rose from 1.2 percent in 1964 to 12 percent in 1989.[7]

The most remarkable achievement in Taiwan's industrialization, however, has been its income distribution. Despite the very high rates of growth and capital formation, income distribution has become much more equal over the past four decades. Improvements in income distribution in Taiwan stem from two important factors: the successful land reform program, which substantially improved the lot of the rural population, and the rapid rise in the demand for nonagricultural labor, which lifted the real wages of urban workers. In 1953, family income among the top 20 percent was estimated at twenty times that of the bottom 20 percent. By 1972, the gap was narrowed to 4.5 times and by 1980, it was further reduced to 4.2 times. In recent years, as stock and real estate speculations flourished, the trend has reversed somewhat. By 1990 the gap widened to 4.9 times, but is still one of the best among the developing nations.[8]

Dramatic changes have also been effected in the economic structure. In 1952, when the ROC embarked on an industrialization drive, agriculture accounted for 32.2 percent of the gross domestic product (GDP). The share dropped steadily to 20.6 percent in 1964, 15.5 percent in 1970, and 4.2 percent in 1990. Concomitantly, the share of industry (including mining, manufacturing, public utilities, and construction) rose from 19.7 percent in 1952 to 42.3 percent in 1990, surpassing the 35 percent attained by most advanced industrial countries.[9]

Taiwan's outstanding economic performance greatly elevated the ROC's role in the world economy. In 1952, on the eve of Taiwan's First Four-Year Economic Development Plan, the value of the island's total foreign trade was only US$326 million. By 1991, it had reached US$139 billion, making it the fourteenth largest trading country in the world.[10]

A Rising World Trade Power

 One component of Taiwan's developmental model has been the pursuit

---

[7]Ibid., 62.

[8]Ibid.

[9]*World Development Report 1991* (New York: World Bank, 1991), 209.

[10]*Ching-chi jih-pao* (Economic Daily) (Taipei), January 7, 1992, 2.

Table 6.1
Foreign Trade as Percentage of Taiwan's GNP (1961-90)

	1961	1966	1971	1976	1981	1986	1990
Exports (US$ millions)	195	536	2,060	8,166	22,611	38,849	67,214
As % of GNP	(11.2)	(17.0)	(31.3)	(44.2)	(47.2)	(51.6)	(41.6)
Imports (US$ millions)	322	622	1,844	7,599	21,200	24,165	54,719
As % of GNP	(18.4)	(19.8)	(28.0)	(41.1)	(44.2)	(31.3)	(33.8)
Dependency Ratio (Trade/GNP)	29.6	36.8	59.3	85.3	91.4	82.9	75.4

Source: *Industry of Free China* (Taipei) 76, no. 5 (November 1991): 6.

of an export promotion scheme. Aware of the limited size of its domestic market, Taiwan has, since the 1960s, employed export expansion as its guiding policy.

As early as the 1950s when import substitution was the main objective of industrial development, a series of export promotion schemes were instituted. One of the most important measures was the devaluation of Taiwan's currency, an act that contributed to reducing the cost of exporting commodities. Another measure was a tax rebate on exportable industrial products. These two measures markedly enhanced the competitive power of Taiwan's products in international markets. The third major measure was the creation of three export processing zones in the coastal exporting centers to attract foreign capital and technology.[11] Under these new policies, Taiwan's foreign trade soared. Between 1952 and 1962, prior to the new policy, foreign trade rose at an annual rate of only 6.1 percent, lower than the GNP growth rate. But between 1962 and 1974, Taiwan's total trade increased twenty-two times, with an annual growth rate of 29.4 percent. The highest growth rate was reached in 1970-74, when the annual rate was 41.5 percent, surpassing Japanese postwar records. In the last decade, Taiwan's foreign trade has accounted for about 80 percent of the GNP and has become the island's engine of growth (see table 6.1).

Between 1961 and 1990, Taiwan's total foreign trade increased 233-fold, from US$517 million to US$121.9 billion. During these three decades, the annual growth rate of foreign trade was about three times the GNP's growth rate. Consequently, Taiwan's dependency ratio (trade/GNP) rose from 29.6 percent in 1961 to a high of 91.4 percent in 1981 before declining

---

[11]Kuai-jeou Wang, "Economic and Social Impact of Export Processing Zones in the Republic of China," *Economic Review* (Taipei), no. 200 (March-April 1981): 10-11.

Table 6.2
The ROC's Changing Rank among the World's Major Trading Countries

Year	Total Trade	Exports	Imports
1979	24	21	25
1980	22	24	21
1981	22	16	22
1982	22	15	23
1983	18	14	20
1984	19	12	21
1985	18	11	22
1986	16	11	20
1987	13	11	17
1988	13	13	16
1989	15	12	16
1990	14	11	16

Source: *Monthly Bulletin of Statistics* (New York, United Nations), various issues.

to 75.4 percent in 1990. The high dependency ratios indicate that the economy of the ROC has become closely integrated into the world economy.

The staggering rise of foreign trade catapulted the ROC to the position of one of the world's major trading countries (see table 6.2). It has been officially projected that by 1996, when the ROC completes its Six-Year National Development Plan (1991-96), Taiwan will be among the top ten exporting countries in the world.[12]

The role of the ROC in world trade can be further evaluated by two other indicators: its share of the world's total trade and its ability to earn foreign exchange.

In the 1950s and 1960s, the ROC's share of world trade was minuscule, and in 1979, it still accounted for less than 1 percent of the world's total. But by 1989, ROC trade accounted for almost 2 percent of the world's total trade and 2.2 percent of the world's total exports (see table 6.3). But in terms of population, the ROC accounted for only 0.4 percent of the world's total. In 1990, Taiwan's total trade value of US$121.9 billion was 2.15 times that of Thailand and 2.56 times that of Indonesia. Although India has a population forty times larger than Taiwan's, its foreign trade value is only one-third that of Taiwan.[13]

---

[12]*Kuo-chi jih-pao* (International Daily News) (Los Angeles), February 18, 1992, 12.

[13]In 1990, Taiwan's exports were worth US$67.2 billion, compared with US$25.7 billion for Indonesia, US$22.8 billion for Thailand, and US$17.8 billion for India. See *Monthly Bulletin of Statistics* (New York, United Nations), June 1991.

Table 6.3
The Share of the ROC's Trade in Total World Trade (1979-90)

US$100 million

Year	Total Trade			Exports			Imports		
	World Total	Taiwan's Total	%	World Exports	Taiwan's Exports	%	World Imports	Taiwan's Imports	%
1979	33,259	309	0.96	16,391	161	1.0	16,868	148	0.88
1980	40,404	395	0.98	19,906	198	1.0	20,498	197	0.96
1981	40,088	438	1.1	19,718	226	1.1	20,370	212	1.0
1982	37,354	411	1.1	18,335	222	1.2	19,019	189	1.0
1983	36,843	454	1.2	18,125	251	1.4	18,718	203	1.1
1984	38,878	524	1.4	19,097	304	1.6	19,781	220	1.1
1985	39,303	508	1.3	21,221	307	1.6	20,082	201	1.0
1986	43,089	641	1.5	21,169	399	1.9	21,920	242	1.1
1987	50,327	887	1.8	24,803	537	2.2	25,524	350	1.4
1988	57,348	1,103	1.9	28,228	606	2.1	29,120	497	1.7
1989	61,517	1,186	1.9	30,205	663	2.2	31,312	523	1.7
1990	69,048	1,219	1.8	33,817	672	2.0	35,231	547	1.6

Source: United Nations, *Monthly Bulletin of Statistics*, various issues.
Note: Trade data are reported on a F.O.B. basis for exports, and a C.I.F. basis for imports.

The strength of the ROC in the world's commodity markets is also illustrated by its capacity to maintain a huge trade surplus. Although Taiwan suffered a trade deficit in the years 1952-77, since then, the island has continuously enjoyed a trade surplus. The surplus for the years 1982-91 added up to US$106.8 billion. By the end of 1991, foreign exchange reserves held by the Central Bank of China totaled US$82 billion, the largest in the world.[14]

The rapid growth of ROC trade and its ability to produce a surplus stems primarily from changes in its industrial structure and the composition of its exports.

In 1961, 32 percent of Taiwan's GNP came from agriculture and 17 percent from manufacturing. By 1990, the share of agriculture dropped to only 4.9 percent while the share of manufacturing rose to 34 percent. The drastic change in the industrial structure led to an alteration in export composition. In 1960, 68 percent of exports were raw and processed agricultural products; industrial products accounted for only 32 percent. By 1990, 95.5 percent of Taiwan's exports were industrial products.[15]

[14]In comparison, Japan had reserves of US$71.1 billion. See *Chung-yang jih-pao* (Central Daily News) (Taipei), June 6, 1992, 1.
[15]*Taiwan Statistical Data Book 1991*, 213.

Table 6.4
Taiwan's Trade Surplus (1981-91)

(US$ million)

Year	Exports	Imports	Balance
1981	21,261	21,441	(−) 180
1982	22,659	19,624	3,035
1983	22,810	18,311	4,499
1984	28,562	21,834	6,728
1985	30,612	21,480	9,132
1986	33,698	21,053	12,645
1987	46,890	28,968	17,922
1988	57,887	43,750	14,137
1989	63,559	50,903	12,656
1990	66,013	53,256	12,757
1991	76,160	62,860	12,300

Source: *Taiwan Statistical Data Book 1991* (Taipei: Council for Economic Planning and Development, 1991), 208.

In 1966, of the five most important exported commodities and services, 23.4 percent were processed food products; 13.1 percent were transport services; 8.8 percent was plywood; and 6.2 percent were animal products. By 1986, the five exported commodities generating the largest revenues were electronics products (15.7 percent), garments (13 percent), textile products (10.2 percent), metal and articles (5.3 percent), and other manufactures (10.8 percent).[16] The change from low value-added products to high value-added products is one of the major factors contributing to the sharp rise in Taiwan's export value.

An Emerging Capital Exporter

Prior to 1977, the ROC was basically a foreign capital recipient. Most foreign capital came from the United States, Japan, and Western Europe (see table 6.5). Although total foreign investment between 1952 and 1990 amounted to only US$11.3 billion (a figure less than Taiwan's trade surplus in one year in the 1980s), the contribution made by foreign capital to the island's economy was far-reaching and profound.

Of all the contributions to Taiwan's economy made by overseas Chinese

[16]Chuang Chia-cheng, "Balance of Payments and Economic Development in Taiwan" (in Chinese), *Industry of Free China* 76, no. 5 (November 1991): 11.

Table 6.5
Foreign Investment in Taiwan (1952-90)

(US$1,000)

Year	Total Cases	Total Amount	United States Cases	United States Amount	Japan Cases	Japan Amount	Europe Cases	Europe Amount	Others Cases	Others Amount
1952-1979	1,191	1,510,336	314	666,192	721	371,575	50	246,112	105	226,457
1980	71	243,380	15	110,093	35	86,081	11	14,428	10	32,778
1981	73	356,294	25	203,213	27	64,623	9	13,196	13	75,262
1982	82	320,286	33	79,606	24	152,164	11	46,570	14	41,946
1983	100	375,382	35	93,294	33	196,770	7	20,746	25	64,572
1984	100	518,971	41	231,175	28	113,978	15	92,242	16	81,576
1985	107	660,703	42	332,760	32	145,236	12	100,011	21	82,696
1986	206	705,574	56	138,428	88	253,596	24	139,642	38	173,908
1987	363	1,223,069	74	414,061	207	399,240	38	234,332	44	175,436
1988	438	1,061,161	60	134,726	212	431,867	75	206,236	92	288,332
1989	478	2,241,026	54	343,002	233	640,552	85	531,420	106	726,052
1990	376	2,081,657	61	540,367	179	826,800	66	348,350	70	366,140
Total	3,586	11,297,839	811	3,291,669	1,819	3,682,482	408	2,010,671	548	2,313,017

Source: Investment Commission, Ministry of Economic Affairs, ROC, *Hua-ch'iao chi wai-jen t'ou-tzu tui wo-kuo ching-chi fa-chan te kung-hsien* (Statistics on overseas Chinese and foreign investments, and their contributions to our economic development) (Taipei), various issues.

122   Chu-yuan Cheng

Table 6.6
Taiwan's Capital Flow (1961-90)

(US$ million)

Year	Balance	Direct Investment and Other Long-term Capital	Short-term Capital
1961-70	915	588	327
1971-80	4,091	4,266	−175
1981	995	886	109
1982	739	1,268	−529
1983	645	1,043	−398
1984	−828	−738	−89
1985	−439	−777	284
1986	13	−1,408	1,421
1987	1,627	−2,386	4,013
1988	−7,512	−6,031	−1,481
1989	−8,303	−7,432	−871
1990	−10,725	−6,402	−4,323

Source: *Chung-hua min-kuo T'ai-wan ti-ch'ü chin-jung t'ung-chi yüeh-pao* (Financial Statistics Monthly, Taiwan Area, the Republic of China) (Taipei), various issues.
Note: Minus sign denotes capital outflow.

and foreign investments, the effect on export promotion was the most conspicuous. In the three years 1977-79, when Taiwan's exports grew extremely rapidly, the share of overseas Chinese and foreign-invested firms in Taiwan's exports was as high as 29 percent. Even as late as 1982, their share still stood at 25 percent of Taiwan's exports. Of Taiwan's major export commodities in 1982, 65.2 percent of electronics and electrical appliances, 63.5 percent of chemicals, and 38 percent of textiles were produced by overseas Chinese and foreign-invested firms.[17] As Taiwan's economic base expanded, the share of these firms shrank. It was 16.7 percent in 1986, 15.52 percent in 1987, and 15.61 percent in 1988, still quite a respectable share.[18]

After four decades of phenomenal growth, Taiwan's economy was by the mid-1980s confronting many formidable problems. Among them were labor shortages, soaring labor costs, sky-high land prices, mounting concerns about pollution, and the sharp appreciation of Taiwan's currency relative to the U.S. dollar. Under growing pressure from the United States, the

[17]Chu-yuan Cheng, "United States-Taiwan Economic Relations: Trade and Investment," *Columbia Journal of World Business* 21, no. 1 (Spring 1986): 87-96.
[18]Liao Ping-tsai (Liao Bingzai), "Mutual Investment between Taiwan and Developed Countries," *Kuo-chi mao-i* (Intertrade Monthly) (Peking), 1991, no. 6:29-32.

Taiwan dollar was allowed to appreciate by 20 percent in 1987, 28 percent in 1988, and another 9 percent in 1989. In January 1989, the U.S. government suspended the benefits of its general system of preference to Taiwan. The ROC no longer enjoys most-favored-nation (MFN) trade status. All these developments substantially increased production costs and affected Taiwan's competitive edge in the international market. Many Taiwan enterprises began to transplant their operations overseas.[19]

The outflow of capital started in 1984, but accelerated after 1987. Prior to 1987, the ROC government strictly controlled foreign exchange, prohibiting the outflow of capital and requiring government approval for foreign investment. In 1987, its huge foreign exchange reserves enabled the government to relax exchange controls. Residents in Taiwan are now allowed to transfer overseas a maximum of US$3 million per person per year, so a family of four can now transfer a total of US$12 million, adequate for a medium-sized operation outside the island. As a result, capital outflow began to surge, with more than US$30 billion reportedly leaving the island from 1987 to 1991.[20]

During the first stage of capital outflow, the prime destination was the United States. Private investment in the United States with government approval rose from US$107 million in 1985 to US$620 million in 1989. But actual investment is widely believed to be many times the official figure.

In the past, most of Taiwan's private investment in the United States was concentrated in restaurants, motels, and real estate. In recent years, as Taiwan entered the era of high-tech, many companies in the fields of computers, petrochemicals, and banking have begun to take over American firms. In 1988, the Pacific Wire and Cable Company in Taiwan purchased thirty-eight American savings and loan associations for a total cost of US$37.5 million. In 1989, the Taiwan Continental Engineering Company acquired American Bridge Co. of Pittsburgh for US$100 million. In 1990, the Chinese Petroleum Corporation purchased Huffco Petroleum. In May 1990, Taiwan President Enterprises acquired Wyndham Foods, the United States' third largest biscuit maker, for US$335 million. In the field of computers, Taiwan Acer Incorporated acquired Altas Computer System in California and Taiwan Wyse Company acquired its U.S. parent company.[21] All of these new ventures are a part of the shift in Taiwan's overseas investment from services to manufacturing, especially in high-tech industries. In November 1991, an aerospace company in Taiwan engaged in negotiations with McDonnell Douglas to buy up to 40 percent of its commercial aircraft business for US$2

---

[19]Chu-yuan Cheng, "Taiwan's Economy in Transition: New Challenges and Prospects," *Asian Outlook* (Taipei) 26, no. 5 (July-August 1991): 5-11.

[20]*Shih-chieh jih-pao* (World Journal) (New York), June 17, 1992, 16.

[21]See note 3 above.

billion. Although the deal has not been consummated, it further reflects the well-known acquisition power of Taiwanese capital.

The injection of Taiwan capital had a significant impact on many sections of the American business community. In the past few years, while the U.S. computer industry was experiencing a slump, Taiwan electronics firms invested US$692 million in Silicon Valley, California, creating 13,545 new jobs.[22] In southern Texas, the building of a US$1.5 billion petrochemical complex by the Formosa Plastics Group also helped to ward off economic woes. However, the most dramatic development has been in the ROC's investment in Southeast Asia and the coastal areas of the Chinese mainland.

Between 1986 and 1990, Taiwan businesses went on an investment spree in Thailand, Malaysia, the Philippines, and Indonesia. Although official statistics on approved investments indicated a total of only US$869 million, data supplied by the host countries added up to US$8.57 billion, almost ten times the official figure (see table 6.7). Recent ROC official sources reveal that during the past six years more than US$13 billion has been poured into Southeast Asia.[23]

In 1990, Taiwan's investment in Malaysia reached a record high of US$2.4 billion, ranking it the number one foreign investor in that country. In 1989, Taiwan's investment in the Philippines ranked second after Japan's, but higher than the United States'. There are now more than 5,000 Taiwanese firms operating in Thailand, Malaysia, Indonesia, and the Philippines and they have become a formidable economic force in Southeast Asia.

Taiwan's investment in mainland China has gained momentum in recent years. Prior to 1987, there was virtually no Taiwanese investment on the mainland. Then, after the lifting of martial law in July 1987, and the subsequent relaxation of foreign exchange controls, some adventurous businessmen began investing in the coastal cities, especially in Amoy (Xiamen), directly across the Taiwan Strait. Initial investments were rather moderate, consisting primarily of small and medium-sized enterprises which would yield a quick return. Mainland Chinese government statistics show that average contracted capital per project was around US$1.6 million in 1988.

Before 1990, 90 percent of Taiwan's investments on the mainland were in manufacturing, with export as their goal. Total investment in 1987 was only US$100 million. The pace accelerated in the following years, partially because of the deterioration of the investment environment in Taiwan and partially because of the preferential treatment offered by the mainland authorities. This "push and pull" effect combined to trigger a "mainland fever" in 1990, when more than US$1.5 billion in Taiwan capital was committed to new ventures in mainland China. By the end of 1991, accumulated

---

[22]*Chung-yang jih-pao* (Overseas edition), February 3, 1992, 4.
[23]*Ching-chi jih-pao*, May 7, 1992, 10.

Table 6.7
Taiwan's Direct Investment in Four Southeast Asian Countries (1986-90)

Country	Year	Host Government Data		ROC Government Data	
		Amount (US$ million)	No. of Cases	Amount (US$ million)	No. of Cases
Thailand	1986	70	21	5.81	3
	1987	300	102	5.36	5
	1988	842	308	11.88	15
	1989	871	214	51.60	23
	1990	761	144	149.39	39
Malaysia	1986	4	15	0	0
	1987	91	37	5.83	5
	1988	313	111	2.70	5
	1989	815	191	158.64	25
	1990	2,383	270	184.88	36
Philippines	1986	0.35	8	0.07	1
	1987	9.04	43	2.64	3
	1988	109.87	86	36.20	7
	1989	148.69	190	66.31	13
	1990	140.65	158	123.00	16
Indonesia	1986	18	N.A.	0	0
	1987	8	3	0	0
	1988	913	17	1.92	3
	1989	158	50	0.31	1
	1990	618	94	61.87	18

Source: *Lien-ho pao* (United Daily News) (Taipei), March 30, 1991, 11.

Taiwan investment on the mainland exceeded US$3 billion. A recent Japanese study indicates that in the past five years, more than US$15 billion of Taiwan capital entered Hong Kong, of which a substantial amount has been channeled into the mainland.[24]

Extensive investment in Southeast Asia and mainland China brought about a rapid increase in intraregional trade. When Taiwan businesses set up new firms in these areas, almost 55 percent of raw materials and 60-70 percent of machinery were imported from Taiwan, making them Taiwan's fastest growing export markets. In the five-year period 1985-90, Taiwan's

[24]*Shih-chieh jih-pao*, June 3, 1992, 14.

exports to Indonesia increased 3 times; to Thailand, 5 times; to Malaysia, 4.7 times; to the Philippines, 2.4 times; and to mainland China 2.3 times.[25] By 1991, the ROC had become the second most influential economic power in Southeast Asia after Japan and the second largest investor in mainland China after Hong Kong.

Compared with other industrial powers, Taiwan's net overseas assets of US$100 billion at the end of 1991 were still relatively small. Japan's overseas net assets in the same period were US$383 billion, about four times greater than those of Taiwan. But since Japan has a population six times as big, Taiwan ranks higher on a per capita basis. When compared with most debt-ridden Third World countries, debt-free, cash-rich Taiwan undoubtedly represents a triumphant example of postwar economic development.

A Model for Third World Countries

In the 1960s and 1970s, the ROC's achievements drew little attention from the West, or from within Asia. Since the late 1970s, however, the Taiwan success story has gained recognition among the world's top economists. Four Nobel laureates, Simon Kuznets, Frederick Hayek, Milton Friedman, and Lawrence Klein, have written articles praising Taiwan.[26] Even the Chinese Communist leaders in Peking (Beijing) have admitted that in the contest of economic growth between the two parts of China, Taiwan appears to be the winner.[27] The experience of Taiwan has since become a model not only for mainland China but also for other developing countries.

Before 1979, the two sides of the Taiwan Strait experimented with two completely different models of industrialization and modernization. While Taiwan pursued a balanced growth and export expansion strategy under a mixed economic system, mainland China followed the Stalinist model of lopsided developmental policies and a highly centralized planned system. The subsequent wide gap between these two economies in terms of per capita income and standard of living prompted the Peking leadership to launch a wholesale reform in 1979. Many of Peking's new policies appear to be quite similar to those implemented in Taiwan.

One major impact of the Taiwan model on mainland China's development has been the abandonment of Mao's self-reliance doctrine and the

---

[25]*Chung-hua min-kuo T'ai-wan ti-ch'ü chin-ch'u-k'ou mao-i t'ung-chi yüeh-pao* (Monthly Statistics of Exports and Imports, Taiwan Area, the Republic of China) (Ministry of Finance, ROC), May 20, 1991, 9-77.

[26]For example, Simon Kuznets, "Growth and Structural Shifts," in *Economic Growth and Structural Change in Taiwan*, ed. Walter Galenson (Ithaca, N.Y.: Cornell University Press, 1979), 15-131.

[27]Ma Hung, *Ching-chi chieh-kou yü ching-chi kuan-li* (Economic structure and economic management) (Peking: Jen-min ch'u-pan-she, 1982), 4-5.

adoption of an open-door policy. In 1979, four special economic zones similar to the export processing zones in Taiwan were set up in Kwangtung (Guangdong) and Fukien (Fujian) provinces. In a novel move in April 1984, the Peking authorities announced that an additional fourteen coastal cities would be opened to the outside world. From Dairen (Dalian) in the north to Peihai (Beihai) in the south, almost all major ports are now open to foreign investors. The government went a step further in early 1985 by opening three more prosperous regions. These are the Yangtze River Delta, the Pearl River Delta, and the Amoy-Changchow-Chuanchow Triangle in Southern Fukien Province. After the CCP's Thirteenth National Congress in October 1987, a new guideline was put forward calling for the opening-up of the entire coast to outside investment.[28] In recent years, the Pearl River Delta has in essence followed the Taiwan model and is designated by the mainland Chinese leaders to become the fifth of Asia's "little dragons" after Taiwan, Hong Kong, Singapore, and South Korea.

Second, in contrast to the previous three decades (1949-78), when foreign trade played only a minor role, the new leadership in Peking has given a leading role to foreign trade. Between 1979 and 1991, mainland China's foreign trade rose 3.6-fold. In 1978, foreign trade accounted for only 9 percent of the country's GNP. By 1990, it accounted for 27.3 percent.[29] Attracting foreign capital has now become an overriding policy goal for Chinese economic planners. From 1979 to August 1991, mainland China absorbed US$21.3 billion-worth of foreign investment and incurred foreign debts of US$52 billion. The Chinese economy has rapidly moved from isolation toward internationalization, a policy Taiwan has vigorously implemented since the 1970s.

Third, in rural areas, the ill-conceived commune system was abolished in the early 1980s and replaced by a household contract system. The new system, although not exactly the same as the "land to the tiller" program in Taiwan, is a total rejection of Mao's collective farming program and a return to individual operation. It has led to the diversification and commercialization of the Chinese rural economy and the emergence of millions of village enterprises which now account for one-third of mainland China's gross industrial output value.

Fourth, radical reforms are under way in the urban economy to enlarge the decision-making power of individual enterprises, to separate government administration from business units, and to combine the market mechanism with central planning. An embryonic stock market and a real estate market

---

[28]He Chunlin, "Eight Years of the Open Policy," *China Reconstructs* (Peking) 36, no. 11 (November 1987): 12-15.

[29]According to the PRC's State Statistics Bureau, mainland China's foreign trade in 1990 was worth 556 billion *yuan* (*jenminpi*), while its GNP was 1.7686 trillion *yuan*. The trade/GNP ratio was 31.4 percent. In terms of U.S. dollars, however, the ratio was 27.3 percent.

have also developed in recent years. The economy is moving toward privatization, another significant departure from the original Stalinist model and a new step in the direction of the Taiwan model.

In Southeast Asia, Taiwan's export promotion and open-door policies have also been widely imitated in the last decade. Most countries have shifted from import substitution to export expansion. The development process in this area has defied the dependency theory advanced by many Latin American economists in the 1960s, which contended that trade between developed capitalist nations and developing nations is a zero-sum game, and that the trade network via the capitalist system and the multinational corporations historically exploited the underdeveloped countries and had harmful social and political ramifications.[30] This anti-trade sentiment has led many Third World nations to pursue an import substitution policy rather than expand exports. The experience of Taiwan and the Southeast Asian countries testifies that trade with advanced capitalist countries is not necessarily a zero-sum game. Insofar as the developing countries can improve technology, control product quality, and fully utilize their comparative advantages, they can penetrate into the capitalist markets. For countries with limited resources, small domestic markets, and a dense population like Taiwan, export expansion proves to be the best way to escape the "low-level equilibrium trap." Expansion of foreign trade and the inflow of foreign capital help to shift the country's production possibilities frontier outward and enable small countries to enjoy economies of scale. By following an outward-looking strategy, both mainland China and Thailand have escaped from stagnation and achieved a high rate of growth in the last decade. Between 1980 and 1989, mainland China's GNP grew at 9.7 percent per year, while Thailand achieved 7 percent annual growth.[31] In recent years, even countries in Latin America, and now the republics of the former Soviet Union, have gained insights from the Taiwan experience. The role of the ROC as a development model for Third World nations has gradually taken root in international society.

The ROC in the Twenty-first Century

Looking ahead to the twenty-first century, the ROC on Taiwan will have a more mature economy and assume a more discernible role in the international community.

First, the ROC has, since 1991, embarked on an ambitious medium-

[30]Gabriel Pulma, "Dependency: A Formal Theory of Underdevelopment or a Methodology for Analysis of Concrete Situations of Underdevelopment," *World Development* 6, no. 7/8 (July-August 1978): 881-924.

[31]*World Development Report 1991*, 206-7.

term plan for national development, the goals of which are to upgrade the industrial structure, promote balanced regional development, and improve the quality of life. Under the current Six-Year Plan, the ROC government has committed a total of US$303 billion for 775 projects. Key projects in the plan include a high-speed railway, rapid transit systems in major cities, highway expansion, petrochemical plants, the island's fourth nuclear power plant, infrastructure for heavy industries, pollution control facilities, housing projects, and the development of science and technology. It is anticipated that by 1996, exports will reach US$122.8 billion and imports US$120.7 billion, placing Taiwan among the top ten trading countries in the world.[32]

Second, as Taiwan's overseas assets continue to grow and income from outward investment increases, the ROC may perform a new role as a foreign aid contributor to less-developed nations. In 1988, an International Economic Cooperation and Development Fund was set up with a modest initial capital of US$400 million. By the end of June 1991, it had granted a total of US$127 million to fifteen countries. A new International Aid Fund is also under consideration. The ROC government is now actively seeking the opportunity to participate in both the "Paris Club" and the European Bank for Reconstruction and Development. In February 1992, at the request of the two governments, Taiwan donated US$15 million-worth of medicines to Ukraine and shipped 100,000 tons of rice to Russia. The ROC government recently decided that in the coming decade, foreign aid will account for 0.17 percent of GNP, slightly higher than the 0.15 percent level attained by most donor countries in recent years.

Third, as Taiwan's investment in Southeast Asia grows by leaps and bounds, and as the island's foreign exchange reserves continue to rise, Taiwan may emerge as a new regional financial center. This goal has been incorporated into the current Six-Year Plan, and both the Central Bank and the Ministry of Finance have set timetables for its realization.[33] Although Taiwan's own domestic market is limited, its financial power in the Far East stands second only to Japan. The island can be regarded and used as a gateway to a much larger East and Southeast Asian regional market by American and West European multinational corporations. Taiwan's expanding supply of skilled technical manpower and its long-standing connections with ethnic Chinese distributors in this region are assets that could make the ROC an Asian economic power in the twenty-first century.

Fourth, as the political atmosphere between the two sides of the Taiwan Strait improves, economic cooperation between Taiwan and the mainland will increase. Mainland China is now Taiwan's fifth largest export market

---

[32]Cheng, "Taiwan's Economy in Transition."

[33]Theodore S. S. Cheng, "Asia-Pacific Regional Cooperation Under the Backdrop of Tripolar Relationship," *Economic Review*, no. 265 (November-December 1991): 8-9.

and Taiwan is the mainland's second largest investor. Trade between Hong Kong and Taiwan has also increased tremendously. Hong Kong is now Taiwan's third largest export market and the principal source of its trade surplus.[34] As interdependency among these three Chinese communities continues to rise, by the end of this century, a "greater Chinese common market" or "Chinese economic sphere" may come into existence with Taiwan as a major partner.

All these new developments are bound to enhance the ROC's economic role in the twenty-first century. As a major trading power with rising overseas financial assets, the Republic of China on Taiwan will become a foreign aid donor, a new regional financial center, and a chief investor in mainland China. All of these developments will make Taiwan a major participant in the world economy.

---

[34]*Ching-chi jih-pao*, August 24, 1991, 2.

Part Three

The ROC and the International Community in the 1990s

CHAPTER 7

The Republic of China and the International Community in the 1990s

Ralph N. Clough

It is already evident that the international community with which the Republic of China (ROC) will interact in the 1990s will be radically different from the 1980s in important respects. Soviet domination over Eastern Europe has ended and the confrontation in Europe between the North Atlantic Treaty Organization (NATO) and the Warsaw Pact is no more. Germany has been unified. The East European nations are struggling to establish market economies and political democracies. The ideological bias that used to determine the foreign policies of these nations has disappeared and they are open to intercourse with states that formerly stood on the opposite side of an ideological divide. Their economies are gradually becoming integrated into the world economy.

The Soviet Union itself has been broken into fifteen separate republics. All of them, to a lesser or greater degree, are struggling to establish market economies and democratic systems, although in several of them bitter ethnic conflicts have preempted the leaders' attention. The Russian Republic retains the bulk of the military forces of the former Soviet Union, but economic distress and domestic politics have compelled the leadership to turn inward. The threat to neighbors posed by the armed forces of the former Soviet Union has been greatly reduced. The military confrontation and ideological contest between the United States and the Soviet Union, known as the Cold War, that dominated world politics since the end of World War II has come to an end, leaving the United States as the world's predominant military power, but sharing economic influence with Japan and the European Community (EC).

The 1990s promise to be a period in which global influence will depend increasingly on economic strength and decreasingly on military power. This shift in the basis of national influence will be felt particularly in the region where the ROC is located. Since the 1960s, East Asian states have enjoyed unparalleled rates of economic growth. Today, five of the ten largest overseas trading partners of the United States are in that region. Two-way trade with Japan is close to three times U.S. trade with Germany, its second largest overseas trading partner. Moreover, during the latter half of the 1980s, the flow of funds from East Asia to the United States reached a high level. While U.S. economic involvement with the region will continue to grow in the 1990s, its military deployments there will decline, under the pressures of budgetary constraints, the loss of Philippine bases, and the sudden weakening of the Soviet threat.[1]

The 1990s began with an unprecedented collective military action under the auspices of the United Nations to defeat Iraq's aggression against Kuwait. Collective action seems likely to remain the preferred method of maintaining peace during the 1990s. The Japanese Diet for the first time has authorized the use of Japan's armed forces overseas in limited peace-keeping operations under the United Nations. The United States and its European allies have cooperated in trying to end the ethnic conflict in the former state of Yugoslavia.

Certain trends that were well under way in the 1980s will continue into the 1990s. These include the growing importance of East Asia in the world economy, the economic domination of East Asia by Japan,[2] the growing concern over the degradation of the global environment, and the increasing integration of the world economy across national boundaries. Global economic integration may, however, be skewed by the formation of regional blocs—the EC and the emerging North American Free Trade Area. Successful completion of the Uruguay Round of the General Agreement on Tariffs and Trade (GATT) negotiations would help to maintain an open world trading system, but the emergence of regional economic blocs in Europe and North America will compel the nations of East Asia to consider how they should react to protect their own national interests.

How will these changes in the international community in the 1990s affect the ROC? Perhaps the most important changes are the disappearance of ideological barriers to international intercourse, combined with the rise in the relative importance of economic power. The ROC, with a dynamic and growing economy, the world's largest foreign exchange reserves, and extensive experience in foreign trade, is well positioned to take advantage of these changes. It has moved rapidly to establish trade and other relations with former Communist states. Even in two of the states still under one-party Communist rule—the People's Republic of China (PRC) and Vietnam—where economic pragmatism is winning out over ideology, businessmen from Taiwan are finding numerous opportunities for trade and investment.

The ROC's increasing economic weight in the world will give it increasing political influence with other trading partners also. They will be

---

[1] The Rand Corporation, *A New Strategy and Fewer Forces: The Pacific Dimension* (Santa Monica, Calif.: R-4089/2-USDP, 1992), 20.

[2] The extent to which the Japanese economy dwarfs the economies of other Asian states is often not fully appreciated. For example, South Korea's gross national product (GNP) is only 6 percent of Japan's. Ibid., 21.

less likely to heed Peking's (Beijing's) protests at steps to raise the level of their relations with Taipei.

The ROC cannot be free of security concerns in the 1990s, despite the general trend toward the overshadowing of security issues by economic issues. The PRC continues to assert its right to use military force if necessary against the recalcitrant province of Taiwan and it has substantially increased its military budget since 1989. Peking's recent purchase from Moscow of high-performance SU-27 fighters has added to Taipei's concerns.[3]

While the ROC probably would not be a match for the PRC's armed forces in an all-out invasion, it continues to maintain a strong military force so as to keep the costs and risks of military action against Taiwan by the PRC as high as possible.[4] The PRC's ability to prevent sales of weapons to Taiwan is weakening in the post-Cold War climate, making it easier for the ROC to procure needed advanced weapons.[5] The trend toward seeking peaceful solutions through collective action also favors the ROC. While Taipei recognizes that most countries would regard a conflict between the PRC and the ROC as an internal affair of China, it believes that they would favor a peaceful resolution and hence would support appropriate action by the United States "in the spirit of the Taiwan Relations Act."[6]

The principal means, however, by which the ROC seeks to prevent the use of military force against Taiwan by the PRC is through the encouragement of people-to-people relations between Taiwan and mainland China, especially trade and investment. Growing economic links between the two sides of the Taiwan Strait, in the framework of a ROC policy aimed at the eventual reunification of Taiwan with mainland China, are a significant deterrent to the use of military force, for expanding interest groups on each side of the Strait have a keen and growing desire to maintain a state of peaceful coexistence between Peking and Taipei.

The ROC's Relations with Former Communist States

At the height of the Cold War, Taiwan had virtually no intercourse with Communist states. Travel and trade were forbidden and the penalties for transgression were severe. In 1979, however, after the United States and most other countries had severed diplomatic relations with the ROC, the government, feeling the need to diversify its trading partners, authorized

---

[3]*China Post* (Taipei), August 7, 1991.

[4]*National Defense White Paper*, excerpts carried in *Chung-kuo shih-pao* (China Times) (Taipei), February 18, 1992, translated in Foreign Broadcast Information Service (FBIS), *Daily Report: China* (hereafter cited as *FBIS-CHI*), 92-039 (February 27, l992): 63-71.

[5]*New York Times*, September 24, 1991; *Far Eastern Economic Review*, July 9, 1992, 8-11.

[6]*FBIS-CHI*-92-039 (February 27, 1992): 65.

indirect trade with seven East European countries: East Germany, Czechoslovakia, Hungary, Poland, Bulgaria, Romania, and Yugoslavia. When
the Communist systems in those countries began to disintegrate, the ROC
loosened its restrictions on trade and travel, authorizing *direct* trade with
the seven East European countries in March 1988. During 1989, it approved
direct investment in these countries, tourist travel, and the opening of offices
there by public and private enterprises. In the spring of 1990, the China
External Trade Development Council (CETRA), a quasi-official trade promotion organization, opened an office in Budapest, its first in Eastern
Europe.

The new governments of these former Communist states showed less
squeamishness than some of the ROC's other non-Communist trading partners
in entering into semiofficial or even official relationships with the ROC.
For example, in March 1992, the director of the ROC's Civil Aeronautics
Administration signed an agreement on the exchange of aviation rights with
the chief of Bulgaria's Civil Aviation Bureau, providing for up to two flights
per week each way by designated airlines of the two countries.[7]

The ROC was slower in warming up to the Soviet Union than to the
East European states, although as early as October 1988, the government
sent officials from the Ministry of Economic Affairs and the Board of
Foreign Trade to accompany a trade mission to Moscow sponsored by the
private Export-Import Association of Taiwan. A CETRA mission followed
in May 1989. Later in 1989, Taipei authorized participation in trade fairs,
business visits, and the opening of branches or representative offices by
organizations of either side on the territory of the other. Finally, in the
spring of 1990, the government approved direct trade and investment and
opened telecommunication links with the Soviet Union.

Once the door was opened, Soviet visitors streamed into Taiwan. They
included a TV crew, a journalist from *Izvestia*, the chairman of the external
trade committee of the parliament of the Soviet Union, the governor of
Sakhalin, the minister of light industry and the deputy minister of finance
of the Russian Republic, and the minister of light industry of Ukraine. The
most prominent visitor was Gavrill Popov, the mayor of Moscow, who called
on the ROC's foreign minister and other officials. Popov's visit prompted
Peking to warn that it was firmly opposed to the development of official
relations between Taiwan and countries having diplomatic relations with
the PRC. Popov, however, dismissed the complaint with the assertion that
his was a private visit.[8]

When the Soviet Union broke up into fifteen separate republics, the
ROC moved quickly to develop relations with the new states. Although

---

[7]*FBIS-CHI*-92-061 (March 30, 1992): 78-79.
[8]*FBIS-CHI*-90-211 (October 31, 1990): 70.

none was prepared to have diplomatic relations with the ROC, several were willing to exceed the strict guidelines that the PRC sought to enforce. For example, Latvia sent its foreign minister to visit Taiwan and agreed to the opening of a ROC consulate general in Riga. Peking spokesmen protested that the Latvians were violating the commitment that they had made in establishing diplomatic relations with the PRC. Peking closed its newly-opened embassy in Riga and withdrew its staff.[9]

The ROC courted the new republics by offering 100,000 tons of rice to Russia and medical supplies to Belarus and Ukraine. China Airlines flew in the medical supplies and the ROC arranged for Russian freighters to load the rice at Keelung. The ROC also contributed US$10 million to a special fund administered by the European Bank for Reconstruction and Development to help finance East European development projects. The ROC has established representative offices in Russia, Belarus, and Ukraine.

During much of the 1990s, the new governments of Eastern Europe and of the former Soviet republics will be feeling their way, readjusting their economic and political relationships with Moscow and seeking out useful ties with other states. Many will be getting to know Taiwan for the first time. A large segment of the world, hitherto closed to contacts from Taiwan, has now been opened, providing an unparalleled opportunity for the ROC to expand its international relationships. Trade will be difficult at first because of the economic ills afflicting all East European countries and former Soviet republics, but Taiwan's traders will probably prove to be efficient at conducting the barter trade that may dominate these countries' international commerce in the early years. The primacy of economics in forging these new relationships will favor Taiwan's efforts to upgrade its relations and hinder the PRC's attempts to interfere.

The ROC's Relations with Vietnam

Vietnam is another country, formerly on the opposite side of the ideological divide in the Cold War, with which the ROC has developed substantial relations in recent years, despite the fact that, unlike the countries of Eastern Europe and the former Soviet Union, it is still firmly controlled by a Communist party. In 1987, Vietnam passed a law to encourage foreign investment. The following year, CETRA sent a mission there to explore trade and investment opportunities. In 1989, a Vietnamese trade mission and the mayor of Ho Chi Minh City visited Taiwan. The ROC authorized direct trade between Taiwan and Vietnam and by the end of 1989, two-way trade for the year amounted to US$41 million.[10]

---

[9]*FBIS-CHI*-92-038 (February 26, 1992): 56.

[10]*Far Eastern Economic Review*, August 30, 1990, 46.

In 1989, the Vietnamese government instituted an economic reform program which stimulated the economy, particularly the agricultural sector, producing a 20 percent increase in rice production that year. Spurred by the need to counter the adverse economic effects of the loss of Soviet aid, the Vietnamese government took steps to encourage the growth of enterprises in the private sector and to improve the climate for foreign investment.[11]

Entrepreneurs from Taiwan responded to the opportunities perceived in Vietnam. Labor was cheap and plentiful and cultural and linguistic affinities between the large overseas Chinese community in Vietnam and the businessmen from Taiwan facilitated cooperation. By the end of 1991, Taiwan had become the leading foreign investor in Vietnam, with US$743 million in approved investments.[12] Two-way trade for the year had soared to US$230 million.[13]

The ROC government encouraged entrepreneurs in Taiwan to trade with and invest in Vietnam, in part to divert them from what officials feared was becoming excessive investment in mainland China. CETRA sent several missions to Vietnam and in March 1991, opened an office in Ho Chi Minh City. Later that year P. K. Chiang, vice minister of economic affairs, visited Vietnam and the following year the two governments agreed on the establishment of a Taipei Economic and Cultural Office in Hanoi with a branch in Ho Chi Minh City and the opening of similar offices by Vietnam in Taipei and Kaohsiung.[14] Negotiations on an investment guarantee agreement and an aviation agreement were under way. The Kuomintang (KMT) itself took the lead in investing in Vietnam. A KMT-owned firm, the Central Trading and Development Corporation, has entered into a joint venture to build an export processing zone near Ho Chi Minh City, which will probably attract a sizeable number of manufacturers from Taiwan.

Assuming that economic reforms and opening to the outside continue in Vietnam, ties between that country and Taiwan should continue to grow during the remainder of the decade. The two economies are complementary in important respects. The establishment of direct air service between the two will greatly facilitate travel and business activities. As one of the world's poorest countries, with a gross national product (GNP) per capita of only US$200, Vietnam will not become a major trading partner of Taiwan, but it provides another useful connection, previously denied to Taiwan for ideological reasons.

---

[11]*Transition* (World Bank) 3, no. 2 (February, 1992): 5-6.
[12]*Far Eastern Economic Review*, May 28, 1992, 50.
[13]*China Post*, July 3, 1992.
[14]Ibid.

The ROC's Relations with Western Europe

Although the PRC has prevented the ROC from having diplomatic relations with the countries of Western Europe, its trade with that region grew rapidly during the 1980s. The ROC actively promoted exports to the EC, in part to reduce excessive dependence on the U.S. market and in part in anticipation of 1992, when the EC was scheduled to become the largest single trading area in the world, with a population of 320 million and conducting 39 percent of world trade. By 1990, the ROC's two-way trade with the EC had reached US$22 billion, equal to the PRC's trade with that region.[15]

The growth of economic ties between Taiwan and the EC caused an increase in other types of links needed to facilitate travel, trade, and investment. More European countries opened offices in Taiwan and those that already had offices there upgraded their status and expanded their functions. Most of the ROC's offices in EC countries obtained quasi-diplomatic status and were able to include "Taipei" in their titles in order to make them more recognizable. Despite Peking's opposition, the ROC was able to establish direct air service between Taipei and Amsterdam. Twenty-two European banks opened branches or representative offices in Taiwan, while five Taiwan banks established eleven branches or representative offices in Europe.

PRC opposition to arms sales to the ROC, which had resulted in the downgrading of Dutch representation in Peking from ambassadorial to the chargé d'affaires level from 1980 to 1984 as a punishment for selling two submarines to the ROC, declined in effectiveness. France sold six frigates to the ROC in 1991, despite PRC protests, and in December 1992 signed a contract for the sale of sixty Mirage 2000-5 aircraft. The PRC strongly criticized this action, threatening reprisals.[16] It later retaliated by ordering the closure of the French Consulate General in Canton (Guangzhou). In 1991, Germany sold the ROC four minesweepers, disguised as commercial vessels.[17] The PRC blocked other arms purchases sought by the ROC in Europe, but further sales during the 1990s seem likely, as European arms manufacturers, their sales to reduced European military forces declining, will increase pressure on their own governments not to stand in the way of sales to customers abroad.

The ROC's US$300 billion, Six-Year National Development Plan (1991-96) has attracted much attention in Europe. The prospects for large contracts for their own firms have caused a number of European countries to disregard PRC protests and send high-ranking officials to Taiwan heading large trade

---

[15] Jong-jen Chiu, "From Economic Relations to Political Ties: The ROC and Western Europe in the 1990s," *Issues & Studies* 27, no. 10 (October 1991): 34-35.

[16] Peking Radio, December 8, 1992, in *FBIS-CHI*-92-237 (December 9, 1992): 64.

[17] *Far Eastern Economic Review*, July 9, 1992, 11.

delegations. Cabinet ministers from France, Ireland, and Italy visited Taiwan, as well as Sweden's vice foreign minister, Denmark's deputy minister of industry, and an undersecretary of the UK's Department of Trade and Industry. Taiwan's growing economic ties with the EC during the rest of the 1990s will cause the upgrading of political relations between the ROC and EC countries to continue, although the PRC probably will be able to prevent the establishment of formal diplomatic relations. The rising economic interdependence of states and the need for official intervention to sustain that interdependence will foster a gradual increase in the officiality of the ROC's relations with the EC.[18]

Other Bilateral Relations

Despite the PRC's interference, the ROC has been able to improve steadily the substantive relations it has maintained with countries with which it lacks diplomatic relations. Taipei even increased the number of its diplomatic partners from twenty-one in 1979 to twenty-nine in 1991. It also maintained seventy-nine representative offices in fifty-one countries with which it had no diplomatic relations.[19] In July 1992, President Lee Teng-hui's activist "pragmatic diplomacy" allowed the ROC to establish relations with Niger, causing the PRC to suspend relations with that country. The following month, however, the PRC more than compensated for that loss by establishing formal diplomatic relations with the Republic of Korea and causing the severance of relations between Seoul and Taipei. South Africa is the only remaining country of significant size and economic power that continues to maintain diplomatic relations with the ROC.

The diplomatic struggle between Taipei and Peking will no doubt continue during the 1990s. The ROC will probably win a few more small diplomatic partners, but more important will be the strengthening of its substantive relations with the principal industrial nations and raw material suppliers of the world.

The ROC's Relations with International Organizations

After the PRC replaced the ROC as China's representative in the United Nations in 1971, it methodically and successfully pushed the ROC out of U.N.-related and most other intergovernmental organizations. The future of the ROC looked dark, as one country after another broke diplo-

---

[18]Bih-jaw Lin, "Rising Political Status from Economic Edge: The Expansion of Taipei's Foreign Relations from the Point of View of Cross-Strait Exchanges," *Issues & Studies* 27, no. 10 (October 1991): 1-18.

[19]Fredrick F. Chien, "A View from Taipei," *Foreign Affairs* 70, no. 5 (Winter 1991-92): 98.

matic relations with it, culminating in the closure of the U.S. embassy in Taipei in 1979.

The ROC was not prepared to give in, however. It worked out with Japan and the United States, its two most important trading partners, arrangements for surrogate embassies, able to perform effectively almost all the normal functions of diplomatic missions. It clung to its membership in the Asian Development Bank (ADB), accepting under protest a change of name negotiated by other ADB members to make possible full membership by the governments in both Peking and Taipei.

Taiwan's increasing economic stature has drawn attention to the desirability of its participation in other international economic organizations. It does participate in two important nongovernmental economic organizations: the Pacific Economic Cooperation Conference (PECC) and the Pacific Basin Economic Council (PBEC). In 1991, after extensive negotiations, it joined the intergovernmental organization for Asia-Pacific Economic Cooperation (APEC), under the name "Chinese Taipei" with the proviso that it would send its economics minister rather than its foreign minister to this ministerial level annual meeting.

In January 1990, Taiwan applied for membership in GATT as "the customs territory of Taiwan, Penghu, Quemoy, and Matsu." The PRC had applied for membership in 1986, but had not yet met the conditions for admission. The PRC's position is that it must be admitted to GATT first, after which Taipei can seek Peking's approval for its admission as a separate customs territory.[20] The ROC authorities reject the idea of seeking Peking's approval and have been soliciting support among GATT members for Taiwan's independent admission as a customs territory.

A GATT working group had been meeting periodically since 1987 to consider the PRC's application and a working group on Taiwan held its first meeting in November 1992. Nearly all GATT members favor participation in the organization by both Peking and Taipei. The ROC would have to make fewer changes in its trade and financial policies than the PRC would in order to qualify for admission to GATT. It is doubtful, however, that the requisite two-thirds of the membership would approve Taiwan's entry before the PRC in defiance of the PRC's strong opposition. Consequently, it is probable that some compromise providing for simultaneous admission of the two governments will be worked out, as occurred in the case of APEC.[21] Because of the importance of economic issues in the 1990s, and the desirability of having both mainland China and Taiwan represented in

---

[20]*Beijing Review* 35, no. 26 (June 29-July 5, 1992): 16.

[21]Arthur Yeh, "Taiwan's Membership in the General Agreement on Tariffs and Trade," in *The Role of Taiwan in International Economic Organizations*, ed. Yun-han Chu and Jennifer Arnold (Taipei: Institute for National Policy Research, 1990), 79-100.

GATT, it is also probable that the compromise on admission will be reached well before the year 2000.

As for the prospects for Taiwan's participation in other international economic organizations, such as the Organization for Economic Cooperation and Development (OECD), the World Bank, or the International Monetary Fund (IMF), these are uncertain in the 1990s. Taiwan's growing economic role in an increasingly interdependent world argues strongly for finding some formula for admitting it to these organizations.[22] Whether that proves feasible depends to a considerable extent on the state of relations between Peking and Taipei, which will be discussed below.

The ROC's Relations with Japan

Taiwan's close economic relationship with Japan is likely to become even closer during the "economics first" decade of the 1990s, as Japan's economic predominance in East Asia becomes more pronounced. In some respects, Taiwan is a competitor of Japan in trade and investment in East Asia, but it has a much smaller population and lacks Japan's economic muscle and technological skills. It will remain dependent on Japan for capital goods and intermediate products essential to its export industry. Moreover, when Taiwan becomes a member of GATT, it will have to remove certain obstacles to imports from Japan which are contrary to GATT rules. Consequently, Taiwan's trade deficit with Japan, which it has complained vociferously about for years, probably will continue to increase. However, so long as Taiwan can continue to compensate for this deficit by maintaining surpluses in its trade with the United States, Europe, and mainland China, its economy will not suffer significantly.

Japan's policy has been to maintain as friendly relations as possible with both mainland China and Taiwan, keeping its relations with Taiwan unofficial and low profile, so as not to annoy the PRC and risk damage to that important relationship. Should the PRC ever use military force against Taiwan, Japan would refrain from intervening militarily, but would work hard behind the scenes for a peaceful resolution of the conflict, which would be damaging to Japan's interests. The possibility of a Taipei-Peking military clash in the 1990s is slight, however.

Japan will be more cautious than the European industrial nations in taking actions toward Taiwan that are offensive to Peking. The sale of weapons is out of the question, for Japan has a total ban on the export of arms to any country. It may follow the European example in upgrading to some extent the level of its relations with Taiwan. A recent small step, of

---

[22]See, for example, Raymond Chang, "The Case for Taiwan's Role in the OECD," in Chu and Arnold, *The Role of Taiwan*, 101-38.

considerable symbolic importance, was the agreement on changing the name of the ROC's representative office in Japan from the "Tokyo Office of the East Asian Relations Association" to "Taipei Economic and Cultural Representative Office in Japan."

The ROC's Relations with the United States

U.S. relations with Taiwan have always been one segment of a triangular U.S.-PRC-Taiwan relationship. Since 1979, the United States, like Japan, has tried to maintain as good relations as possible with both Peking and Taipei. Unlike Japan, however, the United States has assumed a measure of responsibility for Taiwan's security. The PRC authorities have resented the language in the Taiwan Relations Act expressing concern for Taiwan's security and in 1982 compelled the United States to accept restrictions on its supply of arms to Taiwan. The United States accepted these restrictions, however, in response to the PRC's statement that its "fundamental policy" is "to strive for a peaceful solution to the Taiwan question."

In September 1992, President George Bush provoked Peking's ire by approving the sale of F-l6 fighter aircraft to Taiwan, perhaps as many as 150 over the next few years. He justified the sale on the ground that Taiwan's F-5 and F-104 aircraft were outdated, while the PRC had just acquired advanced Russian fighters. A more persuasive reason for his decision was the need to preserve jobs at the F-16 plant in Texas, a state whose electoral college votes were an important prize in the November presidential election. The PRC accused President Bush of violating the 1982 communiqué.

After more than a year of difficult negotiations, Washington and Peking reached an agreement in October 1992 on improving market access in the mainland for American products. Other problems remain, however, particularly the inclination of the United States Congress to make extension of the PRC's most-favored-nation (MFN) status conditional on improvements in the treatment of human rights in mainland China. Most members of Congress took a critical attitude toward Peking after the Tienanmen (Tiananmen) massacre and President Bush had barely been able to retain enough votes in the Senate to sustain his veto of legislation that would have forced the withdrawal of the PRC's MFN status. The willingness of congressmen to make concessions to the PRC on such issues has been diminished by the collapse of the Soviet Union and the resultant decline in the strategic importance of mainland China to the United States. Newly-elected President Bill Clinton indicated in his campaign speeches that he would take a harder line on human rights in mainland China than President Bush did, but as of late January 1993, it is too early to predict just how the new Congress and President Clinton will handle the human rights and MFN issues.

Still another issue affecting U.S.-PRC relations has been mainland Chinese assistance to Iran in building a nuclear power plant. U.S. officials fear that the Iranians may divert some of their growing nuclear expertise into a nuclear weapons program.

U.S.-ROC bilateral relations were good during the first two years of the 1990s. The most prickly economic issues between them had been successfully resolved by negotiations. The rising importance of global economic interdependence during the remainder of the decade is likely to draw the two economies even closer.

Growing tension between the United States and the PRC could, however, have an adverse effect on Taiwan. Withdrawal of MFN treatment toward mainland China could be a heavy blow to Taiwan enterprises that had invested on the mainland. The sale of F-16s to Taiwan will strengthen the views of those within the PRC leadership who see the United States as a prime obstacle to the reunification of China. Should the Taiwan independence movement gain ground in Taiwan's democratic political system, mainland Chinese leaders would be inclined to blame the United States for encouraging it. In an atmosphere of mutual recrimination, Taiwan could again become a high profile issue between Washington and Peking.

Quarreling between Peking and Washington over the Taiwan issue would not necessarily lead to closer relations between Washington and Taipei. On the contrary, concern over the deterioration of U.S.-PRC relations might cause a U.S. administration to be even more cautious than previously, in order to avoid actions toward Taiwan that would damage relations with the PRC further. It is when the PRC's relations with the United States are good that Peking's leaders tend to be more tolerant of moves by Washington to improve relations with Taiwan.

If Taiwan does not again become a highly contentious issue between the United States and the PRC in the 1990s, the United States is likely to follow the examples of its European economic competitors and gradually increase the officiality of its relationship with Taiwan, beginning with the exchange of visits by more senior officials. The process seems already to have begun with the visit to Taiwan of a U.S. assistant secretary of commerce in February 1992, a visit to the United States by Lin Yang-kang, president of the ROC's Judicial Yuan in June 1992, and a visit to Taiwan by the U.S. Trade Representative, Carla Hills, in December 1992. The U.S. government is also actively encouraging the formation of a GATT working group to consider the admission of Taiwan to that organization.

The ROC's Relations with the PRC

As indicated above, the rising importance of economic issues in the 1990s and the growing weight of Taiwan's economy in the global economic system will favor the ROC's efforts to strengthen its substantive relations with countries with which it lacks diplomatic relations and will improve its prospects for admission to intergovernmental economic organizations. It appears likely, however, that the PRC will continue to interfere with the

ROC's efforts to win acceptance by the international community as a political entity fully entitled to the rights of a sovereign state.

Since 1987, the ROC has pursued a policy of increasing engagement with mainland China through people-to-people relations. Residents of Taiwan have made over three million visits to the mainland, two-way trade reached US$5.8 billion during 1991, and cumulative investment on the mainland by Taiwan enterprises probably exceeded US$3 billion. Both the ROC and PRC governments have encouraged the trend, which has substantially reduced tension between the two sides of the Taiwan Strait. The PRC has pressed for direct postal, trade, and transportation links across the Strait, but the ROC has insisted on indirect travel and trade, refusing to open the "three links" until Peking accepts the ROC as a political entity, drops the threat of force against Taiwan, and ends its attempts to isolate the ROC in the international community.

Thus, the ROC has sought to trade the "three links" for political concessions that would improve its status in the world community. The PRC clearly is eager to see the "three links" established, both to accelerate mainland China's economic modernization and, more important, to strengthen the ties between the mainland and Taiwan so as to reduce the influence of the Taiwan independence movement. But whether PRC leaders will pay the price demanded by the Taiwan authorities is questionable. They are aware of the growing pressure on the ROC government from businessmen in Taiwan, who want the "three links" established in order to facilitate their own activities. Businessmen are likely to have a strong influence within the new Legislative Yuan elected in December 1992.[23] Consequently, one or more of the "three links" probably will be established within the next few years, even without political concessions on the part of Peking. Such a development would spur the growth of economic relations between the two sides of the Taiwan Strait and further ease tension in that area unless pro-independence sentiment in Taiwan should increase sharply.

Conclusions

The ROC's position in the international community in the 1990s will be determined by three factors: its own efforts to strengthen its international status, the state of ROC-PRC relations, and trends in the global community.

The ROC's ability to improve its international status by its own efforts is limited by PRC interference. Nevertheless, it has made remarkable progress, despite its exclusion from nearly all intergovernmental organizations and its lack of diplomatic relations with most nations. Using innovative and unorthodox methods, it has steadily strengthened its substantive relation-

---

[23]*Chung-kuo shih-pao chou-k'an* (China Times Weekly) (Taipei), July 5-11, 1992, no. 27:48-50.

ships with a wide variety of trading partners throughout the world, functioning in nearly all important respects as a sovereign independent state. The success of President Lee Teng-hui's "pragmatic diplomacy" in the early 1990s, a diplomacy less trammeled than in the past by questions of nomenclature, foreshadows further gains during the remainder of the decade.

Pro-independence politicians will continue to point to the limits on Taiwan's formal diplomatic relations as a fatal flaw in its foreign policy, correctable only by the establishment of an independent "Republic of Taiwan." The independence issue probably will continue to roil politics in Taiwan for the rest of the decade, but a formal declaration of independence is unlikely. Given the PRC's opposition, it is difficult to demonstrate that a declaration of independence would bring important gains for the ROC in terms of membership in intergovernmental organizations or in bilateral diplomatic relations. A declaration of independence would increase the danger that the PRC would use force against Taiwan and would set back severely the progress being made through people-to-people interaction toward a stable condition of peaceful coexistence between the two sides of the Strait.

Cross-Strait interaction, while not improving the prospects for PRC acquiescence in ROC entry into the United Nations or an increase in formal bilateral diplomatic relations, may well diminish petty PRC interference with ROC efforts to regularize and facilitate its economic and other relations with foreign countries. As the two sides improve their ability to manage their relationship through quasi-official channels, PRC leaders, particularly a new, less ideologically burdened generation, should develop greater understanding of ROC government policies, greater confidence, and less inclination to react with alarm to every small improvement made by the ROC in its management of foreign relations.

As mentioned above, international trends will favor the ROC's efforts to strengthen its international status. The abrupt disappearance of "international Communism" has bolstered those within the PRC leadership who favor continued reform and opening to the outside. The primacy of economics and the growth of international trade will cause those nations with important national interest reasons for wanting official or near-official relations with Taiwan to become more restive at PRC interference. The international community will become increasingly conscious of the fact that the ROC has functioned as an independent state on Taiwan for over forty years. The reality that the "one China" accepted by both Taipei and Peking contains two governments and two systems will gain broader currency in the international community and pressure will increase on the PRC to accept this reality rather than cling to its "one China, two systems" formula, which attempts unrealistically to relegate Taiwan to the status of a province under Peking's sovereignty.[24]

---

[24]Lin, "Rising Political Status," 14-15.

CHAPTER 8

Given a Unique Model of Bilateral Relations, Can Taiwan Be an Actor on the World Stage?

Françoise Mengin

When discussing the presence of the Republic of China (ROC) in the international community one immediately thinks of the country's uniqueness. Its position is ambivalent, combining as it does near nonexistence at the diplomatic level with a strong economic presence. This makes it impossible to fit into any of the usual categories. However, we cannot account for the significance of Taiwan's uniqueness by an analysis of these two components only. It is also necessary to lay great emphasis on how these two components act on each other, that is, to analyze the country's external relations. Such an analysis of Taiwan's external relations should enable the observer to gain a better grasp of the island's political and economic situation, since it will have been filtered through the daily practice of international exchanges which hamper its existence as a state but also token its presence as a trading nation.

Taiwan's bilateral relations are mainly unofficial, as the few countries that accord the ROC official recognition are of little importance on the international scene. These nonofficial links have been developed for more than ten years and mostly involve substantial exchanges with North America, Western Europe, Japan, and the Southeast Asian countries. These relations do not follow any existing pattern and their development has been largely incidental. Therefore, it is particularly difficult to find any coherence in the system.

Analyses of Taiwan's bilateral relations[1] are usually based on a descrip-

---

[1]See among others: William B. Bader and Jeffrey T. Bergner, eds., *The Taiwan Relations Act: A Decade of Implementation* (Indianapolis: Hudson Institute, 1989); Jaw-Ling Joanne Chang, ed., *R.O.C.-U.S.A. Relations, 1979-1989* (Taipei: Institute of American Culture, Academia Sinica, 1991); Jong-jen Chiu, "From Economic Relations to Political Ties: The ROC and Western Europe in the 1990s," *Issues & Studies* 27, no. 10 (October 1991): 19-55; Thomas B. Lee, "Quasi-Diplomatic Relations of the Republic of China: Their Development and Status in International Law," *Issues & Studies* 24, no. 7 (July 1988): 104-17; Françoise Mengin, "Rethinking

tive and empiric approach that stresses substantial exchanges while confining any attempt to characterize these ties to the negative definition "nondiplomatic."

It is easy to understand why no conceptual framework for Taiwan's bilateral relations has been put forward, for they present the observer with a unique situation which everyone thought was only temporary.

Nevertheless, it is only by attempting to conceptualize Taiwan's bilateral relations that we can establish what they are, as opposed to what they are not (diplomatic), and underscore their nature, rather than their substance (commercial, cultural, and scientific links which are easily quantifiable). The usual approach will thus be inverted: an appraisal of the ROC's place in the international community will not be based on the development of tangible exchanges; on the contrary, the scope of these exchanges will be deduced from the possible application of theories of international relations to the case of Taiwan.

It is a question of refusing to elude a conceptual approach under the pretext that Taiwan is a unique and temporary phenomenon in international law, and of weighing up the ROC's international position at the very level where it seems the most hazardous: the theoretical status of Taiwan's bilateral relations.

Different Instruments of Analysis

Analyzing Taiwan's bilateral relations cannot be done within the framework of international law which, in this unprecedented case, has been both infringed upon and inadequately exploited.

The Legal Approach Comes to a Deadlock

The extent to which countries which have recognized the People's Republic of China (PRC) as the sole legal government of China may develop bilateral relations with Taiwan depends on how far the mainland authorities perceive these links as a threat both to their own security and to their reunification policy. Therefore, any relationship which would suggest recognition of the ROC or of a state in Taiwan seems to be prohibited. However, a full range of economic, cultural, and scientific links are permissible.

Although Taiwan's non-diplomatic partners have strived to confine their bilateral relations to the economic, cultural, and scientific spheres, political extensions of these links have inevitably developed. Arms sales—since they are a potential security threat to the PRC—best illustrate the

the Europe-Taiwan Relationship," *The Pacific Review* 4, no. 1 (1991): 25-35, and "The Prospects for France-Taiwan Relations," *Issues & Studies* 28, no. 3 (March 1992): 38-59; Yu San Wang, ed., *The Foreign Policy of the Republic of China on Taiwan: An Unorthodox Approach* (New York: Praeger, 1990).

frequent breaches of the limits imposed on the ROC's foreign relations. Among countries having diplomatic ties with the PRC, the United States alone has clearly defined its policy in this field, toward both Taipei and Peking (Beijing): the amount of American arms that can be delivered to Taiwan is specified by the Taiwan Relations Act (TRA) of April 10, 1979 and the U.S.-PRC Joint Communiqué of August 17, 1982. For all other countries, arms sales could in theory constitute a stumbling block in their commercial relations with Taiwan. Such sales have, however, occurred several times in the past, the most striking examples being the sales of Dutch submarines in 1981 and of French frigates ten years later. Even though the rationale behind these deals was commercial, both sides noted their political implications. Yet it would be wrong to interpret these arms sales as implying some change in Taiwan's status: countries selling arms to Taiwan are in no way disavowing their commitment toward Peking in the political field. The question is only of a limited risk, taking into account national interests—in terms of employment, trade balance, etc.—and a temporary strain in relations with the PRC.

Taipei itself has also exceeded the perceived limits on its foreign relations. Since the Kuomintang's withdrawal to the island in 1949, a one-China policy has been the core of both Peking's and Taipei's foreign policies. As a result, the Hallstein Doctrine[2] was stringently applied in relations with third countries, and neither the PRC nor the ROC would establish diplomatic relations with countries recognizing the rival regime, thus precluding dual recognition. It was not until 1989 that the ROC stopped breaking off diplomatic relations with countries that recognized Peking. The first indication of this shift in Taipei's foreign policy appeared in July that year, when Grenada, which was preparing to establish relations with the ROC, was not asked by the latter to sever diplomatic ties with the PRC as a preliminary. This experiment with dual recognition failed, as Peking took the initiative in severing relations, and the same occurred afterwards with Liberia, Belize, Guinea-Bissau, Lesotho, Nicaragua, the Central African Republic, and Niger. Likewise, Peking insisted that Riyadh break off its diplomatic ties with the ROC after normalizing relations with the PRC, though Taipei had not taken such an initiative. Despite these failures, the ROC has shown that it no longer adheres to the Hallstein Doctrine and wishes to implement a two-China policy.[3]

Actually, this policy has been implicitly followed since the end of 1978,

---

[2]This doctrine, first expressed in 1955 by Walter Hallstein, the then foreign minister of the Federal Republic of Germany, dictated that Bonn would sever diplomatic relations with any state recognizing the German Democratic Republic with the exception of the Soviet Union.

[3]An exception was made in the case of the ROC's diplomatic ties with the Republic of Korea, which were severed on August 22, 1992.

when Washington was preparing to establish relations with Peking.[4] As Hungdah Chiu recounts: "When President Carter sent a delegation headed by Deputy Secretary of State Warren Christopher to Taiwan on December 28-29, 1978, to discuss the post-normalization U.S.-ROC relations, the ROC made several basic demands, namely, that future U.S.-ROC relations be maintained on a government-to-government basis, that the United States fake concrete and effective measures to assure the security of Taiwan, that the United States continue to supply adequate arms to the ROC, and others."[5] The same source reveals that when the two sides resumed talks on maintaining trade, cultural, and other relations in the post-normalization period in early January 1979, "no substantive progress was made for several weeks because the ROC insisted on having official, that is, government-to-government, relations with the United States while the latter insisted, at least formally, on unofficial relations."[6]

Likewise, Taipei's efforts to formalize its links with European countries since the end of the 1970s can be viewed as attempts, not to persuade European governments to switch recognition from Peking, but to implement a two-China policy. While keeping a low profile suited to the occasion, Taipei has endeavored to raise the level of contacts between ROC and European officials, and to establish air links, etc. When these attempts are successful, Taipei sees them as first steps toward official recognition, although in reality—as in the case of arms sales—European countries are simply maximizing commercial relations.

More significantly, this two-China policy has manifested itself in Taipei's willingness to hold memberships in international organizations alongside the PRC. In 1981, the ROC reentered the International Olympic Committee under the name "Chinese, Taipei," and in 1985 it agreed to stay in the Asian Development Bank (ADB) after the PRC's entrance, although it had to change its name to "Taipei, China."

Such examples are numerous. The main point is that as soon as the ROC became radically isolated on the world scene, it stopped acting in accordance with the principle of China's territorial unity, despite its desire to reunify, in the long run, the two sides of the Taiwan Strait. More explicit moves bear witness to attempts to officialize nonofficial relations: in July 1989, the Hallstein Doctrine was abandoned and on May 1, 1991, the so-called Period of Mobilization for the Suppression of Communist Rebellion was ended.

Thus, since derecognition by the United States, while Taipei's nonofficial partners have many a time freed themselves from the restrictive framework imposed by Peking on the island's external relations, Taipei has, for

---

[4]It should be noted that it was Washington, not Taipei, which severed diplomatic ties.

[5]Hungdah Chiu, "The Taiwan Relations Act and Sino-American Relations," in Chang, *R.O.C.-U.S.A. Relations*, 35.

[6]Ibid., 35-36.

its part, gradually modified its foreign policy in order to rejoin the international arena. But what also strikes the observer attempting to assess Taiwan's external relations since 1979 is that beyond a stretching of the rules by Taipei's nonofficial partners or the ROC's alteration of its policy, there has been a failure to adequately exploit all the solutions offered within the framework of international law to cope with this unprecedented case.

When a country is devising its bilateral relations with Taiwan, the question should be: How should Taiwan be defined? As a strict dependent of the PRC, or as an autonomous political entity within Chinese territory? In the former case emphasis is placed on the implicit or explicit commitment to recognize Peking's sovereignty over Taiwan and the offshore islands, and in the latter case on the existence, in these territories, of all the constituent elements of a state, that is to say a territory, a population, and a government. It is a question of reconciling recognition of the PRC as the sole legal government of China with its lack of control over Taiwan. In other words, it is a question of avoiding being trapped in a dilemma where the implicit or explicit recognition of Peking's competency over Taiwan prevails over the existence of an autonomous political entity on the island.

International law may be instrumental in coping with such a situation both as regards the status assigned to Taiwan and the form of bilateral relations.

As to the juridical status of Taiwan, a number of key issues arise. First, even though the thesis that Taiwan is a territory over which the de jure sovereignty is uncertain or undetermined is no longer sustainable since Peking and Washington signed their joint communiqué of January 1, 1979, the fact that the issue is now an internal Chinese problem, and no longer an international one, does not necessarily imply that a third country cannot recognize the division of China into two political entities, even if it is temporary.[7] Therefore, the severing of diplomatic relations must clearly be taken into account. In particular, severance does not necessarily imply derecognition.[8] Thus, although Israel and the Soviet Union severed diplomatic relations in February 1953, this did not mean that Moscow no longer recognized Israel.

---

[7] Hence the interest in applying the concept of multi-system nations to China. See Hungdah Chiu and Robert Downen, eds., *Multi-System Nations and International Law: The International Status of Germany, Korea and China*, Occasional Papers/Reprints Series in Contemporary Asian Studies, no. 8 (Baltimore: School of Law, University of Maryland, 1981), and in particular, chapter 2, Hungdah Chiu, "The International Law of Recognition and Multi-System Nations with Special Reference to Chinese (Mainland-Taiwan) Case," and chapter 3, Yung Wei, "The Unification and Division of Multi-System Nations: A Comparative Analysis of Basic Concepts, Issues and Approaches."

[8] Lucien Sfez, "La rupture des relations diplomatiques," *Revue générale de droit international public*, 3rd ser., 37, no. 2 (April-June 1966): 359-430.

Of course, this argument could not have been put forward in the 1970s, when most Western countries normalized their relations with Peking, since at that time Taipei still held to the Hallstein Doctrine, at least implicitly, and third countries were required to recognize the government of the ROC as the sole legal government of China. So, one can only regret that some countries (the latest being Israel)[9] did not confine themselves to an unconditional recognition of the PRC, but explicitly admitted Peking's sovereignty over Taiwan.[10]

Furthermore, since Peking has most of the time succeeded in insisting on its rights over Taiwan, it was also possible to consider the island as a de facto entity. The United States legislation, for instance, provides that:

> An entity not recognized as a State but meeting the requirements for recognition specified in paragraph 100 (of controlling a territory and population and engaging in foreign affairs), or an entity recognized as a State whose regime is not recognized as its government, has the rights of a State under international law in relation to a non-recognizing State, although it can be precluded from exercising such a right if (a) the right is of such a nature it can only be exercised by the government of a State, and (b) the non-recognizing State refuses to treat the purported exercise of the right as action taken by the government of the other State.[11]

But this solution has not been used in devising relations with Taiwan. The only country which has put its links with Taiwan into a legal framework (the United States) mentions only the "people" of Taiwan.[12]

International law has been inadequately exploited not only as regards the status of Taiwan, but also as regards the form of bilateral relations. Indeed, consular relations seem most suitable for the case of Taiwan.

Consular relations are usually expanded because of international trade and economic links between foreigners and citizens of a particular state. Moreover, consular relations are independent of diplomatic relations or even mutual recognition. As specified in the 1963 Vienna Convention on Consular Relations: "The severance of diplomatic ties does not ipso facto

---

[9]On January 22, 1992, when diplomatic ties were established between Israel and the PRC, Israel recognized Peking as the "sole, legitimate government representing the whole of China." See *Free China Journal* 9, no. 1 (January 7, 1992): 1.

[10]For the French stance, see Mengin, "The Prospects for France-Taiwan Relations," 57.

[11]The Foreign Relations Law of the United States, paragraph 104 (1965), quoted in Aleth Manin, "Taiwan: nouveaux aspects juridiques," *Annuaire français de droit international*, no. 26 (1980): 154.

[12]The Sino-American joint communiqué of January 1, 1979, paragraph 2 provides: "The United States of America recognizes the Government of the People's Republic of China as the sole legal Government of China. Within this context, the people of the United States will maintain cultural, commercial, and other unofficial relations with the people of Taiwan." And the TRA of April 10, 1979 describes itself as "an Act to help maintain peace, security, and stability in the Western Pacific and to promote the foreign policy of the United States by authorizing the continuation of the commercial, cultural, and other relations between the people of the United States and the people on Taiwan, and for other purposes."

lead to severing consular relations."[13] Further, some contractual dispensations may be allowed. Thus, a consular convention was signed between France and the United Kingdom on December 31, 1951, which holds that if diplomatic relations are severed either state will be allowed to require the closing, on its own territory, of the other state's consular posts. Besides this, the text does not specify that the rupture of consular relations will follow the rupture of diplomatic relations; it only makes clear that both states can require it.[14]

There are many examples of such a situation. When the United Kingdom recognized the PRC in 1950, the British retained their consulate in Tamsui. Certainly, for Peking, the retention of this consulate was an obstacle to the full normalization of relations with Britain, and ambassadors were exchanged only after the March 13, 1972 joint communiqué stating that London acknowledged "the position of the Chinese government that Taiwan is a province of the People's Republic of China," and the British consulate in Taiwan was closed.

After Taipei severed diplomatic relations with Paris in 1964, the ROC consulate in Papeete was maintained until 1965.[15] Moreover, General de Gaulle regarded consular relations as an option if the ROC severed diplomatic ties with France after the Paris-Peking normalization.[16] Likewise, after consulates of the German Democratic Republic (GDR) were opened in Phnom Penh and Baghdad, Bonn did not sever its diplomatic ties with Cambodia or Iraq. Bonn also maintained diplomatic relations with the United Arab Republic (UAR) despite the presence of an East German commercial mission and a consulate in Cairo, assuming that these consular links did not imply express recognition of the GDR by the UAR.[17] Further, the severing of diplomatic ties between France and Vietnam was not followed by the rupture of consular relations. A Vietnamese communiqué even specified that both countries would communicate through consular channels.[18]

Despite these precedents, none of Taiwan's commercial partners had resorted to consular relations as a means of formalizing their links with Taipei in the period since Washington switched recognition to Peking, until January 29, 1992, when Latvia, after establishing diplomatic relations with the PRC, started consular relations with the ROC. With this one exception,

---

[13]It is a different matter if the severance of relations brings about a war. In this case, consuls are deprived of the exequatur. See Sfez, "La rupture des relations diplomatiques," 404.

[14]Ibid.

[15]It was closed at the request of the French authorities because nuclear experiments were being conducted in the area. The same request was made to the American consulate.

[16]See Mengin, "The Prospects for France-Taiwan Relations," 58.

[17]Charles Rousseau, "Chronique des faits internationaux," *Revue générale de droit international public*, 3rd ser., 32, no. 3 (July-September 1961): 576.

[18]*Le Monde*, June 26, 1965.

there is no choice but to assume a lack of political willingness on the part of most countries to set up official non-diplomatic ties with Taiwan through various legal solutions. It is now necessary to go beyond such a legal deadlock: the situation calls for a new approach.

Taiwan is an extreme phenomenon in the law of nations and its external relations constitute an original model of bilateral relations. Taiwan's nonofficial partners maintain the fiction that their links with the island are purely private, but one should not be confined to such an observation since it in no way explains the ROC's position on the world scene. Consequently, the question arises as to which paradigm of international relations should be applied when analyzing Taiwan's external relations.

A Paradigm for the Nature of Taiwan's Informal Relations

Taiwan's external relations are often referred to as "transnational relations," a term that has been precisely defined by Robert O. Keohane and Joseph S. Nye as "the movement of tangible or intangible items across state boundaries when at least one actor is not an agent of a government or an intergovernmental organization."[19] The concept of transnational relations does indeed meet the requirements of Taiwan's bilateral relations to a certain extent. Certainly, countries having established diplomatic ties with Peking have strived not only to confine Taiwan's bilateral relations to the economic, cultural, and scientific spheres, but have also excluded the ROC from almost all intergovernmental organizations. This being the case, the basic assumption underlying any review of Taiwan's foreign relations is that they are transnational in nature.

But if Peking's tactic since 1978 has been to confine Taipei's external relations to the transnational level, the institutional framework that has underpinned the expansion of substantial links between Japan, the United States, or Western Europe and Taiwan suggests a more intricate issue.

Nowadays, there is a network of associations, offices, and institutes, both in Taipei and in foreign capitals, that carry out quasi-diplomatic or consular functions, most notably the issuing of visas. Some of these offices are headed by former diplomats or by diplomats temporarily on leave. Finally, contacts between governmental officials are taking place at ever higher levels. In particular, visits by ROC ministers to Europe and by European ministers to Taipei have become commonplace. These developments have prompted some analysts to speak of quasi-diplomatic relations.[20]

---

[19]Robert O. Keohane and Joseph S. Nye, Jr., eds., *Transnational Relations and World Politics* (Cambridge, Mass.: Harvard University Press, 1972), xii.

[20]See, in particular, Lee, "Quasi-Diplomatic Relations of the Republic of China"; Bernard T. K. Joei, "The International Status of the Republic of China and Its 'Quasi'-Diplomacy," in *Taiwan in Transition: Political Development and Economic Prosperity*, ed. Bernard T. K. Joei (Taipei: Tamkang University, 1989), 57-83.

Yet, in setting up these procedures every precaution is taken to maintain the semblance of private relations. As for visas, the conditions of acceptability and the methods of issuing them[21] enable a country to assert that no consular ties have been established and that the facilities are aimed only at reducing delays. In the same way, ministers pay visits in their private capacities only.

It is thus necessary to go beyond the term "private" and the debate aroused by questions about the classic international relations paradigm. This paradigm remains useful for such a study insofar as it provides the theoretical instruments requisite for conceptualizing Taiwan's bilateral relations.

The classic paradigm of interstate politics as theorized by Raymond Aron, Hans J. Morgenthau, or Kenneth N. Waltz,[22] among others, assumes that states are the only relevant actors in international relations. Certainly, this state-centric perspective does include factors such as the economy, science, and culture, but nothing other than the state perspective gives full meaning to their role in international relations. More precisely, this theory argues that since violence is at the core of the interstate system, transnational relations do not significantly affect "high politics," whose business is security and war. Therefore, governments will always prevail in any direct confrontation with transnational actors.

This state-centric perspective has been sharply criticized by those who would set the international society alongside the interstate society. In this view, the classic idea of international relations as an assemblage of sovereign states is challenged by the present expansion of transnational flows avoiding state sovereignty. This could even foreshadow a new world order no longer founded on the artificial and conventional division of the world into sovereign states, but on basic relations.

However, there is no question of participating in this debate since this chapter does not deal with international relations as a whole, only with one segment. What is more, such a debate may appear outmoded on more than one account.

First, it is impossible to draw a very clear dividing line between transnational relations and interstate relations. Not only, in most fields, do private activities precede governmental regulation, but industries in general influence governments too. Moreover, as Keohane and Nye put it: "Transnational organizations are particularly serviceable as instruments of governmental foreign policy whether through control or willing alliance."[23] Generally

---

[21]Visas, though issued in Taipei, are authorized through Hong Kong consulates-general.
[22]Raymond Aron, *Peace and War: A Theory of International Relations*, trans. Richard Howard and Annette Baker Fox (New York: Praeger, 1967); Hans J. Morgenthau, *Politics among Nations: The Struggle for Peace and Power*, 4th rev. ed. (New York: Knopf, 1967); Kenneth N. Waltz, *Man, the State and War: A Theoretical Analysis*, Topical Studies in International Relations no. 2 (New York: Columbia University Press, 1959).
[23]Keohane and Nye, *Transnational Relations*, xxi.

speaking, there is what Evans calls a "contamination of interstate relations by transnational relations."[24]

There is no longer a definite division between high politics and low politics. Stanley Hoffmann, among others, has well underscored this phenomenon. In his words:

> The competition between states takes place on several chessboards in addition to the traditional military and diplomatic ones: for instance the chessboards of world trade, of world finance, of aid and of technical assistance, of space research and exploration, of military technology, and the chessboard of what has been called "informal penetration." These chessboards do not entail the resort to force.[25]

As high and low politics become difficult to distinguish, a country's foreign policy is no longer confined to its ministry of foreign affairs, but is spread out among the ministries of defense, economics, and culture, among others.

Finally, a continuum can be established combining two kinds of distinctions: between transnational relations and interstate relations on the one hand, and between high and low politics on the other. In order to express these complex interplays, some authors have proposed new paradigms for international relations. In particular, Keohane and Nye have devised a "world politics" paradigm that "attempts to transcend the 'level-of-analysis' problem' both by broadening the conception of actors to include transnational actors and by conceptually breaking down the 'hard shell' of the nation-state,"[26] and this seems to fit the Taiwan case. This "world politics" paradigm leads to a new type of interplay: transgovernmental interactions that go beyond the distinction between "transnational interactions" which necessarily involve nongovernmental actors, and "interstate interactions" which take place exclusively between states acting as units.[27]

This concept should be especially operative in the case of Taiwan since it could make it possible to take into account both those aspects of Taiwan's external relations that are similar to interstate relations (mainly a wide range of bilateral cooperation) and the private nature of these relations. This concept could also be helpful in explaining Taiwan's importance on the world scene: because this concept transcends the notion of state, emphasis can be laid on the fact that Taiwan's bilateral relations are substantial rather than formal. Generally speaking, Keohane and Nye have shown that "trans-

---

[24]Peter B. Evans, quoted in ibid., xxiv.

[25]Stanley Hoffmann, "International Organization and the International System," *International Organization* 24, no. 3 (Summer 1970): 401.

[26]Keohane and Nye, *Transnational Relations*, 380.

[27]Keohane and Nye define transgovernmental interactions as "interactions between governmental subunits across state boundaries." In their view, the term transnational relations includes both transnational and transgovernmental interactions—in other words, "all of world politics that is not taken into account by the state-centric paradigm." See Keohane and Nye, *Transnational Relations*, 383.

national relations . . . affect interstate politics by altering the choices open
to statesmen and the costs that must be borne for adopting various courses
of action. In short, transnational relations provide different sets of incentives
or payoffs, for states.''[28] From the angle of nonofficial relations, Taiwan
could thus be reinstated in the world order.

However interesting it may be to call into question the classic paradigm
of interstate politics, one cannot only go this far with regard to a non-rec-
ognized state's bilateral relations, in the conceptualization of which the
distinction between transnational relations and interstate relations remains
instrumental.

The explanatory scope of the classic paradigm in such a case can, at
the outset, be illustrated with an example derived from the Taiwan issue. It
is obvious that in the 1950s and 1960s, there were interstate relations between
the PRC and Western countries which did not recognize the Peking regime,
mainly the United States and France. For instance, the PRC played an important part in the talks on Indochina at the 1954 Geneva Conference. Even
though it was the Soviet Union which arranged the PRC's participation in
the conference, direct talks between the mainland Chinese premier, Chou
En-lai (Zhou Enlai) and his French counterpart Pierre Mendès-France attest
to the existence, at that time, of government-to-government interactions.
Furthermore, from then on it was generally admitted that no solution to
an Asian problem was possible without the PRC's participation.

In fact, representatives of countries having no mutual diplomatic relations can meet in a third country and negotiate and sign intergovernmental
agreements. This was the case for the United States and the PRC prior to
normalization.[29] Likewise, a Franco-Egyptian agreement was signed in Geneva
on August 22, 1958, although diplomatic relations between the two countries
had been severed after the 1956 Suez crisis. While many more examples can
be cited, the main point is that interstate relations between countries having
no diplomatic relations can, and do, exist.

Consequently, the question arises as to whether Taiwan's external relations are purely transnational, or is there a part of them that could be
described as interstate politics as well? In other words, are Taiwan's bilateral
relations instrumental in making Taiwan an actor in international relations
(from the perspective of the classic paradigm) or do they just keep Taiwan
integrated at the transnational level? To what extent is there an area in
Taiwan's external relations that rightly belongs to the political interstate
level?

If it happens that an entity which has all the attributes of a sovereign

---

[28]Keohane and Nye, *Transnational Relations*, 374-75.

[29]In particular, during the Vietnam War, the U.S. ambassador in Warsaw regularly met with
his PRC counterpart. See *Le Monde*, December 31, 1965, 1.

state can be confined outside the interstate realm, then one should resort to the concept of civil society, since the spheres of activity of these transnational relations cover all those of normalized relations, with the exception of those in the strategic field. Although many different meanings can be attached to the term "civil society," it is usually applied to illustrate the state/society dichotomy, which may be particularly instrumental in Taiwan's case. This chapter would opt for Hegel's definition of civil society as the set of institutions that meet the needs of economic life and regulate people's pursuit of their private affairs.[30] Therefore, Taiwan's bilateral relations would be relations between civil societies. Should the word "people," as it appears in the TRA, be understood in such a context?[31]

Thus, political theory provides frames of reference for analyzing Taiwan's external relations and determining Taiwan's part in the world order: an actor in interstate relations or just a unit of transnational relations?

An Original Model of Bilateral Relations: Suppletive Relations

Criteria for the Existence of Interstate Relations

In order to discern signs of interstate relations, several criteria need to be examined; these can be categorized in two major fields: the institutional framework of bilateral relations and the level of contact between governments.

As to the setting up of semiofficial structures, a distinction must be made between Japan and the United States on the one hand, and European countries on the other. Whether or not they had diplomatic ties with Taipei, the latter developed no real exchanges with the ROC before 1978, whereas Japan, followed by the United States, simply continued relations with Taiwan on a nonofficial level after normalizing with Peking. Consequently, it is tempting to conclude that Japan and the United States have only, through several devices, assumed a nonofficial level of intergovernmental relations, and then examine whether, in imitation of this scheme, Europe-Taiwan relations have reached a comparable level during the 1980s.

In fact, Japan's relations with Taiwan were completely relegated to the private sector by the nongovernmental agreement signed on December 26, 1972 by the Japanese Interchange Association and its Taiwan counterpart, the East Asian Relations Association, and they have remained private ever since.

The issue is slightly different (and should be more revealing of the existence of governmental relations) in the American case, since it is a unilateral instrument, that is to say the TRA, issued by a state institution,

---

[30]*Philosophy of Right.*
[31]See note 12 above.

the United States Congress, which has determined how bilateral relations with Taiwan should develop. But because of the circumstances under which the TRA was passed, it does not lead to any conclusion as to the nature of Taipei-Washington relations. First, Teng Hsiao-p'ing (Deng Xiaoping) refused to let the United States establish a liaison office in Taipei, putting forward the official nature of such a body as the reason. Therefore, the United States adopted the private association formula, putting pressure on Taipei's officials to set up a similar organization. This being the case, two interpretations are possible: one can consider either that every effort was made to re-form interstate relations so that they would appear to be private, or that, under Peking's pressure, this plan was dropped and the TRA was a genuine attempt to define transnational relations only. The same applies, all the more so, to Japan's relations with Taiwan, since the Japanese authorities did not directly commit themselves to institutionalizing these links as the U.S. Congress did. Therefore, it is not possible to infer from the transposition of diplomatic ties to the nonofficial level that interstate links have been maintained.

The same ambiguity is present if the chosen criterion is the form of the body in charge of bilateral relations. Even though an overall survey of these structures comes up against the heterogeneity of the legal formulas adopted, it is possible to distinguish two main categories, each suggesting different types of relations: the first category consists of proper chambers of commerce and of private boards representing private industries, the second one of private associations which have been set up on the administration's own authority. In the first category one finds the German Trade Office, the Anglo-Taiwan Trade Committee, the Netherlands Trade and Investment Office, the Italian Trade and Economic Center, the Spanish Chamber of Commerce, the Austrian Trade Delegation, the Swedish Industries Trade Representative Office, the Belgian Trade Association, etc. In the second one: the Japanese Interchange Association, the American Institute in Taiwan, and the two French representative offices, the French Institute in Taipei (FIT) and the France Asia Trade Promotion Association (FATPA). These organizations function as fronts for officials of the ministries in charge of foreign affairs and economic affairs. In particular, these offices are headed by diplomats temporarily attached to them, which would suggest the formation of para-diplomatic or quasi-diplomatic relations. In contrast, organizations in the first category only reveal the industrial sector's interest in the Taiwan market. This presumption is strengthened by the existence, in the American and French cases, of proper chambers of commerce alongside their respective "para-diplomatic" offices. In such cases, the two levels usually existing in normalized relationships seem to have been re-formed into a transnational level, more or less supported by public authorities, and an administrative level where representatives act as the spokesmen of their respective governments and would represent their governments if relations were normalized.

This approach should be confirmed by other evidence since objections can be made to this argument. First, the fact that some unofficial bodies reproduce the pattern of services that normally exist in embassies may be misleading because many embassies have units that represent private interests as much as public ones. For instance, Austrian commercial affairs abroad are handled by trade promotion offices that are part of the Federal Economic Chamber of Austria. Thus, there is no distinction between Taiwan and any other country as to the promotion of Austrian trade. Above all, the fact that diplomatic staff are involved in some organizations does not necessarily imply a commitment of governments to conduct anything other than transnational relations with Taiwan. Examples of private institutions calling on high-ranking civil servants' skills are numerous. Consequently, it is difficult to distinguish whether some institutes and associations in Taipei are engendered by the transnational level or are the component parts of interstate relations.

The same ambiguity is encountered in all other signs of so-called quasidiplomatic relations. Therefore, since it seems impossible to infer from a single criterion the presence of interstate relations with Taiwan, each one will be succinctly reviewed.

At the procedural level, the most striking indication of the establishment of official relations is the issuing of visas. In the past few years, most of Taiwan's non-diplomatic partners have opened "visa offices" in Taipei so that Taiwanese are no longer obliged to travel via a third country to receive a visa.[32] However, no significant conclusion can be drawn from this change. Indeed, since consular relations are independent of diplomatic ones, the fact that the visas are still authorized via consulates in third countries or territories indicates that the purpose was clearly not to officialize bilateral relations. The offending note written down beside visas issued by Australia and New Zealand until 1991 (which said that no credit was lent to ROC passports and the visa did not imply any recognition of the Taipei government) is indicative of this state of mind. From then on, it would seem appropriate to speak, in the case of visas, of the delegation of the public authority's prerogatives to private agencies.

Likewise, some advantages granted to the various so-called representative offices (such as diplomatic privileges and immunities, or communications facilities)[33] can be described as privileges departing from those which by common law are granted to public entities. These privileges and facilities have been granted in a sketchy way, not on the basis of international agree-

---

[32]In 1985, France was the first European country to follow the Japanese and American formula by issuing visas in Taipei, although they are authorized through the Hong Kong consulate. Most other European countries have opened visa offices too; so have Australia, New Zealand, and Canada.

[33]These include the sending of encoded telegrams, installation and use of radio transceivers, and use of the diplomatic bag.

ments,[34] but, in the best case, on the basis of a national law. Except for the United States (the TRA deals with this matter),[35] privileges are granted on the basis of administrative regulations, so the granting is precarious. Moreover, there is often no strict reciprocity, so these various privileges and immunities can be reduced at any time to more customary practices of a functional nature.

Beyond the institutional framework of bilateral relations, the level of contact between officials and politicians is often used as an indicator of growing relations at the interstate level. One of the most striking developments in Taiwan's bilateral relations with Europe in the past months is the increasing number of visits by serving European ministers, even though their trips to Taipei are wholly "private visits." The French minister of Industry and Regional Planning, Roger Fauroux, initiated the change in January 1991, and since then nearly twenty European ministers have been to Taipei.[36] A comparable development can be noticed with other countries, although on a smaller scale and with the exception of the United States and Japan. For instance, at the beginning of 1992, President Corazon Aquino lifted the ban on Philippine officials visiting Taiwan which had been imposed in 1987.[37] It must be stressed that these visits cannot be compared to those of ROC ministers travelling to foreign countries. Certainly, all are private visits; but the implications are clearer when a minister takes the initiative in making a trip than they are when a few meetings are arranged for a visitor from Taiwan, whose visit is usually made under the auspices of one or more large firms. Yet, considered separately, these ministerial visits to Taiwan do not greatly differ from any other kind of support often given by government members to the commercial and industrial sectors. As such, these visits can

---

[34]See the 1961 and 1963 Vienna Conventions on diplomatic and consular relations, respectively.

[35]Section 10 (c) of the TRA states:

Upon the granting by Taiwan of comparable privileges and immunities with respect to the Institute and its appropriate personnel, the President is authorized to extend with respect to the Taiwan instrumentality and its appropriate personnel, such privileges and immunities (subject to appropriate conditions and obligations) as may be necessary for the effective performance of their functions.

[36]January 1991: French minister of industry and regional planning; March 1991: Irish minister and vice minister of industry and commerce; April 1991: Italian minister of public works; June 1991: Swedish vice minister of foreign affairs; July 1991: British under secretary for trade and industry; August 1991: German minister of posts and telecommunications; December 1991: Latvian minister of foreign affairs; January 1992: French secretary of state for foreign trade; February 1992: British minister of state for trade and industry; April 1992: Dutch minister of foreign trade, Danish vice minister of foreign trade and vice minister of industry; May 1992: Ukrainian minister of health, Swedish minister of transport and telecommunications, German vice minister of economic affairs and minister of posts and telecommunications; June 1992: Czechoslovakian vice minister of foreign affairs.

[37]The lifting of the ban does not apply to the president, vice president, minister of foreign affairs, or minister of defense. See *Free China Journal* 9, no. 14 (March 3, 1992): 1.

be taken, primarily, as infrastate relations between the private sector and the administration in charge of it, although it is the alleged interstate dimension of the visits which is highlighted by Taipei. It is this dimension, in turn, which determines the minister's move, since the hypothetical breakthrough in bilateral relations can enable firms to win big contracts. In such cases the governments agree to play (for economic purposes) an interstate game with Taiwan; but the level of contact is not sufficient to infer that foreign countries have truly integrated Taiwan into their game. In this respect it is worth noting that it is mostly ministers in charge of commercial and industrial affairs who come to Taipei.

No single criterion strongly indicates the existence of interstate relations. Each sign of "quasi-diplomatic" relations can be viewed as a progressive organization of the private sector in order to deepen economic ties with Taiwan.[38] When necessary, and in order to compensate for the lack of diplomatic and consular ties, the private sector has assumed some prerogatives of public authority and reproduced some of the services that would come from normalized bilateral relations. From this viewpoint, a foreign state's involvement in bilateral relations with Taiwan remains exceptional: the transnational level is not transcended. Moreover, since these transnational relations cover a wide range of activities and, above all, the institutional frameworks spread their services both horizontally (from advertising the activities of small and medium-sized enterprises to promoting technology developed by big ones) and vertically (from providing information to setting up consular services), it seems useful to speak of relations between civil societies. Indeed, these bilateral links have evolved spontaneously, in a customary way, and independently of international law. Resorting to the concept of civil society therefore enables one to distinguish Taiwan's bilateral relations from transnational relations in general. The latter develop in a specific field (economic, cultural, religious, humanitarian, etc.) while the former aim at developing links with an entity which has all the attributes of a sovereign state but is confined outside the interstate realm.

The simplest and the most obvious way to examine the problem is to look at each indicator of diplomatic ties. But it is also possible to employ a more elaborate argument based on a network of proofs. This will combine two kinds of criteria: the commitment of Taiwan's nonofficial partners in a triangular relationship involving a third country, and all the indicators previously examined.

Only the intervention of a third party enables one to perceive any involvement by a government recognizing the PRC in relations with Taiwan, or any form of institutionalization of the bilateral process, as something more than practical arrangements designed to reinforce transnational rela-

---

[38]The same trend is apparent in cultural and scientific ties although on a smaller scale.

tions. In fact, international relationships in terms of a power struggle are precisely at the core of the classic paradigm.

A political motive can be found in the moralism marking the Washington-Peking-Taipei relationship as established by the U.S. Congress. An examination of the TRA reveals Washington's interest in defending Taiwan against potential external aggression, most particularly from the PRC. Section 2 (b), points (3), (4), (5), and (6), section 2 (c), and section 3 virtually constitute a defense treaty with Taiwan. Certainly, these guarantees are not absolute, but largely depend on the balance of forces in the Taiwan Strait. However, the very fact that the United States accepts the possibility of intervening to protect Taiwan's security and the safety of its people indicates that it is involved in interstate relations.

Although other countries have never expressed concern for Taiwan's security, they have on several occasions been involved in such a triangular game. This is the case when they sell arms to Taiwan. Arms sales generally involve a decision-making process which implies cabinet level consent. When arms are delivered to Taiwan, a government accepts that its (tacit or explicit) commitment toward the PRC not to sell arms to the island will be called into question. Even if such a decision is the result of a zero-sum game in which economic advantages offset a temporary setback in relations with the PRC, a real triangular play takes shape. It becomes clearer when a country renews arms deliveries or when it tries to outbid its rivals. In this way, the recent offers from Paris to sell Mirage 2000-5s and from Washington to sell F-16s are most revealing.

The problem of the destabilization potential of Taiwan's economic strength is halfway between politics and economics. For instance, before the end of the Cold War, one issue was Taiwan's economic and technological relations with the Soviet Union and Eastern Europe. Although Taiwan was not a member of the Coordinating Committee on Export Controls (COCOM), the United States put pressure on Taipei to limit its exports to these countries. This also testifies to the outline of interstate relations. Finally, Taiwan's economic success itself has become an asset in interstate relationships. Indeed, the necessity of Taiwan belonging to some international organizations can determine commitments on a bilateral level. For instance, in 1983, after the PRC asked to join the Asian Development Bank (ADB), the United States and Japan used their political leverage on both Peking and Taipei, so that each would agree to the other's membership: the former agreed to allow the ROC to retain its status and the latter in turn agreed to change its name to "Taipei, China." It was also under United States, Japanese, and South Korean pressure that Taiwan was able to join the Asia Pacific Economic Cooperation (APEC) grouping in 1991, along with the PRC and Hong Kong. At present, the same triangular game is being played by several states (the United States and some European Community members, among others) on the General Agreement on Tariffs and Trade (GATT) issue: they are playing for economic purposes but with political implications. In these instances, Taiwan becomes a part of interstate relations.

It is from the perspective of these triangular interactions that the whole set of indicators of "quasi-diplomatic" relations, previously examined, takes on a new dimension.

The importance of substantial bilateral relations must, above all, be emphasized. It is essential that Taiwan's commercial stake not be limited to a few firms. Furthermore, only big contracts can foster a process of officialization, which can be analyzed as a progressive organization of the transnational level but can, subsequently, serve the interstate one.

The accumulation of procedures which are copied from normalized relations will result in the shaping of reception structures which, as soon as a diplomatic or strategic stake appears, will serve as relay stations for governmental initiatives.

The institutional and political frameworks progressively established when bilateral relations are developed with Taiwan are no longer considered as being transnational, but as re-formed institutions and procedures which are essential to a normalized relationship. Of course, by such reasoning, the United States-Taiwan relationship is a borderline case. Because the United States had substantial interests in Taiwan at the time it established diplomatic relations with Peking, the re-forming of relations with the ROC was achieved beforehand. With Europe-Taiwan relations, however, this re-forming process did not take place until afterward. In this case, governmental authorities are progressively investing in transnational organizations and even expanding their scope.

While relations are becoming broader and more substantial, they are successively growing in two directions: from bottom to top first—as transnational relations assume the prerogatives of public authority or call on government support—and from top to bottom next—where initiatives are governmental and private agencies can be considered as subcontractors of governmental authorities.

From here on, relations which can be described as "suppletive" are being implemented in as much as all the functions of normalized relations except one—the representation of the "accredited" state—are being carried out. Relations are suppletive because they are non-diplomatic interstate relations. Indeed, the different institutes, trade offices, and cultural centers in Taipei fulfill all other duties performed by embassies.

Yet, there are two points which must be noted. First, not all Taiwan's non-diplomatic partners conduct suppletive relations with the ROC. It is difficult to make a clear distinction between those which do and those which are still linked to Taiwan by transnational ties only, since the change from one kind of relationship to the other is progressive. For instance, two European countries whose trade with Taiwan was for a long time of comparable volume, Italy and France,[39] have developed relations of different natures. The two

---

[39]In 1988, Taiwan's trade with Italy and France was worth US$1.4 billion and US$1.5 billion,

French representative offices in Taipei function more or less as fronts for officials of the ministries of foreign affairs and economic affairs, and were established in 1978 (FATPA) and 1979 (FIT). However, the Italian Trade and Economic Center in Taipei was opened as late as September 1989, and only started issuing visas in 1992. It is possible to conclude that Taiwan's relations with Italy are still in the first stage, whereas with France they are already in the second stage. Beyond the fact that these two countries have different foreign policies, one explanation lies in the fact that France-Taiwan bilateral trade is mostly made up of "key contracts"[40] which carry more political implications.

The second point worth noting is that the transition from transnational to suppletive relations is, to some extent, the result of a chain reaction; one country's initiative to win key contracts in Taiwan prompts other governments to accord similar support to their firms. The whole succession of European ministers who came to Taipei in recent months reveals this trend.

Suppletive Relations and Taiwan's Place
in the International System

If Taiwan's bilateral relations are partly conducted on the interstate level—and are suppletive because they are non-diplomatic—the question arises as to whether they can permit Taiwan's reentry into the international community. In other words, are suppletive relations a prelude to diplomatic relations? Insofar as the origin of these relations is generally incidental,[41] it is possible to envisage such a transition. Therefore, forewarning signs and elements of resistance to this will be examined.

It seems that the palliative nature of the suppletive system, which leaves intact the causes of Taiwan's diplomatic position, should prevent any dramatic changes from taking place. Suppletive relations aim to lighten the day-to-day consequences of Taiwan's non-recognition without reopening the question. Consequently, this system tends to uphold the status quo.

Suppletive relations have been arranged in order to avoid taking any definite stand on the PRC/ROC issue. And even if relations largely determined by economic factors can be interstate relations, other nations can choose to remain impervious to political factors.

It can thus be explained how opposite political trends on the two sides of the Taiwan Strait at the end of the 1980s—Taiwan's political liberalization

---

respectively. In 1990, these figures had increased to US$1.8 billion and US$2.2 billion (source: Euro-Asia Trade Organization, Taipei).

[40]These include Airbuses supplied by Aérospatiale, one-third of Taiwan's enriched uranium needs for power generation supplied by Cogema, a large stretch of the mass rapid transportation system constructed by Matra, and the six French-built La Fayette frigate hulls and the ten additional ones to be constructed in Taiwan under a joint-technical agreement.

[41]Except for the United States.

and the June 4, 1989 military crackdown on the democracy movement in the PRC—have not immediately influenced the course of Taiwan's bilateral relations. However, their effects have only been postponed.

The West's reaction to the Tienanmen (Tiananmen) massacre demonstrated its support for the democracy movement in mainland China, but it has not challenged the PRC's membership in the international community. However, in the process, the economic sanctions imposed on the mainland regime after the June 4 massacre have induced a fair number of manufacturers (whether to show support for the pro-democracy movement or for economic reasons) to prospect the Taiwan market. At the same time, it is the economic consequences of Taiwan's political changes which have given a new impetus to Taiwan's bilateral relations, not the changes themselves. Thus, the Six-Year National Development Plan (1991-96), that has attracted the attention of Taiwan's economic partners since it was adopted in January 1991, was devised by the Hau Pei-tsun government to strengthen both domestic and foreign policies implemented since 1989. As to domestic targets, the Six-Year Plan acts as a counterbalance to the regime's democratization inasmuch as it reinforces the image of the Kuomintang as an efficient administrator of Taiwan's economy; on the other hand, it represents the constructive program of Premier Hau whose appointment could only indicate a hardening of the regime after the first stage of liberalization. But the Six-Year Plan is also instrumental in attracting large foreign firms and therefore in strengthening Taiwan's bilateral ties. It is possible to conclude that, up to now, only the economic consequences of political changes on both sides of the Taiwan Strait have reinforced Taiwan's external relations.[42]

The very significant rapprochement between Taiwan and Eastern Europe and the countries of the former Soviet Union is encouraging because it enables Taiwan to diversify its partners and, consequently, increases opportunities for the creation of official bilateral relations. But such a trend can also be viewed as an alignment of these countries with the stand taken by West European countries ten years ago. With the exception of Latvia, the countries of Eastern Europe and the Commonwealth of Independent States (CIS) have all adopted a suppletive relations system comparable, in every respect, with those of Taiwan's other nonofficial partners: trade offices have opened in Taipei, private visits by politicians are taking place, etc.

One can expect that Taiwan's exchanges with Russia, whatever their potential, will at best only approach the level of those the ROC maintains with the United States, Japan, or the West European countries. Moscow's determination to strictly confine its ties with Taipei to the private sphere

---

[42]For an analysis of the impact of political changes in Taiwan and the PRC on France-Taiwan relations, see Mengin, "The Prospects for France-Taiwan Relations."

was clearly expressed a few months ago with regard to the negotiation of a fishing agreement.[43]

Likewise, Israel (another promising trade partner for Taiwan) has reached the same diplomatic deadlock concerning the Taiwan issue.[44] This example is all the more significant as Israel belongs, along with the ROC and South Africa, to the category of isolated states.[45]

Generally speaking, when Taiwan's international position is analyzed from the standpoint of its bilateral relations, caution is advised as to the notion of pragmatism. The successes and potential of informal diplomacy are often attributed to pragmatism, but if the pragmatism shown by Taiwan and its non-diplomatic partners has enabled the development of substantial relations, after a certain stage it may no longer lead to decisive changes. As soon as a complete set of exchanges and their necessary institutional background have been settled, any further "pragmatic" arrangements are aimed only at upholding the status quo, that is to say, at refusing to accept the officialization of relations with Taiwan.

Thus, bilateral negotiations are carried on by senior officials (who pose as ordinary experts) in order to sign agreements involving two governments but binding upon two private firms. This can be seen, for instance, when fishing agreements are signed or in various cases of arms sales to Taipei, which usually require some amount of government negotiation to be approved. In the recent sale of French La Fayette frigates to Taipei, since the vessels are to be sold unarmed, the transaction was not considered to be a genuine arms sale; moreover, the contract was concluded between Thomson-CSF and China Shipbuilding, not by the Paris and Taipei governments. But these tactics cannot hide the fact that, as the frigates are intended eventually to receive ground-to-ground or ground-to-air missiles and artillery, it is indeed an arms sale.

Beyond this rather negative assessment, it is worth examining whether suppletive relations do not after all contain the seeds of future changes.

It is first possible to relativize the previous assessment by integrating the time factor. Then, the establishment of suppletive relations would just be the prerequisite of any process of officialization. Could not suppletive relations be to de facto sovereignty what diplomatic relations are to de jure sovereignty? Several elements justify envisaging the establishment of official relations.

The first element is the progressive awareness of the existence of interstate relations, though without formal recognition. The specific difficulty in the case of Taiwan lies in the fact that the diplomatic and strategic stake

---

[43]See *Free China Journal* 9, no. 15 (March 6, 1992): 1.

[44]See note 9 above.

[45]See Deon Geldenhuys, *Isolated States: A Comparative Analysis* (Cambridge: Cambridge University Press, 1990).

required must be at least equal to the PRC's. This comparison is all the more difficult as the two countries' assets are not of the same nature; therefore, their respective positions on the diplomatic chessboard cannot be the same. And, since Taiwan's strength is estimated in economic and financial terms, Peking supplants Taipei because of a hierarchy of factors which establishes the primacy of politics over economics. In this respect, a parallel can be drawn with the respective positions of the PRC and Japan. While the Gulf crisis won the former increased international legitimacy, the latter contributed US$13 billion, one-fourth the cost of the war, without gaining any political benefit.[46]

In addition, it is possible that European countries are going beyond the United States in their relations with Taiwan. Insofar as these countries are not bound by constraining legal provisions, such as those in the TRA, they are able to take liberties with Taiwan and could be paving the way for more official relations. Visits by ministers and sophisticated arms deliveries have been the most outstanding overtures so far.

Finally, the most encouraging sign of future changes can be seen in Taipei's policy on Chinese unification. Even if the long-term objective is to unify China, everything about the *Guidelines for National Unification* adopted by the ROC government on March 14, 1991, is aimed at normalizing relations between the two sides of the Strait. Taipei subordinates any talks on unification to the recognition by the PRC of the ROC as a legitimate political entity. To this end, Taipei made the first move when the Period of Mobilization was terminated on April 30, 1991: in doing so the ROC government recognized the existence of a legitimate political entity on the mainland. While waiting for a reciprocal gesture, Taipei is developing nonofficial links with the PRC through private bodies: the Straits Exchange Foundation on the island and the Association for Relations Across the Taiwan Straits on the mainland. Therefore, at the Chinese level, suppletive relations are being established in anticipation of normalized relations. However, if the recognition of the ROC by a significant part of the international community could present Peking with a fait accompli, a shorter way for Taipei would be to induce Peking to take the initiative. The general meaning of the national unification policy makes it, in fact, a two-Chinas policy. For the time being, Taiwan is developing substantial and suppletive relations with the mainland.

Conclusion

Taiwan's international relations are still changing and many conclusions

---

[46]Jean-Marie Bouissou, "La Puissance politique: une conquête inachevée," in *L'Expansion de la puissance japonaise* (The expansion of Japanese power) ed. Jean-Marie Bouissou, Guy Faure, and Zaki Laïdi (Brussels: Edition Complexe, 1992), 81-83.

are tentative and speculative. The minimal assessment consists of foreseeing that Taiwan's increasing integration into international economic and financial flows should lead to a crystallization, at the political level, of the ROC's current position on the world scene. However, the basic contention of this chapter—that a mere reference to the classic paradigm of interstate relations is instrumental in conceptualizing Taiwan's non-diplomatic relations—paves the way for a less static appraisal. Given the existence, in the case of the ROC, of all the constituent elements of a state, the concept of statehood remains attractive enough as regards international relations to gradually apply to Taiwan's bilateral ties and make the ROC a full actor in international relations.

CHAPTER 9

Foreign Aid in ROC Diplomacy

Tuan Y. Cheng

Foreign aid, which has been a part of foreign relations for centuries, has become particularly popular in the post-World War II period. The major industrialized states provide large quantities of assistance to the developing and less-developed countries, in the form of cash grants, development loans, and technical assistance. Generally, most foreign aid is the result of bilateral undertakings negotiated between the donor and recipient states, but some is given through multilateral arrangements by international organizations and programs, such as the World Bank, the Asian Development Bank (ADB), and the Inter-American Development Bank.

Aid may be given out of humanitarian concern, as in the case of emergency relief for victims of natural disasters, while some is provided as development assistance to poor states. But most bilateral foreign aid goes to countries from which the donors hope to receive some political, foreign policy, or economic returns, either in the short or long term. Generally, foreign aid is used as a policy instrument for foreign influence.[1]

The Republic of China (ROC) became a foreign aid donor in the early 1960s, when it was still a poor and developing country itself. Yet, within a decade it was providing agricultural and technical assistance to some forty countries in Africa, the Middle East, Southeast Asia, and Latin America. As the ROC developed and became a newly industrialized country in the 1980s, it further expanded its foreign aid programs. In 1988, the ROC government established the International Economic Cooperation and Development Fund (IECDF) with the aim of assisting the developing countries. It also increased its cash grants, development loans, and technical assistance to a number of friendly countries. Whatever the stated purpose of the ROC's past and present foreign aid efforts, however, its main motive has been

---

[1]David A. Baldwin, *Economic Statecraft* (Princeton, N.J.: Princeton University Press, 1985), chap. 10; Robert Gilpin, *The Political Economy of International Relations* (Princeton, N.J.: Princeton University Press, 1987), 310-14; and K. J. Holsti, *International Politics* (Englewood Cliffs, N.J.: Prentice-Hall, 1972), 257-68.

quite clear; that is, to strengthen the ROC's diplomatic ties and expand its foreign relations.

Since the ROC government was forced to withdraw from mainland China to Taiwan in 1949, it has endured a long struggle for diplomatic recognition. In 1971, the ROC suffered a major diplomatic setback when its seat in the United Nations was taken by the People's Republic of China (PRC). Since then, many states and international organizations have followed the U.N.'s lead and switched recognition from Taipei to Peking (Beijing). The ROC's international status was further damaged in 1979, when the United States severed formal diplomatic ties with Taipei. The number of states which recognized the ROC dropped to only twenty-one that year. Under difficult circumstances, the ROC began to adopt a more flexible and pragmatic approach to foreign relations in the 1980s.[2] It no longer refused to coexist with Peking in international organizations, and it increased its economic and commercial contacts with foreign countries. As a result of these efforts, the ROC has been able to improve its foreign relations standing and establish a number of new diplomatic ties. Yet, despite these improvements, Taiwan is still rather isolated internationally.

By contrast, the ROC has been very successful in economic development. For the last three decades, Taiwan has had one of the world's fastest growing economies, with a 9 percent average annual growth rate, and except for the two oil shock years, price levels have remained stable. This sustained economic growth has led to a rise in national income; average per capita income grew from US$160 in 1958, to US$6,000 in 1988, and US$8,000 in 1991. Meanwhile, Taiwan's economy has undergone noticeable structural changes as the ROC transformed from an agricultural into an industrial society. This can be seen most clearly from the decline in agriculture's contribution to national output from 35 percent to only 6 percent over the past thirty years, while industry's contribution has increased from 20 percent to 50 percent.

The ROC today is the world's fourteenth largest trading nation. In 1991, its foreign trade was worth more than US$139 billion, with exports of US$76 billion and imports of US$62 billion. The ROC has the world's largest foreign exchange reserves, valued at over US$80 billion. Its foreign direct investment in the Pacific basin is ranked third after Japan's and the United States', and its investment in the member states of the Association of Southeast Asian Nations (ASEAN) is exceeded only by that of Japan. It has also established an extensive trade network throughout the world. Without a doubt, Taiwan's growing economic strength and expanding international commercial activities have increased the ROC's capability to assist developing countries and raised its confidence in dealing with diplomatic problems.

---

[2]Fredrick F. Chien, "A View From Taipei," *Foreign Affairs* 70, no. 5 (Winter 1991/1992): 93-103.

Foreign Aid to Africa

The initiation of the ROC's foreign aid program was primarily stimulated by the 1960 U.N. General Assembly vote, when there was an increase in the number of countries favoring Peking's admission. Taipei recognized the need for a diplomatic strategy to counteract this development, and its first focus was on Africa. In 1960 alone, seventeen new states were admitted to the United Nations, sixteen of them from Africa. These new African states formed a powerful voting bloc in the U.N. and other international organizations. Consequently, in order to safeguard the ROC's U.N. seat, it was deemed necessary to establish diplomatic relations and develop cooperative working ties with these newly independent nations.

Considering foreign aid relations based on agricultural and technical assistance to be a proper and practical means of approaching African states, the ROC government launched its "Operation Vanguard" program in January 1961.[3] The program's declared objective was to assist the African recipients to develop their agriculture and attain self-sufficiency in food production, but the real purpose was to encourage these countries to extend diplomatic recognition to the ROC and support its claim to the Chinese seat in the United Nations. As the initiator of the program, Ambassador Yang Hsi-kun, has said: "Friendship between two countries, besides relying on diplomatic relations, must also be based on substantial cooperation so that those relations can progress."[4]

Operation Vanguard commenced in 1961, when a fifteen-man agricultural team was sent to Liberia. After that, the ROC rapidly increased its aid missions to Africa. By the end of 1971, the ROC had dispatched over one hundred missions, about one thousand agricultural and technical specialists in all, to twenty-four African countries (see table 9.1). The aid program originally concentrated on agricultural production; it was later extended to include fisheries, handicrafts, veterinary care, sugar refining, and highway building. A technical training program was also established in Taiwan, and this benefitted a total of 583 students and technicians from thirty-one African countries in the years 1960 through 1971.[5]

There are numerous accounts indicating that the ROC's aid program in Africa made a useful contribution to agricultural production and general economic development in the recipient countries, and the ROC agricultural

---

[3]Chiao Chiao Hsieh, *Strategy for Survival* (London: The Sherwood Press, 1985), chap. 5; Bih-jaw Lin, "The Republic of China and Africa," in *Foreign Policy of the Republic of China on Taiwan*, ed. Yu San Wang (New York: Praeger, 1990), 145-54.

[4]From Hai-tu Tsai, *International Agricultural Cooperation* (Taipei: Committee of International Technical Cooperation, 1992), 5.

[5]Hsieh, *Strategy for Survival*, 187.

Table 9.1
Distribution of ROC Technical Missions by Area (1959-91)

Area \ Year	'59	'60	'61	'62	'63	'64	'65	'66	'67	'68	'69	'70	'71	'72	'73	'74	'75	'76	'77	'78	'79	'80	'81	'82	'83	'84	'85	'86	'87	'88	'89	'90	'91
Africa			1	2	5	14	18	20	20	25	29	29	28	26	21	18	12	12	10	7	7	7	7	7	7	3	3	4	4	4	4	9	10
Central America											1	2	3	5	6	8	8	8	8	8	8	9	10	10	10	10	10	9	9	9	9	9	11
South America						1	1	2	2	2	2	5	5	3	2	3	3	4	4	5	6	7	6	6	6	6	4	4	4	3	3	3	3
Caribbean					1	1	1	1	1	1	1	1	1	2	3	3	3	3	2	2	2	2	2	3	4	5	6	6	6	6	7	8	9
Middle East								1	2	2	1	2	1	1	1	1	1	1	1	1	2	3	3	3	3	3	3	3	3	3	3	3	3
Asia & Pacific	1	1	1	1	1	1	1	2	2	2	3	3	2	3	4	4	4	2	2	4	5	7	6	6	7	7	8	8	8	8	9	9	8
Europe									2	2	2	1	2	1																			
Total	1	1	2	3	8	16	22	26	29	33	40	42	42	41	37	36	31	30	27	27	30	35	34	35	37	34	34	34	34	33	35	41	44

Source: Hai-tu Tsai, *International Agricultural Cooperation* (Taipei: Committee of International Technical Cooperation, 1992), 40.

missions earned praise from their host governments. More importantly, the aid program helped the ROC to maintain diplomatic relations with a large number of African countries and win their friendly support in the United Nations. In 1960, Taipei had official ties with only eight African countries, but this number rapidly increased to twenty-four by 1969. Moreover, most African aid recipients tended to vote in favor of the ROC in the United Nations.[6] Although there were other factors working in the ROC's favor during this period, such as continued U.S. support, the Cold War, and Peking's diplomatic blunders during the Cultural Revolution, the ROC's foreign aid program certainly played an important role.

Nevertheless, due to changes in the international environment and the shift in Washington's policy toward Peking, the ROC was eventually forced to withdraw from the U.N. in 1971. Since then, many countries, including African ones, have followed the U.N.'s lead and switched diplomatic recognition from Taipei to Peking. Once the foreign aid program in Africa had lost its utility value, the ROC cut back its agricultural missions and foreign aid to Africa declined. By 1975, Taipei's diplomatic partners in Africa had dwindled to eight, and there were only twelve agricultural missions stationed there.[7] The decline continued, and by 1979, the ROC had official ties with only five countries on the continent (Ivory Coast, Lesotho, Malawi, Swaziland, and South Africa), and had reduced its agricultural missions to seven.[8]

The ROC's first massive foreign aid program ended with this retreat from Africa. The ROC readjusted its political objectives in the wake of withdrawal from the U.N. and shifted its attention to Latin America. Basically, there were three reasons for the change. First, since Taipei's main objective during this period was to secure its relations with the United States, it was thought that aid to Latin America, which was perceived by Americans as their own backyard, might be better appreciated by Washington. Second, out of the twenty-seven countries that recognized the ROC, thirteen were in Latin America, so it was particularly important for Taipei to strengthen its bilateral ties and promote mutual interests in this region. Third, most of the Caribbean and Central American states were poor and underdeveloped, and would thus appreciate agricultural and technical assistance from the ROC.

The ROC's foreign aid to the region continued to grow through the 1970s. In 1975, fourteen agricultural and technical missions, composed of more than 130 Chinese specialists and technicians, were sent on a government-to-government basis to some twelve countries in the Caribbean and

---

[6]Ibid., 190-91.
[7]*The China Yearbook* (Taipei: China Publishing Co., 1976), 353.
[8]*The China Yearbook* (Taipei: China Publishing Co., 1980), 341.

Central and South America.[9] In 1978, although the scale of the ROC technical assistance program was reduced, it still had fifteen technical missions with 141 members in the region (see table 9.1). Nevertheless, the scale of economic aid to Latin America in the 1970s was not so massive as the aid offered to Africa in the 1960s.

Foreign Aid Policy Development

There were new developments in the ROC's foreign aid policy in the 1980s. The first notable change was that aid began to be more important to the ROC's diplomacy. In previous decades, the ROC had depended chiefly on the United States for international support, and foreign aid was generally considered a supplementary means of strengthening diplomatic ties. However, after the rupture of Taipei-Washington diplomatic relations in 1979, foreign aid became a major instrument in the ROC's pursuit of its foreign relations interests, and its scope was greatly expanded. Not only did foreign aid serve to consolidate existing official ties, but it was also broadly employed as a bargaining chip in the negotiation of new foreign relations and in expanding the ROC's participation in the international community.

This increase in the role of foreign aid stemmed from the combination of the ROC's weak diplomatic stance and strong economy. In this period, the ROC was accorded official recognition by less than two dozen states, and was excluded from nearly all the important international organizations. Its economy, in contrast, continued to grow. Expanding trade activities helped Taiwan to become a significant player in the international economy and establish economic links with most countries. This successful economic performance thus reinforced Taipei's interest in using its economic strength to reduce its diplomatic isolation.

Meanwhile, people on Taiwan were becoming more impatient with the ROC's international status. As the fourteenth largest trading nation in the world, the ROC, it was felt, deserved a greater role in the international arena. The government came under mounting pressure from the public to take more effective measures, including the use of foreign aid, to overcome Taiwan's diplomatic predicament.

The second notable development was the rising importance of cash grants or loan grants in foreign aid. In the past, due to a shortage of capital and limited economic resources, agricultural and technical assistance was all that the ROC could offer to Third World countries. Recently, however, the ROC has been able to contribute more to the economic development of other developing countries, and since 1980, loan grants have replaced technical assistance as the main component of Taipei's foreign aid program.

---

[9]*The China Yearbook* (1976), 364.

In 1988, the ROC government established the International Economic Cooperation and Development Fund (IECDF) with an appropriation of US$1.1 billion.[10] The stated goal of the fund is to assist the economic development of developing countries and promote bilateral economic cooperation, but its true purpose is to strengthen the ROC's political ties and expand foreign relations. The IECDF is allowed to (1) provide direct or indirect loans, (2) invest in development projects, and (3) finance technical assistance. Any developing country or country friendly to the ROC is eligible to apply for assistance from the fund, and projects financed by the fund are not required to purchase products from the ROC, or to give ROC products priority in procurement.

Other foreign aid funds besides the IECDF include a number of humanitarian, loan grant, and technical assistance programs administered by the Ministry of Foreign Affairs. Other government agencies are also involved in foreign aid programs, including the Ministry of Economic Affairs, the Ministry of Finance, the Council of Agriculture, the Committee of International Technical Cooperation, and the Export-Import Bank of the ROC.

The third new development was the extension of capital grants to international organizations. In the past, the ROC's foreign aid programs were chiefly directed at nation-states, in accordance with the country's attempts to maintain and increase its diplomatic ties. However, in the mid-1980s, Taipei, recognizing the importance of international organizations to its participation in the international community, adopted a more flexible approach and began seeking membership in these bodies. Capital grants were seen as a useful tool in pursuing this goal. The ROC's economic strength and its substantial input to the ADB's development fund were the main reasons why it was allowed to retain its membership in the ADB. Similarly, a donation of US$150 million helped the ROC become a full member of the Inter-American Development Bank in 1991.[11] The ROC's US$10 million contribution to the European Bank for Reconstruction and Development in September 1991 was also aimed at establishing ties with that organization.[12]

These developments have changed the picture of the ROC's economic aid programs and expanded the scale of their activities. An increasing amount of capital has flowed from the ROC to developing countries in recent years. The government has neither confirmed nor denied reports that it promised to provide low interest loans of US$10 million to Grenada and US$200 million to Liberia in 1989, US$100 million to Nicaragua in 1990, and US$20

---

[10]IECDF, *Regulations and Administrative Guidelines of the International Economic Cooperation and Development Fund* (Taipei: 1989).

[11]*Ching-chi jih-pao* (Economic Daily News) (Taipei), June 22, 1991, 2.

[12]Ibid., June 16, 1992, 2.

million to Guinea-Bissau and US$300 million to the Central African Republic in 1991, when the ROC established diplomatic relations with each of these countries.[13] It was also reported that many soft loans were granted to coincide with high-level official visits. During his trip to Johannesburg in January 1991, the ROC foreign minister, Fredrick Chien, agreed to provide a US$60 million low interest loan to South Africa.[14] Vice President Li Yuan-tzu distributed about US$90 million in loan offers and cash donations during his visits to Costa Rica, Nicaragua, and Honduras in August 1991.[15]

In the meantime, sums expended on humanitarian grants have also increased. Some of these were disinterested offers of international relief, but more were designed to serve foreign policy interests. After the Gulf War, the ROC gave US$20 million in humanitarian aid to Jordan, US$10 million to Kurdish refugees in Iraq, and US$2 million to Turkey. In 1992, the ROC shipped 100,000 tons of rice to Russia, gave US$5 million worth of medical supplies to Ukraine, and donated US$500,000 in aid to Belarus to help that country deal with the after-effects of Chernobyl.[16] The ROC also gave several million U.S. dollars in international relief donations to countries such as the Philippines, Malawi, Sudan, Peru, and Honduras in 1991.[17]

By mid-1992, eleven countries had been granted a total of US$138 million in loans by the IECDF (see table 9.2), while another ten received US$6.2 million in international technical assistance from the same source (see table 9.3). The majority of these countries had diplomatic relations with Taipei, but some, such as Ireland, the Philippines, and Thailand, did not have any official ties. In addition, the IECDF sponsored various technical training programs in Taiwan for developing countries. In 1989 and 1990, 686 people from 62 countries participated in these programs.

Foreign Aid versus Diplomatic Interests

Granting foreign aid has had a positive impact on the ROC's diplomatic status. More developing countries are showing interest in improving relations with Taipei, and since 1988, the ROC has successfully established a number of new diplomatic ties, including those with Grenada, Liberia, the Bahamas, Belize, Lesotho, Guinea-Bissau, Nicaragua, the Central African

---

[13]*Lien-ho pao* (United Daily News) (Taipei), October 5, 1989, 1; *Ch'ing-nien jih-pao* (Youth Daily News) (Taipei), April 28, 1991, 3; *Chung-kuo shih-pao* (China Times) (Taipei), July 14, 1991, 6; ibid., July 21, 1991, 3; and *Far Eastern Economic Review*, November 14, 1991, 34.

[14]*Tzu-yu shih-pao* (Liberty Times) (Taipei), January 23, 1991, 2.

[15]*Chung-kuo shih-pao*, August 30, 1991, 2, 3.

[16]*Free China Journal* 9, no. 11 (February 21, 1992): 1; ibid., no. 26 (April 17, 1992): 2; ibid., no. 28 (April 24, 1992): 1.

[17]Fredrick F. Chien, "New Orientations of the ROC's Foreign Policy in the 1990s," *Wen-t'i yü yen-chiu* (Issues & Studies) (Taipei) 30, no. 10 (October 10, 1991): 8.

Table 9.2
Loan Grants by the IECDF (1988-91)

State	Project	Amount (US$ million)
Costa Rica	Export processing zone	9.0
Panama	Export processing zone	7.8
Ireland	Industrial zone	20.0
Dominican Republic	Products processing zone	2.5
Bahamas	Fish breeding zone	5.0
Papua New Guinea	Community development plan	15.0
Saint Vincent	Domestic construction	8.0
Malawi	Transportation construction	27.0
Honduras	Highway maintenance	20.0
Philippines	Waterworks	20.1
Bahamas	Vegetable and fruit growing project	3.9
Total		138.3

Source: P. K. Chiang (vice minister of economic affairs), *Shen-ch'a "Kuo-chi ho-tso fa-chan chi-chin-hui she-chih t'iao-li" lieh-hsi pao-kao* (Report on the review of the proposed articles for the establishment of the International Cooperation and Development Fund) (Delivered at the first joint meeting of the committees of foreign affairs, economic affairs and budget, 89th session, Legislative Yuan, July 2, 1992) (Taipei: Secretariat of the Legislative Yuan, 1992), 19.

Table 9.3
International Technical Assistance Funded by the IECDF (1988-91)

State	Project	Amount (US$ 1,000)
Philippines	On-job training center at De La Salle University	300
United States	Transfer of milkfish breeding technology for USAID	1,530
Thailand	Tax reforms	250
Venezuela	Export processing zone	350
Guatemala	Export processing zone	940
Paraguay	Alloy iron project	170
Papua New Guinea	Small & medium-sized enterprises development	500
Costa Rica	Small & medium-sized enterprises development	1,500
Mexico	Feasibility studies on export processing zone	100
Bahamas	Spiral shell processing industry	579
Total		6,219

Source: Chiang, *Shen-ch'a "Kuo-chi ho-tso fa-chan chi-chin-hui she-chih t'iao-li" lieh-hsi pao-kao*, 21.

Republic, and Niger. As of 1992, the ROC had diplomatic ties with twenty-nine countries, and it also maintains more than eighty representative offices in fifty-two countries with which it has no official relations.[18] Of course, this improvement is attributable to many different factors, including the adoption of "flexible diplomacy," growing economic strength, and the increasing level of democratization in Taiwan, but foreign aid has certainly played an important part.

However, the extensive use of foreign aid has raised public concern and caused much controversy. The first main argument against it is that it is "dollar diplomacy" (i.e., funds for friends). If the new bilateral relations are based on aid alone, there will be no substantial links or common interests involved. Once a better price is offered from the other side of the Taiwan Strait, the ties may be broken again, making the effort futile.

Second, almost all of the ROC's new diplomatic partners are small, poor, and insignificant in international relations. They are geographically distant from Taiwan, and politically incapable of helping the ROC expand the scope of its international participation. They help boost the number of official ties, but only to an insignificant degree.

Third, the ROC spends a great deal of money on establishing and maintaining new foreign ties, but the countries with which it does have official relations generally do not interact closely with Taiwan. They constitute less than 5 percent of the ROC's total foreign trade, and except for a few countries like South Africa, people-to-people contacts are minimal. Most countries that do have close contacts with Taipei lack official ties. It is argued that it is unnecessary to spend so much for such a small return.

Fourth, the current policy does nothing to remove the main obstacle to the expansion of Taipei's foreign relations, that is, the attitude of Peking. The Chinese Communists may gradually change their stance, however, as growing trade and investment links with Taiwan and the inflow of information about Taiwan's development experience and way of life encourage liberalization in mainland China.

Some pro-foreign aid arguments have been put forward in response to these criticisms. Advocates of aid for diplomacy contend that nearly all industrialized states give foreign aid in exchange for diplomatic gains. This is what the United States does with its Western allies and the developing countries, and what Japan is doing in Southeast Asia. The ROC, while politically weak and diplomatically isolated, is thus fully justified in applying economic means to win friends.

It is further argued that although the ROC has expanded its foreign aid program, it is still modest in scale. According to official reports, the

---

[18]*Chung-hua min-kuo pa-shih-nien wai-chiao nien-chien* (1991 yearbook of the ROC's diplomacy) (Taipei: Ministry of Foreign Affairs, 1992), 860-79.

ROC only spends about US$35 million a year on foreign aid; that is a mere 0.02 percent of Taiwan's gross national product (GNP), which is below the government's own goal of 0.17 percent, and far less than the goal of 0.7 percent set by the United Nations.[19] It is also claimed that the IECDF is under-utilized. In the past three years, the fund has granted just US$140 million in soft loans to eleven countries, nowhere near its full allocation.

The number of Taipei's official ties is thought to be important to public opinion and the country's international status. Economic aid has already made a difference in this respect; it helped to raise the number of countries which recognize Taipei from twenty-two in 1988 to twenty-nine in 1992. If the number can be increased to forty or fifty in the near future, then the ROC's international position will be greatly enhanced. Although some countries with which the ROC has recently established diplomatic relations are small and poor, others are quite influential in their own regions, like Nicaragua, the Central African Republic, and Niger.

In addition to serving foreign policy interests, aid is also a way of repaying the international community for its role in Taiwan's economic success. As a former underdeveloped country and an aid recipient, the ROC is well aware of the many problems faced by the Third World, and it can play a useful role in supplying financial and technical assistance there.

The Foreign Aid System

Regardless of all the arguments for and against foreign aid, nearly everyone agrees that the government should open up the policymaking process and publicize its foreign aid decisions. At present, all information about foreign aid is kept from the public, and all decisions are made by just a few top government officials. The Legislative Yuan plays no role in deciding foreign aid programs, nor does it have any control over how much is spent on each one. The foreign aid budget is treated as a lump sum within the budget of the Ministry of Foreign Affairs (MOFA), and secrecy is maintained in the name of national security.

The need to establish a comprehensive and well-organized system to regulate foreign aid is widely accepted. The new system should be free of national security concerns and placed under legislative supervision. It should be a permanent system with long-term plans for the further development of foreign aid programs. The new system should recruit more aid specialists, regional experts, and scholars to participate in foreign aid administration.

Under the current system, foreign aid can be classified into three main types: humanitarian grants, loans, and international technical assistance (see table 9.4). These come out of three funds—the International Relief and

---

[19]*Lien-ho pao*, August 24, 1991, 2.

Table 9.4
The ROC's Foreign Aid Framework

Type of aid	Purpose	Agency in charge	Legislative status	Source
Humanitarian grant	Diplomatic	MOFA	None	MOFA budget
	General	MOFA (implemented by MOFA and Red Cross)	None	MOFA budget
Low-interest loan	Diplomatic	MOFA	None	MOFA budget
	Economic	MOFA (implemented by IECDF)	Proceeding	IECDF
International technical assistance	Diplomatic	MOFA (implemented by CITC)	None	MOFA budget
	Economic	MOFA (implemented by IECDF and CITC)	Proceeding	IECDF

Source: Chiang, *Shen-ch'a "Kuo-chi ho-tso fa-chan chi-chin-hui she-chih t'iao-li" lieh-hsi pao-kao*, 26.

Humanitarian Fund, the International Affairs and Activities Fund, and the International Technical Cooperation Fund—under the direct control of the MOFA.[20] All three funds are appropriated from the government budget. According to official reports, an estimated US$35 million is allocated to the MOFA each year for foreign aid.

Foreign aid grants can also be classified into those given for diplomatic reasons and those for economic and general purposes. Grants given for diplomatic purposes are controlled by the MOFA. It has the right to propose cases, review applications, and, in consultation with other related agencies, decide on aid allocation. For example, when a request for a loan is received from a friendly state, the MOFA will first review the case and submit it to the Executive Yuan for approval. Once consent is given, the MOFA will inform the Ministry of Finance (MOF) and authorize the state-owned banks, such as the Export-Import Bank of the ROC or the Inter-

---

[20]*Chung-yang jih-pao* (Central Daily News) (Taipei), August 24, 1980, 2.

national Commercial Bank of China, to make loans to the applicant states. Since most of these loans are low interest, the MOFA makes up the difference to the lending bank out of the International Affairs and Activities Fund. If the recipient state defaults on its payments, the MOFA is responsible to the lending bank.[21]

Several agencies are involved in grants for economic and general purposes. The MOFA is responsible for international relief assistance, but the Ministry of Economic Affairs (MOEA) is in charge of administering the IECDF. The political vice minister of economic affairs runs the fund's day-to-day activities, and the minister of economic affairs chairs its seven-member management council, the other members being the ministers of foreign affairs, finance, and communications, the governor of the Central Bank of China, the chairman of the Council for Economic Planning and Development, and the secretary-general of the Executive Yuan. The Committee of International Technical Cooperation (CITC), a semiautonomous government agency, is the main agency in charge of implementing technical assistance programs.[22] Its governing board includes representatives from the MOFA, the MOEA, the Council of Agriculture (COA), and the Taiwan Provincial Government. Since technical assistance usually involves agricultural projects and is closely related to diplomatic interests, the MOFA and the COA play important roles in the development of the CITC's policies and programs.

The distinction between diplomatic and economic purposes in grants is generally determined by the intentions of the recipient and the nature of the aid project. However, the MOFA is empowered to classify all grants and to decide which type of aid to provide. In fact, the MOFA is involved in all aid programs, even those which are purely economic in nature. As indicated above, the minister of foreign affairs is a leading member of both the IECDF management council and the board of the CITC, and the MOFA has the final say on all aid decisions. It is hardly surprising, therefore, that most loans and technical assistance offered by these two organizations go to countries that have diplomatic relations with Taipei.

The predominant role of the MOFA in granting foreign aid has often been the cause of disputes with the MOEA and the MOF. Officials in these ministries complain that they are treated as subordinate agencies in matters of foreign aid. The MOFA rarely consults other ministries before making a decision, and then requires them to cooperate in the name of national interest. Although the IECDF was initiated by the MOEA, it has now become a political tool of the MOFA. Some have blamed the IECDF's lack of ef-

---

[21]Fu P. Chao, "The MOFA Spreads Money," *Shang-yeh chou-k'an* (Business Weekly) (Taipei), no. 241 (July 5, 1992): 19-25.

[22]Tsai, *International Agricultural Cooperation*, 9.

ficiency on excessive political interference and too little concern about economic factors.

Similar charges have been laid against the MOFA by the state-owned banks which are required to make the foreign aid loans. Given the fact that many of these loans are politically risky and unprofitable, the banks show little interest in undertaking the business. Even though all the loans are guaranteed by the MOFA and its counterpart in the recipient state, the lending banks are afraid that they would have to get involved in a lengthy and complicated law suit if a country did default.

Recently, the MOEA attempted to have the IECDF reorganized as a corporate body rather than a government agency, in an effort to improve its management, reduce recruitment restrictions, and increase its autonomy.[23] However, the ministry was forced to withdraw its reorganization bill from the Legislative Yuan, and it was replaced by a similar bill introduced by the MOFA. The new bill proposes the creation of a new International Cooperation and Development Fund to take the place of the IECDF, and for all foreign aid programs to be put under the administration of the MOFA. A new Department of Economic and Trade Affairs has already been established within the MOFA, which it is assumed will take over all future foreign aid programs.

According to the proposed legislation, the new fund will incorporate all foreign aid funds currently administered by the MOFA and the IECDF. It will be organized as a corporate body subject to legislative review. The fund will be financed from the government budget, fund profits, and other revenues. MOFA officials claim that the new fund will permit public participation in foreign aid decisions and enable Taiwan to increase its aid to needy nations. The fund's corporate nature will allow it to recruit more professionals and specialists.

Conclusion

Basically, there is a policy consensus both inside and outside the government that the ROC, as a country with abundant capital, a booming export trade, and a wealth of experience in economic development, should provide foreign aid to developing countries. Also, almost everyone agrees that there is nothing wrong with using foreign aid to win friends and influence people. Where disagreements do arise, however, is on the issues of how much the ROC should spend on foreign aid programs, how it should increase public

---

[23]The ROC Legislative Yuan, Committee Hearings, "Review of the Proposed Articles for the Establishment of the International Cooperation and Development Fund," *Li-fa yüan kung-pao ch'u-kao* (Preliminary reports of legislative proceedings), July 2, July 4, and July 11, 1992 (Taipei: Secretariat of the Legislative Yuan, 1992).

control over foreign aid spending, and whether it is appropriate to emphasize diplomatic interests in foreign aid.

The amount of money spent on foreign aid is shrouded in secrecy, and few people take seriously what government officials say about the cost of foreign aid programs. The announced figures often lack supporting data and are contradicted by media reports. People, including members of the Legislative Yuan, believe that the MOFA can always find some way to procure funds for diplomatic purposes. A broad gray area is seen to exist in the foreign aid process in which the MOFA can easily maneuver.

The increasing power of the MOFA in foreign aid programs worries some people. Although the recently proposed legislation seems to be quite open as to the features of the new fund and attempts to systematize foreign aid programs, many people are concerned because it puts the MOFA in firm control of foreign aid. The legislature can only decide the total foreign aid budget, it has no say in how the money is distributed. The governing board of the new fund will consist of eleven to fifteen members, of whom ten will be government officials.

Moreover, there is some concern that the emphasis on diplomatic interests might harm the development of foreign aid programs. This will distort the nation's image and make aid efforts unproductive. It will also encourage recipient states to ask for more aid from Taipei without bothering to promote mutually beneficial relations. Short-term diplomatic gains might thus be obtained at the expense of the nation's long-term interests.

Although the government has made some efforts to respond to demands for an improvement in foreign aid management, as shown by the newly proposed legislation, these initiatives have not been sufficient to reduce confusion and increase public confidence. Currently, the biggest challenge comes from the imbalance between diplomatic interests and foreign aid. No easy solution will be found on the issue as long as the ROC remains in its present diplomatic predicament. For the time being, the ROC, as a democratic country, should have a more open foreign aid policymaking process and increased public participation in foreign aid activities.

Part Four

Cross-Strait Relations:
Current Developments and Prospects

CHAPTER 10

Taipei-Peking Relations: The Sovereignty Issue

An-chia Wu

President Lee Teng-hui's proclamation of April 30, 1991 terminating the Period of Mobilization for the Suppression of Communist Rebellion marked a turning point in relations between the two sides of the Taiwan Strait. It was a, clear indication that the government of the Republic of China (ROC) was determined to end the hostility between Taiwan and mainland China and it heralded new developments in cross-Strait relations. The government subsequently abrogated both the Temporary Provisions of the Constitution, which had been in force while the country was technically in a state of civil war, and the Statute for the Punishment of Rebellion.

The ROC government had already made a number of institutional changes to cope with the rapid development of exchanges with mainland China. In October 1990, the National Unification Council (NUC), a presidential task force, was set up, and this was followed in January 1991 by the establishment of the cabinet-level Mainland Affairs Council (MAC), charged with formulating, coordinating, and implementing the government's mainland policy. Routine problems arising from Taiwan-mainland exchanges are handled by the semiofficial Straits Exchange Foundation (SEF), supervised by the MAC, which was set up in February 1991.

Also in February 1991, the NUC adopted the *Guidelines for National Unification*, which after being approved by the president and the Executive Yuan, formed the basis for developing relations across the Taiwan Strait. The "Statute Governing Relations Between the People of Taiwan and Mainland Areas" has established a legal basis for a wide range of contacts between Taiwan and mainland China, including direct trade and communications.

In response to Taipei's new policy initiative and the corresponding legal and institutional changes, Peking (Beijing) consolidated Party and government agencies in charge of Taiwan affairs and established the Association for Relations Across the Taiwan Strait (ARATS) as a counterpart to Taipei's SEF. Since its establishment, the SEF has had frequent contacts with mainland Chinese agencies and conducted negotiations on a number of issues, all of which are rooted in the fundamental question of political sovereignty.

188   An-chia Wu

The Major Obstacle: The Sovereignty Issue

Although both sides maintain that there is only one China, they obviously interpret the term "one China" differently. To Peking, the term refers to the People's Republic of China (PRC) with its capital in Peking. Taiwan is only a province, or possibly a "special administrative region," of China which may be permitted to participate in the international community as an economic and cultural entity but should not engage in international political activities.

In addition to consistently denying Taiwan a political status in the international community, Peking has also refused to renounce the use of force against Taiwan as a solution to the unification issue.[1] In justification of this, Peking says that an undertaking not to use force against Taiwan would limit its options in the event of foreign intervention in the China question. They also claim that reserving the right to use force has a deterrent effect on advocates of Taiwan independence and that it is only the threat of force that will induce the Kuomintang (KMT) to agree to negotiations on reunification.

However, these arguments are not convincing to people in Taiwan. They do not feel they are in any imminent danger from outside forces, nor do they believe that independence advocates would be able to muster sufficient political support to attain their goal. In these circumstances, the threat of force is only delaying the process of China's unification, because neither the people of Taiwan nor the ROC government is willing to yield to Peking's military pressure.

The ROC government's attitude on the unification issue is that "one China" refers to the Republic of China which was founded in 1912. The ROC admits the existence of two political entities (one in Peking, one in Taipei) within this "one China," and holds that issues concerning China's unification should be resolved through government-to-government talks. Peking has totally rejected this proposal; it refuses to recognize Taipei as an independent political entity, fearing that would lead to "dual recognition" and the permanent division of China.[2]

Peking's answer to the China issue is still the "one country, two systems" formula under which Taipei would become a semiautonomous "special ad-

---

[1]Information Bureau of the Taiwan Affairs Office under the State Council, *Liang-an kuan-hsi yü ho-p'ing t'ung-i—I-chiu-chiu-i nien chung-yao t'an-hua ho wen-chang hsüan-pien* (Cross-Strait relations and peaceful unification—Selection of important talks and articles made in 1991) (N.p.: Hua-i ch'u-pan-she, January 1991), 58, 127, 137. This book is printed in traditional Chinese characters and so obviously meant for a Taiwan readership. Also see T'ang Shu-pei's speech in Los Angeles, *People's Daily* (Overseas edition), May 19, 1992, 5.

[2]"On Taiwan's *Guidelines for National Unification*," *People's Daily* (Overseas edition), March 18, 1991, 1.

ministrative region," in effect a local government. Peking's leaders have proposed party-to-party talks within this framework between the Chinese Communist Party (CCP) and the KMT. From the ROC's point of view, however, this proposal is totally unrealistic. The CCP, which operates a one-party dictatorship, may consider itself the legal representative of the mainland Chinese people, but the KMT is only one of many political parties in Taiwan. In a society like Taiwan, such a proposal by the ruling party would justifiably provoke the wrath of the opposition and lead to unrest. In this situation of stalemate, Peking is seeking to increase its influence in Taiwan through the establishment of direct postal, transportation, and trade links between the two sides. It has also urged Taipei to allow more mainlanders to visit Taiwan.[3]

Peking's regulations governing exchanges with Taiwan have been framed with the intention of emphasizing Taipei's status as a local government. For example, mainland departments in charge of foreign affairs are not allowed to receive visitors from Taiwan or to sign agreements with them. If groups from Taiwan use any title which might imply that the ROC government is the central government of China, they will not be accorded an official reception by any government department or unit (although the persons in charge of these delegations may be received if necessary). Letters and documents mailed from Taiwan with the title "Republic of China" on them are handled in different ways: those containing material considered to be provocative propaganda are returned to sender, while senders of ordinary mail are advised to use the title "Taiwan" or "China Taiwan" in their address. In addressing ROC parliamentarians or government officials, mainland agencies are instructed not to use their official titles.[4] Leaders in Taipei have been looking for a more pragmatic and rational response from the mainland—especially for Peking to renounce the use of force as a solution to the unification issue and to give Taiwan more scope to operate in the international community.

The different positions adopted by the two sides on the question of Taipei's status have been the source of a lot of disputes that have arisen in the course of exchanges. One example is the case of a Taiwan fishing boat which was boarded by crewmen from two mainland fishing vessels in the Strait thirty miles off the coast of Taiwan. The mainlanders allegedly took money and valuables from the Taiwan vessel as "reparation" for alleged damage done to their nets by the Taiwan boat. Since the alleged crime occurred on an ROC vessel, Taipei claimed jurisdiction over the case under Article 3 of the ROC Criminal Code. Regardless of this, the mainland authorities demanded the right to send officials to Taiwan to negotiate the

---

[3] *People's Daily*, June 8, 1991, 1.

[4] *Chung-kung nei-pu ts'an-k'ao tzu-liao* (Internal reference materials of the Chinese Communist Party).

matter. That is, they intended to interfere in judicial proceedings within the ROC's jurisdiction and force Taiwan to accept their conditions regarding a case of piracy. When their demand was rejected, they asked that the deportation of the mainland fishermen be delayed until mainland Red Cross officials and reporters had been given an opportunity to interview them. The ROC government agreed in principle, but disagreed over the specific number of people that could be sent to Taiwan.

In another example, during November 1991 talks on combating crime at sea between the SEF and the State Council's Taiwan Affairs Office (TAO) in Peking, the TAO refused to authenticate any documents submitted to them by agents of the ROC government on the ground that the submission of such documents was a deliberate attempt by Taipei to create a government-to-government relationship which would imply the existence of two Chinese governments.

Once again, in March 1992, when the SEF had its first meeting with ARATS to discuss the problems of document verification and an indirect registered mail service, the latter insisted that the terms "the principle of one China" and "China's internal affairs" should be included in all agreements to be signed between the two sides. As Peking obviously uses "one China" to refer to the PRC, such proposals were of course unacceptable to Taipei. As a result, the talks broke down. Two months later, ARATS wrote a letter to the SEF demanding that the press certificates issued by the ROC's Government Information Office to eighteen visiting mainland journalists be "amended" because they carried the title and map of the "Republic of China."

In a final example of Peking's attitude on this issue, in May 1992 President Yang Shang-k'un (Yang Shangkun) categorically rejected a proposal advanced a few weeks earlier by Cheyne Chiu, ROC presidential spokesman and NUC executive secretary, that Taiwan and mainland China sign a non-aggression pact modeled after the 1972 treaty between East and West Germany.[5] Yang's argument was that signing such a pact would imply recognition of the existence of two Chinese governments. He insisted that government-to-government negotiations between the two sides are "absolutely impermissible."

The Link Between Economics and Politics

Official statistics on economic exchanges between Taiwan and the mainland reveal increasingly strong ties between the two sides. The total value of trade via Hong Kong rose from US$5.793 billion in 1991 to US$7.406 billion in 1992, an increase of 27.86 percent (see table 10.1). Up to the end

---

[5]*Wen Wei Po* (Hong Kong), May 31, 1992, 2.

Table 10.1
Indirect Trade Between Taiwan and the Mainland via Hong Kong

Unit: US$ million

Year	Total Volume	Taiwan to Mainland			Mainland to Taiwan		
		Volume	Growth Rate	Dependence Ratio	Volume	Growth Rate	Dependence Ratio
1979	77.76	21.47	—	0.14	56.29	—	0.41
1980	311.18	234.97	994.41	1.17	76.21	35.39	0.42
1981	459.3	384.15	63.49	1.74	75.18	-1.35	0.34
1982	278.47	194.45	-49.38	1.01	84.02	11.76	0.38
1983	247.69	157.84	-18.83	0.74	89.85	6.94	0.40
1984	553.20	425.45	169.55	1.55	127.75	42.18	0.49
1985	1,102.73	986.83	131.95	2.34	115.90	-9.28	0.42
1986	955.55	811.33	-17.78	1.8	144.22	24.43	0.46
1987	1,515.47	1,226.53	51.18	2.84	288.94	100.35	0.73
1988	2,720.91	2,242.22	82.81	4.06	478.69	65,67	1.01
1989	3,483.39	2,896.49	29.18	4.09	586.90	22.61	1.12
1990	4,043.62	3,278.26	13.18	6.14	765.36	30.41	1.23
1991	5,793.11	4,667.15	42.36	7.32	1,125.95	47.11	1.57
1992	7,406.90	6,287.93	34.73	7.80	1,118.97	-0.62	1.32

Source: Kao K'ung-lien, *Liang-an ching-mao hsien-k'uang yü chan-wang* (Trade and economic exchanges across the Taiwan Strait: Current situation and prospects) (Taipei: Mainland Affairs Council, March 1993), 49. The figures are based on statistics issued by the Hong Kong government and the mainland Chinese customs authorities.

of February 1992, the ROC government had approved 2,783 mainland investment projects worth a total of US$1.7 billion.[6] Indirect trade and investment is expected to increase in the foreseeable future, as mainland China prepares to open its economy still wider to the outside world. In response to this development, the ROC government has relaxed the ban on investment in mainland China's service sector. The first service businesses permitted to invest there will be wholesalers, retailers, restaurant chains, law firms, newspapers, and movie companies.[7]

The nature of Taiwan investment in the mainland and the behavior of investors has changed notably in the past few years. Whereas in the past, Taiwanese tended to make small-scale, short-term investments in labor-intensive processing industries, mostly in the provinces of Fukien (Fujian) or

---

[6]*Lien-ho pao* (United Daily News) (Taipei), May 18, 1992, 3.
[7]*China News* (Taipei), June 13, 1992, 1.

Kwangtung (Guangdong), they are now committing larger amounts of capital for periods as long as fifty or even seventy years in capital- or technology-intensive industries or the production of raw materials. Geographically, they are looking farther afield, to Shanghai, Peking, the northeast, or even the inland provinces. More and more investments are being made by consortia rather than on an individual basis. Instead of providing only capital and production equipment, investors are providing raw materials and spare parts, as well as their own management personnel, and using well-established international sales networks. Some investors are even including periphery industries and satellite plants in their investment projects. In the past, Taiwan investors were attracted by the mainland's cheap labor, land, and raw materials; now the chief motivation is the prospect of access to the vast mainland Chinese market. When economic exchanges were first opened with the mainland, Taiwan businessmen purchased goods there to fill overseas orders. Later, they began processing products on the mainland and selling them via Hong Kong. Recently, products processed on the mainland have been sent to Taiwan via Hong Kong for further processing before being dispatched to overseas markets.[8]

Taiwan's trade dependence on the mainland rose from 0.74 percent in 1983 to 7.80 percent in 1992 (see table 10.1). The trade relationship between Taiwan and the mainland is an asymmetrical one which makes Taiwan both sensitive and, in the longer run, vulnerable to policy changes in Peking.[9] For example, Taiwan's economic development would be affected if mainland China were to close its market to Taiwan. Generally speaking, the higher the trade dependence of country A on country B, the more likely it is that any sanctions imposed by B on A will be successful. According to the findings of Hufbauer, Schott, and Elliott, in cases where sanctions have been successful, the sanctioner "accounts, on average, for over a quarter of the target's total trade." Any interruption of that trade will force the target country to change its policies or risk greater repercussions.[10] For these reasons, the sharp increase in trade and investment with the mainland has

---

[8]Lu Wei, "The New Trend of Economic Exchanges Across the Strait," *Chiao-liu* (Exchange) (Taipei), March 1992, no. 2:60-61.

[9]See Robert O. Keohane and Joseph S. Nye, *Power and Interdependence* (Boston: Little, Brown, 1989), 13. According to Keohane and Nye,

> Sensitivity means liability to costly effects imposed from outside before policies are altered to try to change the situation. Vulnerability can be defined as an actor's liability to suffer costs imposed by external events even after policies have been altered. Since it is usually difficult to change policies quickly, the immediate effects of external changes generally reflect sensitivity dependence. Vulnerability dependence can be measured only by the costliness of making effective adjustments to a changed environment over a period of time.

[10]Gary Clyde Hufbauer, Jeffrey J. Schott, Kimberly Ann Elliott, *Economic Sanctions Reconsidered: History and Current Policy*, 2nd ed. (Washington, D.C.: Institute for International Economics, 1990), 64.

been an issue of great concern to the ROC government. There are, however, those who maintain that trade interdependence is neither a necessary nor a sufficient condition for political influence, because the relationship between asymmetrical interdependence and political power is better represented by bargaining than by threat.[11] No matter which theory stands the test, it is interesting to note that the Japanese government has also been cautious about possible dependence on the mainland China market. It has set a ceiling on Japan's trade with mainland China of 10 percent of Japan's total foreign trade, and individual companies are not allowed to export more than one-third of their products to the mainland. In contrast, some Taiwan firms send up to 70 percent of their products to the mainland.[12]

It cannot be denied that there is a close link between economics and politics. At a seminar held in Peking in May 1992, Chao Yao-tung, a former ROC minister of economic affairs, proposed that the two sides of the Taiwan Strait should deal with political and economic matters separately, as this would enable them to reach a consensus through further economic cooperation.[13] The mainland news media, however, completely ignored Chao's suggestion.

Students of political economy would argue that it is impossible to separate politics from economics. If there were no relationship in the first place, there would be no need for scholars to demand a separation. Just as economic factors influence politics, so political factors influence economics. According to Joan Edelman Spero, there are three ways in which political factors affect economic outcomes: (1) the political system shapes the economic system; (2) political concerns often shape economic policy; and (3) international economic relations are themselves political relations.[14] This inseparability is particularly obvious in Peking's policy toward Taiwan. Documents circulated within the CCP indicate that Peking's efforts to intensify trade ties with Taiwan have a twofold purpose: to curb separatist tendencies in Taiwan and to force the ROC government to the negotiating table by creating conditions in which Taiwan businessmen, heavily dependent on the mainland market, will pressure their government to make political concessions.[15] As Yang Shang-k'un has said,

---

[11]R. Harrison Wagner, "Economic Interdependence, Bargaining Power, and Political Influence," *International Organization* 42, no. 3 (Summer 1988): 465.

[12]The author's interview with Liu T'ai-ying, president of the Taiwan Economic Research Institute.

[13]Chao Yao-tung, "The Experience of Taiwan's Economic Development and Relations between the Two Sides of the Taiwan Strait" (Keynote speech delivered at the symposium, Economic Relations between the Two Sides of the Taiwan Strait in Retrospect and the Prospects for Future Cooperation, Peking, May 16, 1992), 14. The seminar was attended by scholars and business representatives from both sides of the Taiwan Strait. Chao is currently an advisor to the Chung-Hua Institution for Economic Research and a senior advisor to the ROC government.

[14]Joan Edelman Spero, *The Politics of International Economic Relations* (New York: St. Martin's Press, 1990), 4.

[15]Documents circulated within the Chinese Communist Party.

> Our economic work toward Taiwan should be handled in line with the strategy of the peaceful unification of our motherland. Developing mutual economic relations and promoting linkages between the two sides are the forceful means of curbing separatist tendencies in Taiwan and realizing [China's] peaceful unification. While economic laws are to be observed, economic work toward Taiwan should serve the political task of realizing peaceful unification.[16]

Policy disputes within the CCP provide further evidence that Peking cannot keep politics out of economic affairs. The reformist faction in the Party maintains that the regime's best safeguard is to promote economic growth so as to achieve a significant rise in living standards. The conservatives argue, however, that the top priority is to strengthen ideological indoctrination in order to prevent "peaceful evolution." This debate is not only hindering economic reform, it is also making it impossible for the CCP to deal with economic and political questions separately. One can anticipate the kinds of obstacles the conservatives would put in the way of Taiwan investors were they to gain power in mainland China. Recently, the authorities obstructed the formation of a Taiwan businessmen's association in Shanghai, as they feared it would be used to carry out infiltration activities.[17]

Cultural Exchanges

In November 1991, President Lee Teng-hui said that cultural exchanges should be given top priority in future relations with the mainland. So far, contacts have included academic, sports, and religious exchanges, the publication of mainland Chinese literature in Taiwan, and TV and press coverage. Academic exchanges have been particularly frequent. Scholars from the two sides take part in international conferences overseas, Taiwan scholars attend international or bilateral conferences on the mainland and mainland scholars attend conferences in Taiwan, and prominent mainland scholars visit Taiwan at the invitation of private foundations. Cultural exchanges have become more frequent now that Taipei no longer regards Peking as a rebel regime and has revised its sedition laws. Members of the CCP are permitted to visit Taiwan by invitation, as long as they do not engage in subversive activities. In one prominent example, six members of a group of seven mainland scientists who visited in June 1992 were members of the CCP, and some were even delegates to the National People's Congress or members of the Chinese People's Political Consultative Conference.

Cultural exchanges have become increasingly frequent. In 1989, there

---

[16]Yang Shang-k'un, "Speech at the National Conference on Taiwan Work" (December 6, 1990), in *Chung-kung tui T'ai cheng-ts'e tzu-liao hsüan-chi (1949-1991)* (Mainland China's policy toward Taiwan: Selected documents, 1949-91), 2 vols., ed. Kuo Li-min (Taipei: Yung-yeh ch'u-pan-she, 1992), 1143.

[17]Internal reference materials circulated within the Chinese Communist Party.

were 70 visits in both directions, involving a total of approximately 260 individuals. In 1990, the numbers increased to about 100 visits and 500 individuals, and in 1991 to 130 visits and 900 individuals. The content of exchanges has also expanded. Whereas they were originally limited to stage performances, they now include visits and lectures by experts in the fields of scholarship, literature, music, dance, and the mass media.

There is now a growing trend toward two-way exchanges. According to statistics issued by the mainland Chinese authorities, as of November 1991, only eighteen mainlanders had visited Taiwan under eighteen cultural exchange programs, whereas exchanges in the other direction totaled 110 programs involving over 800 individuals. According to statistics compiled by the SEF in Taiwan, however, approximately one hundred mainland people visited Taiwan during this period under fifty exchange programs.

The level of institutional involvement in cultural exchanges has also risen in recent years, with more high-level officials in academic institutions visiting on either side. In May 1992, for example, Wu Ta-you, president of the Academia Sinica, led a delegation to the mainland. However, the kinds of individuals participating in cultural exchanges have tended to differ on the two sides. Whereas the ROC authorities have restricted invitations to mainland scholars or artists who are particularly outstanding in their field, the cream of the cultural and academic community in Taiwan has until recently been prevented from going to the mainland, either by government restrictions or personal reluctance. This has meant that the mainland visitors have been able to exert an influence on people in Taiwan quite out of proportion to their numbers.[18]

Cultural exchanges have a greater impact on people than any other kinds of exchanges. Although this impact cannot be evaluated quantitatively, it is possible to draw some conclusions. Cultural exchanges have enhanced understanding between the two sides of the Strait, although they still differ in many respects, and both sides are aware that this understanding is a prerequisite for negotiations leading to China's unification.

Cultural exchanges across the Taiwan Strait have, nevertheless, caused some vexing problems for Taiwan. The most obvious negative impact is that people have relaxed their vigilance against the threat posed by the CCP regime which in essence is still hostile to Taiwan. The introduction of Communist ideology into Taiwan in the form of publications exchanges is also noteworthy. There is also fear in the entertainment business, for example, that Taiwan will be swamped by mainland stage shows, TV programs, and films, leaving little room for homegrown talent. Furthermore, the ROC

---

[18]*Liang-an wen-hua chiao-liu hsien-k'uang chien-chieh* (A brief introduction to cross-Strait cultural exchanges) (Taipei: The Straits Exchange Foundation, August 1991), 6-58.

government is concerned that mainland programs and performances might carry some political content.

Peking has imposed strict political controls on mainland China's cultural exchanges with Taiwan, and exchanges at all levels are overseen by the TAO.[19] For example, while publications exchanges are handled by the State Press and Publications Administration, and literature and arts exchanges by the Ministry of Culture, all these departments must brief the TAO on exchange activities. All invitations to participate in local-level activities have to be issued by the corresponding branch of the TAO.[20] A strict watch is kept on all mainlanders travelling overseas, whether to Taiwan or foreign countries. Their passports and other documents are held by accompanying foreign affairs personnel and delegates attending international conferences usually meet each night to discuss questions they have been confronted with.

It is obvious that Peking is using cultural exchanges with Taiwan to achieve political ends by spreading propaganda about "one country, two systems," the reform and opening-up policy, and peaceful unification. Meanwhile, the regime is conducting a publicity campaign to emphasize the achievements made by the mainland so as to win the support of people in Taiwan.[21] To this end, exchanges on the mainland side are deliberately concentrated in the fields of scientific research and traditional Chinese medicine, because these are areas in which mainland China has been relatively successful. Peking's strategy is summarized in the ·following statement from a CCP document:

> In relations between the two sides of the Strait, there is both tension and a kind of rapprochement. Struggles exist though exchanges have increased, and there are still obstacles to a closer relationship. . . . We should not let up on our work toward Taiwan just because it is a long-term job. . . . The longer we put off the Taiwan issue, the more complicated it will become and the more difficult it will be to solve. Therefore, we should do a solid job in a spirit of "racing against time."[22]

By using cultural exchanges to serve political ends, the CCP regime has obstructed any attempt to question the superiority of socialism and Communist rule. For example, a paper written by a Hong Kong scholar, Huang Yü-min, was rejected by the symposium, "Sun Yat-sen's Ideology and China's Modernization," which was held in Peking in June 1992 under joint Taiwan-mainland sponsorship, because it claimed that there are disputes within the CCP over the question whether or not it would be better for mainland China

---

[19]Documents circulated within the Chinese Communist Party.
[20]Ibid.
[21]Ibid.
[22]Ibid.

to base its current program of accelerated economic growth on Sun Yat-sen's principle of "people's livelihood" rather than on capitalist principles. At the meeting, scholars were prohibited from using the title "Republic of China" in discussions of post-1949 history. Although cultural exchanges across the Strait have been frequent, the CCP regime has censored information about progress in Taiwan and prevented the mainland Chinese people from achieving a clear understanding of the situation there. In contrast, Taiwan has given full coverage both to the situation on the mainland and to mainland visitors in Taiwan. Cultural exchanges conducted under these conditions have provided mainland China with more opportunities to exert its influence in Taiwan.

Solutions

For the time being, disputes between the two sides of the Taiwan Strait over the question of sovereignty will continue to be the major obstacle in their mutual relations. However, since both sides agree on the common goal of reunification, there are a number of approaches that could be adopted to promote the smooth development of contacts between them. The first of these is to develop mutual relations within the framework of "one China, two political entities." This would be a workable formula for the transitional period (after unification, of course, there would be only one "political entity") as it recognizes the political and historical realities on the two sides. Since 1949, the ROC government has controlled Taiwan, Penghu (the Pescadores), Kinmen (Quemoy), and Matsu, while the PRC has ruled the rest of China, and neither side has made any territorial gains at the expense of the other. Both sides behave as political entities and have participated as such in various international organizations and activities. Such a framework would dispense with disputes over which is the "central government" and which the "local government," or whether there are "two Chinas," or "one China, one Taiwan." This framework would have the important advantage of enabling Taipei to have government-to-government contacts with Peking.[23]

Another useful approach would be to apply the "divided nations" model to China. Up to now, the ROC government has refrained from using the terms "two Chinas" or "one China, two governments" in order to avoid provoking Peking. Instead, it has opted for "creative ambiguity" and used the term "two political entities." Peking, though, still insists on "one country, two systems," under which Taipei would be relegated to the status of a regional authority. This is a deliberate refusal on Peking's part to acknowledge the fact that the Republic of China has existed since 1912 and

---

[23]An-chia Wu, "The ROC's Mainland Policy in the 1990s," *Issues & Studies* 27, no. 9 (September 1991): 9.

that it is still recognized by twenty-nine countries. Furthermore, the current state of the mainland's political, social, and economic development gives the ROC no reason whatsoever to abandon its claim to be the legitimate government of the whole of China.

China has many important characteristics in common with other divided nations, such as Korea and pre-unification Germany. These include differences between the two entities in terms of political and economic systems and levels of development, intense competition in the international community, the lack of a consensus as to whether unification should be carried out peacefully, and a strong desire on both sides to realize unification through exchanges. Since unification is a long-term goal, it would be useful if the two sides would recognize the reality of division. Only when they do this will it be possible for them to take concrete steps toward unification.

It would also be constructive if the two sides would seek to create an atmosphere of mutual trust before proceeding to discuss political issues. Without trust, peaceful unification will be very difficult. Peking has set up CCP branches in enterprises in which Taiwan businessmen have invested, and it criticizes Taipei's "pragmatic diplomacy" as an attempt to create "two Chinas." On the grounds that there is still a danger that Taiwan will declare independence, Peking refuses to renounce the option of using force to reunify China. This continued military threat, as well as the CCP's determination to maintain one-party rule on the mainland, has been the major cause of the lack of trust in Peking among the Taiwan public.

Finally, the two sides should try to keep political issues, including the possibility of official visits, an armistice agreement, and unification in general, separate from nonpolitical exchanges, such as the need for joint action to combat crime at sea, and the possibility of a trade and investment guarantee pact and the establishment of direct transportation links. Politically sensitive issues should be shelved for the time being, and the two sides, through the SEF and ARATS, should work out solutions to practical problems.

In short, the two sides should try to solve their disputes in a pragmatic way and not engage in wishful thinking. Only when mutual understanding and trust are built up through expanded exchanges will it be possible to bring about the peaceful unification of China in a way that will ensure the country's sustained political stability and prosperity.

CHAPTER 11

The Future of
Taiwan-Mainland Relations

Maria Hsia Chang

Beginning in 1987, after decades of alienation, relations between the Republic of China (ROC) on Taiwan and the People's Republic of China (PRC) underwent a significant transformation. That year saw the two sides embark on an expanding series of unofficial and semiofficial contacts. By 1991, some 2.5 million residents of Taiwan had visited the mainland, and 40 million pieces of mail and 10 million phone calls and telegrams had been exchanged across the Taiwan Strait.[1]

Other forms of interaction may be even more impressive. Bilateral indirect trade between Taiwan and the mainland increased by 100 times in twelve years, from US$70 million in 1979 to US$7 billion in 1991. Today, the mainland has become Taiwan's fifth largest trading partner, and the ROC is the PRC's sixth largest trading partner.[2] Despite the state-engineered violence at Tienanmen (Tiananmen) Square in June 1989, Taiwan was the largest foreign investor in mainland China in 1990.[3] Today, Taiwan's entrepreneurial investments in the mainland may be as much as US$6 billion.[4]

The complex and tortuous forty-three-year history of relations between Taiwan and the mainland may be regarded as a continuous, though unsuccessful, effort at negotiating the reunification of China.[5] The term "negotiation" is defined as "a process in which explicit proposals are put forward ostensibly for the purpose of reaching agreement on an exchange or on the realization of a common interest where conflicting interests are present."[6]

---

[1]Michael Chang, "MAC's First Year Rates High Marks," *Free China Journal* 9, no. 6 (January 28, 1992): 7.

[2]*Shih-chieh jih-pao* (World Journal) (New York), July 20, 1991, 11; July 2, 1991, 3.

[3]Ibid., May 4, 1991, 4.

[4]David Chen, "Politics Taking Backseat to Economy," *Free China Journal* 9, no. 68 (September 18, 1992): 7.

[5]The interactions between Taiwan and the mainland have conformed to the five characteristics that together make up a genuine bargaining or negotiation relationship. See Jeffrey Z. Rubin and Bert R. Brown, *The Social Psychology of Bargaining and Negotiation* (New York: Academic Press, 1975), 32.

[6]Fred C. Ikle, *How Nations Negotiate* (New York: Harper & Row, 1964), 3-4.

In any future negotiations between Taiwan and the mainland, their respective power will be a primary determinant. The realist school of international politics emphasizes the central role of power in all international politics, including the politics of negotiation. "Power" is defined in absolute terms by state capabilities—military, political, economic—and in relational terms by influence. A state's negotiating position is dependent on its power relative to other states. According to Druckman and Hopmann, "States with greater capabilities have an advantage in negotiations."[7]

The Past

In the past, the relative power of Taipei and Peking (Beijing) affected their relations and policies on reunification. Three periods can be discerned in the forty-three-year history of Taiwan-mainland relations.[8] They are the periods of military confrontation (1949-70); peaceful competition (1970-87); and peaceful interaction (after 1987).

During the first period of Taiwan-mainland relations, from 1949 to 1970, the two sides shunned all forms of official contact. Whatever "relations" the two engaged in were unremittingly hostile, punctuated by two episodes of military violence: the first in 1949, the second in 1958-59. In both cases, the violence was instigated by Peking but successfully repelled by ROC forces. After the second armed conflict, relations between the two gradually relaxed. Although Peking continued to shell the ROC offshore islands of Quemoy (Kinmen) and Matsu, the bombardment became ritualistic, taking place on a regular odd-number-day basis.

In effect, the first period of ROC-PRC relations was characterized by an approximate balance of power between the two rivals. Neither side seemed to have an advantage over the other. Each had the backing of a powerful patron and ally: Peking had the Soviet Union; Taipei was shielded by the United States. The roughly equivalent power of Taiwan and the mainland probably accounted for the military stalemates of 1949 and 1958-59.

By the second period (1970-87) of their relations, both sides had lost their patrons. The rift between Peking and Moscow, begun in 1956, culminated in the open rupture of relations in 1960. That, in turn, alleviated Washington's apprehensions about a monolithic international Communist bloc, leading to an adjustment in the United States' conception of the relative strategic importance of Peking and Taipei. On August 10, 1969, the

---

[7]Daniel Druckman and P. Terrence Hopmann, "Behavioral Aspects of Negotiations on Mutual Security," in *Behavior, Society, and Nuclear War*, ed. Philip E. Tetlock et al. (New York: Oxford University Press, 1989), 100-101.

[8]See, for example, Milton D. Yeh, "Taiwan-Mainland Relations: An Analysis of International and Domestic Factors" (Paper presented at the annual conference of the American Association for Chinese Studies, Charlottesville, Virginia, November 9-10, 1991), 3.

U.S. Seventh Fleet was withdrawn from the Taiwan Strait. More than that, a conviction coalesced in Washington concerning the "China card"—the belief on the part of American policymakers that, through better relations with Peking, the United States could use the PRC as a strategic counterweight against Moscow.

With that, the balance of power between mainland China and Taiwan shifted in favor of the PRC. Peking further enhanced its advantage through skillful maneuvering in the international arena. Not only did Peking manage to win international recognition, it also succeeded in increasingly isolating its rival in Taipei.

For the ROC, the decade of the 1970s was bracketed by two traumatic setbacks in international diplomacy. One was its expulsion from the United Nations in 1971; the other was the termination of official ties with the United States in January 1979. Both were a direct result of Peking's pursuit of a zero-sum game strategy in its dealings with other countries and international organizations.

To international bodies (such as the United Nations) that wanted the PRC as a member and to foreign governments (such as the United States) that desired diplomatic intercourse, Peking presented them with an either/or option: They must choose between Peking and Taipei; they could not pursue official relations with both. Confronted with this dilemma, most chose the PRC. By the end of the 1970s, all the world's major nations had severed formal relations with Taipei. The ROC was recognized by only twenty-two states, all of which were marginal powers.

Emboldened by its diplomatic successes, Peking in 1981 put forth a proposal for reunification with Taiwan. Comprised of nine points, the proposal envisioned a reunited China in which Taiwan would be a regional entity subordinate to Peking. Despite all the preferential conditions the reunified Taiwan would enjoy as a "special administrative region"—such as being able to retain its armed forces—the PRC Constitution is unambiguous on the subordinate status of such regions. Article 31 of the Constitution states that the "systems to be instituted in special administrative regions shall be prescribed by law enacted by the National People's Congress. . . ." Article 5 specifies that "no law or administrative or local rules and regulations shall contravene the Constitution."[9] According to Peking, the reunited China would be "one nation" with "two systems." Taiwan and the mainland would retain their respective societal arrangements of capitalism and socialism. Two different systems would coexist within a single nation, each "not hurting" the other.[10]

---

[9]*The Constitution of the People's Republic of China* (Peking: Foreign Languages Press, 1983), 27, 13.

[10]*Chung-kung chung-yao wen-t'i ts'an-k'ao tzu-liao: Chung-kung t'ung-chan lan-yen* (Reference

Peking's importunings for reunification were categorically rejected by Taipei, an unsurprising response given the diplomatic reversals it had endured. Taipei's response was formalized in the "three nos" policy: Taiwan would have no official contact, make no compromises, and engage in no direct negotiations with the Communists on the mainland.[11]

In 1987, as the third period of Taiwan-mainland relations commenced, Taipei had managed to reverse its fortunes by becoming an economic and political success. Taiwan had become a newly industrialized country with an average per capita income more than fifteen times that of the economically retarded mainland. Politically, Taiwan was demonstrably more democratic than the mainland, providing for greater individual liberties as well as political competition.[12]

In other words, as the 1980s drew to a close, through its own endeavors, Taiwan had won for itself a significant measure of economic and political power. That power, in turn, gave Taipei the self-confidence and security to embark on a rapid series of democratizing reforms that included the opening, on November 2, 1987, of unofficial (people-to-people) relations with the mainland.

Taipei's enhanced sense of confidence also accounted for its new assertiveness toward Peking. Eschewing its former demeanor of passivity and avoidance, in March 1991, Taipei offered a counterproposal for reunification: that of "one nation, two political entities."[13] Taipei acknowledges Peking as "a political entity," but regards itself equally as "the government" on Taiwan.

Peking's formula of "one nation, two systems" would provide for a reunified China in which Taiwan would be a junior partner, subject to Peking's control. Such an arrangement clearly could not assure the safeguarding of Taiwan's interests. In proposing an alternative formula of "one nation, two political entities," Taipei is seeking to negotiate with Peking as an equal. As ROC Premier Hau Pei-tsun put it, if two "entities" of equal status were to be reunified, it could not be through the absorption of one "entity" by the other.[14]

---

material on important problems of Chinese Communism: CCP's united front disinformation) (Taipei: Government Information Office, 1988), 46-47, 25.

[11] For an account of Taipei's policy, see Maria Hsia Chang, "Taiwan's Mainland Policy and the Reunification of China," *Strategic Study Series* (Claremont Institute: Asian Studies Center, 1990).

[12] In Taiwan's national elections of December 1986, for example, independents or "nonparty candidates" captured some 25 percent of the votes.

[13] For a complete text of Taipei's new policy, see *Guidelines for National Unification*, drafted by the National Unification Council and approved by the ROC government on March 14, 1991.

[14] A statement made by Premier Hau to the Legislative Yuan on February 21, 1992. *Shih-chieh jih-pao*, February 21, 1992, A2.

As a "political entity," it is entirely appropriate for the ROC to engage in "pragmatic diplomacy" with countries with which it has no formal relations, as well as participate in international political and economic bodies.[15] As long as Peking treats Taiwan as less than equal, evinced through such behavior as refusing to renounce the use of force against Taiwan, obstructing Taipei's arms purchases, and blocking the ROC's "pragmatic diplomacy," Taipei cannot trust the Peking regime. "Mutual trust" can only be derived from "concrete evidence" of Peking's "cooperative goodwill."[16] As long as there is no mutual trust, there can be no "direct linkages" of mail, transport, and commerce, and exchanges of high-ranking officials, nor can there be formal negotiation for reunification.

Thus far, Peking has responded to Taipei's initiative with a softening of rhetoric but no change of substance.[17] The PRC's policy toward Taiwan and reunification still adheres to the "nine-point proposal" and the "one nation, two systems" formula.

The Future: Endogenous Determinants

If, as stated by Druckman and Hopmann, states with greater power capabilities—absolute as well as relational—indeed have an advantage in negotiations, a more powerful Taiwan will be in a better position to bargain with the mainland over reunification. Any increase in Taiwan's power will hinge on a number of endogenous and exogenous factors that could affect the ROC's future economic, political, and military capabilities, as well as its international status and influence. The endogenous factors include: (1) the ROC economy; (2) domestic politics; and (3) governmental policies.

The ROC Economy

Among the factors that affect Taiwan's power capabilities, none is perhaps as important as its economy. To begin with, like any other nation, the ROC's overall stability depends on the continuation of economic growth and expansion. More than that, Peking has long maintained that one of the conditions that would precipitate its deployment of lethal force against Taiwan is if instability and chaos should develop on the island.[18]

---

[15]From a speech by Ying-jeou Ma, on June 11, 1991, at the Twentieth Sino-American Conference on Contemporary China, Columbia, South Carolina.

[16]"Ma Explains Unification Dispute," *Free China Journal* 8, no. 55 (July 19, 1991): 7.

[17]*Shih-chieh jih-pao*, February 16, 1992, A1.

[18]In a paper delivered at a symposium in Washington, D.C. in March 1985, Li Shen-chih, director of the Institute of American Studies of the PRC's Chinese Academy of Social Sciences, stated: "Once there is internal disorder in Taiwan, [Communist] China will have to resort to force. . . ." *Pai-hsing* (Paishing Semi-monthly) (Hong Kong), no. 93 (April 1, 1985): 7.

Since the Nationalist (Kuomintang or KMT) government moved to Taipei in 1949, it has accomplished nothing less than an economic miracle. Under the KMT government, Taiwan progressed from economic backwardness to the status of a newly industrialized country. Today, Taiwan is on the verge of becoming a fully mature industrial power. In 1991, Taiwan replaced Germany as the economy with the world's second largest trade surplus, with an annual surplus of US$13.3 billion.[19] The ROC is now first in the world in foreign exchange reserves, which totaled US$82.4 billion in December 1991.[20]

In 1992, while the global economic growth rate was estimated to be about 2.8 percent, Taiwan's rate of growth was over 7 percent.[21] In 1992, Taiwan was estimated to have a gross national product (GNP) of more than US$211 billion, making it twentieth in the world in GNP. Taiwan's per capita GNP reached US$10,242, ranking it twenty-fifth in the world.[22] Taiwan's total bilateral trade approached US$150 billion, making it the world's fourteenth largest trading nation.[23] By the year 2000, the ROC will be able to claim membership in the elite group of advanced industrialized countries.

Taiwan's economy has a direct effect on the ROC's international status and influence. Simply put, the wealthier Taiwan becomes, the more attractive it is to the nations of the world: as a market for the exports of other nations, including the arms-exporters;[24] as a locus for investment by developed nations;[25] and as a source of foreign aid and investment to less developed and post-Communist nations.

Its reserves, in turn, had transformed Taiwan from an importer of capital into a major foreign investor nation. A third of Taiwan's overseas investment is in the United States,[26] especially in U.S. Treasury debt instruments.[27] Taiwan has over US$12 billion invested in East Asia.[28] In Southeast Asia, Taiwan is the largest foreign investor in Vietnam, the third

---

[19]*Shih-chieh jih-pao*, May 23, 1992, A2.

[20]*Free China Journal* 9, no. 3 (January 17, 1992): 1.

[21]Song Su-feng, "Solid Growth Charted for 1992," ibid., no. 1 (January 7, 1992): 3.

[22]"Record Per Capita GNP Predicted for Taiwan," ibid., no. 60 (August 18, 1992): 2.

[23]*Shih-chieh jih-pao*, January 19, 1992, A5.

[24]See "Western Firms More Willing to Sell Weapons to Taiwan," *San Francisco Chronicle*, September 30, 1991, A13.

[25]In 1992, Taiwan's business environment was ranked third in the world by an American firm, Business Environment Risk Information, after Switzerland and Japan. *Shih-chieh jih-pao*, June 19, 1992, A18.

[26]*Shih-chieh jih-pao*, February 13, 1992, A6. An estimated 1,395 Taiwan entrepreneurs have invested in the United States.

[27]*San Francisco Chronicle*, February 12, 1992, A9.

[28]*Shih-chieh jih-pao*, February 21, 1992, A18.

largest in Indonesia, and the seventh largest investor in the Philippines.[29] In the five years between 1986 and 1990, Taiwan invested some US$19 billion overseas, making the ROC the world's ninth largest foreign investor.[30]

The ROC is also becoming a significant provider of foreign aid and loans. In 1988, Taiwan established the International Economic Cooperation Development Fund (IECDF) to help forge closer ties with countries friendly to the ROC.[31] In 1991, Taiwan repaid all its debts to the Asian Development Bank and became a creditor instead, with a 1.2 percent capital share. In 1992, the ROC provided US$12 million worth of medical aid to Ukraine; it pledged US$500,000 to aid Belarus's recovery from the Chernobyl nuclear disaster; and it promised US$5 million in humanitarian aid for drought relief to Malawi, Swaziland, and Lesotho.[32] Taiwan is prepared to provide US$1.1 billion in low-interest loans to aid development in Central America, Central Europe, Eastern Europe, and the Commonwealth of Independent States.[33]

In Southeast Asia, the ROC has agreed to lend the Philippines US$20.1 million to develop its water supply system, and is considering another US$50-100 million loan to fund its industrial zone development. To Vietnam, Taiwan is prepared to lend US$30-100 million for a highway expansion project, and is considering another loan of US$15 million to develop Vietnam's small and medium-sized enterprises. Taiwan is poised to grant Indonesia a US$10 million low-interest economic development loan.[34] By 1995, Taiwan aims to increase its foreign aid budget to 0.25 percent of its GNP—78 percent of Japan's foreign aid budget.[35]

All of this has affected other nations' perceptions and assessments of the ROC. As one Taiwan businessman put it, "Now, Taiwan has money and when it talks, people start listening."[36] More recently, an official of the Danish Foreign Ministry explained his government's plan to develop economic and other relations with Taiwan by saying that "money rules this world."[37] Commensurate with the rise of Taiwan's economic "stock" in the world is the enhancement of the ROC's international power and status,

---

[29]As of May 1992, Taiwan businesses have invested a total of US$3.37 billion in Indonesia. *Shih-chieh jih-pao*, May 7, 1992, A14; February 25, 1992, A14.

[30]*Shih-chieh jih-pao*, April 1, 1992, A6.

[31]Song Su-feng, "Indonesia Given Preliminary OK to Tap into ROC Assistance Fund," *Free China Journal* 9, no. 59 (August 14, 1992): 3.

[32]Ibid., no. 23 (April 7, 1992): 1; no. 26 (April 17, 1992): 2; and no. 30 (May 1, 1992): 1.

[33]"ROC to Gain ADB Clout by Boosting Capital Share," ibid., no. 32 (May 8, 1992): 2.

[34]See note 31 above.

[35]Japan's foreign aid expenditures constitute 0.32 percent of its GNP. Among the European nations, Norway ranks highest in foreign aid expenditures, at 1.2 percent of its GNP. *Shih-chieh jih-pao*, July 19, 1991, 1.

[36]See note 24 above.

[37]*Shih-chieh jih-pao*, April 11, 1992, A5.

resulting in a perceptible improvement in Taipei's fortunes in the global diplomatic arena. In 1989, for example, the Bahamas, Grenada, and Belize established formal diplomatic relations with the ROC, followed by Nicaragua in 1990.

Taipei arguably has experienced the greatest diplomatic success in the former Soviet bloc. As part of its non-ideological "pragmatic diplomacy," the ROC began to actively cultivate commercial relations with the Soviet Union and the nations of Eastern Europe in 1988. By the beginning of December 1991, Taiwan's trade with the Soviet Union exceeded US$201 million, an increase of 89.1 percent from the previous year. Taiwan exported US$59.6 million to the Soviet Union, but imported US$141.8 million—an increase of 163.6 percent from 1990.[38] All of this apparently convinced Moscow of the importance of its ties to Taipei. In February 1992, the government of the Russian Federation stated that it did not feel compelled to consult with Peking on its relations with the ROC, since "contact with Taiwan is both necessary and helpful for Russia."[39] Half a year later, in September 1992, the two governments officially announced that representative offices will be established in each other's country.[40]

Taipei has had even greater success with Latvia, one of the former Baltic Soviet republics. On January 29, 1992, Latvia upgraded Taipei's office in Riga to consulate level, becoming thereby the first country to engage in a dual recognition of both Peking and Taipei. Despite threats from Peking, the Latvian government held onto its position, resulting in Peking's closure of its embassy in Riga on February 25, 1992.[41]

Latvia's move seemed to have set a precedent. In April 1992, a member of Estonia's Supreme Council, Tiit Made, also indicated that notwithstanding Peking's predictable objections, Estonia intended to establish formal diplomatic relations with the ROC.[42] In June 1992, Niger reestablished formal diplomatic relations with the ROC, leading Peking to sever its official ties with the west African nation on July 30.[43]

Where Taipei encountered diplomatic stalemate and reversals was in its relations with other Asian nations. In 1990, Indonesia and Singapore established diplomatic intercourse with the PRC and broke off formal relations with the ROC. In February 1992, Vietnam indicated that its relations with Taipei could not go beyond the unofficial level, despite the substantial

---

[38]*Free China Journal* 8, no. 95 (December 13, 1991): 3.

[39]*Shih-chieh jih-pao*, February 12, 1992, A2.

[40]Tammy C. Peng, "Office Pact Hardens Moscow-Taipei Ties," *Free China Journal* 9, no. 67 (September 11, 1992): 1.

[41]See Tammy C. Peng, "Latvia Squeezed over ROC Pact," ibid., no. 8 (February 11, 1992): 2; and *Shih-chieh jih-pao*, February 25, 1992.

[42]*Free China Journal* 9, no. 23 (April 7, 1992): 1.

[43]Susan Yu, "Niger's 41-Day Ties with Taipei and Peking End," ibid., no. 56 (August 4, 1992): 1.

trade and investment benefits Hanoi derived from the ROC.[44] In August 1992, the ROC ended diplomatic relations with South Korea two days before Seoul's official recognition of Peking.

All these Asian states apparently are persuaded by considerations of national security to pursue closer ties with Peking, at the cost of formal relations with the ROC. Other reasons aside, the geographical proximity of the PRC—Asia's largest and most powerful nation—would counsel such a course of action.

Domestic Politics

Taiwan's stability is not simply dependent on its economy, it is also contingent on the domestic political situation. Nowhere is such a generalization more trenchant than in the case of Taiwan's leading opposition party, the Democratic Progressive Party (DPP).

Since 1975, when the PRC State Council established a Taiwan Affairs Office, Peking's fundamental policy on Taiwan has been one of adamant opposition to any development that could lead to the formation of "two Chinas," "one China, one Taiwan," or "an independent Taiwan."[45] Peking has consistently threatened it would employ lethal force against Taiwan should the latter attempt independence.

On October 13, 1991, at its fifth national convention, the DPP adopted an amendment of its party platform calling for the creation, through a national plebiscite, of a "Republic of Taiwan" separate from mainland China.[46] The response from Peking was swift and unambiguous.

On October 17, the *People's Daily* published an article condemning the DPP amendment, accusing the DPP of "a conspiracy" to "splinter the nation" and "betray the Chinese people." The article warned that unless the DPP refrained from its advocacy of independence, its fate would be that of "total destruction."[47] In November, the Hong Kong journal *Cheng Ming* reported that PRC military regions contiguous to Taiwan had been ordered to stand at "battle readiness."[48] Another Hong Kong journal, *Kuang-chiao*

---

[44]For the first three quarters of 1991, bilateral trade between Vietnam and Taiwan totaled US$152.8 million, an increase of more than 28 percent from 1990. The ROC, with a total investment of US$172 million, was Vietnam's largest foreign investor in 1991, accounting for more than 15 percent of the country's total foreign capital. Allen Pun, "Vietnam Blooms as Green Pasture for Taiwan Business," *Free China Journal* 8, no. 97 (December 20, 1991): 8.

[45]King C. Chen, "Chinese Communist Tactics Toward Taiwan and Peaceful Unification," in *Chung-kuo t'ung-i yü Kuo-Kung ho-t'an wen-t'i yen-chiu lun-wen chi* (Essays on issues concerning China's unification and KMT-CCP peace talks), ed. Hungdah Chiu et al. (New York: Shih-chieh jih-pao she, 1982), 72.

[46]Ann Scott Tyson, "Taiwan Opposition's Independence Bid Sets Tone for Vote," *Christian Science Monitor*, October 24, 1991, 4.

[47]*Shih-chieh jih-pao*, October 17, 1991, . 3.

[48]Ibid., November 1, 1991, 1.

ching, reported that the commander of the PRC navy had indicated that Peking would install a naval blockade of Taiwan if the latter sought independence.[49]

As it turned out, public opinion in Taiwan obviated Peking's resort to force. The DPP amendment met with strong public disapproval. A poll conducted on October 14, a day after the DPP vote, showed that the party was trusted by only 13 percent of those surveyed—a sharp drop from the previous month's 50 percent. Only 8 percent supported the DPP, compared to 16 percent a month before.[50] Not surprisingly, given the DPP's unpopularity, it lost to the ruling Kuomintang (18.61 percent versus 78.91 percent) in the historic elections for a new National Assembly on December 21, 1991.[51]

The choices that the ROC electorate made in that election proved to be a felicitous affirmation of the democratic transformation of Taiwan. Political democratization, however, carries with it attendant costs. Politicians and government officials must increasingly address and satisfy the needs and concerns of various interest groups within Taiwan, groups that are not primarily concerned with larger national interests. The small and medium-sized businesses of Taiwan comprise just such a group.

Beginning in the 1980s, Taiwan's economy underwent a significant transition from being a newly industrialized country to becoming a more mature economy. New capital and skill-intensive industries were replacing labor-intensive ones; the service sector was burgeoning. This transition, never easy in itself, was made all the more difficult by labor disputes, wage increases, and the appreciation of the new Taiwan dollar—all of which seriously impaired the competitiveness of Taiwan's export-oriented industries.[52] Many of Taiwan's small and medium-sized exporters were threatened with extinction.[53]

In Taiwan's increasingly open and competitive political environment, threatened business interests began to aggregate in voluntary associations to articulate their concerns, including their desire to establish economic contact with the mainland. For Taiwan's smaller businesses, mainland China seemed to offer a solution for their problems, being a source of cheap labor and raw materials as well as a potential market for ROC products.

---

[49]Ibid., November 14, 1991, 10.

[50]"DPP 'Trust' Slips in Poll," *Free China Journal* 8, no. 80 (October 18, 1991): 2.

[51]Susan Yu, "ROC Voters Give KMT Whopping Mandate," ibid., no. 98 (December 24, 1991): 1.

[52]For more on this subject, see Chang, "Taiwan's Mainland Policy and the Reunification of China."

[53]As of March 1992, Taiwan had a total of 770,000 small and medium-sized companies, 150,000 of which are export-driven manufacturers. "Seminar Heeds Small Firms' SOS," *Free China Journal* 9, no. 17 (March 13, 1992): 3.

The predicament of Taiwan's smaller businesses could have played a role in President Chiang Ching-kuo's decision in September 1987 to lift the official restrictions on travel to the mainland for the purpose of visiting relatives. Taiwan's entrepreneurs quickly took advantage of the opening to strike deals with mainland contacts. Bilateral indirect trade between Taiwan and the mainland rapidly grew to US$1.5 billion in 1987, US$2.5 billion in 1988, US$3 billion in 1989, US$4.04 billion in 1990, and US$7 billion in 1991.[54] Nor are Taiwan's private entrepreneurs the only ones engaged in the mainland trade. In March 1991, the ROC government gave its permission for state-run enterprises to import raw materials, such as coal and tin, from the mainland.[55]

Almost nonexistent before 1987, Taiwan's investments on the mainland rapidly increased to US$520 million in 1988, and an estimated US$2 billion in 1990.[56] Today, investments by Taiwanese entrepreneurs in the mainland may be as much as US$6 billion, making Taiwan the PRC's fourth largest investor.

In effect, the economies of Taiwan and mainland China are becoming increasingly involved and interdependent. That reality poses both risks as well as opportunities to the ROC. One opportunity that Taiwan could encourage and exploit is the growing phenomenon of regionalism (*ti-fang chu-i*) in mainland China. An unintended by-product of the economic reforms after 1979 has been the increasingly independent disposition of mainland China's regional and local authorities.[57] Investments made by Taiwan's entrepreneurs may be intensifying this phenomenon, particularly as it pertains to the mainland's southeastern coastal provinces.

ROC investments are concentrated in the two coastal provinces closest to Taiwan: Fukien (Fujian) and Kwangtung (Guangdong). Taiwan's investments in Fukien accounted for more than half of the province's total foreign investments in 1991. Fukien's officials now "openly acknowledge that they have hitched their fortunes to Taiwan."[58] In the case of Kwangtung, as of July 1991, Taiwan accounted for 8.13 percent of the province's total foreign investments of US$12.3 billion. The growth rate of Taiwan's investments in Kwangtung now exceeds that in Fukien.[59] Nor are Taiwan's entrepreneurs

---

[54]*Shih-chieh jih-pao*, July 20, 1991, 11; July 2, 1991, 3. See also Chu-yuan Cheng, "Trade and Investment Across the Taiwan Strait: Economic Consequences and Prospects," *Strategic Study Series* (Claremont Institute: Asian Studies Center, 1990), 1.

[55]*News Digest* (New York: Government Information Office, CCNAA), March 26, 1991, 1.

[56]Estimates made by Peking. *Shih-chieh jih-pao*, May 4, 1991, 4.

[57]For a discussion of regionalism, see Maria Hsia Chang, "China's Future: Regionalism, Federation, or Disintegration," *Studies in Comparative Communism* 25, no. 3 (September 1992): 211-27.

[58]According to Hong Kong's *South China Morning Post*, April 1, 1991, as cited by *News Digest*, April 2, 1991, 2.

[59]*Shih-chieh jih-pao*, July 7, 1991, 7; September 25, 1991, 10.

limiting themselves to these two provinces. They are rapidly expanding their investment activities to other parts of mainland China—to the Yangtze River area, to central and southern China, and to the northeast.

Opportunities for Taiwan aside, there are potential risks in the expanding economic transactions across the Strait. One danger is that Taiwan might grow too dependent on its trade with the mainland. Since the surge in indirect trade between Taiwan and the mainland began, that trade consistently has been in Taiwan's favor. Taiwan's trade surplus with the mainland accounted for 26 percent of the ROC's total trade surplus in 1991, although the mainland trade was only 3 percent of Taiwan's total global trade.[60]

If Taiwan becomes overly dependent on trade with the mainland, the ROC economy could be adversely affected by the inherent volatility of the mainland economy. The ROC could also become susceptible to Peking's political pressure and manipulation. For example, Peking could abruptly reduce its imports from across the Strait, drastically decreasing Taiwan's trade surplus and hurting ROC exporters. They, in turn, might exert pressure on the government to make unwise concessions to Peking. An example of an imprudent concession would be permitting direct trade and investment with the mainland, which is favored by a growing majority of Taiwan's entrepreneurs.[61]

Aside from trade, ROC investments in the mainland also harbor potential risks. As early as April 1990, ROC economics minister, Chen Li-an, commented on several investment trends that could be deleterious to Taiwan. One was the increasing tendency of Taiwanese businesses to export more than mere capital to the mainland. Entire operations were being uprooted from Taiwan and transplanted to the mainland.[62]

At the same time, instead of helping the ROC economy, Taiwan's investments in the mainland's export industries may be undermining the international competitiveness of ROC exports. In 1990, for example, 10.8 percent of Taiwan's exports to the United States competed with similar exports from the PRC. That percentage is expected to increase to 16.5 percent in the future.[63]

Taiwan investments in the mainland are also beginning to benefit the economy of the PRC more than that of the ROC. The investments initially served the interests of Taiwan's labor-intensive smaller businesses. Since that time, however, ROC investments in mainland China have not only in-

---

[60]See note 1 above.

[61]See the results of two surveys as described in "Trade Growth with Mainland Worrisome," *Free China Journal* 8, no. 47 (June 21, 1991): 3.

[62]*Shao-nien Chung-kuo ch'en-pao* (Young China Daily) (San Francisco), April 17, 1990, 4.

[63]Ibid.

creased in scale, they have become more sophisticated, diversifying into capital and technology-intensive production, building forward and backward linkages in the mainland economy. The duration of Taiwan's investments is also increasing, from the earlier "quick profit" ventures to commitments of as long as fifty to seventy years.[64]

ROC Governmental Policies

In all this—the maintenance of stability and economic prosperity at home; the conduct of international diplomacy; the "dialogue" with Peking on reunification; the management of the DPP, independence advocates, and business interest groups—the government in Taipei plays a pivotal role. All the available evidence seems to indicate that Taipei's policies are on track.

In international politics, Taipei has eschewed ideology-driven diplomacy for a more pragmatic "flexible diplomacy." Toward the mainland, Taipei has replaced the untenable "three nos policy" with one that is at once more realistic as well as protective of ROC interests. The opposition party, the DPP, is being managed with consummate skill, included in important political discussions (such as the National Affairs Conference), but properly sanctioned when it oversteps legitimate boundaries.

The government in Taipei is also dealing with the potential dangers of Taiwan's economic transactions with the mainland. A trade warning system has been instituted, effective since the second half of 1991. The ROC Board of Foreign Trade is monitoring the shipping activity of some 205 export items from Taiwan to the mainland, and 218 mainland export items to the ROC. A warning system of colored "signal lights" (blue, amber-blue, green, amber-red, and red) indicates the frequency and rate of growth in the shipment of an item. A red light signifies an overheated trade in a particular item exceeding the normative 80 percent level. This means that Taiwan exporters or importers of that product could become dependent on their mainland counterparts. Depending on other considerations, the government would move to suspend shipments of that item.[65]

Aside from controlling the risks of trading with the mainland, Taipei is also mindful of the opportunities inherent in these contacts. Taiwan could use economics as a leverage to influence Peking. As an example, Taipei could propose a quid pro quo: Taiwan would be prepared to extend a large sum of aid to Peking if the latter would sign a nonaggression treaty with Taipei.[66] Another quid pro quo might be Taipei's relaxation of its ban against

---

[64]Ibid.; *Shih-chieh jih-pao*, December 30, 1991, A14.

[65]"Trade Warning System Gearing Up," *Free China Journal* 8, no. 48 (June 25, 1991): 3.

[66]An idea proposed by a DPP legislator, Hsü Kuo-t'ai, who suggested diverting up to a quarter of the ROC's defense budget (or US$68 billion in 1992) to aid the mainland. *Shih-chieh jih-pao*, November 16, 1991, 6.

direct trade to areas on the mainland that instituted private ownership, free markets, and guarantees for foreign investments.[67]

Taiwan can also exercise indirect influence over the mainland simply through its people-to-people contacts by visiting relatives, tourists, traders, and investors. Along with the export of capital and products, Taiwan is also exporting an alternative model of societal arrangements to the Communist mainland—"the Taiwan experience." In this manner, Taiwan may hasten the "peaceful evolution" of the PRC away from Communism.[68]

The Future: Exogenous Determinants

Despite the efficacy of the ROC government, there are forces and factors outside of its control or influence. These include: (1) the global economy; (2) the disposition of arms-exporting nations to sell to the ROC; and (3) the PRC.

The Global Economy

By necessity—being an island that is resource-poor as well as having the world's second densest population, now exceeding 20 million—Taiwan is an exporting economy. Any export-oriented economy is vulnerable to the vicissitudes of the global economy. As an example, recessionary pressures could reduce the consumer market for ROC exports, particularly in developed countries.

Thus far, Taiwan has been remarkably successful at weathering these cyclical fluctuations in the world market, amassing the world's largest foreign exchange reserves. Ironically, however, that very success is creating problems for the ROC in that countries with large trade deficits with Taiwan may resort to protectionist measures.

Aside from these problems, a structural transformation is under way in the global economy with potentially grave implications for Taiwan. Regional trading blocs are being formed in the world, with the European single market leading the way. The future will only see more such regional entities being created. Already, there is talk of a North American economic monolith, as well as an Asian common market. Unless Taiwan gains membership in an Asian economic bloc, or forms a regional bloc with Hong Kong, Kwangtung, and Fukien, it might find its exports excluded from the world's markets in the future.

Arms-Exporting Nations

In any future negotiations with Peking, it is important that Taipei bargain from a position of strength. Given that, the maintenance of Taiwan's

---

[67]An idea of Yang Shih-chien, director general of the ROC government's Industrial Development Bureau. "Taiwan Could Use Trade Clout to Push Mainland," *Free China Journal* 8, no. 59 (August 2, 1991): 2.

[68]From a statement made by ROC Premier Hau. *Shih-chieh jih-pao*, July 5, 1991, 2.

defensive capabilities becomes critical. Despite Taiwan's efforts at self-sufficiency in arms production—developing an indigenous fighter airplane (the Ching-kuo), a surface-to-air missile (the Sky Bow), and a 4,000-ton frigate with missile and anti-submarine helicopter capabilities[69]—the ROC still depends on purchases of advanced weaponry from foreign countries to maintain its defensive capabilities against the mainland.

Ironically, this issue has become even more critical with the demise of the Soviet Union and the end of the Cold War. In 1992, the PRC once again increased its military budget for the third consecutive year. The People's Liberation Army's budget in 1992 increased 52 percent from 1989. It was reported that Russia would transfer MiG-31 and Su-27 fighters, Ilyushin-76 long-range transport planes, and T-72M tanks to the PRC. Peking was also negotiating with Ukraine for the purchase of an aircraft carrier, the acquisition of which will significantly upgrade the PRC's navy.[70]

In the past, Peking has been successful in frustrating Taipei's attempts to purchase arms. The PRC's greatest triumph was in bringing the Reagan administration to sign the August 17, 1982 joint communiqué, in which the United States agreed not only to put a ceiling on its arms sales to Taipei, but to gradually reduce those sales to a point of "final resolution."[71] In 1989, and again in 1990, Peking succeeded in blocking plans by France to sell Lafayette-class frigates to Taiwan.[72] In February 1992, the planned US$2.7 billion sale by the Netherlands' Rotterdam Dockyard Co. of six Sea Dragon-class submarines to Taiwan fell through because of pressure from Peking.[73] In June 1992, Peking punished France for its planned sale of as many as 100 Mirage 2000-5 fighters by informing Paris that the PRC will bypass France on its buying mission to Europe.[74]

The ROC has had some success in arms procurement. In July 1991, in an effort to offset the sale of twenty-four Su-27s by the Soviet Union to the PRC, the United States agreed to make available to Taiwan an unspecified number of used F-16A and F-16B fighter airplanes.[75] In August, the ROC succeeded in contracting for the purchase of six unarmed Lafayette-class frigates for a total of US$2 billion.[76] In November 1991, a Japanese newspaper reported that Taipei managed to negotiate a US$119 million sale of

---

[69]*Shih-chieh jih-pao*, November 13, 1991, 4.

[70]For a more detailed discussion, see A. James Gregor, "China's Shadow over Southeast Asian Waters," *Global Affairs*, Spring 1992, 1-13.

[71]"Text of U.S.-China Communiqué on Taiwan," *New York Times*, August 18, 1982, A12.

[72]See note 24 above.

[73]Susan Yu, "Peking Pressures Dutch out of Sub Deal with Taiwan," *Free China Journal* 9, no. 10 (February 18, 1992): 1.

[74]*Shih-chieh jih-pao*, June 23, 1992, A10.

[75]Ibid., July 29, 1991, 1.

[76]Ibid., May 15, 1992, A2.

three M-60A combat vehicles from the United States, as well as other un-specified advanced armaments from Germany and Italy.[77]

In January 1992, it was reported that Moscow was willing to transfer ninety of its high performance MiG-29 fighters to Taipei.[78] There were also unconfirmed rumors that Washington had agreed to the sale of Patriot missile parts.[79] In February, news from Amsterdam indicated that Holland would sell Taiwan about three Fokker-50 reconnaissance aircraft.[80] In March 1992, Washington agreed to increase the number of AH-1W Cobra helicopters it would transfer to Taipei from eighteen to forty-two, and the number of OH-58D Chinook reconnaissance helicopters from twelve to twenty-six.[81] That was followed in July by Washington's approval of a five-year lease of three Knox-class frigates to the ROC navy.[82]

On September 3, 1992, the United States reversed a ten-year-old policy when President Bush announced to Texan aerospace workers that he would allow the US$6 billion sale of 150 F-16s to Taiwan. In so doing, the Bush administration argued that the sale did not represent a betrayal of the August 17, 1982 U.S.-PRC agreement on limitations of American arms sales to Taiwan because the Reagan administration communiqué "cannot bind any future president of the United States."[83] Bush's announcement of the sale of F-16 jet fighters was followed three weeks later by another announcement of the sale of twelve anti-submarine (LAMPS) helicopters to Taiwan.[84]

According to Japanese military analysts, what transpires in the next ten years will be decisive. By the year 2000, Taiwan—with its capital and technological assets, supplemented with appropriate arms transfers from other nations—could surpass mainland China in defensive military capabilities.[85]

The PRC

In all this, the PRC has a decisive role. Were it not for Peking's ob-structions, Taiwan would not be impeded from membership in international political and economic organizations, nor would the ROC be excluded from diplomatic relations with other nations. Were it not for Peking's objections, the weapons-manufacturing nations would have no reason not to sell arms

---

[77]Ibid., November 13, 1991, 4.

[78]The sale was delayed because Taipei preferred that the United States sell the ROC its F-16C fighters. *Shih-chieh jih-pao*, January 19, 1992, A2.

[79]*Shih-chieh jih-pao*, January 14, 1992, A2.

[80]Ibid., February 19, 1992, A2.

[81]Ibid., March 17, 1992, A5.

[82]Tammy C. Peng, "Bush Sells ROC Helicopters to Defend Taiwan," *Free China Journal* 9, no. 70 (September 25, 1992): 1.

[83]Gary Klintworth, "F-16 Sale Good for US and ROC," ibid., no. 66 (September 8, 1992): 7.

[84]See note 82 above.

[85]*Shih-chieh jih-pao*, November 13, 1991, 4.

to foreign-exchange rich Taiwan. Were it not for Peking's oft-repeated threat to use force against Taiwan, the ROC would have little reason to fortify its defensive capabilities in the first place.

What the PRC will do about all this is contingent on its internal politics. How impatient is the mainland's gerontocracy about reunifying Taiwan with "the motherland"? How will the succession to Teng Hsiao-p'ing (Deng Xiaoping) be resolved? What is the disposition of the next generation of leaders, in particular the emerging elite group of "princes"? Will the reformist faction within the Chinese Communist Party (CCP) gain decisive ascendance over the conservatives? Will the phenomenon of regionalism in the mainland continue to intensify, perhaps eventuating in the virtual autonomy of the southeastern coastal provinces, who would join Taiwan and Hong Kong in a "Greater China Economic Community"?

What is clear is that peaceful relations between Taiwan and the mainland are in their mutual interest. More than that, in important ways, Taiwan and the mainland complement each other. The CCP's professed goal is the economic modernization of China. The mainland is poor and backward, but rich in labor and natural resources. Taiwan is land and resource-poor but rich in capital and technology. In an ideal world, the two Chinese entities would cooperate with each other, each contributing its unique talents and assets, complementing the other for its deficiencies. Together, Taiwan and the mainland could rebuild China into a modern world power, restoring it to its historic prominence.

CHAPTER 12

Recent ROC-PRC Unification Policies in the Light of the German Experience

Gottfried-Karl Kindermann

The Concept of Unity in Historical Perspective

Crossing the threshold from the nineteenth to the twentieth century, China and Germany both constituted unified nation-states, one justly considering itself as Asia's "central empire," the other one forming the geopolitical center of the European continent. However, through many centuries and dynasties, China—in spite of many periods of division—has experienced a far longer and more intensive history of unity than Germany. China's unification was accomplished in the second century B.C. by the Ch'in (Qin) Dynasty, and impressively expanded by the succeeding Han Dynasty. Yet starting from this early period, China experienced recurring phases of division and reunification. Chinese experts have calculated that before the inauguration of the Republic in 1912, imperial China had been a unified state for altogether 1,963 years and divided for a total of 1,134 years.[1] The last two dynasties before the Republic, the Ming (1368-1644) and the Ch'ing (Qing) (1644-1911), represented 543 years, or half a millennium, of unbroken unity. More than that, ever since the institutionalization of Confucianism as the official state doctrine in A.D. 136, China had an overarching element of continuity in the sphere of its political culture.

By comparison, Germany only emerged as a state in the ninth century A.D. from the eastern half of the vast Franconian empire of Charlemagne. The German empire's functioning as an effective political state system, however, ended in the thirteenth century. In subsequent centuries, political power continuously shifted from the royal center to the periphery, into the hands of a multitude of regional dukedoms, principalities, and autonomous cities.

---

[1]Yung Wei, "Zyklen von Teilung und Wiedervereinigung der Geschichte des chinesischen Reiches," in *Chinas unbeendeter Bürgerkrieg. Im Spannungsfeld Peking-Taiwan-USA 1949-1980* (China's unending civil war: The electric field among Peking, Taiwan, and the USA 1949-1980), ed. Gottfried-Karl Kindermann (Vienna and Munich: 1980), 17-26, and Dun J. Lee, *The Ageless Chinese: A History*, 2nd ed. (New York: Scribner, 1965), 562-68.

Although the titles, symbols, laws, and institutions of the so-called Holy Roman Empire were preserved in name at least, the emperor's de facto influence depended exclusively on his dynastic power base (*Hausmacht*).[2] Contrary to the developments in France, Great Britain, and Russia, where the power of the feudal lords was tamed or crushed, the German imperial center did not succeed in breaking the power of those centrifugal forces of state and society. The Reformation, followed by the Thirty Years' War (1618-48) between Protestants and Catholics, added a cultural and confessional dimension to Germany's ongoing fragmentation. More than one century of conflict between Prussia and Austria—interrupted by the wars of liberation against Napoleon and by the national and democratic revolutions of 1848-49—finally ended in 1866 with a Prussian victory, followed by the Prussian-led foundation of the Second German Empire in 1871.

Though it was neither planned nor intended by the four major World War II allies, the division of Germany developed between 1946 and 1949 as a major by-product of a worldwide power contest between the West and the Soviet Union. In 1949, the same year that saw the establishment of a West and an East German state, China was also divided as a result of civil war, leading to the proclamation of the People's Republic of China (PRC) by Mao Tse-tung (Mao Zedong) on October 1, 1949, and to the withdrawal to Taiwan of major components of the Nationalist government. In both these different cases, Communism—self-reliant in mainland China and imposed by outsiders in East Germany—played a key role. China and Germany, as well as Korea and later Vietnam, thus became *bisystemic divided nations*. In other words, the fact of national division in the two countries was aggravated by confrontation between mutually exclusive sociopolitical and economic life-styles and ideologies.

Codetermining Factors of World Politics

In the period between the victory of Mao Tse-tung in mainland China and the start of the Korean War, U.S. intelligence estimates assumed, not without plausibility, that Taiwan was likely to be conquered by Peking's (Beijing's) People's Liberation Army (PLA) by fall 1950.[3] Early in 1950, hoping for an early normalization with Peking, and especially also for a "Titoization" of the PRC's foreign policy, the United States explicitly proclaimed its disengagement from Taiwan as well as from any defense commitment with regard to the countries of continental East Asia. All that was

---

[2]Wilhelm Treue, *Deutsche Geschichte* (German history) (Stuttgart: 1958), 192-93. From the thirteenth to nineteenth centuries, for instance, the imperial crown of the German empire was mostly held by the Austrian Habsburg dynasty, whose dynastic power base in central and southeastern Europe was composed of eleven different nationalities.

[3]*Foreign Relations of the United States 1950*, vol. 6, *The China Area*, 330, 340-41.

suddenly changed by the outbreak of the Korean War on June 25, 1950. After a seventy-two-hour information gathering, analysis, and decision-making process in Washington, the Truman administration radically altered its East Asian policy to include intervention in Korea, commitment to protect Taiwan, and massive aid for the French war in Vietnam. Each of the two systems, in divided China and divided Germany, was subsequently integrated into larger alliance systems. In East Asia, the Moscow-Peking axis confronted Washington's newly created chain of alliances aimed at the peripheral containment of mainland China through defense pacts concluded with Japan in 1951, South Korea in 1953, and Taiwan in 1954, and further extended through the creation of the Southeast Asian Treaty Organization (SEATO) in 1954. In Europe, West Germany was admitted to the North Atlantic Treaty Organization (NATO) in 1955, while East Germany became a member of the newly created Warsaw Pact.

In the case of the two Chinas, this pattern of integration into confronting alliance systems was dissolved by two globally significant trends of development: the progressive disintegration of the Sino-Soviet alliance and the related Sino-American rapprochement, which resulted in an understanding between Washington and Peking at the expense of Taiwan. The negative impact on the latter was, however, somewhat softened by America's continuing commitment, as expressed in the Taiwan Relations Act of 1979, though this was somewhat reduced in substance by the Washington-Peking Communiqué of August 17, 1982.[4]

The terminal crisis of the Soviet Union, which brought about internal reforms and drastic changes in Soviet foreign policy, affected the division of China and of Germany, although in rather different ways. In the West, Mikhail Gorbachev's abandonment of the Brezhnev style of interventionist imperialism encouraged democratic liberation movements in Eastern Europe and became a primary determinant for the success of the bloodless revolution and system transformation in East Germany. In East Asia, the Soviet crisis produced the twin effect of Sino-Soviet normalization in 1989, and the consequent end of Moscow's material support for Vietnamese hegemonism in Cambodia. Peking was thus freed from the pressure of the Soviet-Vietnamese alliance, which had been concluded against Peking in 1978 and which functioned indirectly as a security factor in favor of Taiwan.

Next to the United States, which regained its world supremacy, and to Germany, which accomplished national unification, the PRC has therefore to be considered one of the major beneficiaries of the recent change in global

---

[4]Taiwan Relations Act, Public Law No. 96-8, 93 Stat. 14 (1979), U.S. Congress SS 3301-3316 (1982). See also Lori Fisler Damrosch, *The Taiwan Relations Act after Ten Years*, Occasional Papers-Reprints Series in Contemporary Asian Studies (School of Law, University of Maryland), 1990, no. 4. For the text of the Washington-Peking communiqué on arms sales to Taiwan, see *New York Times*, August 18, 1982, and *Beijing Review* 25, no. 34 (August 23, 1982): 14-15.

power configurations. As a result of the "ping-pong diplomacy" of 1971-72, it had already won admission to the United Nations (from which Taiwan was excluded), normalization with Japan, and diplomatic recognition by a large number of countries. Sino-American normalization occurred when Washington, after years of hesitation, finally gave in to all Peking's major demands: derecognition of the Republic of China (ROC) on Taiwan and renunciation of the U.S.-ROC defense pact, and withdrawal of remaining U.S. military units from Taiwan. This was followed by the Sino-British and Sino-Portuguese agreements on the transfer of Hong Kong and Macao before the end of this century. In 1989, Gorbachev, like Richard Nixon before him, traveled to mainland China after Moscow had submitted to another set of Peking's demands: the end of support for Vietnam's policy in Cambodia, withdrawal from Afghanistan, and a thinning out of Soviet forces along the northern frontiers of China. Having lost a considerable amount of support from Moscow, India today poses less of a problem for Peking than at any other time in the postwar period. Thus, apart from securing its claim to the Spratly Islands, only one major foreign policy objective seems to remain for Peking: the solution of the Taiwan problem.

Building up Contacts and the Question of Single or Dual Representation: The Cases of China, Germany, and Korea

One typical question for peoples and governments within divided countries, as well as for third states and international organizations, is whether there exists any governmental authority legitimately entitled to represent the entire divided nation or even one of its politically separate entities. This question is complicated by the conflicting claims of the competing governments within the divided country and by the problem of effective de facto control. In the case of China, Chiang Kai-shek, following the model of Sun Yat-sen's policies in Kwangtung (Guangdong) after 1917, withdrew to Taiwan in 1949, not only with his government and parts of the armed forces, but also with large segments of the Republic's three parliamentary bodies, elected in China's first relatively free elections in 1947-48. Emergency legislation settled the quorum problem in a manageable way and a ruling by the Council of Grand Justices allowed the mainland-elected parliamentarians to keep their mandate until the mainland had been recovered by the ROC government. Initially assisted by the fact that it held the seats reserved for China in all major U.N. institutions until 1971, the ROC government in Taipei claimed de jure legitimacy and referred to the PRC government as a rebel regime. However, in the ROC's first two major treaties—its peace treaty with Japan in 1952 and its treaty of alliance with the United States in 1954—explicit reference was made only to the territories under the de facto control of the ROC government.[5] Essentially, the ROC has maintained this claim to the whole of China despite its recent recognition that although it is the only legitimate government of China, the country now has two political entities. In spite of the ROC's loss of de facto control over mainland China, it still insists on its de jure legitimacy since its rule is based on the constitution that emerged in 1946 from the democratically elected National Assembly.[6]

The PRC's claim to be the legitimate government of mainland China and Taiwan is based on its 1949 conquest of the mainland, its continuous effective control of that area, and the fact that Taiwan is widely recognized in the international community as forming an integral part of China.[7] Here, then, are two mutually exclusive claims to be the legitimate government of the whole of China in a situation in which one side does not have any de facto control over Taiwan and its adjacent islands and the other side has no control over the Chinese mainland.

In the case of Germany, the 1949 Basic Law (constitution) of the Federal Republic of Germany (FRG) claimed in its preamble that one of the main purposes of the new state and of its constitutional order was to maintain Germany's unity as a nation and as a state, that the legislators having adopted this constitution "for a transitional period" (*Übergangszeit*) were also acting on behalf of the unfree citizens in East Germany, and that the entire German nation was charged with the mission of achieving, on the basis of free self-determination, the unity and freedom of the whole of Germany.[8] This was interpreted as meaning in theory and practice that West Germany claimed the right of "sole representation" (*Alleinvertretungsanspruch*) for the entire German nation. In connection with their "general treaty" which restored West Germany's sovereignty as a state, the three Western former occupying powers stated in a joint declaration of October 3, 1954 that they regarded the FRG government "as the only German government that has been freely and legally formed and that is therefore entitled to speak on behalf of

---

[5]The Exchange of Notes that accompanied the ROC's peace treaty with Japan of April 28, 1952 stated that "the terms of the present Treaty shall, in respect to the Republic of China, be applicable to all territories, which are now, or which may hereafter be, under the control of its government." See Hungdah Chiu, ed., *China and the Question of Taiwan: Documents and Analysis* (New York and London: 1973), 247 (Document 40). Article 6 of the U.S.-ROC Mutual Defense Treaty of December 2, 1954, says that the territories in question shall mean, in respect to the ROC, "Taiwan and the Pescadores." Ibid., 251 (Document 42).

[6]"'One China' Policy Defined," *China News* (Taipei), August 2, 1992.

[7]"Yang Shangkun on China's Reunification," *Beijing Review* 33, no. 48 (November 26-December 2, 1990): 7-13. See also "Mainland and Taiwan: Formula for China's Reunification," ibid. 29, no. 5 (February 3, 1986): 18-25.

[8]"Das Grundgesetz für die Bundesrepublik Deutschland vom 23. Mai 1949" (The basic law of the Federal Republic of Germany, May 23, 1949), chap. 6 in *Deutsche Verfassungen* (German constitutions), ed. Rudolf Schuster (Munich: 1978), 137.

Germany as representative of the German people in international affairs."[9] In contrast to the West German Basic Law, the first constitution of East Germany (the German Democratic Republic, GDR) of 1949 declares in article 1 that "Germany is an indivisible democratic republic. . . . There is only one German citizenship," while article 118 states, "Germany forms a united customs and trade area, surrounded by a common customs border." The second East German constitution of 1968, however, claims in its preamble that it was U.S. imperialism in collusion with West German monopoly capital that had divided Germany. Article 8 of that same constitution stipulates that the establishment of "normal relations" and "cooperation between the two German states on the basis of equality," and the achievement of a "step by step rapprochement" (schrittweise Annäherung) until the achievement of "their unification on the basis of democracy and socialism," comprised a major purpose of the GDR.[10] Only as the result of the 1974 amendment to the 1968 constitution were all references to the imposed division of Germany and to the basic objective of overcoming this division deleted.[11] The amended constitution (1974) contained a new paragraph (article 6) stating that the GDR was "irrevocably allied with the Soviet Union," and "an inseparable component part of the socialist community of states."[12] As far as the right to govern the whole nation was concerned, there existed, in the case of China, an antithetic symmetry at least insofar as both Chinese governments agreed that there was only one China, including Taiwan, and only one legitimate Chinese government. In the case of Germany there existed in this respect a changing asymmetry. Only West Germany claimed, until 1972, to be the legitimate spokesman for the entire nation, while until the end of the 1960s the East German government, nominally at least, opposed the division of Germany without claiming to represent all of Germany. Menaced by the continuous flight of its citizens to the West, East Germany in 1961 built a fortified wall along its border with the Federal Republic to isolate its population from the West, and especially from West Germany. A decade later, the West German Liberal-Social Democrat coalition government of Willy Brandt and Walter Scheel decided to break through this isolation on the basis of a quid pro quo. West Germany's claim to "sole representation" was sacrificed and East Germany was recognized as a sovereign state in order to give millions of West Germans the chance to travel to the East. There remained, however, an essential difference in definition and level.

---

[9]Text of the joint statement in Dokumente des geteilten Deutschland (Documents of the divided Germany), ed. Ingo von Münch, vol. 1 (Stuttgart: 1968), 246-47.

[10]For the texts of the East German constitutions of 1949 and 1968, including the 1974 amendments to the 1968 constitution, see Schuster, Deutsche Verfassungen, 198-249.

[11]For the relevant passages, see ibid., 243-49.

[12]Ibid., 219.

According to the West German definition, the Inter-German East-West Treaty on the Basis of Relations had legally institutionalized the coexistence of *two states within the German nation*, states which, therefore, could not be "foreign countries" to each other. East Germany from then on, however, claimed that the two Germanies had no special connections with each other whatsoever and that for the GDR, West Germany was not only a "foreign" country, but even worse than that it was an "imperialist foreign country."[13] Thus unification did not become a common objective when the two German governments concluded the treaty on their mutual relations in 1972. But the treaty did reopen the gates to an increasing flood of inter-German people-to-people and institutional contacts, which were considered by Bonn as more promising tools for the restoration of national unity than the legal claim to "sole representation." As far as the level of contacts was concerned, there had been even in the Adenauer era occasional unofficial exchanges of letters between the chiefs of the two German governments. The intensification and institutionalization of East-West German relations began, after preliminary correspondence, with a meeting between Chancellor Brandt and Prime Minister Willi Stoph on March 19, 1970. In view of the above-mentioned differences of approach with regard to the character of mutual relations, the chief of the East German permanent mission to West Germany was accredited with the chancellor's office, while the chief of the West German mission in East Germany was accredited with the GDR's Foreign Ministry.

Some aspects of the Inter-German Treaty of 1972 that may be of interest to other still divided countries are as follows:

Article 3

. . . the Federal Republic of Germany and the German Democratic Republic shall settle their disputes exclusively by peaceful means and refrain from the threat or use of force. They reaffirm the inviolability now and in the future of the border existing between them and undertake fully to respect their territorial integrity.

Article 4

The Federal Republic of Germany and the German Democratic Republic proceed on the assumption that neither of the two States can represent the other internationally or act in its name.

. . .

Article 6

The Federal Republic of Germany and the German Democratic Republic proceed on the principle that the jurisdiction of each of the two States is confined to its own territory. They shall respect each other's independence and autonomy in internal and external affairs.

---

[13]On this difference of opinion, see Gottfried-Karl Kindermann, *Grundelemente der Weltpolitik* (Basic elements of world politics) (Munich: 1986), 334-39.

Article 7

[The signatories] . . . state their readiness to regulate practical and humanitarian questions in the process of normalization of their relations. They will conclude agreements with a view to developing and promoting cooperation in the fields of economics, science and technology, traffic, judicial relations, post and telecommunications, health, culture, sport, environmental protection and in other fields on the basis of the present Treaty and for their mutual benefit.

Article 8

The Federal Republic of Germany and the German Democratic Republic will exchange permanent missions.

Article 9

[The signatories] . . . are agreed that the present Treaty does not affect the bilateral and multilateral international treaties and agreements previously concluded by them or concerning them.[14]

This treaty was preceded by the Bonn-Moscow Treaty of August 12, 1970, which broke the ground for West Germany's new *Ostpolitik*. An authentic interpretation by the German side which accompanied this treaty declared that it "does not conflict with the political objective of the Federal Republic of Germany to work for a state of peace in Europe, in which the German Nation will recover its unity in free self-determination."[15]

By comparison, inter-Korean contacts started in May 1972, without any government-to-government preliminaries, with the daring trip to North Korea by the director of South Korea's Central Intelligence Agency during which he had direct consultations with the North Korean president, Kim Il-sung. Vice Premier Pak Song-chol of North Korea then paid a return visit to Seoul. On July 4 that year the famous North-South Communiqué, until recently regarded by both sides as the "Magna Carta of Korean unification," was signed. It is true that subsequent high-level talks produced no conclusive results, but after eight government-to-government "preliminary meetings" from February 1989 to July 1990 and six "high-level talks," the two premiers were able on December 13, 1991 to sign the Agreement on Reconciliation, Nonaggression, and Exchanges and Cooperation between the South and the North. Some of the most salient points of this agreement are as follows:

> The preamble stresses "the yearning of the entire Korean people for the peaceful unification of the divided land," and recognizes that current North-South relations "not being a relationship between states, constitute a special interim relationship, stemming from the process toward unification."

---

[14]Treaty on the Basis of Relations between the Federal Republic of Germany and the German Democratic Republic of December 21, 1972, in Press and Information Office of the Government of the Federal Republic of Germany, *Documentation Relating to the Federal Government's Policy of Détente* (Bonn: 1974), 71-74.

[15]Letter on German Unity, ibid., 16.

Article 1

The South and the North shall recognize and respect each other's system.

Article 2

The two sides shall not interfere in each other's internal affairs.

. . .

Article 4

The two sides shall not attempt any actions of sabotage or overthrow against each other.

. . .

Article 6

The two sides shall cease to compete or to confront each other and shall cooperate and endeavor together to promote national prestige and interests in the international arena.
      The two sides shall not use force against each other and shall not undertake armed aggression against each other.

It is further stipulated in the same agreement that a "South-North political committee" shall be established to discuss measures required for the implementation of the agreement, that a "joint military commission" shall work toward military confidence-building, and that direct rail, sea, and air links shall be opened as well as direct postal and telecommunications services.[16]
      In an official comment, the South Korean National Unification Board said that this agreement would open up a new era of North-South reconciliation and cooperation that was intended to form a stage of development preceding a North-South "commonwealth," an interim phase leading to more advanced forms of national reunification.[17]
      As far as divided China is concerned, the PRC was the first to suggest negotiations between the two sides. Following its rather unsuccessful military offensive during the first Taiwan Strait crisis of 1954, Chou En-lai (Zhou Enlai) stated on July 30, 1955, that the Peking government was willing to enter into negotiations with "responsible local authorities of Taiwan" to discuss "Taiwan's peaceful liberation." On a note that has remained until this day a leitmotif of Peking's attitude in this respect, Chou added: "It should be made clear that these would be negotiations between the central government and local authorities. The Chinese people are firmly opposed to any ideas . . . of the so-called 'two Chinas'."[18]

---

[16]Kim Hak-joon, "Toward National Unification: South and North Korean Approaches," in *Korea: A Nation in Transition*, ed. Kim Se-jin and Kang Chi-won (Seoul: 1978), 285-86.

[17]National Unification Board, Republic of Korea, *An Era of Reconciliation and Cooperation Begins* (Seoul: 1992), 18.

[18]The Chinese People's Institute of Foreign Affairs, ed., *Oppose U.S. Occupation of Taiwan and "Two Chinas" Plot* (Peking: 1958), 36.

In the following years, Peking's psychological strategy toward Taiwan endeavored to exploit the shock of the Sino-American rapprochement of 1972 and full normalization between Washington and Peking in 1979. In February 1972, a number of leading figures on the Peking side, such as Liao Ch'eng-chih (Liao Chengzhi) and Fu Tso-i (Fu Zuoyi), warned that the Nixon-Mao summit had opened an era of understanding and cooperation between Peking and Washington, and that the government on Taiwan should understand that the United States could not be relied upon. It should therefore enter into public or secret talks with the PRC leaders.[19] Explicitly pointing to the PRC's Treaty of Peace and Friendship with Japan (1978) as well as to its normalization with Washington, the Standing Committee of Peking's National People's Congress (NPC) suggested on January 1, 1979 the establishment of postal, economic, and people-to-people relations between Taiwan and the mainland, announcing also that the ritual bombardment of Quemoy (Kinmen) would be stopped.[20] The same offer was made in greater detail by NPC Chairman Yeh Chien-ying (Ye Jianying) on September 30, 1981, this time combined with another proposal:

> After the country is reunified, Taiwan can enjoy a high degree of autonomy as a special administrative region and it can retain its armed forces. The central government will not interfere with local affairs on Taiwan. . . . Taiwan's current socio-economic system will remain unchanged, so will its way of life and its economic and cultural relations with foreign countries.[21]

In the following decade, in spite of a great variety of statements, Peking did not substantially alter its basic position, except to add Teng Hsiao-p'ing's (Deng Xiaoping's) slogan "one country, two systems" (*i-kuo liang-chih*), that had originally been applied to Hong Kong.

One year after the NPC's appeal to Taiwan, this author interviewed Ambassador Hao Te-ch'ing (Hao Deqing), chairman of the People's Institute of Foreign Affairs, in an effort to elicit Peking's attitude toward the Kuomintang (KMT). The interview ran, in part, as follows:

Kindermann: Do you consider the Kuomintang as a national all-Chinese party or as a local Taiwanese party?
Hao: Of course as a national all-Chinese party. Our party has, in the past, repeatedly cooperated with it in important historical phases.

---

[19] *Twenty-sixth Anniversary of the "February 28" Uprising of the People of Taiwan Province* (Peking: 1973), 12, 18. Fu Tso-i, referring to Mao Tse-tung's trip to and negotiations in Chungking in 1945, added that now it was the Kuomintang's turn to come and negotiate peace.
[20] *Beijing Rundschau* (Beijing Review), January 9, 1979, 16-18.
[21] Text of Yeh Chien-ying's message in British Broadcasting Corporation, *Summary of World Broadcasts*, FE/6842 (October 1, 1981): A3/1. In addition, on October 10, 1981, CCP general secretary, Hu Yao-pang, invited President Chiang Ching-kuo and other Taipei leaders to pay private visits to the mainland, where, if they so wished, they could also talk with CCP leaders about China's reunification. See *Beijing Review* 24, no. 42 (October 19, 1981): 20.

Kindermann: If the KMT decided to unify with the mainland, would it be permitted to establish a party headquarters in Peking and branch offices throughout the country?
Hao: Of course, why not? Besides the CCP, there are several other parties on the mainland as well.
Kindermann: And would the KMT have the chance to print and distribute newspapers, pamphlets, books, etc., and would it be given broadcasting time on radio and television?
Hao: If the KMT embarks on a policy of reunification, it would of course obtain all those chances.
Kindermann: And if there were elections, would the KMT be permitted to compete openly and critically with the CCP?
Hao: Actually, why not? The other parties are always invited to correct the working style of the CCP.
Kindermann: But if the KMT could freely compete in elections with a theoretical chance of winning them, would you not have to change those passages of the PRC's constitution which characterize its system of government as a "socialist state of dictatorship of the proletariat" with the CCP being "the nucleus of leadership of the Chinese people" and which stipulate the guiding role of Mao thought?
Hao: Almost like an examining teacher you have been asking many questions and I begin to feel that foreigners should not intervene too much in purely Chinese matters!

After maintaining a rigid attitude on the unification issue for almost four decades, the ROC, in the years 1987-92, began to take the initiative in inter-Chinese relations. Only a few months prior to his death, President Chiang Ching-kuo of the ROC eased his government's thirty-eight-year ban on travel to the mainland. And in 1988, Taiwan residents were permitted to send letters to the mainland via Hong Kong.[22]

In the year of German unification, Chiang Ching-kuo's successor, Lee Teng-hui, announced his intention to abrogate the anticommunist emergency legislation that had impeded the development of democracy in Taiwan, and said that the existing constitution would be revised with due regard to changing circumstances. In the course of his inaugural speech on May 20, 1990, Lee— referring to possible progress in inter-Chinese relations—declared:

> If the Chinese Communist authorities can recognize the overall world trend . . . , implement political democracy and a free economic system, renounce the use of military force in the Taiwan Straits and not interfere with our development of foreign relations on the basis of a one-China policy we would be willing, on a basis of equality, to establish channels of communication and completely open up academic, cultural, economic, trade, scientific and technological exchange.[23]

A few days earlier, when one legislator who had just returned from mainland China mentioned that Peking's vice premier, Wu Hsüeh-ch'ien

---

[22]The division between the two Germanies was never as rigid as that between the two Chinese governments prior to 1987.
[23]Full text of President Lee Teng-hui's inaugural address in *China Post* (Taipei), May 21, 1990.

(Wu Xueqian), had declared his government's readiness to enter into "party-to-party contacts and talks with Taiwan," President Lee had replied that, as far as the ROC government was concerned, only "government-to-government talks" could be considered, because only at this level would the two sides have equal status. Otherwise, Peking would again try to treat Taipei as a subordinate local government. In a subsequent comment, presidential spokesman Cheyne Chiu explained that President Lee had meant to say that the ROC would consider talks with the Peking government "only if they are conducted on an equal government-to-government basis. The president had not meant to say that those talks could be initiated immediately."[24] In November that year, the ROC vice premier, Shih Chi-yang, said that his government had relaxed its "three nos" policy insofar as private organizations would be permitted to have direct contacts with PRC officials. The private Straits Exchange Foundation (SEF), operating under the government's Mainland Affairs Council (MAC), headed by himself, would serve as an institution for handling those contacts. This newly created foundation would be permitted to have direct technical and business contacts with Chinese Communist organizations. At the same time, government-to-government contacts were to be avoided.[25]

Peking's reaction to Taipei's new approach was rather critical. For instance, President Yang Shang-k'un (Yang Shangkun) said:

> Taiwan has done well in developing . . . and it has US$70 billion in foreign reserves. But that means nothing to us, because we have done well in developing our heavy industry. . . . We have 70 million tons of steel, coal and oil. We have nuclear bombs, missiles and many submarines. Nevertheless, we still want peaceful reunification, but while we sit down to talk, preconditions and equal status are out of the question. We have 1.1 billion people; Taiwan has only 20 million. We cannot be considered as equals, because the figures are not in proportion. . . . If Taiwan tries to gain independence, we will not rule out the possibility of using force.[26]

Yang added that President Lee Teng-hui's proposal was tantamount to advocating "two Chinas." The best way to intensify contacts between Peking and Taipei, he said, was to hold talks between the CCP and the KMT.[27] Shortly thereafter CCP general secretary Chiang Tse-min (Jiang Zemin), talking to a one-hundred-member delegation of Taiwan industrialists in Peking, argued that maintaining the PRC's threat of a military invasion against Taiwan could help to promote China's reunification by exercising pressure

---

[24]"Taiwan President Calls for Government-to-Government Talks with Mainland," *Summary of World Broadcasts*, FE/0767 (May 18, 1990): A3/1.

[25]*China Post*, November 19, 1990.

[26]"Yang Shang-k'un Says, Peking and Taipei Cannot Have Equal Status in Talks," *China Post*, June 9, 1990.

[27]Ibid.

on the forces of separatism and preventing foreign interference to the disadvantage of China. He said that representatives of other political parties besides the two ruling parties could participate in the party-to-party talks. When asked whether Peking would approve of an exchange of semiofficial offices for the purpose of handling bilateral relations, Chiang replied: "Anything can be discussed, if Mr. Lee Teng-hui is willing to send representatives here to talk with us. We cannot discuss this issue thoroughly with civic groups."[28]

Chiang's remark about the participation of smaller parties in inter-Chinese talks referred to Taipei's argument that party-to-party talks were out of the question because neither of the ruling parties could represent the entire people. Asked whether Peking would oppose Taiwan's entering the General Agreement on Tariffs and Trade (GATT), Chiang answered that only after the PRC itself had become a member would Peking consider supporting Taiwan's admission. Terminologically speaking, Taiwan's membership in GATT should follow the model of its membership in the International Olympic Committee, where the ROC is registered under the name "Chinese Taipei."[29] Other reservations on the Peking side were revealed in the overseas edition of the *People's Daily* of May 5, 1990, where an article on the timing of peaceful unification observed that "China's Kuomintang" would eventually become "Taiwan's Kuomintang" in an ongoing process of regionalization, unless unification could be achieved in the near future.[30]

Taipei's policy on unification reached a new stage in February-March 1991 when the National Unification Council—a presidential task force set up in October 1990—and the Executive Yuan Council adopted the *Guidelines for National Unification*.[31] In the words of the chairman of the Mainland Affairs Council, the *Guidelines* envisage unification as a phase-by-phase process "without being subject to a timetable." Their aim is to achieve "parity, reciprocity, gradual and measured progress in improving existing relations between the two sides of the Taiwan Straits."[32]

Envisaging unification as an evolving process rather than an act of will, the *Guidelines* define three phases of unification. In phase one, the two sides will work toward reciprocal elimination of hostility and the establishment of mutually beneficial exchanges, while "not denying the other's existence as a political entity." Intermediary organizations will be set up on both sides

---

[28]"Chiang Tse-min: Peking Won't Renounce Use of Force Against Taiwan," *China Post*, July 2, 1990.

[29]Ibid.

[30]*Summary of World Broadcasts*, FE/0768 (May 19, 1990): A3/1.

[31]Huang Kun-huei, *The Key Points and Content of the Guidelines for National Unification* (Taipei: 1991), 17-19. Huang is chairman of the Mainland Affairs Council under the ROC Executive Yuan.

[32]Ibid., 5.

to handle practical problems arising from exchanges. The two sides will allow each other to participate in the international community under the principle that there is only "one China." In the second phase, the two sides will open official channels of communication on an equal footing. This phase will see the inauguration of direct postal, transport, and commercial links and joint development of the southeastern coastal area of mainland China. Taiwan and the mainland will assist each other and cooperate in international organizations. Phase three will see the creation of a joint consultative organization charged with developing an all-Chinese constitutional system adhering to democracy, economic freedom, and social justice.

In the course of a press conference with 150 local and foreign reporters in Taipei on April 30, 1991, President Lee Teng-hui cautioned that the implementation of the *Guidelines* was conditional. If the PRC did not abandon its threat of military force against Taiwan and if it continued to isolate the ROC internationally, Taiwan would treat the PRC as "a hostile political entity." One thing that was particularly emphasized in the *Guidelines* was that "the two sides of the Taiwan Strait should not deny each other as political entities under the 'one China' principle."[33] When asked what the ROC would do if there was no positive response from the Peking side, the president replied that his government would wait patiently. In a way reminiscent of the beginning of Sino-American "ping-pong diplomacy," Lee said that if PRC President Yang Shang-k'un was willing to visit the ROC, he might invite him for a "sight-seeing trip" as president of the ROC, and if Yang was willing to invite him to the mainland as president of the ROC, he might "give it a try."[34] On May 1, 1991, ROC legislation came into effect which terminated the Temporary Provisions of the ROC Constitution relating to the "Period of Mobilization for the Suppression of Communist Rebellion," promulgated in May 1948. President Lee indicated his hope that the termination of the Temporary Provisions would facilitate both the process of democratization within the ROC and the development of relations with the mainland.[35] From now on the PRC would no longer be regarded as a rebel regime, but rather as "a political entity that controls the mainland area," and it would be referred to either as the "mainland regime" or the "Chinese Communist regime."[36]

In an early reaction to the ROC's new initiative, a *People's Daily* commentary said that with the decision to end the "period of mobilization," the Taiwan authorities had formally put an end to the state of civil war between the KMT and the CCP, and this would contribute to the develop-

---

[33]"ROC Ends 43 Years of Hostility with Peking" (Text of question and answer sessions with President Lee Teng-hui), *China Post*, May 1, 1991.
[34]Ibid.
[35]Ibid.
[36]Ibid.

ment of relations between the two sides. The commentator said that it was "unrealistic" for the Taiwan authorities to seek the position of a "parallel political entity," and to try to expand their "international space" by pursuing their flexible pragmatic diplomacy. Referring to a related statement by President Lee Teng-hui, the paper said that Taiwan's leaders were cherishing the illusion that they could peacefully transform the mainland with the "Taiwan experience." All this of course would lead nowhere.[37] Almost simultaneously with Lee Teng-hui's above-mentioned press conference, Yang Shang-k'un was reported to have said ,in an "internal speech on Taiwan affairs" that at the present moment particular stress had to be laid on economic exchanges and trade, so that "economic exchanges would promote political relations and unofficial contacts will promote official contacts." It was, however, necessary "to strengthen propaganda and education among cadres, the masses, and the personnel responsible for handling Taiwan affairs, and let them correctly approach Taiwan, overcome admiration for Taiwan, and enhance their consciousness in safeguarding national security and guarding against infiltration and corruption." Ideological education among workers ought to be strengthened in enterprises with Taiwan investment or management.[38]

On June 7, 1991, a spokesman of the Taiwan Affairs Office of the CCP Central Committee announced the following proposals: (1) the establishment of the "three direct links" (postal, shipping, and commercial), along with other kinds of two-way exchanges; (2) unification talks among representatives of the CCP and the KMT, supplemented by representatives of other parties; and (3) for the KMT Central Committee to nominate members and others to visit the mainland as guests of the CCP Central Committee and for leading members of the CCP to visit Taiwan on a similar basis to "discuss state affairs" with KMT leaders.[39]

The following day, Ma Ying-jeou, vice chairman of the ROC's Mainland Affairs Council, sarcastically but realistically commented that Peking's overtures to Taipei had essentially not gone beyond those of Yeh Chien-ying in September 1981, and they simply did not deserve comment.[40] Even so, the director-general of the ROC's Government Information Office argued that the "three links" demanded by Peking, which according to Taipei's *Guidelines* were scheduled to be established only in the second phase of unification,

---

[37]*China Daily* (Peking), May 13, 1991. On June 14, President Lee indeed had said: "While we want national reunification, it does not mean we should be reunified by the Chinese Communist Party; we must bring our Taiwan experience to the mainland and build our country into one where people can enjoy freedom, democracy, and common prosperity." *Summary of World Broadcasts*, FE/1101 (June 18, 1991): A3/4.

[38]"*Chiu-shih nien-tai*: Chinese President's 'Top Secret' Speech on Taiwan Policy," ibid., FE/1068 (May 10, 1991): A3/5.

[39]Ibid., FE/1094 (June 10, 1991): A3/11.

[40]Ibid.

could be hastened if Peking would respond promptly to Taiwan's first-phase goals.[41] On the eve of the eightieth anniversary of China's 1911 revolution, Yang Shang-k'un issued a stern warning to Taiwan, where preparations for National Assembly elections were in full swing:

> We are deeply concerned about the unfinished task of reunification. If any action is taken to sever Taiwan from China, we shall never just sit back and watch. Let me sternly warn the handful of those actively advocating the "independence of Taiwan": Do not misread the situation. Those who play with fire will be burnt to ashes.[42]

At the end of 1991 there was a feeling of considerable relief, not only in KMT circles in Taiwan but also in Peking, Washington, and Tokyo, when the opposition Democratic Progressive Party (DPP), which was running on a pro-independence platform, obtained only 23.94 percent of the popular vote in the National Assembly elections, a drop of 16.86 percent compared to the legislative election of 1989.[43]

A new degree of symmetry in Taipei-Peking relations was achieved on December 16, 1991, when Peking established its Association for Relations Across the Taiwan Strait (ARATS), the mainland counterpart of the SEF.[44] The second SEF delegation to visit the mainland in early November 1991 was even received by Vice Premier Wu Hsüeh-ch'ien.[45] On the other side, it was considered a historic event when two representatives of the PRC's Red Cross organization and two mainland journalists were allowed to pay a three-day visit to Taiwan in August 1991, where the Red Cross officials negotiated the release of detained fishermen and the reporters interviewed Chen Charng-ven, the secretary-general of the SEF.[46] ARATS and the SEF have begun cooperating on an array of practical and operational issues in inter-Chinese relations, such as crime control, travel and residency regulations, fishing disputes, and cultural and economic exchanges.

On the mainland side, Premier Li P'eng (Li Peng) signed on January 6, 1992 exhaustive and detailed regulations governing visits by PRC citizens to Taiwan,[47] while in July the ROC legislature passed the Statute Governing

---

[41]Ibid.

[42]"Yang Shangkun Warns Taiwan over Independence," *Korean Herald* (Seoul), October 10, 1991. See also *Summary of World Broadcasts*, FE/1199 (October 10, 1991): i.

[43]Jürgen Domes, "Taiwan in 1991: Searching for Political Consensus," *Asian Survey* 32, no. 1 (January 1992): 49.

[44]Yang Yuanhu and Li Dahong, "Promoting Exchanges Across the Taiwan Straits," *Beijing Review* 35, nos. 5-6 (February 3-16, 1992): 30-31. Also see *China aktuell*, December 1991, 761.

[45]*China aktuell*, November 1991, 700.

[46]Ibid., August 1991, 506; *Free China Journal* (Taipei) 8, no. 66 (August 27, 1991): 1; *China Post*, August 13 and 14, 1991.

[47]"Regulations for Citizens Visiting Taiwan Issued," *Beijing Review* 35, no. 3 (January 20-26, 1992): 5-6.

Relations between People in the Taiwan Region and People in the Mainland Region.[48] The preamble of this document describes its contents as being "based on the situation that the country is not unified," and on "the normative principle of 'one country with two regions'." Article 6 of the statute declares that the ROC Executive Yuan may, "based on reciprocal principles, allow legal persons, organizations or other units of the mainland region to establish branches in the Taiwan region." In other words, the statute envisages the exchange of semiofficial representative offices between Taipei and Peking. The law encompasses numerous aspects of nonofficial relations between the two sides and, potentially at least, grants the ROC government the authority to consent, on certain conditions, to the opening up of direct air and shipping links and to visits by members and officials of the CCP. These measures are, however, conditional. "Everything," ROC Premier Hau Pei-tsun told the ROC legislature, "hinges on the state of relations between the two sides. . . . We will not take measures that endanger Taiwan's 20 million people."[49] Peking initially reacted in a negative tone to the new statute. In a Hsinhua interview, Li Ch'ing-chou (Li Qingzhou), spokesman for the State Council's Taiwan Affairs Office and the CCP's Taiwan Affairs Office, claimed that in fact Taiwan was seeking to implement a policy of "one country, two governments," which was against the "one China" principle.[50] When Li further argued that Taiwan's new cross-Strait statute had "no validity" because the ROC's legal and judicial system had "ceased to exist" when the PRC was established in 1949, Ma Ying-jeou replied that the Peking side had overlooked the historical fact of a concrete division of China into two regions since 1949.[51]

Taiwan's recently intensified policy of institutionalizing nongovernmental operational cross-Strait relations was overarched early in August 1992 by the ROC's official interpretation of the "one China" concept. After four months of study and debate the National Unification Council, personally chaired by President Lee Teng-hui, officially declared on August 1, 1992 that the term "one China" referred to the Republic of China as established in 1912, whose territory, since 1949, had been temporarily divided into two

---

[48]Text of the Statute in *Summary of World Broadcasts*, FE/1448 (Special Supplement) (August 1, 1992): C2/1-C2/7.

[49]"New Law to Help Open Beijing Ties: Passage of Cross-Strait Relations Bill to Bolster Political, Economic Links," *China Post*, July 17, 1992. See also "Law: Taiwan-Mainland People, Authority 'Equal'," *Free China Journal* 9, no. 52 (July 21, 1992): 1, and Julian Baum, "Good Neighbors: Taipei Overcomes Another Barrier to Mainland Ties," *Far Eastern Economic Review*, April 23, 1992, 32-33.

[50]*China Daily*, July 23, 1992.

[51]"Ma Refutes PRC's Criticism," *China News*, July 23, 1992. For a more detailed CCP criticism of Taiwan's new law on cross-Strait relations, see "Beijing Radio Says, Taiwan's New Straits Law 'Long on Restriction'," *Summary of World Broadcasts*, FE/1447 (July 31, 1992): A2/6-A2/7.

regions and two political entities. The expression chosen was: "one China, two regions and two political entities."[52] While stressing the objective reality of a historically and systemically conditioned division of the country, the authors of this definition avoided earlier definitions such as "one country, two governments" or "multi-system nation." The interpretation of this concept also implies that the ROC government, though aware of the de facto limitation on the territory under its control, nevertheless considers itself as the de jure government of all of China.[53]

In China's modern history there is a lot of evidence that the coexistence of competing governments and systems was not interpreted as implying or aiming at a de jure division of China. When the founding father of Republican China, Dr. Sun Yat-sen, established a "national government" in Kwangtung Province between 1917 and 1925 for the purpose of working for the unification of China, he never claimed that China was a de jure divided country. At the Versailles Conference, the whole of China was represented by delegates from the northern warlord government in Peking as well as by representatives of Sun Yat-sen's southern "national government."[54] In 1923-24 three Chinese governments concluded separate agreements with the Soviet Union, each without claiming that thereby China had ceased to be an unbroken de jure entity.[55] The octogenarian CCP leadership may recall that in 1931-32 a "Chinese Soviet Republic" was established by the CCP in Kiangsi (Jiangxi) Province as a separate political entity, having its own constitution, laws, and army, waging civil war against the Chinese central government in Nanking, and—according to article 9 of its constitution—seeking to extend its social, economic, and ideological system "over all of China."[56]

---

[52]See note 6 above and "Unification Body Defines 'One China': NUC Proclaims China One Country, Separately Ruled by Two Political Entities," *Free China Journal* 9, no. 56 (August 4, 1992): 1.

[53]*China News* of August 2, 1992, thus wrote: " 'One China' refers to the Republic of China, established in 1912, whose sovereignty extends to mainland China, although currently only Taiwan, the Pescadores, Kinmen, and Matsu are under its direct rule."

[54]On China's dual representation at the Paris Peace Conference, 1919-20, see Chu Pao-chin, *V. K. Wellington Koo: A Case Study of China's Diplomat and Diplomacy of Nationalism, 1912-1966* (Hong Kong: 1981), 13-14.

[55]These were the Joint Statement by Sun Yat-sen and Adolph Joffe that established the Canton-Moscow entente of 1923, Moscow's treaty with Peking of 1924, and Moscow's parallel treaty with the Manchurian warlord regime of Chang Tso-lin who was in de facto control of China's northeastern provinces. Text of the Sun-Joffe Joint Statement of January 26, 1923 in *The China Yearbook 1924-25*, 863. On Sun Yat-sen's policies in Kwangtung, see Gottfried-Karl Kindermann, *Sun Yat-sen: Founder and Symbol of China's Revolutionary Nation-Building* (Munich and Vienna: 1982), 53-62. On Sino-Soviet treaty policies in 1924, see Allen S. Whiting, chap. 6 in *Soviet Policies in China, 1917-1924* (Stanford, Calif.: Stanford University Press, 1954), 208-35.

[56]For the constitution and policies of the Kiangsi Soviet, see part 4 in *A Documentary History of Chinese Communism*, ed. Conrad Brandt, Benjamin I. Schwartz, and John King Fairbank (New York: Atheneum, 1966).

Gottfried-Karl Kindermann

In the case of Germany, the government of the Federal Republic continuously upheld the concept of Germany's de jure unity, although in 1972 it modified this position by legally recognizing that, due to historical developments and contrary to the will of the German people, there had emerged two German states, each having only partial control over different areas of Germany.[57]

Fearing that any parallel recognition of two German governments by a third state might psychologically and legally contribute to a deepening of Germany's division, the Adenauer government coupled the claim to "sole representation" with the "Hallstein Doctrine," which implied a categorical warning that Bonn would regard any such acts of dual recognition as a move inimical to the national interest of the German people and that it might react with a termination of diplomatic relations with that state or with economic sanctions against it.[58] Except for the interlude in the 1970s in which an ROC embassy coexisted with the PRC's diplomatic liaison office in Washington, D.C. (and an American embassy in Taipei with a U.S. diplomatic liaison office in Peking), the two Chinese governments have, for decades, applied a kind of Chinese Hallstein Doctrine against each other. Peking has maintained this policy with comparative rigidity, although it has, on recent occasions, consented to Taiwan being represented in certain international organizations such as the Asian Development Bank and the Asia-Pacific Economic Cooperation (APEC) organization, provided that Taiwan's delegation appears under the name "Chinese Taipei." A similar solution might apply if and when the PRC and the ROC should become members of GATT. Reportedly, the ROC government may be prepared to consider allowing "indirect transportation" across the Taiwan Strait (with a stopover in the territory of a third country) if Peking in return was ready to abandon its policy of seeking to prevent the ROC from joining international organizations such as GATT.[59] Maintaining as of January 1992 normal diplomatic relations with only twenty-nine countries (sixteen in Latin America, seven in Africa, four in the South Pacific, one in East Asia, and one in Europe), Taiwan has developed "pragmatic diplomacy," which involves establishing substantive, though formally nongovernmental, relations with a great number

---

[57]See ruling of the Constitutional Court of the FRG on the legality of the Inter-German Treaty on the Basis of Relations of June 4, 1973. Text in *Dokumente des geteilten Deutschland* (Documents of the divided Germany), vol. 2 (Stuttgart: 1974), 355-83.

[58]Auswärtiges Amt (Foreign Office of the FRG), *Die Auswärtige Politik der Bundesrepublik Deutschland* (Foreign policy of the FRG) (Cologne: 1972), 314-15 (Document 76).

[59]"Mainland Links Considered: Plan Hinges on Approval of ROC's Right to Join GATT," *China Post*, August 1, 1992. See also "China Reportedly Ready to Join GATT Simultaneously with Taiwan," *Summary of World Broadcasts*, FE/1352 (April 10, 1992): A3/6, and David S. Chou, "Multi-System Nations and International Organizations" (Paper delivered at the Vanguard Foundation's International Conference on Unification of Multi-System Nations, Taipei, September 1991).

of other countries. However, as new states have emerged in recent years—for instance, after the disintegration of the Soviet Union or of Yugoslavia—they have come under pressure from Peking, which could use its position as a U.N. Security Council member to veto their admission to the United Nations. The ROC can and does, however, use its considerable economic power for the purpose of maintaining or expanding existing diplomatic relations.[60] Regardless of how many states accord it full diplomatic recognition, the ROC, being the fourteenth largest trading nation in the world, and having foreign exchange reserves of US$85 billion and a gross national product more than one-third that of mainland China, is a significant player in the field of international trade and investment.[61]

Renouncing or Maintaining the Threat of Military Force

The question of a mutual renunciation of force came up recently when President Yang Shang-k'un of the PRC rejected outright the suggestion of a PRC-ROC nonaggression agreement, patterned after the renunciation of force agreements between the two Germanies in 1972. This proposal was put forward by Cheyne Chiu, presidential spokesman and convener of the Research Committee of the ROC's National Unification Council, in May 1992.[62] On May 30, Yang Shang-k'un personally rejected the proposal, arguing that the signing of such a treaty would imply recognition of the existence of two Chinese governments. "Talks between two governments are absolutely out of the question," he said.[63]

Actually, one of Washington's key motives in normalizing relations with Peking at the expense of Taiwan in 1978 had been the hypothesis, advanced by Richard Solomon who was until recently U.S. assistant secretary of state for East Asian and Pacific affairs, that the United States was not likely to go to war with the PRC over the issue of Taiwan. A recently issued ROC defense white paper also expressed the view that the international community was not likely to intervene if PRC military forces should take action against Taiwan.[64] When U.S.-PRC normalization was approaching in 1978, the deputy chief of the general staff of the PLA, General Wu Hsiu-ch'üan

---

[60]See Fredrick F. Chien, "A View from Taipei," *Foreign Affairs* 70, no. 5 (Winter 1991-92): 93-103, and Hungdah Chiu, *The International Legal Status of the Republic of China*, Occasional Papers-Reprints Series in Contemporary Asian Studies, 1990, no. 1.

[61]Chien, "A View from Taipei," 98. See also "ROC Foreign Aid Not Free Lunch," *Free China Journal* 9, no. 52 (July 21, 1992): 6.

[62]"Official Suggests Signing Peace Accord with Peking," *China Post*, May 11, 1992.

[63]"Chinese President's 'Authoritative' Rejection of Taiwan Non-Aggression Proposal," *Summary of World Broadcasts*, FE/1399 (June 5, 1992): A1/4.

[64]"No Help Likely if Peking Invades, White Paper Says," *China Post*, January 30, 1992. For Washington's normalization motive, see Richard H. Solomon, "Thinking Through the China Problem," *Foreign Affairs* 56, no. 2 (January 1978): 324-56.

(Wu Xiuquan), told Japanese military experts that the PRC might seize Taiwan by force if two conditions were met—if the international situation was right and if the PLA could build up its forces to the extent that it could achieve air and sea superiority in the Taiwan Strait area.[65] Militarily, the PRC's material superiority is quite considerable.[66] While both sides keep a suspicious eye on each other's military purchases from third countries, Peking has far more leverage to prevent or impede foreign military sales to Taiwan. Up to now the ROC government has not been too active in seeking to convince Peking of the psychological damage done to the claim of all-Chinese unity and brotherhood by the continuous threat of war.

In the process of inter-German relations, the renunciation of force always played an important role. Chancellor Adenauer defined West Germany's top policy priorities in terms of three concepts: "freedom, peace, and unity," which meant that the maintenance of peace was—in inter-German relations—more highly valued than unification by means of a civil war. The renunciation of force was a key element in the Bonn-Moscow Treaty of 1970, the first and most significant of the treaties of the new *Ostpolitik* of the Brandt-Scheel administration, and it was, both practically and psychologically, an indispensable element of the 1972 Treaty on the Basis of Relations between the two German states. This inter-German renunciation of force was reconfirmed within the framework of the Helsinki Agreement of 1975 as signed at the institutionalized Conference on Security and Cooperation in Europe (CSCE).

Separatism—Conditional and Unconditional

The concrete way in which Taiwan's return to China, as envisaged by the conferences of Cairo (1943) and Potsdam (1945), was to be brought about gave rise to a new phenomenon in Chinese politics, i.e., Taiwanese separatism. As a minor political trend it emerged from the tragic events on Taiwan in February 1947. Facing large-scale civil war activities in many provinces of China, and having been surprised by the sudden end of the war against Japan, the mainland authorities were ill-prepared for the delicate tasks involved in the administrative takeover and psychological reintegration of the island province of Taiwan, which since the Sino-Japanese War of 1895 had been for half a century under Japanese rule. The indigenous Taiwanese, who had in the first weeks and months of the Chinese takeover of Taiwan and the end of Japanese rule welcomed Taiwan's return to China, were very soon alienated by the overbearing attitude of the mainlanders who treated Taiwan more like a conquered province than one that was returning to the

---

[65]*Korean Herald*, April 30, 1978, and *Frankfurter Allgemeine Zeitung*, October 25, 1978.
[66]*China aktuell*, July 1990, 573-75.

motherland. Wartime poverty caused many of the arriving mainland administrators and soldiers to engage in acts of corruption or extortion. There was a severe language barrier, because few of the arriving mainlanders were able to speak or to understand the local Taiwan dialects, while the Taiwanese had mostly not beeń taught to speak Mandarin. For the mainlanders, there was a provocative Japanese flavor to many aspects of life on Taiwan. The breakdown of the Japanese administration was followed by inflation and economic chaos. The mainlanders, who were seeking to assert their leadership role in all spheres of public life, lacked the knowledge and competence necessary for dealing with this particularly difficult situation. Thus millions of Taiwanese very soon felt disappointed and antagonized. In February 1947, minor incidents snowballed into a major uprising, which turned into a kind of civil war when the Taiwan authorities under the corrupt governor, Ch'en I, responded with utmost brutality.[67]

Among certain strata of the local Taiwanese population there emerged the feeling of a special and oppositional identity in contrast to the life-style and behavioral patterns of the mainlanders. American policy planners, being confronted in 1949 with the deterioration and defeat of the KMT's central government in China and yet seeking to prevent the Chinese Communists from taking over Taiwan, were discussing among themselves the possible removal of the mainland administration from Taiwan and the holding of a plebiscite under U.S. or U.N. auspices in which the Taiwanese population was expected to opt for an independent state of Taiwan which might then be placed under U.N. trusteeship.[68] Yet the speed and energy with which the Nationalist Chinese government carried out basic reforms on Taiwan and the outbreak of the Korean War put an end to such speculations. There developed, nevertheless, between the mid-1950s and the mid-1960s the so-called Formosan Government in Exile, located in Tokyo and headed by the American-trained Dr. Liao Wen-i (Thomas Liao), who was elected president of this "government" in February 1956.[69] In the course of a conversation

---

[67]For details of the 1947 incident, see Günther Whittome, *Taiwan 1947: Der Aufstand gegen die Kuomintang* (Taiwan 1947: The revolt against the Kuomintang) (Hamburg: 1991); Lai Jeh-hang, Ramon H. Myers, and Wei Wou, *A Tragic Beginning: The February 28, 1947 Uprising in Taiwan* (Stanford, Calif.: Hoover Institution Press, 1991); and George H. Kerr, *Formosa Betrayed* (Cambridge, Mass.: Houghton Mifflin, 1966).

[68]See, for instance, memorandum by the director of the Office of Far Eastern Affairs to the deputy undersecretary of state (Dean Rusk) dated June 9, 1949, in *Foreign Relations of the United States 1949*, vol. 9, *The Far East: China* (Washington, D.C.: U.S. Government Printing Office, 1974), 346-50; as well as statement by the secretary of state at the thirty-fifth meeting of the National Security Council on the Formosan problem, ibid., 296; and memorandum by the deputy special assistant for intelligence dated May 31, 1950, in *Foreign Relations of the United States 1950*, vol. 6, *East Asia and the Pacific*, 347-49.

[69]On Liao, see Douglas Mendel, *The Politics of Formosan Nationalism* (Berkeley and Los Angeles: University of California Press, 1970), 147-54. Also see Thomas W. I. Liao, *Inside Formosa: Formosans versus Chinese since 1945* (Tokyo: 1956, 1960).

Gottfried-Karl Kindermann

with this author in Tokyo in January 1960, Liao said that, for biological reasons, a re-Taiwanization of the political and military system on Taiwan was unavoidable. But he stressed that in the case of a PRC attack, his adherents would join with the hated KMT to defend Taiwan and that while his first option was the creation of a Republic of Taiwan, his second option would be the return of the KMT to the Chinese mainland, because that would open chances for genuine Taiwan autonomy.[70]

When due to the historic initiative of Chiang Ching-kuo the process of democratization gained momentum in Taiwan, the KMT discovered that in practice freedom always means freedom for political adversaries. For any opposition to the ruling KMT on Taiwan it was and still is tempting to utilize antagonism between sections of the indigenous population and the mainlanders, who were, until a few years ago, dominant in politics and administration. Ever since the DPP was formed on September 28, 1986, it has endeavored to stress its championship of indigenous interests as opposed to the mainland-oriented KMT. In its first electoral contest, in December 1989, the DPP was able to score impressive results on the national and local level.[71] A DPP party conference in April 1988 led to an intensive debate on the question of Taiwan's independence. The then chairman of the party, Yao Chia-wen, described the KMT regime as a mainland Chinese "refugee regime," having no roots and no native identity on Taiwan. Although the radical wing of the DPP, the New Tide faction, suggested a clause in the party's platform that would give people the right to advocate Taiwan independence, this was rejected, as at that time it was illegal to advocate or practice separatism in Taiwan. Instead, the party delegates agreed on a rather interesting and shrewdly phrased resolution defining four conditions under which the DPP would demand Taiwan's independence: (1) if the KMT should seek a compromise with Peking; (2) if the ruling party should "sell out" the interests of the people of Taiwan; (3) if the PRC should endeavor to take over Taiwan by force; or (4) if the KMT should fail to implement genuine political reforms.[72]

In the early 1990s, prominent DPP leaders proposed the creation of a "South China common market," patterned after the European Economic

---

[70]On this author's contact with Liao Wen-i, see Gottfried-Karl Kindermann, "Peking und Taipeh in der Weltpolitik: Eindrücke einer Fernostreise. 2. Teil" (Peking and Taipei in world politics: Impressions from a trip to the Far East), *Europa Archiv*, no. 18-19 (1960): 602.

[71]Oskar Weggel, *Die Geschichte Taiwans vom 17. Jahrhundert bis heute* (History of Taiwan from the seventeenth century to the present) (Cologne: 1991), 268-75.

[72]Shim Jae Hoon, "Muted Independence Talk," *Far Eastern Economic Review*, April 28, 1988, 16. See also "Oppositionsresolution über die Unabhängigkeitsfrage Taiwans" (Opposition resolution on the problem of Taiwan independence), *China aktuell*, April 1988, 276-77. Text of the "Resolution of the First Additional Conference of the Second Congress of the Democratic Progressive Party" (April 17, 1988) in *DPP* (a brochure issued by the DPP's headquarters in Taipei) (1990), 28-29.

Community (EEC), while an official resolution at the party's fourth congress demanded that the ROC's claim to sovereignty should not include mainland China and Mongolia.[73] In a sensational move at the end of August 1991, a DPP conference, preceded by a two-day seminar attended by many legal scholars, produced a draft "Constitution of Taiwan." According to this document, the ROC should officially be renamed the "Republic of Taiwan," and should be a sovereign state, independent from mainland China.[74] At the DPP's fifth congress on October 12 and 13, 1991, the radical New Tide faction became the mainstream force in the party, replacing the more moderate Formosa faction. After heated debates, two-thirds of the delegates approved a new passage in the party's platform calling for a plebiscite on the establishment of a "sovereign Republic of Taiwan."[75] The DPP also organized large-scale demonstrations demanding that Taiwan be admitted to the United Nations.[76] The DPP endeavored to use the ethnic disintegration process in the former Soviet Union and Yugoslavia to gather support for its independence demands. With positions and attitudes such as these, the DPP, among other motives, hoped to attract an unusually large portion of the popular vote in the National Assembly election on December 21, 1991. Yet, as mentioned above, the DPP's share of the total vote dropped by 16.44 percent, while the ruling KMT won a landslide victory. It remains to be seen whether this election defeat will change the party's stand in favor of Taiwan separatism. The results of the election contributed, in any case, to a relaxation of inter-party relations in Taiwan as well as of relations between Taiwan and the mainland. When asked in a 1992 interview with William F. Buckley Jr. whether the advocacy of separatism was permissible in Taiwan, ROC Premier Hau Pei-tsun replied as follows:

> Political separatism by means of violence or coercive behavior is still prohibited under the National Security Law. However, the advocacy or discussion of separatism itself does not constitute a criminal offense now. Since the recent revision of article 100 of the Criminal Code, some people, who had advocated separatism and were punished under the original Criminal Code, have had their cases dropped. Except for those using violence, all others have been released.[77]

In Germany, a different type of separatism developed as one of the negative by-products of the inter-German détente. Frightened by the prospect of an increase in the number of West German visitors and institutionalized inter-German contacts, the ruling East German Socialist Unity Party (SED)

---

[73]"DPP Proposes Chinese Common Market in Asia," *China Post*, February 19, 1990, and "DPP Passes Resolution Calling for End to Sovereignty Claims," ibid., October 9, 1990.
[74]"Constitution Proposal Polished," *China News*, August 26, 1991; "DPP Draft Constitution Backs Taiwan Independence," ibid., August 19, 1991.
[75]*China aktuell*, October 1991, 641.
[76]Ibid.
[77]"Buckley Interviews Hau on U.S. TV," *Free China Journal* 9, no. 56 (August 4, 1992): 7.

abruptly decreed that not only were there two German states, but also *two German nations*. The party's argument was that since classical Marxism had claimed that man's social consciousness depends on the socioeconomic base of society, the collectivized economic base of East Germany and the capitalist base of West Germany were bound to produce great differences in the national consciousness. Due to the laws of history, a socialist type of national consciousness, and with that a socialist German nation, had developed in East Germany, while an antagonistic and utterly alien German national consciousness had emerged in West Germany. The two German states were thus foreign to each other.[78] After the East German Communists had reacted to the 1989-90 revolution in their country with the opening of the border, their prime minister, Hans Modrow, presented a new plan on February 1, 1990, entitled "For Germany, United Fatherland," that envisaged a development process from an inter-German "contractual community" via an all-German confederation to a final all-German federation.[79] The ongoing revolution in their own country and Moscow's denial of support made free general elections in East Germany unavoidable. As a result, the Communists and a few other leftist separatist groups obtained in 1990 only about 21 percent of the total vote, the rest going to other parties, the overwhelming majority of which were advocating the unification of Germany at the earliest possible moment.[80] With that, the way was opened to unification negotiations between two democratic German governments and the final national reintegration was accomplished by the end of 1990. Thus the forces of very differently motivated separatism—regionalistic in Taiwan and systemic in East Germany—were in 1989 and 1991 almost equal in terms of voting strength.

Conclusions and Prospects

Both China and Germany have experienced in their premodern past prolonged periods of dynastic division and have been faced since 1949 with the problem of systemic division. In both countries in the post-1949 period, a prolonged phase of acute Cold War confrontation—in the case of China even interrupted by two military collisions in the 1950s—gave way to a new era of détente and mutual rapprochement, in Germany since 1970 and in China since 1987. In Germany, a partially competitive and partially cooperative coexistence between the two systems was—as in the case of divided

---

[78]Gottfried-Karl Kindermann, "The Peaceful Reunification of Germany," *Issues & Studies* 27, no. 3 (March 1991): 57-58.

[79]See Deutschland Archiv, ed., *Chronik der Ereignisse in der DDR* (Chronicle of events in the GDR), 4th ed. (Cologne: 1990), 60-61.

[80]Severin Weiland et al., eds., *9. November. Das Jahr danach. Vom Fall der Mauer bis zur ersten gesamtdeutschen Wahl* (November 9, the year after: From the fall of the wall to the first all-German election) (Munich: 1990).

Korea—inaugurated through top-level government-to-government contacts and agreements. The same holds true for reintegrating Cambodia. The cases of three divided countries, Germany, Korea, and Cambodia, do indicate that bisystemic equality and even dual representation in the United Nations does not constitute an obstacle to eventual national reintegration. Although, as indicated above, there are several illuminating cases in China's early Republican history in which the coexistence of various Chinese governments was not assumed by any party to imply a de jure division of China, the PRC government, for hierarchical and systemic reasons, has so far rejected inter-Chinese government-to-government contacts, while the ROC government, also for opposite reasons of hierarchy, has refused to accept Peking's proposal of party-to-party talks. Instead of moving, as in the German or Cambodian case, from top to bottom, the two Chinese systems are managing their current rapprochement through exchanges between semigovernmental institutions with the expectation that this process will one day be upgraded. Since 1949 the ROC government on Taiwan has worked through education and the mass media to create among the Taiwanese population an all-Chinese national consciousness. Simultaneously, Chiang Ching-kuo initiated a Taiwanization of the KMT's leadership, followed by democratization of the political process on Taiwan. This has set free forces of Taiwanese separatism that were until 1992 not very successful in terms of voting strength. In 1991, constitutional interpretation no. 76, made by the Council of Grand Justices, allowed for the dissolution of the ROC's three parliamentary bodies. The ROC's claim to an all-Chinese legitimacy from now on rests upon its constitution. Most, though not all, of the clauses of that 1946 constitution were supported by the CCP. As far as the restoration of national unity in Germany was concerned, West German governments since the 1970s proceeded on the assumption that the reestablishment of people-to-people contacts and an increase in cooperation on a technical level were more conducive to reunification than the right to "sole representation" by one side. Prior to the revolutionary systemic change in East Germany, *both* German governments had in 1989 and early 1990 developed similar schemes for a process that would lead from an intersystemic "contractual community" via a confederation to an eventual all-German federation. In China something resembling a contractual community in the sphere of legal, commercial, cultural, and other interaction has begun to develop.

In Germany as in China, intensified operational contacts between the two sides have not led to any systemic destabilization of either. There is in China now a certain amount of apprehension on both sides—in Taiwan with regard to overdependence on the mainland market, and in the PRC concerning psychological and economic penetration of southeast China by Taiwan. Chinese and foreign observers wonder what can be done in a situation in which one side rejects government-to-government talks, while the other side refuses to consent to party-to-party negotiations. One interim solution might be the formation of a mainland-Taiwan nongovernmental consultative body, composed—on the basis of parity—of representatives of the two intermediary organizations, Taiwan's SEF and the mainland's ARATS, and enlarged by an equal number of parliamentarians from both sides. This organization might be called the "All-Chinese Interim Consultative Council," and it would be chaired by a mainland and a Taiwan representative in turn. It might also include, either as observers or as regular members, representatives from Hong Kong and Macao. The primary objective of this interim council would be to coordinate and to expand activities involving the two intermediary organizations in operational spheres and to explore the possibility of creating a Chinese common market and establishing a "Chinese commonwealth." These institutions would then serve to intensify inter-Chinese contacts and cooperation until such time as the shared objective of national unification can be achieved.

Part Five

Internal Political Development in Mainland China: "Peaceful Evolution" and "Anti-Peaceful Evolution"

CHAPTER 13

New Authoritarianism, Neo-Conservatism, and Anti-Peaceful Evolution: Mainland China's Resistance to Political Modernization

Wen-hui Tsai

For over forty years, the People's Republic of China (PRC) has been a totalitarian state. From its establishment in October 1949, to the Teng Hsiao-p'ing (Deng Xiaoping) regime of the 1990s, the leadership of the Chinese Communist Party (CCP) has never relaxed its tight control over the people of mainland China. Numerous political campaigns and mass mobilizations have been launched to promote government policies in the name of the CCP and to crack down on any dissidents who opposed those policies or threatened the rule of the CCP.[1]

If there was any hope that mainland China was to enjoy a taste of freedom and democracy after the death of Chairman Mao Tse-tung (Mao Zedong) and the emergence of Teng Hsiao-p'ing in the 1970s, it was shattered by the June 4, 1989 Tienanmen (Tiananmen) massacre.

This essay will discuss the emergence in mainland China in the 1980s of "new authoritarianism," a doctrine which aroused tremendous interest among Chinese intellectuals. Advocates of new authoritarianism believed that this line of thought represented a compromise that would appeal to the leaders of the CCP, especially the reform-oriented leaders such as Teng and Hu Yao-pang (Hu Yaobang). The opponents of new authoritarianism, however, charged that its theorists had betrayed the ultimate goal of complete

---

[1] For discussions on mainland China's totalitarian political and social control, please see Wen-hui Tsai, *In Making China Modernized: Comparative Modernization between Mainland China and Taiwan*, Occasional Papers/Reprints Series in Contemporary Asian Studies (Baltimore: School of Law, University of Maryland, forthcoming); Jürgen Domes, *The Government and Politics of the PRC: A Time of Transition* (Boulder, Colo.: Westview Press, 1985); Richard Bernstein, *From the Center of the Earth: The Search for the Truth about China* (Boston: Little, Brown, 1982); Charles P. Cell, *Revolution at Work: Mobilization Campaigns in China* (New York: Academic Press, 1977).

democracy in mainland China by calling for the concentration of power in the hands of a few top leaders of the CCP.

Although the CCP did not officially endorse new authoritarianism, it seemed to welcome this line of thought as long as it did not challenge the legitimacy of Communist rule in mainland China, or become part of a conspiracy to promote "peaceful evolution" toward capitalism. In the aftermath of the 1989 student democracy movement and in the wake of the collapse of the Soviet Union, the leaders of the CCP are very sensitive about anything that could weaken their power.

Can the conservatives in the CCP leadership succeed in stopping peaceful evolution and return to the days of totalitarianism? Can reform-oriented leaders like Teng and his followers insulate themselves from the effects of peaceful evolution while continuing their economic openness? The central focus of this essay will be the nature and scope of peaceful evolution and the CCP's strategies in the anti-peaceful evolution campaign.

The essay will begin with a discussion on the meaning of new authoritarianism and the rationale behind this school of thought. Then, it will give a thorough analysis of peaceful evolution, from its historical development to the current anti-peaceful evolution campaign. Finally, the essay will look into the inevitability of peaceful evolution in mainland China's future economic development and the inevitable consequences of partial peaceful evolution in mainland China.

The Nature and Scope of New Authoritarianism

The Emergence of the Doctrine

The 1980s were a turning point in the history of the CCP. During this decade, we saw the struggles between a planned economy and a market economy, between a totalitarian political order and a decentralized social structure, between rural areas and urban centers, and between government control and democratic movements.[2] The decade began with an exciting openness in both economics and politics under Teng's economic reform policy, and ended in the bloodshed of Tienanmen.

New authoritarianism emerged in the second half of the 1980s, in the midst of what seemed like social and economic disorder. The confusion over the "two-track price system," the growing black market, the corruption

---

[2]For discussion on changes in mainland China in the 1980s, please see Elizabeth J. Perry and Christine Wong, eds., *The Political Economy of Reform in Post-Mao China*, Harvard Contemporary China Series, no. 2 (Cambridge, Mass.: Harvard University Press, 1985); Harry Harding, *China's Second Revolution: Reform After Mao* (Washington, D.C.: The Brookings Institution, 1987); An-chia Wu, ed., *Chung-kung cheng-ch'üan ssu-shih nien te hui-ku yü chan-wang* (The Chinese Communist regime at forty: Retrospect and prospects) (Taipei: Institute of International Relations, 1990).

of government and Party officials, and rising inflation in the mid-1980s were all indications that Teng's reform policy was not working. After more than thirty years of tightly controlled political and economic order, mainland China was in chaos. As new leaders of mainland China's ideological front, intellectuals engaged in a thorough analysis of the country's problems and began to look for alternatives.

Although the term "new authoritarianism" was coined by Hsiao Kung-ch'in (Xiao Gongqin) of Shanghai Normal University in 1988, discussion on the concept of "strong-man" politics had already been sparked in 1986, when Professor Wang Hu-ning (Wang Huning), a member of the International Politics faculty at Futan (Fudan) University, published an essay calling for the concentration of power in guiding economic reform. In that same year Chang Ping-chiu (Zhang Bingjiu), a graduate student at Peking (Beijing) University, proposed a theory to explain the transformation from a traditional society to a modern one. According to Chang, this transformation takes place in three stages: the first stage is characterized by a planned economy and authoritarian politics; in the second stage a developing commodity economy is combined with semiauthoritarian politics; and the third stage would see a mature commodity economy and decentralized politics. Chang maintained that mainland China's economy was at a crossroads between the first and second stages, and thus a semiauthoritarian political leadership was needed to guide economic reform. Chang insisted that it would be a terrible mistake for mainland China to bypass this second stage by jumping directly into the third stage.

Although this theory had its critics, the idea of semiauthoritarian rule attracted a great deal of attention in mainland China's young intellectual circles. Hsiao Kung-ch'in called this line of thought "new authoritarianism." He argued that the political romanticism of Sun Yat-sen was not useful in mainland China's circumstances because it had originated in the West and also because mainland China does not have a strong middle class to support it. Tai Ch'ing (Dai Qing), a reporter for the *Kwangming Daily* and the adopted daughter of Marshal Yeh Chien-ying (Ye Jianying), supported Hsiao's theory, pointing out that the iron rule of Chiang Ching-kuo was responsible for Taiwan's economic miracle. Later that year, Professor Chang Wu-chan (Zhang Wuzhan) of the University of Hong Kong took a similar stand by arguing that a wise and benevolent authoritarian government was much better than any democratic system and that mainland China's problems in economic reform were caused by the lack of authoritarian rule. Chang argued that if Chao Tzu-yang (Zhao Ziyang) had the same kind of authoritarian power, mainland China's economic reform would be smoother. The publication of an article on new authoritarianism by top CCP theoretician Wu Chia-hsiang (Wu Jiaxiang) in the Shanghai journal *Shih-chieh ching-chi tao-pao* (World Economic Herald) in January 1989 was seen as a sign of unofficial approval from the Party leadership. It was also reported in March of that year that Teng had said: "This is what I have advocated," after a

briefing from Chao Tzu-yang on the theory of new authoritarianism.[3]
In early 1989, the stage seemed set for new authoritarianism to become
the leading ideology in mainland China. It was generally agreed by young
Chinese intellectuals that mainland China needed a strong man and that
Teng was the ideal man to lead mainland China into the twenty-first century.
They argued that authoritarian rule by a single strong man was a small price
to pay for the eventual realization of total democracy.

Unfortunately, the outbreak of the student demonstrations in the spring
of 1989, and the subsequent massacre of the demonstrators on June 4, all
but destroyed the young intellectuals' hopes for a smooth transition from
new authoritarianism to democracy. Many of the young intellectuals who
had been strong supporters of new authoritarianism were involved in the
student movement and had to flee abroad.

The discussion of new authoritarianism took a new twist in the post-
June 4 period. As the leading thinkers of new authoritarianism scattered
around the world to escape from political persecution, the idea was picked
up by the so-called "Legion of Princes," children of high-ranking Party
officials. They espouse new authoritarianism under the guise of "neo-conservatism," and call for power to be transferred from the old guard to themselves, excluding other contenders such as technocrats and students newly
returned from abroad.

The Debate on New Authoritarianism

At the core of new authoritarianism is the belief that mainland China
needs strong leadership to guide its economic reform from a planned to a
market economy. Mainland China had been implementing Teng Hsiao-p'ing's
economic reform since the late 1970s, but the country's economy was clearly
in chaos by the middle of the 1980s—highlighted by rising inflation, a widening gap between rural and urban areas, increasing government corruption,
and social disorganization. There was a widespread fear among young intellectuals that Chinese civilization would collapse altogether. New authoritarianism seemed to be an excellent cure for an ailing China.

Young intellectuals like Wang Hu-ning, Chang Ping-chiu, Tai Ch'ing,
Jung Chien (Rong Jian), and Hsiao Kung-ch'in examined the economic
success stories of Taiwan, South Korea, and Singapore, as well as the failure
of many other developing nations, and decided that a semiauthoritarian
government is necessary for economic growth. They found that developing
countries with strong rulers had all been able to achieve a much higher rate

---

[3]This section of the history of "new authoritarianism" was taken from the account given by Ch'i
Mo, in Ch'i Mo, ed., *Hsin ch'üan-wei chu-i: Tui Chung-kuo ta-lu wei-lai ming-yün te lun-cheng*
(New authoritarianism: The debates on the future fate of the Chinese mainland) (Taipei: T'ang-
shan, 1991), 234-44.

of economic growth than those ruled either by a democratic government or by a totalitarian regime. For instance, a cross-nation study of economic growth by Chao Tzu-yang's think-tank, the Research Institute for Economic System Reform, discovered that many developing nations have experienced greater social and political instability than developed nations. The Research Institute concluded that this instability is caused by the raising of popular expectations in developing nations. When a nation suffers food shortages and hunger problems, it is relatively easy to meet people's basic expectations for food, but when their hunger is satisfied, people will demand more consumer goods, democracy, human rights, freedom, etc., which are not so easy to provide, and thus social unrest may come about. Such instability did not occur in the "four little dragons" of Asia (Hong Kong, Singapore, Taiwan, and South Korea) because their authoritarian governments suppressed demands for material goods and political freedom. It was concluded that authoritarianism was responsible for the steady economic growth and sociopolitical stability experienced in the "four little dragons."[4]

New authoritarianism is also called by other names—such as "elite rule" and "strong-man politics." It is built upon the following assumptions:

1. Stability in society and politics is a necessary precondition for economic growth.
2. The success of economic growth in the "four little dragons" and the instability suffered by other developing nations clearly indicate the necessity for a strong government.
3. Democracy would not work in mainland China because its people are ill-educated and ill-prepared for the decentralization of power.
4. The experience of rule by the people during the Cultural Revolution was a lesson that mainland China ought not to repeat.
5. The social and economic disorganization in mainland China during the first half of the 1980s was caused by the decentralization of power within the CCP.
6. Mainland China's reform should not be built on a democratic system; it must depend on a strong authoritarian political system to force reform programs forward.

The supporters of new authoritarianism held that mainland China must pass through a stage of authoritarian rule to promote economic reform. Authoritarian rule would be replaced by a true democratic system when the reform is completed. Any call for a democratic system of government previous to this would mean instability and chaos. The goal of new authoritarianism

---

[4]The study was cited in Yü Kuang-hua, "The Social Foundation and Fantasy of the New Authoritarianism," in Ch'i, *Hsin ch'üan-wei chu-i*, 85.

is to establish a strong government while at the same time opening up the economy; or what Ch'en I-tzu (Chen Yizi) and his colleagues have called a "hard government-soft economy" development model.[5] The idea of authoritarian "strong man" rule appealed to Teng and other reform-oriented leaders prior to the 1989 student unrest because it neither challenged the legitimacy of CCP rule nor did it threaten Teng's power.

However, new authoritarianism met with strong resistance from a small group of young intellectuals who advocated the immediate installation of true democracy in mainland China. They saw new authoritarianism as a betrayal of freedom and human dignity. Hsü Liang-ying (Xu Liangying), for example, called new authoritarianism "an anti-democratic reflux."[6] Hsü insisted that the implementation of democracy is the only guarantee for stability and integration and that mass participation in policymaking is the best way to avoid mistakes and errors in the process of economic reform. From Hsü's point of view, it would be a historical tragedy if mainland China were to return to dictatorship. In "Does China Need Another Emperor?" published in 1988, Shao Yen-hsiang (Shao Yanxiang) criticized the followers of new authoritarianism for trying to create another Chinese emperor. Shao said mainland China's severe underdevelopment in the past was the result of authoritarian leadership, not a democratic government.[7]

The Tienanmen massacre further proved that strong-man rule was dangerous as well as anti-democratic. Since then, many supporters of new authoritarianism have changed their views and joined the critics in calling for the overthrow of Teng and his power clique.

The Legion of Princes and Neo-Conservatism

An article published in the Hong Kong magazine *Paishing* in March 1992 indicated that new authoritarianism has now been adopted by the "Legion of Princes" and renamed "neo-conservatism":

> The theoretical preparation for this was long before the Soviet coup. In December 1990, the theoretical section of *China Youth Daily*, one of the original fortresses of new authoritarianism, sponsored a conference on "Traditional Chinese Culture and Socialist Modernization." Participants in this conference included Yuan Mu, Xu Weicheng [Hsü Wei-ch'eng], He Xin [Ho Hsin], and a bunch of the *China Youth Daily* theoretical elite. It was during this conference that the theoretician Xiao Gongqin, the reported architect of new authoritarianism in mainland China, changed the name of "new authoritarianism" to "neo-conservatism."[8]

---

[5]Ch'en I-tzu, Wang Hsiao-ch'iang, and Li Chün, "Establishing a 'Hard Government-Soft Economy' Development Model," in Ch'i, *Hsin ch'üan-wei chu-i*, 80-82.

[6]Hsü Liang-ying, "China's Anti-Democratic Reflux," in Ch'i, *Hsin ch'üan-wei chu-i*, 59.

[7]Shao Yen-hsiang, "Does China Need Another Emperor?" in Ch'i, *Hsin ch'üan-wei chu-i*, 64-68.

[8]"Behind the CCP Princes Party," *Pai-hsing* (Paishing) (Hong Kong), no. 260 (March 16, 1992): 32-35. Translated in *Inside China Mainland* (Taipei) 14, no. 5 (May 1992): 7.

Neo-conservatism calls for gradual modernization based on respect for the historical continuity of the traditional order; it opposes "bourgeois liberalization" and upholds the "four cardinal principles." To the "Legion of Princes," the idea of power being concentrated in the hands of a few is attractive, for it would not only help them to gain control of central power, but also help slow down Teng's more liberal and radical economic reform measures.

Members of the "Legion of Princes" realize that trying to reverse the economic reform is unrealistic, yet they are also aware that the pace of Teng's reforms must be slowed to allow them time to seize power. Under the leadership of Ch'en Yün's (Chen Yun's) son, Ch'en Yüan (Chen Yuan), the "Legion of Princes" with their ideology of neo-conservatism have begun to undermine the economic reform. Along with their parents, they have resisted Teng and his reform-oriented faction.

Anti-Peaceful Evolution and Mainland China's Fear

The Origin of Peaceful Evolution

The adherents of new authoritarianism, neo-conservatism, and Teng's economic reform policy may be fighting each other for power, but they all share the common goal of maintaining the power of the CCP. In the aftermath of the 1989 Tienanmen massacre, new authoritarianism gradually lost its appeal to the CCP leadership under the campaign of anti-peaceful evolution. The foreign elements in new authoritarianism made it an object of suspicion to the regime which had blamed foreign influence for the recent disturbances.

The concept of peaceful evolution can be traced back to the 1950s, at the height of the worldwide spread of Communism. John Foster Dulles, then U.S. secretary of state, proposed in a speech he made in Los Angeles in 1958, that the Western world adopt a peaceful strategy to change Communism in the Soviet Union and mainland China. Dulles believed that the power struggles and internal conflicts inherent in Communism would likely worsen, and that Western nations must increase people-to-people contacts and cultural and scientific exchanges, and find other peaceful means to influence Communist nations.

Changing the Communist system through peaceful evolution subsequently became the main strategy of United States foreign policy in dealing with the Soviet Union and the PRC. President John F. Kennedy, for example, said in 1959 that the Communist world was no longer an unbreakable stone and that the West ought to gradually, carefully, and peacefully approach Communist nations to plant the seeds of freedom. President Lyndon B. Johnson echoed this same line of thought in 1964, when he said that the main purpose of U.S. policy on Eastern Europe was to encourage peaceful efforts to reduce control from Moscow, and that trade with the United States and

other free world nations would be one of the fundamental means for East
European countries to resist Soviet control.[9]

Mao Tse-tung took these statements very seriously. He believed that
it was possible for this strategy of peaceful evolution to erode the CCP from
within. In his attempt to block the process, Mao closed mainland China's door
almost completely to foreign contact, while engaging in constant campaigns
against "revisionists" and "capitalist roaders" at home to keep alive the
spirit of class struggle among his Communist cadres. Although Mao was
successful in blocking peaceful evolution, under his rule mainland China
became totally isolated from the rest of the world and economically underdeveloped. In an article recently published in the mainland it was said that
"the Western bourgeoisie's peaceful evolution strategy found little opportunity for infiltration when our nation was closed unto itself in the days of
ceaseless class struggle. The influence of peaceful evolution on intellectuals'
ideology was at that time absolutely minimal. . . . Suspension of all exchange with the outside prevented the Western world from penetrating ideological and cultural infiltration by using its people to spread the seeds of
freedom."[10] The price was certainly high,[11] but the CCP under Mao was
in firm control of the country and peaceful evolution was never a threat.

The Emergence of Peaceful Evolution

The PRC is currently undergoing tremendous changes. As new elements
are being introduced, peaceful evolution has begun to take hold. Among
the factors that have contributed to the recent peaceful evolution in mainland
China, the following stand out as the most significant:

First, mainland China's economic reform and open-door policy under
Teng has created an environment conducive to foreign influence, especially
American influence. According to one author,

> With the great expansion in exchange which the new order has ushered through
> our open doors, developed Western nations have, on the strength of their eco-

---

[9]Excerpts from the speeches of Dulles, Kennedy, Johnson, Richard Nixon, Ronald Reagan,
and George Bush were translated in Li Ch'uan-hua et al., eds., *Chung-kuo ssu-hsiang cheng-
chih kung-tso ch'üan-shu* (Encyclopedia of Chinese ideological and political work) (Peking:
Chung-kuo jen-min ta-hsüeh ch'u-pan-she, 1990), 1:1239-62.

[10]"Intellectuals in a New Era of Ideological and Political Work," *Ssu-hsiang cheng-chih kung-tso
yen-chiu* (Ideological and Political Work Studies) (Peking), December 8, 1991, 15-17. Translated in *Inside China Mainland* 14, no. 3 (March 1992): 46-47.

[11]For discussions on mainland China's underdevelopment under the closed-door policy, see:
Bernstein, *From the Center of the Earth*; Dennis Bloodworth, *The Messiah and the Mandarins*
(New York: Atheneum, 1982); Stuart R. Schram, *Mao Zedong: A Preliminary Reassessment*
(Hong Kong: Chinese University Press, 1983); Tang-tai Chung-kuo hsüeh-hui (Society for the
Study of Modern China), ed., *Chung-kuo te wei-chi: Ssu-shih nien-lai te cheng-chih, ching-
chi, ho she-hui yün-tung* (China's crisis: Politics, economy, and social movements during the
past forty years) (Hong Kong: Shu-kuang t'u-shu kung-szu, 1990).

nomic and technological superiority, stepped up their pursuit of peaceful evolution. . . . The gradual lifting of restrictions on listening to overseas radio programs has provided peaceful evolution with a chance to divide and disintegrate the people's fighting will without resorting to bullets or bombs. Increased economic collaboration, technical cooperation, foreign trade and cultural exchanges have presented an opportunity for peaceful evolution to make use of intellectuals as seeds of freedom for the propagation of Western thought, culture, and values. In sum, opening up to the outside has brought us prospects for learning from and about the advanced technology and management experience of developed nations, but it has also provided inroads for hostile Western forces and peaceful evolution.[12]

In the eyes of the CCP leadership, the United States is the major player in this peaceful evolution conspiracy against mainland China. An internal document which the CCP Propaganda Department distributed to cadres at the provincial and local levels said: "The U.S. has already gone from opposing Communism to making an all-out effort to promote its own values and ideals to establish a 'new world order'."[13] The document went on to outline the extent of U.S. strategies to foster peaceful evolution in mainland China. It said that, politically, the United States has used human rights as an excuse to create international anti-Peking sentiment, to attack mainland China's population control practices and "slander" Peking's military actions against Tibetans. The economic measures adopted by the United States, the document said, include threatening to revoke the PRC's most favored nation status, accusing Peking of exporting goods produced in labor camps, listing mainland China as one of the "key countries" which fails to protect American intellectual property rights, and complaining about the U.S.-mainland China trade imbalance.[14] In the military field, the document continued, the United States has banned the export of advanced technologies to mainland China and set punishments for other nations that did export them. The document also accused the United States of using the news media and cultural and academic exchange channels to introduce new ideas to mainland China and of attempting to isolate the PRC and prevent it from having high-level diplomatic contacts with Western nations.[15]

Second, Peking sees the collapse of the Soviet Union and the East European Communist regimes as proof of the effectiveness of the peaceful evolution strategy. Kao Ti (Gao Di), publisher of the *People's Daily*, condemned Mikhail Gorbachev and Boris Yeltsin as "traitors" during one internal speech. Kao termed Gorbachev's dissolution of the Soviet Communist Party as the

---

[12]See note 10 above.

[13]"Behind the Anti-U.S. Secret Document," *Tung-hsiang* (The Trend Magazine) (Hong Kong), no. 77/78 (January-February 1992): 6-8. Translated in *Inside China Mainland* 14, no. 3 (March 1992): 19.

[14]Ibid., 19-20.

[15]Ibid.

"greatest betrayal" of international Communism. Kao said: "Gorbachev is by no means a Communist, but a traitor and an agent of the West. They handle everything according to the Western system and the U.S. agenda. However, Western Europe and America are still not satisfied. They still wish for the Soviet Union to become a 'de-fanged lion', which is the same as in the past when they wanted China to become a sleeping lion."[16]

The collapse of the Soviet Union was a tremendous shock to the Chinese Communist leadership. The Soviet Union had served as a model for Communist China for the past forty years; the PRC's economy, politics, and many of its social institutions were all copied from the Soviet Union. Although the two had their differences, they were both part of the Communist world and mainland Chinese were reminded that the Soviet Union was like an "elder brother." Now, this "elder brother" had been destroyed by peaceful evolution, and those in power in Peking feared that the same thing could happen to them.

Third, the student demonstrations and democracy movement of 1989 made the mainland Chinese leaders aware of dissatisfaction among students and the general population. Teng said on June 9, after the military crackdown at Tienanmen Square:

> This incident was definitely going to come; it was inevitable. It is better for us to have it happen now because we still have a large group of elderly comrades alive who had experience in dealing with this type of disturbance. They all know what is good for the Party and they all support the Party in taking firm action against the demonstrations. Although there are a few comrades who still do not understand, they will eventually support the Party center in taking such an action.
>
> As soon as the incident exploded, it became very clear to us that their [foreigners'] two major items of propaganda are: overthrowing the Communist Party and destroying the socialist system. Their goal is to establish a bourgeois republic, totally dependent on the West.[17]

Without any doubt, the 1989 student demonstration was the largest mass movement against the PRC regime in its forty years of existence. The government's legitimacy was seriously challenged and the CCP's leadership was critically questioned. The students' calls for democracy and freedom reflected a long accumulation of human suffering in mainland China. More importantly, though, the student demonstration proved that Western efforts to bring about peaceful evolution had begun to influence the minds of many young Chinese students.

Fourth, the regime is worried that the revival of religion in mainland China has weakened the influence of Communist ideology. In a report to the Central Party School, T'ao Ssu-chü (Tao Siju), the minister of public security, listed the increasing prominence of religion as one of the main

---

[16]Quoted in ibid., 83.

[17]Quoted in *Chung-kuo ssu-hsiang cheng-chih kung-tso ch'üan-shu* 1:1237.

forces behind peaceful evolution in mainland China. T'ao said that the majority of religious activities are supported by Christian groups abroad and that they are "using the Bible to defeat Communism in China," in the hope of making religion evolve into an anti-government force which answers to foreign forces.[18]

From Communist China's very beginning, Mao saw religion as an "enemy without guns." Religious beliefs and practices, especially those of Western origin, were feared for their ability to undermine Communist ideology and threaten the CCP.

The Communist attacks were focused on Western religions under the influence of foreigners. The Catholic Church was singled out because Catholic bishops, priests, monks, and nuns owe obedience to the Pope in the Vatican. In Mao's eyes, Western religions were an institution that could be used by foreigners to further peaceful evolution in mainland China.[19]

The CCP believes that the United States especially is using religion to promote peaceful evolution in mainland China. A December 5, 1991 article in *Hsüeh-hsi yü yen-chiu* (Learning & Study), a journal published by the Peking Municipal Party Committee, argued that "heavyweights in U.S. political circles attach great importance to using religious forces to carry out ideological subversion against socialist countries."[20] It implied that the United States and the Vatican were the main forces responsible for the collapse of Communism in Eastern Europe and are currently trying to penetrate into mainland China.

Although a religious revival is currently under way in mainland China under Teng's open-door policy, the repression of religion has never been completely relaxed. Every sign indicates that the Chinese Communists are conducting a ruthless campaign of suppression of home-based church groups, which have mushroomed in the relatively liberal atmosphere of recent years. The CCP leadership fears that if religion is allowed to develop, loyalty conflicts will arise, making it impossible for them to exercise complete control. Liu Chung-te (Liu Zhongde), a deputy secretary-general of the State Council, was quoted in the *People's Daily* (January 21, 1990) as saying that "in the anti-pornography, anti-six-evil campaigns, local authorities in some places have castigated religious activities and scriptures and relics of feudal super-stition. This behavior is mistaken and measures are being taken to correct

---

[18]See "Guard Against Six Kinds of Hostile Forces—T'ao Ssu-chü's Report at the Central Party School," *Chiu-shih nien-tai* (The Nineties) (Hong Kong), January 1992, 26-28. Translated in *Inside China Mainland* 14, no. 3 (March 1992): 8-14.

[19]James T. Myers, *Enemies Without Guns: The Catholic Church in China* (New York: Professors World Peace Academy, 1991).

[20]Excerpts from this article were translated in *Inside China Mainland* 14, no. 3 (March 1992): 60-62. The quote here is from page 60.

it."[21] This was followed by a rash of reports about harassment of clergy, especially Christian priests and nuns.[22]

Finally, the successful economic development of Taiwan and Hong Kong has become the envy of every Chinese on the mainland. In particular, the democratization that has taken place in Taiwan since the death of President Chiang Ching-kuo has also provided new hopes for human dignity and freedom among mainland Chinese intellectuals.

For nearly forty years, Taiwan and mainland China have been separated and people on both sides of the Taiwan Strait were prohibited from visiting each other. Their image of the other side was built purely on the propaganda supplied by their own respective governments. The breakthrough came on November 2, 1987, when Taipei first allowed its citizens to travel to the mainland to visit their relatives. Since then, Taipei has also permitted visits for tourism and academic and professional conferences, and indirect trade with mainland China. The increase in contacts with people from Taiwan and Hong Kong has opened the eyes of the ordinary Chinese on the mainland to the economic wealth and political freedom these two Chinese communities enjoy.[23]

Strategies in the Anti-Peaceful Evolution Campaign

It is clear that the leaders of Communist China are very worried about peaceful evolution. Premier Li P'eng (Li Peng), in a report to the third session of the Seventh National People's Congress held in Peking in March 1990, cautioned his audience that the CCP is under threat from peaceful evolution. A year later, Li warned again: "In the next ten years, the international situation will change dramatically, and thus the foreign opposing groups will not end their conspiracy to promote peaceful evolution in China."[24] Communist leaders are worried that peaceful evolution will increase foreign influence in mainland China, both economically and culturally, and lead to the eventual death of the Communist system.

Peaceful evolution has become a major preoccupation of the Peking leadership and action has been taken in several areas to combat it.

Indoctrination: Chinese Communist leaders believe that the fight against peaceful evolution will be determined by the CCP's ability to indoctrinate

---

[21]*K'ai-fang* (Open) (Hong Kong), March 1990, 21-23. Translated in *Inside China Mainland* 12, no. 6 (June 1990): 27.

[22]A news item reported in *Chung-kung wen-t'i tzu-liao chou-k'an* (Weekly Materials on Chinese Communist Problems) (Taipei), no. 411 (April 9, 1990): 24-25 listed several prosecutions and harassments of religious personnel after June 4, 1989.

[23]For a detailed discussion of the recent contacts between mainland China and Taiwan, please see Wen-hui Tsai, "Convergence and Divergence Between Mainland China and Taiwan: The Future of Unification," *Issues & Studies* 27, no. 12 (December 1991): 1-28.

[24]Quoted in Lung Fei, "A Discussion of Communist China's Cadre Policy as Seen from 'Anti-Peaceful Evolution'," *Chung-kung wen-t'i tzu-liao chou-k'an*, no. 516 (April 24, 1992): 39.

its members. The focus of this indoctrination campaign is intellectuals and university students.

Mainland officials admit that there are three "much's" in the PRC's higher education: "much resentment, much dissatisfaction with the status quo, and much unrestrained demand for freedom."[25] At a meeting with college and university presidents and Party secretaries in October 1991, Ho Tung-ch'ang (He Dongchang), vice chairman of the State Education Commission, said: "The authority to lead our nation's institutions of higher learning must rest in the hands of those who believe firmly in Marxism, who are resolute in following the socialist road, and who dare to wage a struggle against bourgeois ideology."[26]

Since intellectuals and students are the most likely targets of peaceful evolution efforts, they are now required to take additional courses on Marxism and Maoism to learn the "truth" of Communism. In addition, students returning from abroad must be reindoctrinated so that they will appreciate the "greatness" of Communism. Ho also said that "criticism of bourgeois liberalization and criticism of corrupt bourgeois ideology must be required curriculum in every institute of higher learning. Anyone who fails these courses does not make the grade as a builder of socialism. We must maintain guard over the gates."[27]

Anti-corruption: The PRC leadership believes that peaceful evolution could enter mainland China through corrupt government officials at various levels of the administration. Under the open-door policy, there have been more incidents of corruption among government and Party officials who take bribes or are involved in the embezzlement of funds, and such corruption was one of the main targets of the 1989 student demonstrations.

A campaign against corruption in the Party and government is being carried out and ideological correctness is now required of all key officials. Corrupt officials are being punished and an aggressive campaign is under way to remove all bad elements from the Party. According to a report in the *People's Daily* on January 29, 1992, the CCP expelled nearly 40,000 members for corruption in 1991 and hailed the "house cleaning" as a new success in boosting its image.[28]

The Legion of Princes: As students, intellectuals, and technocrats are believed to have been "polluted" by Western liberal capitalist ideology, a section of the Peking leadership is convinced that only their own children can be trusted to uphold the absolute power of the CCP. They advocate

---

[25]*Inside China Mainland* 14, no. 3 (March 1992): 50.
[26]Quoted in ibid., 53.
[27]Ibid.
[28]Quoted in ibid., 94.

the recruitment of the "Legion of Princes" to succeed the present Party leadership.

Evidence of this scheme for passing power from the old guard to the "Legion of Princes" may be found in two important documents. One is a letter written by Ch'en Yün to the CCP Politburo in which he suggests that children of high-ranking cadres be recruited into the leadership. As Ch'en said, "With our children our hearts are at ease. At least they will not totally deny their own fathers."

The other document is the "Theoretical Guidelines for National Governance," written by Ch'en Yün's son, Ch'en Yüan, which details mainland China's responses and strategic choices in the wake of the fall of the Soviet Union. The General Office of the CCP Central Committee printed it as an internal document for circulation among its top leadership. It supports the "iron-fisted" method of dealing with the student demonstrators on June 4 and blames the demonstrations on Western ideas of freedom and democracy. It also argues that all the people's and the nation's property must be held by the Communist Party, and advocates the internationalization of the "class struggle."[29]

Response to Taiwan: The CCP is taking a firm stand against Taiwan's efforts to bring about peaceful evolution in the mainland. The economic prosperity and political freedom enjoyed by people in the West can be dismissed by the CCP leaders as products of a different tradition and culture that will not work in mainland China, and the Chinese people may be persuaded to accept this point of view for nationalistic reasons. The situation in Taiwan, however, cannot be dismissed in this way. Until the mid-1980s, ordinary people in mainland China were not aware of Taiwan's economic success. They were told that life in Taiwan was harsh and terrifying and that Communism, being people-oriented, was better than Sun Yat-sen's Three Principles of the People and the tyranny of the Kuomintang.

The Taipei government's decision in 1987 to allow its citizens to visit mainland China has changed all that. Armed with tremendous wealth, Taiwanese visitors have been bringing gifts of cash and consumer goods to their relatives and friends on the mainland. Between 1987 and 1990, more than half a million Taiwan residents visited the mainland, an average of five hundred every day. It has been estimated that Taiwanese visitors infuse some US$2 billion in foreign exchange into mainland China each year. In addition, Taiwanese businessmen invested around US$400 million on the mainland in 1988 alone, in more than eight hundred joint business ventures and 10,584 Taiwanese managed individual businesses.[30] As restrictions on travel and trade with the mainland have been relaxed, Taiwan's success story

---

[29]*Inside China Mainland* 14, no. 5 (May 1992): 6-8.
[30]Tsai, "Convergence and Divergence," 21-24.

has been repeatedly told to people on the mainland. Educational materials, TV programs, and material goods from Taiwan have become sought after items in mainland China. Peaceful evolution from Taiwan has slowly and steadily spread through mainland China.

The leaders of the CCP realize that, in the eyes of the mainland people, the Taiwan success story is more convincing than any Western example could be. As a result, the CCP has consistently tried to downplay Taiwan's success and has taken a firm stand against Taipei's demand for peaceful coexistence. Its leaders have rejected Taipei's repeated calls for Peking to forswear military aggression against Taiwan, to allow the Republic of China (ROC) to participate in international organizations, and to hold government-to-government negotiations on reunification.[31]

CCP leaders and several mainland Chinese social scientists have continued to downplay Taiwan's achievements. They maintain that the ROC government had very little to do with the Taiwan miracle, and instead attribute Taiwan's economic growth to such factors as its smaller territory and population, U.S. aid, Japanese colonial education, the pre-1949 industrial base, and the gold allegedly stolen by the Kuomintang from the mainland when they retreated to Taiwan in 1949. Moreover, the CCP leaders also overemphasize the seemingly chaotic process of Taiwan's transition to democracy as evidence of Taiwan's failure.

In addition to the above-mentioned strategies, other measures have also been taken by the CCP to block peaceful evolution. These include keeping tighter controls on students abroad, denouncing racial conflicts in America, exaggerating the incidence of violence and crime in America and other Western nations,[32] accusing the West of trying to overthrow the Communist system, and discouraging marriages between Chinese and foreigners. All these are aimed at the preservation of Chinese Communism and shutting out "spiritual pollution" from the West. In view of the success of peaceful evolution in the Soviet Union and its East European Communist allies, the Peking leaders realize that they must do everything they can to halt the process of peaceful evolution in mainland China.

Conclusion: Mainland China's Future

Can mainland China successfully stop peaceful evolution while continuing its economic reform? The answer is a clear *no*. Peaceful evolution

---

[31]Ibid., 2-13.

[32]Two columnists on the *Fa-chih jih-pao* (Legal System Daily) in Peking are reported to have criticized violations of human rights in dealing with the Los Angeles riot of May 1992. See *Chung-kuo shih-pao* (China Times) (Taipei), May 7, 1992. The original report appeared one day earlier.

is a complex process that involves changes in internal and external aspects of a society. Although the Communist Chinese leaders seem to view peaceful evolution purely as the result of foreign infiltration, domestic factors such as the erosion of the CCP's political leadership, population pressure, uneven development of the urban and rural sectors, and the rising expectations of the masses have all contributed to peaceful evolution on the Chinese mainland.

Peking's attempt to block foreign influence will inevitably prove fruitless. Already, the process of peaceful evolution has begun in mainland China as a result of business and trade, tourism, and academic and cultural exchanges. China's ignorance of international affairs in the nineteenth century was one of the main causes of its many defeats at the hands of foreign powers, while Mao's closed-door policy was responsible for mainland China's underdevelopment. Today, mainland China cannot afford to close its door to outsiders again.

It is clear that mainland China's attack on foreign influence is a smoke screen for its resistance to overall change that could have a lasting impact on the CCP's hold on power. Recently, Hsü Chia-t'un (Xu Jiatun), the former chief of the New China News Agency's Hong Kong branch who is now in exile in the United States, proposed changing the Chinese translation of the term "peaceful evolution" from "*ho-p'ing yen-pien*" to "*ho-p'ing yen-chin*," as the latter implies mild peaceful progress rather than radical change. Hsü believes this new translation will ease the CCP's fears and make change more acceptable.[33]

The dilemma faced by both Teng's reformist clique and the other more conservative cliques is to allow economic openness while at the same time preserving the authoritarian rule of the CCP. This is nothing new, for the same dilemma was faced earlier by Chinese intellectuals and the Ch'ing government in the second half of the nineteenth century. Adopting only Western technology while preserving the "Chinese essence" was the goal of late-Ch'ing reformers also. The late-Ch'ing Westernization programs were aimed at upgrading China's technology and economy without touching the political foundation of the Manchu court. This effort failed, however, and the Manchu Dynasty was overthrown by the revolution of 1911. Apparently, Teng and the current CCP leadership are in search of the same goal that eluded the Ch'ing. If history is any indication, continued economic reforms will eventually bring about political change in mainland China.

The future leaders of the CCP, whether they be technocrats or members of the "Legion of Princes," will all have to make adjustments to the new openness that peaceful evolution will bring. Modernization involves all aspects of a society's infrastructure; it introduces changes in economic, po-

---

[33]Hsü Chia-t'un, "On Peaceful Evolution," *Shih-chieh jih-pao* (World Journal) (New York), June 3, 1992, 19.

litical, social, cultural, and religious institutions. Changing economic practices will eventually change other aspects of the Chinese way of life. Thus, the success of economic modernization will be dependent on its coordinated interplay with other noneconomic systems of society. A process of political modernization—characterized by the political participation of citizens, the decentralization of the decision-making process, and fairness in distributive justice—must accompany economic reform. In any case, the attempts to limit economic reform will prove to be fruitless. Peaceful evolution in mainland China's political system will eventually occur.

Mainland China is now the "orphan" of the Communist world. It may take several years, but the current anti-peaceful evolution campaign will gradually fade away and allow mainland China's seeds of democracy to grow and mature.

CHAPTER 14

Comprehensive Security in the Information Age: Internal Factors of "Peaceful Evolution" and "Non-Peaceful Evolution" in Mainland China

Gerrit W. Gong

In ways more subtle and devastating than ever before, politics, strategy, and technology come together in today's management of competition and in today's conduct of conflict. The management of the interface between the political-military context (which establishes perceptions and expectations, and thereby provides support, legitimacy, and coalition cohesion) and the military-technical prosecution of conflict on the battlefield seems increasingly and decisively to favor countries able to accommodate the underlying trends of the information age.

This chapter thus addresses mainland China's concept of comprehensive security in the information age, as evidenced in the dynamic interplay of internal and international factors of "peaceful evolution" and "anti-peaceful evolution."

Information Age Trends as Factors of "Peaceful Evolution"

Revolutionary, global information age trends affect mainland China, as every other country, and form an inescapable framework as factors of "peaceful evolution."[1] One characteristic of the age of information is the

---

[1]Elements of this argument are set forth in George P. Shultz, "The Shape, Scope, and Consequences of the Age of Information," *Bulletin* (Washington, D.C., U.S. Department of State), March 26, 1986, 86:40-43. See also Gerrit W. Gong, "Information, Secularization, and the 'Crisis of Belief': Fundamental Dynamics of Change in China," in *Forces of Change in Contemporary China*, ed. Bih-jaw Lin and James T. Myers (Taipei: Institute of International Relations, 1992), 189-95.

unprecedented convergence of the factors necessary for success in political, economic, and social areas. As part of a deep-rooted historical trend, people expect higher standards of living, directly linked to their own level of work performance. They also expect a greater say, through some form of direct or indirect representation, in their political futures.

The increasing inseparability of politics, economics, and basic social structures and values poses a particular, fundamental dilemma for socialist countries. Now more than ever, it seems impossible to foster a globally competitive, market-oriented economy while at the same time tightly centralizing control of the information and authority necessary to make decisions. Economically efficient distribution systems seem to demand politically pluralistic ones; both depend on the same real-time, open channels of information to be competitive.

Thus, the information revolution in the People's Republic of China (PRC) transcends cross-border flows of information by fax, satellite, radio, and readily-available printed materials—though each independent source of facts forces a closed system to open or adjust that much more. Even more fundamental aspects of the information revolution challenge mainland China's socialist system; for this reason, such factors inadvertently serve as factors of "peaceful evolution." For example, a key to Party control is the restricted flow of information through printed *nei-pu* or internal documents. Even retired cadres insist on retaining access to controlled Party documents as a means of keeping informed. Indeed, like charting the circulation of radioactive barium in the bloodstream in a medical test, one could gauge the acceptance (or not) of Teng Hsiao-p'ing's (Deng Xiaoping's) reformist speeches as they made their way to various levels through different Party, government, and military structures.[2]

Yet, the control of paper flow on a national scale as a means of regulating political decision-making seems increasingly anachronistic, and susceptible to jolting change, in an age of electronic media. The charges on which Chao Tzu-yang's (Zhao Ziyang's) advisor Pao T'ung (Bao Tong) was sentenced to seven years in prison included "revealing state secrets,"

---

[2]For example, see Hu Hsiu-yuen, "Leading Leftists Remain in Power," *Ming Pao* (Hong Kong), April 26, 1992, 20, cited in Foreign Broadcast Information Service (FBIS), *Daily Report: China* (hereafter cited as *FBIS-CHI*), 92-082 (April 28, 1992): 24; Shih Chun-yu, "Deng Xiaoping Line Will Remain Unchanged for 100 Years," *Ta Kung Pao* (Hong Kong), March 13, 1992, 2, cited in *FBIS-CHI*-92-050 (March 13, 1992): 19; *FBIS-CHI*-92-089 (May 7, 1992): 18-22, etc. For example, page 19 of this last reference notes that "in accordance with Yang Shangkun's proposal, the CPC Central Committee's Political Bureau held an enlarged meeting to discuss the spirit of Deng's speeches; after that, Yang Shangkun again proposed that the Political Bureau relay Deng's speeches during his trip to the south to all high- and intermediate-level party cadres. The version of Deng's remarks to be disseminated was examined and approved by Deng himself. The aim was to bring the thinking of all high- and intermediate-level cadres in line with Deng's speeches."

the same charge leveled against Chao himself. Still, widening exchange with international sources and conduits of news will necessitate a continued opening of internal means of handling news and information, eventually making charges of "leaking state secrets" increasingly difficult to maintain.

Access to the television media by other than state-controlled sources seems a political explosion waiting to happen in mainland China. Indeed, it was partly the potential of mobilizing the Chinese countryside through emotional, televised pictures of gaunt hunger-striking students and their weeping mothers which led to the abrupt cessation of Tienanmen (Tiananmen) Square coverage in the days prior to the declaration of martial law.

Nevertheless, mainland China's efforts to develop information technologies, including computers, telecommunications systems, and so on, are inescapably embedded in its imperative toward overall science and technology modernization. Discrete problems of applied physics and engineering are the challenges of the industrial age. These are the sometimes large, but focused tasks on which centrally managed systems could and did successfully concentrate human and physical resources, as the Soviet Union and mainland China did in respectively developing their atomic bombs in 1949 and 1964.

Yet, as the information age promises to reveal further, higher levels of competitive productivity leading to more prosperous and fulfilling life styles are only possible if societies draw on the capital of codified knowledge called information (as opposed to mere data) through technologies which both require and foster open systems.

Thus goes my general argument.

More specifically, as a striking example of conflict in the information age, the Persian Gulf War set off a new self-examination in mainland China about how Peking (Beijing) establishes itself relative to the scientific-technological revolution. Some of the elements of this discussion may thereby provide a useful prism for considering the interplay of internal and international factors of "peaceful evolution" and "anti-peaceful evolution" in mainland China, affecting directly and indirectly as they do key Chinese institutions (including the People's Liberation Army [PLA]) at a time when mainland China must set its future economic and political orientation while in the midst of a watershed generational and leadership transition.

Conflict in the Information Age:
The Persian Gulf War as "Smart War"

Well before the Persian Gulf conflict, mainland Chinese strategists successfully argued for a basic concept of comprehensive national strength. This concept linked mainland China's domestic and international interests and imperatives. The comprehensive strength argument provided a compelling rationale for systemic modernization and economic invigoration. It also provided guidelines and priorities for developing key capabilities, including among the so-called "fourth generation" technologies.

Yet, the Gulf War, in ways mainland Chinese analysts are still realizing, underscored not only the essential need for comprehensive strength, but also how far mainland China lags in the technologies necessary to wage war under modern, high-intensity conditions.

Three basic points can be made about conflict in the information age, as represented by the Gulf War, which mainland Chinese analysts continue to painstakingly analyze and spiritedly debate.

First, the Gulf War was the first major military conflict of the post-Cold War period; it also marked a possible new era of "smart war."[3] "Smart war" is characterized as the competition to manage the interface between the political-military objectives which set the context for conflict and the technical-military means which determine the outcome of battle. What further marks the Gulf War as "smart war" is the central role played by information technologies in the management of the interface between technological means and political ends, and thus in shaping the ability to both effectively wage war on the battlefield and authoritatively define its purpose.

Second, with an effectiveness which surprised mainland Chinese analysts, the United States and its coalition partners were able to (1) concentrate technical-military resources, (2) maintain the initiative, and (3) determine the parameters of conflict sufficient to win decisive military victory within the period of public expectation and well within the scope of publicly-acceptable losses.

By definition, the theaters of "smart war" range from the way the political-technical interface of war is justified to one's own people and coalition or alliance partners, to the way the interface is carried out against one's identified and potential enemies. The very speed of decision-making placed a premium on pre-existing common perceptions and values, personal familiarity and thereby personal trust among individuals, and established avenues and experience of exchange and cooperation. All this underscores how mainland China might increase its leverage through its U.N. Security Council seat, though it may also indicate how isolated Peking is in many ways from current international thinking and multilateral decision-making venues.

Third, while many analysts focus on the political-military aspects of the "smart war" interface, the industrial and scientific-technological bases which produce the technical-military means necessary to prosecute conflict on the battlefield cannot be underestimated.

---

[3]See Gerrit W. Gong, "Managing Conflict in the Information Age: Lessons from the Gulf War" (Paper contributed to the Center for National Security Studies, Los Alamos National Laboratory project "Gulf War Lessons Learned"), *Strategic Review* (forthcoming). See also, among others, Martin van Creveld, *Technology and War: From 2000 B.C. to the Present* (New York: The Free Press, 1989), 235-310.

An inescapable message for mainland Chinese observers is that the ability to inflict unacceptable damage on the vital interests of a declared enemy or potential foe—the extension of political objectives by other means—remains the fundamental objective of conflict. In this regard, battlefield superiority based on the maximum combination of weapons and strategy is an obvious sine qua non for winning wars, especially when quality consistently outperforms quantity in modern conditions. (Quality is defined as durability and other performance standards beyond simple incorporation of state-of-the-art technology, though the Gulf War may not have lasted long enough to represent a full endurance test of U.S. weapons.) In this regard, some reports suggest that certain PLA commanders despair of ever indigenously developing integrated weapons systems that would be competitive on the modern battlefield.

The PLA and Gulf Lessons Learned

The lessons that mainland Chinese analysts learned from the Gulf War were very much those based on information technologies.

Peking followed all aspects of the Gulf War—diplomatic preparation, conduct of actual hostilities, international post-War analysis—in great detail.[4] Mainland China's senior leaders reportedly watched with fascination and horror at the backwardness of mainland China's capabilities as the realities of modern warfare were instantaneously and globally broadcast over CNN.[5]

Mainland Chinese analysts noted: (1) the coalition's ability to project power through logistics and lift; (2) the combined arms operations which coordinated maneuver ability and firepower; (3) the superiority of high-technology weaponry in open battlefields; and (4) for economic and moral reasons, the difficulty of any single country independently conducting high-intensity warfare for an extended period beyond its borders.[6]

The sobering conclusion for some mainland Chinese analysts may be that, in the conduct of conflict in the information age, the management of the interface between the political-military context (which establishes perceptions, expectations, and thereby provides support, legitimacy, and coalition cohesion) and the military-technical prosecution of conflict on the battlefield

---

[4]See, for example, Liu I-ch'ang, Wang Wen-ch'ang, and Wang Hsien-ch'en, eds., *Hai-wan chan-cheng* (The Persian Gulf War) (Peking: Military Science Press, 1991).

[5]Author's conversations with observers in Peking. This section also draws on "Rapporteur's Report," seminar on Gulf War Lessons Learned (East Asia), Center for National Security Studies, Los Alamos National Laboratory held at the Center for Strategic and International Studies (CSIS), Washington, D.C., May 29, 1992. Views expressed are solely those of the author.

[6]She Duanzhi, "Gulf War Implications Linger," *Beijing Review* 34, no. 28 (July 15-21, 1991): 12-14.

may increasingly favor countries able to conform to the underlying trends of the information age.

Indeed, not surprisingly given the volume of contradictory data Peking was trying to interpret through its own particular national and current ideological perspectives, mainland China's assessment of the Gulf War underwent several evolutions. Initially, Peking assumed a settlement would be brokered in the Persian Gulf, perhaps at the last minute. When conflict loomed closer, mainland Chinese analysts smugly assumed the United States and its coalition partners could win a military confrontation only by suffering tremendous losses.[7]

Peking saw opportunities to leverage its potential veto at the U.N. Security Council (which would have precluded necessary consensus on the U.N. use of force veto) for increased diplomatic influence in the Middle East (which Foreign Minister Ch'ien Ch'i-ch'en [Qian Qichen] sought to develop in his visits) and with Washington (including a meeting in the Oval Office). Yet, after the coalition decisively routed the Iraqi forces, mainland Chinese commentators began warning that the United States had become a single, ideological superpower in a unipolar world.

Some younger mainland Chinese analysts now argue the central lesson of the Gulf War should not be a desperate, economically infeasible Chinese "great leap" attempt to catch up with a technologically superior West. Rather, these circumspect observers suggest, mainland China needs to target electronics and other selected sectors with multiplier payoffs to enhance its ability to conduct war under modern conditions. Heated internal debate continues in mainland China over how to maximize scarce defense resources at a time when the demands of high-intensity warfare in a changing world have yet to produce precise threats or mission requirements.

Not surprisingly, mainland Chinese observers focus on traditional areas of Chinese military analysis, even while seeking modern lessons learned. Thus, they focus on what some call the special features and laws of high-tech wars and the proper concepts and military theories necessary for a well-trained force. They seek a comprehensive use of mobility, striking power, protection, and command-control-communication-intelligence (C^3I) capability.

Mainland Chinese analysts must walk a narrow line between proposing potentially necessary but overly ambitious military modernization programs and calling for more targeted (and potentially achievable) emphasis on priority areas such as electronic technology, including reconnaissance and probing, command and communications, electronic warfare, and weapons control and guidance.

---

[7]Author's interviews. This was clearly the prevailing view during the time the author attended the U.N. Security Council debate on the use of force resolution (Security Council Resolution 660) in November 1990.

Also, PRC force structure and organization may be more immediately amenable to revision than equipment acquisition. Thus, some PRC military commentators argue after the Gulf War that mainland China should balance its force structure better by paying less attention to ground forces and more attention to its air force and, especially, to its navy; should seek quality over quantity in equipment and professional personnel; and should emphasize general, comprehensive reform instead of improvement in individual fields.

While seemingly straightforward on the surface, each of these recommendations takes a side in some of the fundamental, long-standing debates over the future direction of the strategy and disposition of the PLA. It is unclear how much influence will ultimately be gained by arguments for increasing the PRC's ability to (1) strike behind enemy lines with air power and stand-off weapons; (2) deter war during crisis and quickly fight should war erupt; and (3) wage joint army, air force, and navy operations.

In any case, PRC commentary on the Gulf War reveals many of the internal battle lines within mainland China over the PRC's future orientation in strategy and technology.

The importance of technologically sophisticated, independent intelligence-gathering capabilities has been underscored by the Gulf War, though the full political and military implications have yet to be drawn. Technologically, independent intelligence capabilities may rewrite the parameters of surprise and make more complex the regional information context. Politically, independent intelligence capabilities may create ambiguities of evidence, change the time-frames necessary for action or coalition building, and deepen the added value of cooperative operations. Paradoxically, indigenous intelligence capabilities might enhance an East Asian country's willingness to join a U.S.-led coalition by allowing local decision-makers to argue independent corroboration of key findings.

In some cases, PRC analysts note specific tactical features of the Gulf War, for example, Iraq's lack of submarines and Baghdad's inability to disrupt coalition supply lines. It will be interesting to see if specific lessons are drawn relative to potential Washington options in the event of various Northeast Asian conflict scenarios.

The PLA in the Information Age:
Resisting "Peaceful Evolution"
While Preparing to Fight Under Modern Conditions

An interesting way to ask the question of how the PLA can resist "peaceful evolution" while preparing to fight under modern conditions is this: To what extent will the PRC choose in the coming years to operate within (as a rule-abiding member) or outside the established international system?

The concept of mainland China "in or out of the system" raises an intriguing play on words. Initially, the term refers to the important issue of the extent to which mainland China will define and pursue its primary interests as a responsible member within the current international system. But the idea of "in or out of the system" also points to the fundamental debate now taking place within mainland China regarding its domestic structure. As much as ever, the domestic parameters of mainland China's decision-making and external Chinese foreign policy behavior are inextricably linked.[8]

In 1978, Teng Hsiao-p'ing identified the promotion of mainland China's fundamental interests within the international system. The thrust of reform and openness was to undertake domestic change while reversing the legacy of mainland China's international disengagement during the Cultural Revolution period. What has been clear since then is that if the positive aspects of reform and openness can be mutually reinforcing, so can the negative ones. Thus, on the one hand, an enlivened domestic economy benefits from mainland China's broadened international interaction; on the other hand, domestic barriers to international market access inherent in the structure of mainland China's command economy can and have become a major bilateral trade issue with the United States.

It is the increasing political and economic disjunctions of socialist systems in the information age that most challenge mainland China today. In the realist tradition of power politics, the highest political decision-making levels in Peking have always been sensitively attuned to perceived international realities; decisions and behavior in specific international situations have thus inevitably reflected perceived national interest as much (if not more) than statements of mainland Chinese ideological principle.

Yet, the paradox of mainland China's current situation is that the resilience of hardline socialist ideology (the so-called "inner environment") has become a kind of blinder on otherwise realist interpretations of the external international environment (the so-called "outer environment").

The divergence between the perceived ideological necessity of maintaining domestic stability and the realist assessment of the current international environment thus remains a fundamental dilemma for those who see the PRC losing valuable development time. There is no legitimacy for the current regime in Peking if it does not move to fulfill the deep-seated nationalistic sentiment that mainland China become strong and take its appropriate place in the world. The more (and the more open) engagement into which mainland China enters across the spectrum of activity with the international system, the greater the reality check on seemingly anachronistic claims that the PRC is under attack by sinister forces of "peaceful evolution."

---

[8]This section draws on Gerrit W. Gong, "China and the New Emerging Order in Asia in the Twenty-first Century" (Unpublished manuscript, March 9, 1992).

It is thus not surprising that the concept of "in or out of the system" provides a key term of reference in mainland China's internal debate over future direction. This was true both prior to, and after, the Tienanmen incident. This debate was further intensified in light of developments within the former Soviet Union. The crux issue has been whether systemic change is necessary in mainland China, and whether such change can or should occur "within the system" (*t'i-chih-nei*) or whether it requires a change in systems (*t'i-chih-wai*).

The terms of reference inherent in the *t'i-chih-nei/t'i-chih-wai* debate are more than simply linguistic or semantic. They go to the heart of the inevitable domestic roots of Chinese foreign policy decision-making. These involve ongoing changes in Peking's decision-making process and its evolving foreign policy approaches. They are also closely related to the fundamental question of whether mainland China's external behavior will contribute in a constructive manner to the international order. Clearly, mainland China's future internal organizational (substance) and ideological (form) orientations are determining elements in what mainland China will do externally. Domestic dynamics that influence the way the PRC will address these fundamental issues include Peking's perceptions of threat; sources of international influence; Party-army-government relations; and leadership succession. It may be useful to make several broad assertions about each of these factors.

Threat Perceptions

Today the PRC's perception of threat has shifted from concern for military encirclement by a then-Soviet "south forward" strategy and coalition to one for encirclement by potential forces of "peaceful evolution." Hong Kong accounts of Chinese Politburo debates make this point abundantly clear. In this view, a primary objective of PRC policy encompasses not only the traditional assertion of sovereignty and territorial integrity (as in the Spratlys), but also maintenance of the current governmental system. This shift in policy focus also underpins the acute concern regarding the organizing principles that will underpin any "new world order."

For those concerned about "peaceful evolution" (that is, system preservation), the primary threat is the United States. In this perspective, the United States emerges as the lone superpower, superconfident after the Gulf War in the superiority of its technology and—more threateningly—in its values. These values include individual human rights and liberal democracy, market-oriented economy, and Washington-centric regimes for imposing a new security order on the world.

For those in mainland China concerned about direct military threats, Japan's potential is the primary issue. The Marco Polo Bridge incident and its aftermath, the Sino-Japanese War, are within living memory of many current leaders. Vivid depictions of Japanese atrocities in popular, award-winning movies like *Red Sorghum* keep it alive for the next generation.

In any case, the mainland Chinese argue in good dialectical tradition, the potential contradiction in the world's largest debtor country guaranteeing the security of the world's largest creditor country suggests the status quo of Japan deliberately taking a circumspect role in East Asia cannot be guaranteed in perpetuity. This is especially true, the Chinese say, because Japan is itself in the midst of generational and political transition, with the United States urging Tokyo to play a more assertive international role.

In any emerging order leading to the twenty-first century, the threat mainland China perceives from the United States is not so much military as political and cultural. Two major implications for mainland China flow from this conclusion.

First, Peking must ensure that, drawing on their different cultural traditions and approaches, Washington and Tokyo continue to take divergent approaches to human rights and other values issues. This is why Peking works so assiduously to deal with Tokyo in neighborly political and economic terms; Peking cannot afford to have Tokyo become an active agent of "peaceful evolution," including in political forums such as G-7 meetings. Thus far, the PRC's "containment by guilt" approach to constrain Japan by keeping Tokyo on the defensive has worked well.

Second, the PRC must maintain the established balance of power in the Pacific, at least until Peking is better able to assert itself. This requires a continued U.S. regional presence. For this reason, Peking has quietly indicated its interest in the United States maintaining an appropriate military presence in the Asia-Pacific necessary for peace and stability, and therefore potentially contributing to prosperity. While Peking has also welcomed a gradual drawdown of U.S. forces consistent with post-Soviet threats, it prefers that such developments occur in a cautious, deliberate fashion, not precipitously in a possibly destabilizing way.

Changing Sources of International Influence

In many ways, the PRC has enjoyed international influence disproportionate to the organization and wealth of its polity and economy. Traditionally, China's influence has derived from a careful blending of two sources: a central position in the regional balance of power; and the assertion of moral or cultural superiority. Now neither is clear.

With respect to global or regional power balances, mainland China's geostrategic size and location automatically give it some influence. But the collapse of the Soviet Union makes many mainland Chinese strategists nostalgic for the days when Moscow threatened the world. In many ways, the PRC's natural advantages in a geopolitical world of balance-of-power diplomacy are diminished in what appears to be an emerging geoeconomic era.

The traditional pattern of Chinese regional and global influence by means of culture and moral superiority has been undermined by mainland China's perceived economic backwardness and ongoing political challenges. Indeed, at a time when competitiveness is based on scientific and technological infrastructure and the ability to interact through globalized information and capital flows, the PRC may find itself increasingly less able to influence the international environment—a factor that over time may influence its leadership succession. The extent to which the PRC government will recover domestic and international credibility (in moral terms or in terms of trusted official statements) after Tienanmen and ongoing revelations about convict labor, arms sales, and other perceived fabrications or distortions of the truth remains an unresolved question.

Other basic dilemmas are clear. If the PRC does not open to economic exchange with South Korea, Taiwan, and the member states of the Association of Southeast Asian Nations (ASEAN), it will fall further behind. If the PRC does open up, it risks playing with the fire of change that may increase standard of living differentials (a challenge to a socialist system) or affect the economic loyalty of its provinces (an emerging challenge as traditional definitions of territory and new definitions of sovereignty diverge). The "Radio Free Asia" issue is an example of this kind of conundrum.

Thus the PRC has made efforts and had some successes in improving relations with its immediate neighbors on a state-to-state basis. This reduces any remaining traditional security threats and increases the opportunities for mutually beneficial economic exchange. At the same time, Peking sees Japan declaring conditionality for official development assistance (ODA) programs— another potential sign that playing within the international system may carry insidious risks.

Army-Party-Government Relations

Despite the clear dictum that even if "power comes from the barrel of a gun, the Party controls the gun," institutional tensions among the Party, army, and government are long-standing, perhaps rooted in perpetuity in mainland China's bureaucratic structure. Some recent assessments suggest that the PLA has, after twenty years, come to terms with itself as a professional organization with a modern vision for its future. This orientation no doubt influenced the PRC's position regarding the Persian Gulf War. It also underlies the ongoing PLA concern that command-economy policies may never provide sufficient budget resources for the PRC to field the equipment necessary to fight successfully under modern battlefield conditions.

Arguably the strongest institution in the PRC today, no group is more clear than the PLA regarding the high stakes inherent in the PRC's central dilemma: that a closed, rigid centrally planned economic system is uncompetitive in today's global economy. Whether politically authoritarian regimes are likewise anachronistic remains among the most sensitive of topics. Thus, while reform and opening up remain the public banner of modernization, behind-the-scenes battles over the pace and scope of reform and degree of openness mix questions of policy, philosophy, personality, and raw power. The debate within the PLA over its role is now encapsulated in the provocative expression popular among some mid-level, professional PLA officers: "marketize economics, liberalize thinking, pluralize politics, and nationalize the army."

Some within the PLA may feel that mainland China's national leaders may be sacrificing opportunities for the PRC to move ahead in a strengthened fashion. With a coherent sense of what it considers mainland China's best future course, the PLA may become a factor for unity and continued reform, and therefore a factor arguing for the PRC to play an active and responsible role within the international system. Otherwise, the PLA's burden of defending a potentially isolated and backward PRC becomes increasingly heavy.

Still, well-informed about the world around them, few in the PLA desire to rush into battlefields from which few politicians have emerged unscathed. Having fought to depoliticize the army, most people in the PLA do not want overt responsibility for navigating the political and economic quagmires inherent in mainland China's future orientation. The PLA is especially loathe to involve itself in problems the government has been unable to resolve. But, some say, the PLA must circumspectly prepare itself should a collapse occur in the ability or authority of mainland China's current system to govern itself.[9]

The prestige of the Party is already low; popular complaints about Li P'eng (Li Peng), Chiang Tse-min (Jiang Zemin), and others express what many see as discontent with mainland China's entire governing system. If precipitous change should arise in mainland China akin to what occurred in the former Soviet Union and Eastern Europe, the PLA knows a single institution stands between mainland China and chaos, and that institution has learned its own lessons from Tienanmen.

The enunciation of the concept that the PLA might have to play a national organizing role suggests the notional underpinning of a potential shift in institutional alignment in the coming period—a shift in the center of gravity of mainland China's decision-making. Nor should it be assumed that such a shift, in the current unlikely eventuality the PLA takes a major organizing role, would imply more hostile PRC attitudes toward key international structures such as those regarding trade and proliferation. As already noted, a PLA determined to provide itself the capability to fight wars under modern conditions could well be more flexible in seeing that mainland China is not isolated and thereby has direct access to the economic and technological means the PLA deems necessary to fulfill its mission.

Leadership Succession

As the political maneuvering attendant to the Chinese Communist Party's Fourteenth National Congress demonstrated, the current process of leadership succession is a rolling one. It will not come all at once by political

---

[9]Willy Wo-lap Lam, "Rallying Cry for Total Obedience," *South China Morning Post* (Hong Kong), January 13, 1993, 9.

fiat or by a sudden actuarial change of leadership generation. Rather, it will continue to combine the elements of a soap opera played out in the sometimes dark corridors of power. It is a continuous play of numberless acts, which could be called "No Waiting for Godot."

A certain attention has been paid to the significant increase in Central Committee members with military background since the Fourteenth Party Congress. In particular, some observers have noted Liu Hua-ch'ing's (Liu Huaqing's) elevation to the Politburo, though the suggestion that the appointment of a senior navy official is indicative of mainland China's blue water, power projection ambitions seems strained. More fundamental is the need for strong civil-military relations at a time when the Long March generation, whose personal prestige and experience spans the "Party" and the "gun," is now increasingly passing leadership responsibility to successors with less comprehensive experience. This is most recently underscored by the calls by Liu Hua-ch'ing and other senior PLA officers for a return to the "Yenan Spirit" and the "glorious tradition" of unity and sacrifice.

Western observers sometimes partially misdefine the key question as when mainland China will again begin reform. Reform continues, but in a manner more circumscribed and cautious according to the imperative of maintaining stability. Mainland China's real dilemma is not reform or no reform, but how to reform. This brings us full circle to the crucial question of whether fundamental reform can occur without restructuring mainland China's political system.

As noted above, a key question in Peking's future approach to proliferation issues will be the position of the PLA relative to reform and openness and, more particularly, the extent to which the PLA will seek or welcome gradually renewed ties with the United States. It is certainly possible that more progressive elements within the PLA, acting out of perceived self-interest in terms of the PRC's defense future, may find themselves at odds with conservative political leaders bent on viewing mainland China's external relations through the ideological prism of fear of "peaceful evolution."

Peking is now actively assessing shifting international attitudes regarding transfers of weapons and technologies of mass destruction in light of the collapse of the former Soviet Union, of the Persian Gulf War, and of U.N. and other efforts to strengthen global non-proliferation regimes. These efforts include more detailed study of the exact provisions (including legal loopholes) in treaties or conventions that Peking may choose to join or be pressured into adherence of.

Conclusion

This chapter has tried to examine the impact of the most recent, vivid example of conflict in the information age on mainland China as a means of analyzing internal and international factors of "peaceful evolution" and "anti-peaceful evolution."

It has noted the always close connections between traditional, cultural, bureaucratic, and other domestic parameters of Chinese decision-making and the impact of the realities of the changing international environment. Moreover, it has argued that the gap between potential domestic ideological blinders (that is, preoccupation with "peaceful evolution") and international competitive, development, and security realities may be increasing in the PRC's case.

In this view, the PRC has yet to confront the possibility that systemic changes may be required, and how those structural economic and political adjustments should be carried out in practical terms. Within this debate, the PLA is characterized, based on calculated self-interest, as having a major interest in the long-term approach of openness and reform, and it may therefore serve as an element of continuity for economic construction. Yet, mainland China's real challenge is not reform, but how to reform in a way that maintains stability, promotes growth, and preserves governability.

Part Six

The Collapse of the Communist World and Mainland China's Foreign Affairs

CHAPTER 15

The Collapse of the Communist World and Mainland China's Foreign Affairs

Kenneth Lieberthal

The period since mid-1989 has witnessed the greatest peacetime change in international affairs since the beginning of the industrial revolution. Many have viewed this change as the "collapse of Communism," as the topic of this chapter indicates. This somewhat misstates the issue, however. Communist states still exist in North Korea, the People's Republic of China (PRC), Indochina, and Cuba. What collapsed during 1989-91 was not "Communism" so much as the Soviet empire itself. With the erosion of the will to maintain the empire in Moscow, all the former states of the Soviet imperium from the German Democratic Republic (GDR) to the Mongolian People's Republic (MPR)—including the territories within the former Soviet Union itself—underwent major change.

Analysis of the effect of the collapse of the Soviet empire on mainland China's foreign policy is complicated by the fact that, virtually simultaneously, Peking (Beijing) had to cope with the consequences of its bloody suppression of the Tienanmen (Tiananmen) protests on June 4, 1989. During the mid- and late 1980s, Peking had pursued a foreign policy that seemed best characterized by a term that formerly applied to Japanese external affairs in the 1970s, "omnidirectional." That is, Peking sought improved relations with countries around the globe, virtually without regard to their domestic political and social systems. The repression summed up by the term "Tienanmen massacre" interfered with this omnidirectional foreign policy approach in two ways: it prompted sanctions by the major powers that offended Peking's pride and upset concrete ties; and it facilitated the rise of hardliners within mainland China who sought a less open and expansive policy toward the international arena.

Between June and December 1989 peaceful (and, in Romania, violent) revolutions occurred against Communist rule throughout Eastern Europe. These generally further enhanced the domestic position of hardliners in mainland China, as the leaders feared that the Chinese Communist Party (CCP) might be swept away in the flood tide of anticommunism seemingly sweeping the socialist world. The Romanian violence itself played an important role in shaping mainland China's longer-term foreign policy. Peking was committed to making concrete responses to President George Bush's initiative of dispatching National Security Advisor Brent Scowcroft and Under Secretary of State Lawrence Eagleburger to mainland China in December 1989. But, evidently due to the alarm in Peking caused by the Romanian events, mainland China's leaders reneged on these promised steps, thus creating deep problems for Peking-Washington relations in the ensuing years.

More generally, though, Peking's response to its diplomatic problems caused by Tienanmen is difficult to sort out from its reaction to the changed environment produced by the collapse of the Soviet empire. It is probably the former that accounts more for mainland China's concentrated effort after June 1989 to strengthen its ties with the member states of the Association of Southeast Asian Nations (ASEAN) and with other countries in Asia.[1] While this continued a trend in mainland China's foreign policy that had been evident for years, there appeared to be renewed energy in this aspect of mainland China's foreign relations after mid-1989. These Asian countries had, in general, not reacted strongly against Tienanmen, and thus they formed a natural diplomatic bridge for the country's reentry into the halls of international diplomacy.

In broad terms, though, the changes in world politics resulting from the collapse of the Soviet empire are profound. In particular, four dimensions of this collapse have been particularly salient to Peking. This chapter first considers each of these four dimensions and then takes up the resulting issues for Peking and the PRC's responses to this dramatically new situation. Just as the Soviet collapse meshed domestic and international affairs, so some of the issues raised for the PRC blur the boundaries between internal and external concerns. Following this broad discussion, this chapter considers the one set of concrete diplomatic issues for Peking that clearly grew directly out of the collapse of the Soviet empire: the PRC's relations with the former socialist states.

Collapse of the Soviet Imperium:
The Issues Raised

The four broad areas in which the collapse of the Soviet imperium created major issues of concern to Peking are the end of the Cold War, the proliferation of new states and the redefinition of existing political entities, the heightening of ethnic tensions, and the global assumption that the era of Communism is over.

---

[1]In broad terms, the Republic of China's active diplomacy during this period probably provided an additional spur to Peking's efforts.

End of the Cold War

The Cold War ended with the collapse of the Soviet Union in late 1991 and its replacement by the loose Commonwealth of Independent States (CIS). With the former Soviet states themselves in internal turmoil, none of the successor states has the will or intention to contend with the United States for global leadership. Virtually all have repudiated the very notion of an ideological divide with the West, and most have sought instead to join the Western trading system in order to participate in the bounty that they see there. To a greater or lesser extent, each also now advocates changes in the direction of democracy and of private property and a free market economy.

This fundamental reorientation has broken down the raison d'être for the discipline that had countries within each of the two major blocs submerge their frictions in favor of a united show of strength against the enemy. The United States and the Soviet Union led their respective blocs on the basis of military, economic, and ideological resources, all three of which provided key components of power in the Cold War era.

The end of the Cold War has not rendered this mix of elements irrelevant to calculations of power, but it has created significant uncertainty about the long-term balance that should be struck among its various components. It has also raised questions about just what constitutes the best measure of power in the new era.

Certainly, the strategic nuclear forces of the United States and the Soviet Union no longer carry the political weight that they did until 1991. The major purpose of each of these arsenals was to checkmate the other, and with this central competition concluded, these strategic weapons possess little other value. Rarely has so much firepower counted for so little political muscle as is the case with possession of strategic nuclear weapons in the wake of the Cold War.

Even with tactical nuclear weapons and with conventional arms, though, the United States in 1992 has absolute superiority over any other country. Only America possesses the ability, demonstrated in the Persian Gulf War, to project large-scale conventional forces over long distances. The United States in 1992 has the world's largest military budget and possesses the most advanced military technologies and military research and development systems.

Economic problems have, however, raised the question of whether America's huge military establishment confers power or, ironically, weakens the country in the international system over the long run.[2] Washington had to seek financial support (along with contributions of forces) from many countries in the Persian Gulf War. The country is running a budget deficit

---

[2]Paul Kennedy outlines the fundamental argument in his analysis of "imperial overstretch": Kennedy, *The Rise and Fall of the Great Powers* (Lexington, Mass.: D.C. Heath and Company, 1987).

of four hundred billion dollars per annum, and servicing the national debt has itself become a major financial burden. Thus, many have begun to question the balance that should be struck between military and economic investment as sources of power in determining the shape of the future international system.

To the extent that economic prowess has grown in relative importance in the post-Cold War world, Japan has emerged as an important power in and of itself. East Asia (from Japan through Burma) is the most rapidly growing economic region of the globe, and this relative economic dynamism is likely to continue at least until the turn of the century. But Japan alone accounts for more than 70 percent of the total gross national product (GNP) of all of East Asia.[3] To the extent that economic factors are replacing military might as a determinant of international authority, Japan's role in East Asia is growing larger.

Thus, the end of the Cold War has brought two fundamental changes that inevitably impact on mainland China's global position. With the dissolution of political blocs, mainland China has lost its critical role in the "strategic triangle." One could doubt in the past whether such a triangle really played a major role after the early 1970s, but it carried sufficient weight in the minds of American and Soviet leaders to lend mainland China an important increment in its international stature. And by shifting power more broadly from military to economic resources, the end of the Cold War highlights the tremendous potential of Japan to exercise greater influence in East Asia.

Indeed, there are now legitimate questions being raised as to the extent to which major trading blocs will form in the wake of the dissolution of the former Free World and Communist World blocs.[4] Europe is moving rapidly toward consolidation of a market based on the European Community (EC), and there is a possibility that in the coming years this will expand to a Gaullist conception of the continent (extending from the Atlantic to the Urals). Germany is the predominant economic power of this region. The United States has a free trade agreement with Canada and is likely to develop a parallel agreement with Mexico. America will be the predominant economic power of this North American region.

In Asia, during 1990 and 1991 intraregional trade and foreign direct investment exceeded transactions involving countries from outside the region for the first time since World War II.[5] Thus, while less far along this path

---

[3] *Asia 1990 Yearbook* (Hong Kong: Review Publishing Company, 1990), 6-7.

[4] See, for example, Du Gong, "A Year of Final Breakup of Bipolarity in the World," *Foreign Affairs Journal*, no. 23 (March 1992): 17-19.

[5] Trade figures presented by Professor Daniel Okimoto at the conference, "Asian Security Issues in Transition to the Twenty-First Century," Monterey, California, March 19-20, 1992.

than the other two major regions, East Asia is itself showing signs of forming increasing regional ties.[6] If this trend continues, Japan is well positioned to become the predominant economic power of this region. Such a development would raise important questions for the PRC's foreign policy.

As the above discussion of the incipient development of regional trading blocs indicates, moreover, the United States-Japan relationship may be undergoing a basic change. With the Soviet threat no longer binding the countries together, underlying strains are now emerging with greater force than would otherwise be the case. While these remain the two economies with the greatest two-way trade in the world, fissiparous tendencies are such that it is difficult to predict with certainty the future dynamics of United States-Japanese relations—and therefore of the larger U.S. role in the East Asian region.[7] These issues, though, are of the greatest importance for the PRC's international position.

In sum, the end of the Cold War has reshaped the global environment, and the future contours of the international system are at this point quite uncertain. But the basic changes already evident—the reduced importance of strategic nuclear forces, the dissolution of the major Cold War political/ military/economic blocs, a shift in the direction of increasing importance of economic power, greater United States-Japanese strains, and the glimmerings of movement toward the development of major regional trading blocs (that would place mainland China in Japan's bloc)—have altered dramatically the international environment and the challenges facing Peking in the coming years.

Proliferation and Redefinition of States

The concept of state sovereignty has been the key organizing idea in international relations for centuries. Except for the aftermath of war itself (and, of course, the aftermath of decolonization), there are relatively few instances since the late 1940s of changes in the boundaries of states, despite the high levels of civil disorder and violence that have occurred during the years since World War II.

Against this background, the proliferation of new states and the attitudes adopted by the international arena in this process since 1989 have been striking. Many countries recognized the Baltic states before the Soviet Union formally granted them independence in late 1991.[8] In similar fashion,

---

[6]Nigel Holloway et al., "An Insurance Policy," *Far Eastern Economic Review*, July 25, 1991, 52-56; and Shim Jae Hoon, "Growing-up Pains," ibid., November 14, 1991, 27.

[7]For a wide-ranging, very balanced assessment of the U.S.-Japan relationship and its future, see Howard Baker, Jr. and Ellen Frost, "Resuming the U.S.-Japan Alliance," *Foreign Affairs* 71, no. 2 (Spring 1992): 97-113.

[8]"Soviets Recognize Baltic Independence," *Washington Post*, September 7, 1991, A1.

Germany successfully demanded recognition of the independence of Croatia and Slovenia, even while Belgrade was fighting a civil war to keep them within the federation.[9] The United Nations has sent forces into Yugoslavia where the distinction between civil war, inter-state war, and genocide is difficult to draw. And the U.N. admitted all the former Soviet republics as independent countries, even before Russia dispatched embassies to the newly independent former Central Asian republics.[10]

In short, since 1989 countries have broken apart piece by piece, and the international community has at times gotten ahead of the leaders of the former countries in recognizing fully the independence of their various parts. A number of cases of quasi-independence have also emerged during this process, involving varying degrees and types of international involvement.[11]

As of mid-1992, no clear norms have emerged to provide a consistent framework for these international activities, but taken as a whole they have softened the previous reluctance of international organizations to become involved in disputes over the actual composition of existing states. Given the dynamics of change in Eastern Europe and the CIS (and, possibly, in Black Africa) during the coming few years, it is likely that international actions with regard to groups that for one reason or another claim independence will increase.

The PRC is potentially affected by this trend of development in two ways: it has large disaffected minorities with clear territorial identities (e.g., Tibetans, Uighurs); and it faces an anomalous situation with regard to Taiwan. Peking places enormous stress on what former U.S. Ambassador James Lilley has characterized as "a nineteenth century notion of sovereignty,"[12] and the willingness of the international community to soften its views toward that notion must be discomfiting to the PRC's leaders. These international actions might also encourage dissatisfied groups in the Chinese mainland to press their grievances more emphatically.[13]

---

[9]"Yugoslavia's Breakup: Slovenia Is Secure, Croatia Is Uncertain; Europeans Confer Recognition on the New Order," *New York Times*, January 16, 1992, A1.

[10]See "UN Session to Bring Rise in Membership," in *Christian Science Monitor*, September 17, 1991, 5; and "Five Asian Republics Join Slavs in Plan for Commonwealth," *New York Times*, December 14, 1991, 1.

[11]This was especially notable throughout 1991 in the Soviet Union, where various republics held referenda, declared sovereignty, and took other steps toward full independence. Even as of the summer of 1992, moreover, Russia has 130,000 troops in the independent Baltic countries, and there is disagreement over the timetable for their withdrawal. Russia also still has troops in the former German Democratic Republic which, as part of a united Germany, is already a member of NATO.

[12]"China Attacks Ex-U.S. Ambassador for His Comments on Taiwan," *New York Times*, August 18, 1991, 4.

[13]Tibetans, for example, are reported to be very much aware of U.S. Congressional actions in support of Tibet and of President Bush's 1991 meeting with the Dalai Lama at the White House: Harold Saunders et al., "Tibet: Issues for Americans," *National Committee China Policy Series*, no. 4 (New York: National Committee on US-China Relations, April 1992), 21.

Increase in Ethnic Tension and Conflict

The dynamics of change that brought down the Soviet empire have also produced sharply increased ethnic strife in their wake. Soviet-style Communism had severely repressed ethnic conflict without, however, doing anything to mitigate it. When repression eased in the late 1980s, ethnic assertiveness became increasingly the norm. This is producing bloodshed and tragedy in Yugoslavia, Nagorno-Karabakh, and many other regions, and the prospects favor increased rather than diminished ethnic tensions in the coming few years. This widespread upsurge in ethnic sentiment has, moreover, been a key factor feeding the changes in state boundaries noted above. Indeed, ethnic passions have run so high since 1989 that state boundary changes have even taken place in locales such as Czechoslovakia where the predictable result is increased hardship for the population involved.

As noted above, the PRC contains important ethnic minorities. Peking fears that ethnic unrest in the former Soviet Union could spark problems on the Chinese side of the border, including the border with the Mongolian People's Republic.[14] While mainland China's ethnic minorities constitute far less than 10 percent of the population (unlike the former Soviet Union's roughly 50 percent), they nevertheless by rough count number some sixty million people and form a substantial proportion of the population in vast border regions from the Southwest through the Northwest to North China.[15]

Global Assumption that the Era of Communism Is Over

Despite the fact that to date the collapse of Communist systems has occurred only in areas that directly formed part of the former Soviet empire, these developments have produced a virtual international consensus to the effect that the era of Communism as a historical force on the world stage is over. The dissolution of the Soviet empire certainly does weaken most of the remaining Communist states, as subsidized trade, security assistance, and other Soviet help has evaporated.[16]

While the PRC was not dependent on these Soviet props—and thus is less directly weakened by the turnabout—Peking no longer enjoys the prestige of being seen as the leader of reform among Communist states. Indeed, these changes in the Soviet empire have made many view the PRC

---

[14]See Lincoln Kaye et al., "Bitter Medicine," *Far Eastern Economic Review*, September 5, 1991, 10-12; Kaye, "China Feels the Chill," ibid., January 9, 1992, 14; and Kaye, "Faltering Steppes: China Looms Large in Ethnic Upsurge among Mongols," ibid., April 9, 1992, 16-18.

[15]June Dreyer, *China's Forty Millions* (Cambridge, Mass.: Harvard University Press, 1976); Dru Gladney, *Muslim Chinese* (Cambridge, Mass.: Council on East Asian Studies, Harvard, 1991).

[16]The Soviet collapse has, for example, produced severe economic problems in North Korea, pressured Vietnam to adopt economic reforms and seek a settlement of the Cambodian issue, and brought the Cuban economy to the brink of collapse.

system as backward, almost quaint in its continuing adherence to an outmoded doctrine. Within mainland China itself, moreover, the leaders must
confront the fact that the mother of all Communist parties has been repudiated by its own people. While no public opinion polls are available to
validate this fact, it is virtually certain that the result has been to weaken
further the legitimacy of the CCP within its own country. The Party can
no longer claim to represent a doctrine that is recognized by many even in
the West as putting mainland China at the head of the queue of countries
marching toward the future.[17]

Summary

The collapse of the Soviet empire has thus created serious problems in
the international environment for the PRC, and it has also produced forces
that challenge the stability of the Chinese Communist system domestically.
The resulting difficulties are both direct and indirect, ranging from a change
in mainland China's former strategic position between the United States and
the Soviet Union to important—and for Peking generally unfavorable—changes
in the international system as a whole.

The Chinese reaction to the collapse of the Soviet empire thus should
be seen in a broader context than merely Peking's effort to adjust its diplomatic stance vis-à-vis the former Communist states of the Soviet Union and
Eastern Europe. This response has required Peking to think in new terms
about both foreign and internal policies on a broad front.

Peking's Overall Reaction
to the Collapse of the Soviet Empire

In the broadest terms, Peking has taken up two issues in response to
the above changes in its environment. One concerns the dissolution of the
strategic triangle and its implications, especially for Peking-Washington relations; the other regards how best to prevent mainland China from following
the same path as the Soviet Union. In addition, Peking has confronted an
array of specific diplomatic issues as a result of the dynamics of the post-Soviet
world. The most important of these directly attributable to the Soviet collapse
concern relations with states along what used to be the Sino-Soviet border.

Aftermath of the Strategic Triangle

The collapse of the Soviet Union obviously removed a framework for
international politics that Peking had been able to use to increase its own

---

[17]As Joseph R. Levenson demonstrated, this formed one of the major bases of Marxism's appeal
in mainland China: Joseph R. Levenson, *Confucian China and Its Modern Fate: A Trilogy*
(Berkeley: University of California Press, 1968), 134 et seq.

importance. Even in the early 1970s when the PRC was an extremely minor factor in international economics, had virtually no conventional power projection capability, and had a nuclear arsenal that was too small even to be calculated in the U.S.-Soviet nuclear balance, Peking's posture vis-à-vis the United States and the Soviet Union was considered an important factor in the global struggle between the two superpowers. The global reaction to the Nixon and Kissinger trips to Peking in 1971-72—including Moscow's virtual state of panic over this initiative—highlights the leverage mainland China gained via the strategic triangle notion.

The Soviet Union's collapse meant both the end of the strategic triangle and the removal of any major military threat to mainland China from its north. The remaining threats emanating from the successor states are those of ethnic fervor and, in the case of the former Soviet Central Asia, the possible spread of Muslim religious fundamentalism and a radically changed power balance in that region. These issues are considered below.

The major immediate Chinese concern as the Cold War wound down became the role and power of the United States in the post-Cold War world. In the wake of the Tienanmen massacre in June 1989, Peking-Washington relations ran into deep trouble. While all major powers chastised Peking for its brutality and imposed some types of sanctions, by late 1991 only the United States maintained sour relations with the PRC and continued (indeed, debated increasing) its sanctions. This unique American behavior reflects, inter alia, the fact that Peking-Washington relations became entangled in other contentious issues in the U.S. Congress, including human rights, fair trade, and proliferation. In addition, the Peking-Washington relationship became—for the first time since 1972—a partisan issue that Democratic leaders sought to use against the Republican President Bush.

As the Soviet Union crumbled, Peking became alarmed at the prospect that a confident, moralistic America might dominate a unipolar world. President Bush's vague comments during 1991 about the formation of a "new world order" heightened Chinese concerns, and the smashing victory of the American-led coalition in the Gulf War added more worries.[18] Peking has in the past tended to appreciate Washington's capabilities and instincts when the United States is in a mood of self-doubt on the world stage. At such times, mainland China finds the United States to be refreshingly pragmatic, open, and sincere.

But there is also a moralistic streak in American foreign policy that Peking dreads. This element in American policy has periodically cast Peking as morally obnoxious and has thus created enormous obstacles to a *realpolitik* approach in Washington to policy toward mainland China. A confident

---

[18]See *Liao-wang chou-k'an* (Outlook Weekly), April 8 and June 10, 1991, and *Ta Kung Pao* (Hong Kong), April 8, 1991. More broadly, see *FBIS Trends*, May 2, 1991, 30-35.

America too often, in Peking's eyes, becomes a moralistic America, and that is rarely in mainland China's immediate interests.[19]

The Chinese leaders saw precisely this set of developments unfolding in 1991. Americans felt very good about the victory of democratic ideology and of free market principles in the struggle against the Soviet empire. They believed the world was headed for a far better international system that would be guaranteed by the only remaining superpower, the United States, and that would embrace basically American values. And all this occurred during a period of great tension in Peking-Washington relations, when America directed great attention to the political dimensions of human rights in the PRC.

Mainland China responded to this situation in several ways. Domestically, the CCP stressed propaganda to criticize what it claimed were American attempts to undermine mainland China's socialist system, an American strategy that Peking dubbed "peaceful evolution." Those Chinese leaders such as Ch'en Yün (Chen Yun), Teng Li-ch'ün (Deng Liqun), and Li P'eng (Li Peng), who wanted in any case to slow down economic reform, also manipulated this threat so as to enhance their own leverage over domestic policy.

Internationally, mainland China sought in part to balance the power of the United States by bolstering the position of the United Nations. This tactic had several advantages. It stressed moving international security decisions into a forum in which mainland China formally enjoyed the position of being one of the top five participants (ahead, for example, of Japan, Germany, and India). This is also a forum in which major security actions are subject to Peking's veto. And support for the U.N. positioned Peking so that it did not appear to be too inward-looking and self-centered. Rather, it could articulate support for greater internationalism in the post-Cold War world while at the same time moving issues into an arena in which Peking's own power is maximized.

The fundamental problem with a pro-U.N. strategy is that Peking does not want the United Nations to become involved in what mainland China considers to be the domestic affairs of various countries. The U.N. Charter, for example, contains strong human rights provisions, and the PRC fears that these could be turned against the Chinese mainland. Premier Li P'eng, therefore, stressed in his January 1992 address to a special meeting of the heads of state of the "Perm Five" that mainland China had its own views on human rights and that the United Nations had no authority to intervene in domestic affairs on this issue.[20]

---

[19]Harold Isaacs captured some of the reasons for this in his *Scratches on Our Minds* (Cambridge, Mass.: MIT, 1958).

[20]"Full Text of Speech by Premier Li Peng at UN Security Council Meeting in New York on 31 January," *People's Daily* (Overseas edition), February 3, 1992, in Foreign Broadcast Information Service, *Daily Report: China* (hereafter cited as *FBIS-CHI*), 92-022 (February 3, 1992): 2-4.

Mainland China's tilt toward the United Nations, therefore, has been a strategy with both advantages and risks. Peking has been drawn into supporting sanctions against Iraq and supporting the dispatching of U.N. forces to other trouble spots, such as Yugoslavia. Given Peking's previous costly experience with United Nations actions in the early 1950s in Korea, these current activities must create some anxieties among PRC leaders. Indeed, mainland China abstained from the vote on U.N. Resolution 678 of November 29, 1990, which authorized the use of force against Iraq, and it abstained again in late May 1992 from the U.N. vote authorizing severe economic sanctions against Yugoslavia.[21] Peking's support of the U.N.—like that of the other major countries—is thus limited and conditional, and this forms at best only a part of the reaction to dealing with the post-Cold War world.

Peking's concerns about American global leadership surfaced during 1990 and became especially acute in 1991. Many articles in PRC specialist journals during 1990 and 1991 pointed with some confidence to the emergence of a five power world: the United States, Germany (or the EC), the Soviet Union, Japan, and mainland China. America and the Soviet Union qualified because of their superior military power (and, in America's case, also because of its economic might). Germany and Japan joined this company because of the increasing importance of economic performance. The reasons for mainland China's being included in this elite group were generally left for the reader to provide, reflecting Peking's uncertainties about the fundamentals of its own participation in the emerging world order.

As the Soviet Union crumbled during the course of 1991 and the Gulf War demonstrated America's preeminent position that spring, mainland China's press increasingly devoted itself to expressions of concern about emergent hegemonism and the dangers of a unipolar world.[22] In off-the-record conferences, knowledgeable Chinese government advisors expressed deep concern about the content and implications of President Bush's declaration of intent to construct a ''new world order.'' Whereas many Americans took this presidential rhetoric as little more than sloganeering, key Chinese saw in it the precursor to an operational doctrine with ominous consequences for the PRC's interests.

This view led the PRC to develop a conscious strategy of preparation for a worsening of relations with the United States. In part, this strategy entailed trying to improve relations with other countries in Asia. During these years, the PRC worked assiduously and skillfully to normalize fully its relations with Singapore (October 1990) and Indonesia (August 1990), to improve its ties with the newly-democratic Mongolia, Vietnam, and

---

[21]See, respectively, "Mutual Abstainers," *Far Eastern Economic Review*, December 13, 1990, 10; and *New York Times*, June 1, 1992.

[22]*FBIS Trends*, May 2, 1991, 30-35 summarizes this literature.

India, and to cultivate its already-good relations with the other countries in ASEAN.

At the same time, mainland China worked to prepare for a significant deterioration in Peking-Washington bilateral relations by building up its foreign exchange reserves to cushion the shock from the most likely American change in policy toward the PRC, termination of most-favored-nation (MFN) tariff treatment. It is difficult to assess the extent to which Peking's policy of promoting exports in general while sharply limiting imports during 1990-91 reflected its domestic policy of cooling down inflation and bringing the economy back under control, but mainland China's foreign exchange reserves grew very rapidly during these two years to more than US$40 billion by the end of 1991.[23] These foreign exchange reserves would cushion the shock of sudden partial loss of access to the U.S. market.

But mainland China's evaluation of the potential for an American-led unipolar world shifted noticeably during the winter of 1991-92. By the spring of 1992 a new consensus appeared to be emerging to the effect that internal economic difficulties and external tensions with other countries would likely limit America's leadership to levels tolerable to Peking.[24] In this new context, the leadership in mainland China is anxious to retain American involvement in Asia as a source of stability (and an offset to Japan) and to sustain practical direct ties with the United States in order to assure continuing access to the American market.[25]

Perhaps reflecting this changing evaluation of America's future role, mainland China in early 1992 asserted anew its claims to sovereignty over the Paracel Islands and over Tiaoyutai (Diaoyutai, called Senkaku by the Japanese). The National People's Congress (NPC) on February 25 adopted a law on territorial waters[26] that predictably created frictions with Vietnam, Indonesia, and the many other countries that claim all or part of the Paracels, and also with Japan over Tiaoyutai. CCP General Secretary Chiang Tse-min (Jiang Zemin) then visited Japan on April 6-10, but the visit failed to produce agreement on a date for Emperor Akihito to travel to Peking, which had been one of Chiang's major goals in undertaking the trip.[27] Mainland China's changed view of the need to cultivate other Asian countries in order to offset the power of a hegemonical United States in the region thus appears to have cleared the way for Peking to assert more of its own claims around its periphery at the possible cost of some rising friction with its neighbors.

---

[23]*China Daily* (Business Weekly), May 7, 1992, 1.

[24]See, e.g., Qian Qichen's (Ch'ien Ch'i-ch'en's) article in *Beijing Review* 34, no. 52 (December 30-January 5, 1992): 7-10.

[25]*Liao-wang chou-k'an*, June 10, 1991 and *Shih-chieh chih-shih* (World Affairs), no. 1090 (November 1, 1991).

[26]AFP, February 26, 1992, in *FBIS-CHI*-92-038 (February 26, 1992): 19.

[27]NCNA, April 6, 7, and 10, 1992.

In sum, it appears that the PRC is now satisfied that the end of the strategic triangle does not mean that the United States will play an over-weening global role. Peking, therefore, is free to pursue a foreign policy that seeks the continued engagement of the United States in Asia and con-tinued bilateral trade and other activities. Mainland China has not yet, however, determined the basis of its own power in the emerging world order and the role that it should play. Chinese articles in the first half of 1992, indeed, are quite candid in acknowledging Peking's uncertainty about the directions in which the world is heading.[28]

Assuring Domestic Stability

The collapse of the Soviet Union and the moves in almost every former constituent republic to repudiate Communism and outlaw the Communist party tremendously heightened fears among the PRC's leaders about whether the same developments could occur on the Chinese mainland. These con-cerns, already high in the wake of the Tienanmen movement and its violent suppression, acquired new urgency as the Communist Party of the Soviet Union traversed from power to oblivion in a matter of months.[29]

The public record does not reveal the full range of views articulated to and by mainland China's leaders concerning how best to cope with this crisis situation. Some, such as Ch'en Yün's son Ch'en Yüan (Chen Yuan), are said to have advocated a peculiar mix of policies that stresses jettisoning Marxist ideology, retaining control over a strong state sector in industry, opening wide to the international economy, and maintaining an avowedly development-oriented authoritarian government. This "neo-authoritarianism" bears a passing resemblance to the "new authoritarianism" floated in 1988 and early 1989 by some of Chao Tzu-yang's (Zhao Ziyang's) supporters, but it seems to pay less attention to socialist ideology and also to place more stress on nurturing the state sector of the economy than did the Chao-era version.

Ch'en Yün himself, though, fundamentally held the view that the Soviet developments reflected a too rapid adoption of reform measures by Mikhail Gorbachev, thus letting the situation get out of control and the economy collapse. For the elder Ch'en and his followers, therefore, the prescription was to stress ideological education, secure the Party's control over the major levers of the economy, remain open to the international economy but keep control over foreign trade and over the scale of interaction with the inter-

---

[28]For example, Luo Renshi, "Tremendous and Profound Changes and Complex Contradic-tions," *International Strategic Studies* 1 (1992): 8-14; and Chen Xiaogong, "The World in Transition," *Beijing Review* 35, nos. 5-6 (February 3-16, 1992): 13-15.

[29]Ironically, the civil disorder and declining standard of living in the CIS and parts of Eastern Europe appear to have lessened the popular appetite for major political change on the Chinese mainland as of the summer of 1992. See, e.g., *New York Times*, June 5, 1992.

national economy, and utilize the press to encourage values of patriotism and frugality. These views, dubbed "hardline" in the Western media, predominated in Chinese policies and rhetoric from the time of the failure of the coup against Gorbachev in August 1991 to early 1992. In a nutshell, these views argued that reform is itself a slippery slope and that one must be very cautious lest the slide accelerate and produce calamity.

In late January 1992 Teng Hsiao-p'ing (Deng Xiaoping) set out on a trip to Kwangtung (Guangdong) and Shanghai during which he articulated a very different version of the imperative of maintaining stability. He argued forcefully that stability will result only if economic progress is rapid enough to meet the expectations of the population. The obstacle to achieving this, Teng asserted, is too great a tilt toward leftism. The key to success, by contrast, is acceleration of reform and opening to the outside world. In sum, Teng implicitly said that the Soviet Union collapsed because Gorbachev had pursued reform too slowly and thus had raised expectations but then had utterly failed to meet them.

Teng pressed successfully for Politburo endorsement and wide circulation of the views he expressed on this trip, and some of his key slogans were inserted into Li P'eng's "Government Work Report" at the NPC meeting in spring 1992, evidently over Li's personal objections.[30] While Teng as of mid-1992 has thus succeeded in generating media momentum behind his views concerning the best way to avoid a Soviet-type collapse, his victory is at the time of this writing by no means either complete or secure. The CCP's Fourteenth National Congress in the fall 1992 should provide a good indication of the state of play via both its personnel appointments and the general ideological line that it formally adopts.[31]

Thus, the Soviet collapse increased domestic tensions over the fundamental tempo of mainland China's economic reform and the scope of its interaction with the international economy. Teng and Ch'en Yün have supported significantly different trajectories for mainland China based in part on their very different readings of the causes of the Soviet collapse. Ultimately, of course, the key players in this will be the "younger" officials who will take over as the octogenarians pass from the scene, and we do not have good independent information on the real views of the most important of these future leaders.

These basic assessments of how best to maintain stability inevitably have a broad and important impact on the PRC's foreign policy. To the extent that Teng's basic perception wins out, mainland China can be ex-

[30]"Li Peng Presents Government Work Report at NPC," Peking Central People's Radio, March 20, 1992, in *FBIS-CHI*-92-055-S (March 20, 1992): 1-13; and "NPC Adopts Government Work Reports, Bills," NCNA, April 3, 1992, in *FBIS-CHI*-92-065 (April 3, 1992): 26-33.

[31]An-chia Wu, "On the Renewed Promotion of the 'Teng Hsiao-p'ing Line'," *Issues & Studies* 28, no. 5 (May 1992): 1-12.

pected to place greater priority on maintaining good access to the American and other markets and to encourage more wide-ranging contact with the non-Communist countries in Asia and with the West. Ch'en Yün's approach, by contrast, would produce rougher going, both because of its greater distrust of international contact and because its more cautious approach to domestic economic development would hold down somewhat the PRC's demand for foreign imports.

Relations with the Former Socialist States

One of the few really concrete new issues raised by the collapse of the Soviet empire (beyond those discussed above) was how to deal with the new non-Communist states in both the former Soviet Union and Eastern Europe. Where East European states had simply changed their type of government, mainland China invariably shifted quickly to recognition and expressions of a desire for good working relations with the new authorities.[32]

Peking treated this type of change publicly as simply a continuing application of the policy it had espoused throughout the 1980s whereby its ties with another country should not depend on that country's domestic political and social systems. In actuality, of course, some of these transitions were painful and embarrassing for the Chinese. Ch'iao Shih (Qiao Shi) had visited Bucharest and expressed support for Nicolae Ceausescu almost on the eve of the coup there, and it seems very likely that Peking would have been acutely embarrassed had the new authorities chosen to release their notes of the comments Ch'iao had made while in Bucharest on his official visit.[33] In similar fashion, it was rumored that Yao I-lin (Yao Yilin) had advised the Honecker government to suppress popular demonstrations in Leipzig in the fall 1989,[34] and this was in fact ordered (only the refusal of the official dispatched to carry out this order prevented a Tienanmen-type massacre). Presumably, the post-Honecker leaders could have fundamentally embarrassed Peking. Also, Peking has worried about the willingness of some of these successor governments to deal directly with the Republic of China (ROC) and has expressed its concerns about this. Overall, though, clear-cut transitions found mainland Chinese diplomacy marching in step, and the Chinese consistently sought good ties with the new authorities. In this, Chinese diplomacy was facilitated by the stand Peking had adopted during the 1980s of seeking good diplomatic ties virtually across the board,

---

[32]This was true even in the case of Romania, where Peking had grave misgivings over developments there. See: NCNA (Peking), December 26, 1989, in *FBIS-CHI*-89-246 (December 26, 1989): 12.

[33]Seth Faison, "Qiao Shi Meets Nicolae Ceaucescu," *South China Sunday Morning Post*, November 19, 1989, in *FBIS-CHI*-89-224 (November 22, 1989): 17-18.

[34]On Yao's trip, see: "Further on Yao Yilin Group's Visit to GDR," NCNA, October 9, 1989, in *FBIS-CHI*-89-194 (October 10, 1989): 19.

regardless of the domestic political and economic systems of the other countries.

A different issue arose, as noted earlier in this chapter, in the cases where parts of countries sought independence, such as occurred in the Soviet Union and Yugoslavia. Mainland China sought improved relations with the central government in Moscow until August 1991, and Chinese leaders voiced support for maintaining the territorial and political integrity of the Soviet Union.[35] When the Baltic states declared independence, mainland China did not grant immediate recognition. Rather, it waited until Moscow itself recognized this independence (as had most European countries—and the ROC) and then granted its own recognition on September 7, 1991. In a similar fashion, mainland China refused to recognize the declarations of "sovereignty" or "independence" made by various other Soviet republics until Peking announced on December 27, 1991—upon the formal dissolution of the Soviet Union—that it recognized all twelve remaining republics as independent countries. It established formal diplomatic relations with most of them the following week.[36]

Finally, we see a similar pattern in Peking's policy toward recognizing the former Yugoslav republics. Like other countries, mainland China did not recognize Slovenia and Croatia immediately upon their declarations of independence in June 1991. But unlike other countries, neither did Peking change that policy in response to the descent into civil war; after all, a "civil war" between Han Chinese and Tibetans would not be good enough reason for foreign powers to recognize an independent Tibet. Instead, Peking waited until April 27, 1992 to recognize Slovenia and Croatia; that was the day the Yugoslav parliament approved a constitution for a new Yugoslavia consisting of only Serbia and Montenegro.[37]

As of late May, mainland China had not yet recognized the independence of either Bosnia-Herzegovina or Macedonia. Probably in the former case the Chinese are waiting for the new, rump Yugoslavia to cease aiding the Serb guerrillas so that the situation can be stabilized and the borders of the new state established. Here, mainland China's policy is inconsistent with those of the European Community and the United States.

Finally, the collapse of the Soviet Union itself has created potentially complex new political alignments and opportunities around mainland China's periphery from northeast to west. In the west, the newly independent states that had formed part of Soviet Central Asia (Kazakhstan, Uzbekistan,

---

[35]E.g., Li P'eng told visiting Soviet defense minister, Dmitri Yazov, in May 1991 that mainland China hoped Moscow "will preserve the stability and unity of the USSR." Peking Radio, May 7, 1991, in *FBIS-CHI-91-094* (May 15, 1991): 14.

[36]*People's Daily*, January 8, 1992, in *FBIS-CHI-92-005* (January 8, 1992): 8.

[37]"Government Recognizes Slovenia, Croatia," NCNA, April 27, 1992, in *FBIS-CHI-92-081* (April 27, 1992): 20.

Kyrgyzstan, Tajikistan, and Turkmenistan, the first three of which border China) have not yet defined either their domestic political systems or their external alignments.[38] The possibilities here are wide-ranging and consequential, affecting the future power and influence of Turkey, Iran, Afghanistan, Pakistan, India, and mainland China, among others, in this region. It is too early to determine whether any of these new states will become a new source of Islamic fundamentalism, whether any will become a nuclear threat (Kazakhstan as of mid-1992 is the world's third largest nuclear power, after the United States and Russia), and whether a powerful regional subsystem will be stitched together. At least some of these states are likely to seek warm water ports through Pakistan, creating new regional dynamics.[39] Overall, developments here present important unknowns to Chinese diplomacy, and Peking has, after a brief hesitation, begun to pursue an active diplomatic effort in the region, especially in Kazakhstan.[40]

To its northeast, mainland China must consider the extent to which the Russian maritime provinces will slip from Moscow's tight control. This will affect the prospects for regional development (encompassing mainland China, North Korea, Japan, Russia, and probably South Korea) currently under discussion.[41] Slightly to the west, Mongolia's rapid shift toward democratization occurred as a direct result of the weakening of the Soviet Union. This dramatic set of changes creates some risk that it will produce increased tensions between the Han and the Mongols in the Inner Mongolian Autonomous Region on the PRC side of the border.

Overall, therefore, mainland China must now deal with a far more complex and fluid set of circumstances along its former borders with the Soviet Union and Mongolia. While immediate military threats from these vast areas have subsided, new regional groupings and dynamics are developing, with potentially great consequences for mainland China's security and well-being. Peking has generally tried to develop diplomatic and economic ties with these new entities, but the big issues about regional developments here lie in the fairly near future.

Conclusion

The collapse of the Soviet imperium profoundly and adversely affected the PRC's position in the international arena, raising pressing questions

---

[38]*New York Times*, May 31, 1992, 8.

[39]A wide-ranging, controversial set of ideas on future regional dynamics here is provided in an interview with Dr. M. Nasir Gazdar in *Asia-Pacific Briefing Paper*, 14 (Honolulu: East West Center, May 1992).

[40]See, e.g., the successful visit by Prime Minister Tereschenko of Kazakhstan to Peking on February 24-28, 1992: NCNA releases on February 24, 26, and 28, 1992.

[41]See, e.g., *Wall Street Journal*, June 10, 1992.

both about the broad directions of the international arena and about how best to maintain CCP control domestically. Mainland China initially feared the development of a unipolar world dominated by the United States, but it has since reevaluated and downgraded the probability of this outcome. Peking has thus devoted itself to coping pragmatically with the new diplomatic challenges it confronts on various concrete issues. It has, however, not yet reached a consensus on the broad directions in which the international arena is headed, the bases of power in that new system, and mainland China's own role as that system emerges.

The global changes have struck at some of the fundamentals of mainland China's pre-1989 foreign policy. The PRC can no longer position itself in a strategic triangle, and it greatly fears any changes in international norms concerning the sanctity of national sovereignty. Yet, with the decline of Peking's fears of American global domination—fears that had peaked in the spring of 1991—the PRC's *concrete* foreign policy activities have not changed dramatically from those before 1989. The most noticeable changes during this period have, in fact, probably reflected primarily the ascendancy of hardline leaders and the harsh international condemnation of the Tienanmen repression. If Teng Hsiao-p'ing's ideas win out during 1992, then in many respects mainland China's 1993 foreign policy, other than placing somewhat greater emphasis on strengthening its Asian regional position, should resemble quite closely that of 1988.

CHAPTER 16

Peking's Foreign Policy Conundrum Since Tienanmen: Peaceful Coexistence vs. Peaceful Evolution

David Shambaugh

When Richard Nixon visited Peking several months after the Tienanmen (Tiananmen) tragedy in an attempt to arrest the downward spiral in U.S.-mainland China relations and inform the Peking (Beijing) leadership of the ostracism their nation faced in Washington and other Western capitals, the former president's stern words were greeted with an even tougher barrage of criticism from senior Chinese leaders, including Teng Hsiao-p'ing (Deng Xiaoping). Teng chastised Nixon for America's role in fomenting the "counter-revolutionary turmoil" (*fan-ke-ming pao-luan*) in Peking and across main-land China during the spring of 1989, and he warned that the United States should cease its policy of "peaceful evolution" (to peacefully evolve Chinese socialism into capitalism and "bourgeois democracy").

When Premier Li P'eng (Li Peng) took his place at the table of a special summit meeting of the United Nations Security Council in January 1992, the People's Republic of China (PRC) was welcomed as one of the nations key to shaping the post-Cold War world order. Premier Li's visit to the U.N., following state visits to several West European countries, also symbolized the PRC's reemergence from nearly three years of international ostracism following the Tienanmen massacre of June 1989.[1]

Peking's Foreign Policy Conundrum

These two vignettes encapsulate the principal dilemma confronting the makers of the PRC's foreign policy since 1989: to pursue an offensive policy

---

[1]With the exception of a continuing ban on military exchanges with Western nations, all of the sanctions imposed by the Group of Seven (G-7) countries following the bloodshed in Peking had been lifted by the time Li P'eng visited the U.N. The sanctions had been lifted progressively over the previous two years with Japan taking the lead and bringing pressure to bear on the United States and West European states to relax strictures on lending and investment, while enforcing the ban on military exchanges and sales of weapons and defense technologies.

of peaceful coexistence or a defensive one of countering "peaceful evolution." Surely no policy choice is zero-sum, and Peking has pursued a
variegated policy mix of both elements since 1989, and some policy thrusts
represent a two-track approach. Indeed, Peking (notably Foreign Minister
Ch'ien Ch'i-ch'en [Qian Qichen]) has fashioned a rather sophisticated strategy
for overcoming its near-universal ostracism. PRC leaders and diplomats have
adroitly used all the instruments of diplomacy at their disposal, and they
have tactically maneuvered in a perceptive manner to probe openings and
consolidate incremental gains. An equally important consideration is that
their policies are at least as much reactive as they are proactive. The choice
of pursuing a policy of peaceful coexistence versus anti-peaceful evolution
was, in large part, a choice foisted upon Chinese leaders by the varying
policies pursued by the Group of Seven (G-7) nations and other countries.
A principal argument of this chapter is that the United States has pursued a
China policy at extreme variance with its G-7 partners and the rest of the
world. In brief, the United States has pursued a policy of "peaceful evolution" toward mainland China, while its G-7 partners and other nations have
taken pains to distance themselves from this policy and instead have pursued
a policy of peaceful coexistence with Peking. This dichotomy and the reasons
for it are the subject of this chapter.

The PRC's status as one of the five permanent members of the U.N.
Security Council mandated Li P'eng's attendance at the U.N. summit, but
it bespoke much about the tenacity and success of Peking's campaign to
overcome its pariah status following the tragic events of 1989. It also said
much about mainland China's increasing importance in the world due to
its growing economic and military strength, even if the PRC's global strategic
significance has decreased with the end of the Soviet Union, the Cold War,
and the strategic triangle. The world's major powers all have to reckon
with Peking as a growing economic and military power and as a significant
player in international trade and arms markets. The PRC's growing economic
and military strength is of particular concern to its regional neighbors. In
the short and medium term, these neighbors are worried about the poten-
tialities of a stronger and more assertive People's Liberation Army (PLA),
capable of projecting military power beyond China's shores. In the long
term, mainland China's economic power looms large. Not only is the PRC
central to the reconfigured balance of power in Asia, but Peking also has
a role to play in other parts of the world. It would, however, be inaccurate
to paint the PRC simply in threatening and disruptive terms. Despite its
sometimes roguish behavior and the aforementioned concerns, the lure of
the mainland China market remains a major attraction for many nations,
and mutual commercial interests have served to sustain a policy of "peaceful
coexistence" between the PRC and most countries. As Teng Hsiao-p'ing
wryly observed after suppressing the 1989 demonstrations, mainland China
was a "big piece of meat" that Western nations covet and would have to
return to sooner or later.

The PRC's diplomatic offensive since 1989 has scored numerous gains for Peking—notably the normalization of diplomatic relations with South Korea, Indonesia, Singapore, Saudi Arabia, Israel, and the new states of the Commonwealth of Independent States (CIS), and the expansion of ties with South Africa (which may soon lead to full diplomatic relations). The PRC's adroit statecraft, accommodating policy of peaceful coexistence, and growing power status have reaped significant gains for Peking. Equally important, these gains have been the result of these and other nations' belief that their national interests are best served by a policy of peaceful coexistence with the PRC. At the same time, domestic political trends in mainland China following Tienanmen have combined with the collapse of the international Communist community to introduce a distinctly xenophobic and paranoid element in Peking's foreign policy. After 1989, mainland China's Communist leaders felt their personal and institutional power threatened by hostile forces inside and outside the country who sought either to undermine (by peacefully evolving the system to one dominated by market economics and political pluralism) or to overthrow (by organized, violent opposition) the Chinese Communist Party (CCP).

The PRC's struggle to regain international acceptance has been an arduous yet incomplete one. While the vast majority of its international relationships have returned to "normal," relations with the United States remain severely strained. Thus, since 1989, a dichotomy is clearly apparent in Peking's foreign relations—a tense and acrimonious relationship with the United States, on the one hand, but a more accommodating relationship with the rest of the world. What are the reasons for this dichotomy in the PRC's foreign relations?

Sources of Peking's Conundrum

Peking's foreign policy conundrum stems in part from the fact that the Cold War has not ended in Peking or Washington. While many of the irritants in Sino-American relations are non-ideological in nature (the trade deficit, market access, arms sales, etc.), this chapter argues that ideology remains an important variable in explaining U.S.-mainland China tensions. Many American policymakers, notably in Congress, wish to bring the Cold War to a final close by accelerating the demise of Communist rule in mainland China, Cuba, Vietnam, and North Korea. They believe that various diplomatic instruments should be brought to bear on Peking in order to hasten the demise of its Communist autocracy. This chapter also argues that the lingering Cold War atmosphere has mixed together with a century-long American "missionary complex," resulting in policies aimed at transforming China in America's image.

For the PRC, this "peaceful coexistence" versus anti-"peaceful evolution" conundrum is the result of several underlying forces that give rise to Chinese foreign policy. Foreign policies in all nations are fashioned by a combination of internal and external factors. In the case of the PRC, three principal factors have served to shape its dichotomous foreign policy of pursuing peaceful coexistence while countering peaceful evolution.

The first factor is the world view of the PRC's octogenarian leadership. Their collective world view after 1989 was a throwback to the class-based, two-camp struggle between socialist and imperialist systems that was dominant during Mao's lifetime.[2] This is an insecure and defensive world view that envisions a Manichaean struggle between social systems and an active conspiracy of domestic and foreign "hostile forces" to undermine and overthrow the CCP. As then Politburo Standing Committee member Yao I-lin (Yao Yilin) warned at an emergency enlarged Politburo meeting following the Tienanmen massacre,

> We must on no account take the Polish road or the Hungarian road that the American Dulles designed in the 1950s for the gradual transformation of communist countries. Over the past decades, the imperialists have never changed their original design. They came to cooperate with us and express friendship not only for the purpose of making money but also for the purpose of changing the nature of our country and remodeling our country to become a capitalist society.[3]

The conspirators who pursue a policy of "peaceful evolution" allegedly use all the tools at their disposal: military pressure; various punitive economic measures (sanctions, high tariffs, protectionism and dumping, withholding loans, restricting technology transfers, etc.); cultural exchange programs; and the infiltration of corrosive "bourgeois" ideas via the electronic and print media.

For mainland China's political elite this state of paranoia and sense of international class struggle is fused together with a world view of immutable state sovereignty and strict noninterference in internal affairs. This Westfalian definition of international relations that domestic and foreign affairs are clearly distinguishable and national borders shall not be transgressed is firmly rooted in modern China's historical and revolutionary experience. These Manichaean and Westfalian world views have reinforced each other in the minds of PRC leaders in the wake of Tienanmen.

The second factor contributing to the PRC's foreign policy dilemma following Tienanmen has been the vast and fundamental changes in the international landscape that began with the overthrow of Communist regimes across Eastern Europe, continued during the Gulf War against Iraq, and

---

[2] The origins of this world view are explored in David Shambaugh, "The Soviet Influence on China's Worldview," *The Australian Journal of Chinese Affairs*, no. 27 (January 1992): 151-58.

[3] "Comrade Yao Yilin's Speech at the Conference Held by the CCP Central Committee and Attended by Responsible Comrades of Various Departments" (June 1989), *Hsüan-ch'uan tung-t'ai* (Propaganda Developments), no. 21 (June 20, 1989), translated in "The Making of the Big Lie: Content and Process in the CCP Propaganda System," *Chinese Law and Government* 25, no. 1 (Spring 1992): 49.

culminated in the collapse of the Soviet Union. These events served not only to reinforce the paranoid world view of the PRC leaders noted above, but also radically reconfigured the global strategic system and mainland China's place in it.

For almost two decades the PRC had enjoyed a central position in the "strategic triangle," but with the collapse of the triangle between 1987 and 1989, and the bipolar system that sustained it, Peking was forced to grope for a redefined position in global strategic affairs. Peking could no longer premise its foreign policy on the continued confrontation between the super-powers. Nor, indeed, was the existence of two superpowers any longer a defining characteristic for Peking's foreign policy. The breakup of the Soviet Union and the victory of the American-led coalition during the Gulf War suggested to many strategic analysts in Peking that a unipolar world of American hegemony was emerging in the post-Cold War period. From the PRC's perspective, the prospect of unipolarity was an alarming state of affairs far worse than bipolarity. Peking's preference is for a multipolar world in which regional powers, such as the PRC, play defining roles in their regions and are able to resist external intervention and interference in internal affairs. In short, the fundamental change in the international system undercut the very essence of the foreign policy strategy Peking had practiced since the early 1970s, and forced the PRC's leaders to pursue a more variegated policy of interest maximization.

The third determining factor was the growth of mainland China's domestic economy and its growing interdependence with the global economy. Both phenomena operated, to a significant extent, independently of Peking's control. Despite a harsh economic austerity program implemented by central economic planners in 1989 to cool off an overheated economy, mainland China's economy has continued to grow at a healthy rate in the three years following Tienanmen. From the fourth quarter of 1990, the domestic economy began to roar out of the doldrums and resume its pre-Tienanmen growth rates. The gross.national product (GNP) grew at an average annual rate of 7 percent in 1989-91, and will post a growth rate of at least 10 percent for 1992. Exports have boomed, causing mainland China's trade surplus and foreign currency holdings to expand rapidly (US$9 billion and US$42 billion respectively in 1991). After an initial downturn in 1989-90, direct foreign investment also reached new levels with many foreign investors reaping record profits. Much of the new investment came from Taiwan and Hong Kong commercial concerns. Agricultural output attained record levels (435 million metric tons in the 1990 harvest), and energy production was also up. At the same time, the austerity program brought inflation down to 3-4 percent. To be certain, various (and serious) structural imbalances continue to plague the economy—most notably the inefficient and heavily subsidized state industrial sector, a rising budget deficit, and slack consumer demand. But, on the whole, mainland China's economy exhibited robust vitality between 1989 and 1991, while containing inflation and not overheating. State Statistical Bureau figures for the first three quarters of 1992 reveal impressive figures across the board—10.6 percent overall GNP growth, 19.3 percent growth in gross industrial output, a 36.3 percent rise in investment in fixed assets, a retail sales increase of 14.4 percent, a rise in bank deposits to US$185 billion, a 13 percent increase in state revenue, 52 percent growth in foreign investment, and a 19 percent increase in foreign trade. These statistics confirm Teng Hsiao-p'ing's call for acceleration of economic reform. The danger of such robust growth, of course, is rekindled inflation and renewed overheating. The signs of overheating and creeping inflation are present, but a series of macroeconomic adjustments and limited price reform undertaken since 1989, taken together with approximately US$225 billion in personal savings that can cushion and absorb price increases, argue that the situation is not analogous to 1988-89.

The major catalyst of mainland China's impressive economic growth has, of course, been the non-state sector concentrated along the southeastern "Gold Coast." Fukien (Fujian), Kwangtung (Guangdong), and Hainan provinces serve simultaneously as the principal export platforms and magnets for foreign investment. The lower Yangtze (Yangzi) River basin encompassing Chekiang (Zhejiang), Kiangsu (Jiangsu), Shanghai, and the Putung (Pudong) development zone, as well as the Shantung (Shandong) and Liaotung (Liaodong) peninsulas further up the coast, serve the same purposes vis-à-vis Japan, Korea, and the United States. The integration of these regional economies into the East Asian regional and global economy is accelerating, and with it the PRC's overall external interdependence with the outside world.[4] In economic terms, the PRC is actually more dependent on, than interdependent with, the world economy. Concomitantly, these coastal economies are becoming more independent from Peking with every passing day.

This inexorable trend has important foreign policy implications. Mainland China's dependence/interdependence means that foreign nations—particularly Japan and the United States—and international financial institutions—such as the International Monetary Fund (IMF), World Bank, and Asian Development Bank (ADB)—possess leverage over the PRC should they decide to exercise it.[5] Since the United States and Japan hold the preponderance of voting shares on the directorates of these institutions, pressure can be brought upon Peking in these multilateral institutions as well. During the 1980s, the PRC became the world's leading recipient of international aid from international and national lending bodies (from accepting no foreign

---

[4]See Thomas W. Robinson and Wendy Frieman, "Costs and Benefits of Interdependence: A Net Assessment," in *China's Economic Dilemmas in the 1990s: The Problems of Reforms, Modernization, and Interdependence*, ed. Joint Economic Committee of the U.S. Congress (Washington, D.C.: U.S. Government Printing Office, 1991), 2:718-40.

[5]Mainland China now owes international creditors approximately US$52 billion.

aid in 1979, to being the recipient of more than US$50 billion in 1990[6]); this leverage was exercised with the post-Tienanmen sanctions, and subsequently over human rights and other concerns. Foreign direct investment is another important dimension of the PRC's financial interdependence. Foreign capital is pouring into mainland China from Hong Kong, Taiwan, Japan, the United States, Europe, and overseas Chinese at an unprecedented rate.[7] The PRC is also interwoven into regional and international trading regimes, and the domestic economy is increasingly driven by its external component.[8] Mainland China's foreign trade sector now accounts for more than one-third of the country's gross domestic product (GDP). The importance of foreign trade and export markets also provides the PRC's partners with certain leverage in bilateral and multilateral political relationships, as is demonstrated by the annual debate in Washington over renewal of most-favored-nation (MFN) trading status for the PRC, the "super 301" U.S.-mainland China trade negotiations, and the European Community's (EC's) linkage of trade preferences to human rights concerns.

In short, the PRC is now linked inexorably to the global trading and financial systems. Withdrawal from these systems and the pursuit of an autarchic path of development is no longer an option. To the contrary, participation in these systems mandates distinct obligations and behavioral standards for the PRC.

These three factors—the world view of the PRC leaders, change in the international system, and developments in the Chinese economy—collectively underlie and have greatly influenced foreign policy options for the Peking leadership since 1989. They have had the effect of pulling the PRC's foreign policy in opposite directions. The antiquated Westfalian world view of the leadership outlined above, taken together with the radical change in the international system, have tended to strengthen the "peaceful evolution" end of the PRC's foreign policy continuum, while the rapid development of the economy and growing interdependence have pulled foreign policy toward the "peaceful coexistence" dimension. The Peking leadership has been pulled in both directions. From 1989 to 1991, the predominant opinion favored the defensive anti-peaceful evolution world view, but following Teng Hsiao-p'ing's tour of southern China in early 1992, the balance of political power began to shift. A fierce intra-leadership struggle took place throughout the year during the run-up to the Fourteenth Congress of the CCP in October.

---

[6]*Economist*, March 24, 1990, 1.

[7]Foreign direct investment in 1991 totaled US$11 billion. Commitments for the first half of 1992 had already matched this figure. *Economist*, July 18, 1992, 24. Peking's State Statistical Bureau revealed that the total contracted value of direct investment for the first three quarters of 1992 stood at US$36.4 billion. *Asian Wall Street Journal*, October 26, 1992, 4.

[8]See Nicholas R. Lardy, *Foreign Trade and Economic Reform in China, 1978-1990* (Cambridge: Cambridge University Press, 1992).

The Congress enshrined a new leadership far more technocratic and reformist than ideological in nature, and many of the octogenarians in the leadership stepped down. This changing of the guard reinforced the "peaceful co-existence" end of the PRC's foreign policy continuum, while the ideological hardliners who had pressed the campaign against "peaceful evolution" declined in power. To be sure, the problems with the United States endure, particularly following President Bush's decision to sell 150 F-16 fighters to Taiwan, but in general both the rhetorical tone and the substance of foreign policy shifted in a less-defensive direction following Teng's southern tour.

Reactions to Tienanmen

The tug and pull between peaceful coexistence and peaceful evolution in PRC foreign policy reflects not only domestic policy proclivities in Peking, but also the varying approaches of different nations toward the PRC. No nation makes its foreign policy in a vacuum; foreign policies are at least as reactive as they are proactive. It is therefore instructive to take note of the policies that different nations have pursued toward the PRC since Tienanmen.

The differing policies reflect these countries' varying national interests vis-à-vis the PRC, and these differences have been exploited by Peking in its attempt to overcome the ostracism and sanctions imposed following Tienanmen.

Governments around the world were by no means united in their response to the Peking massacre, although there was collective shock and outrage among all those who witnessed the military suppression on television or in person. Satellites beamed the horrors of June 1989 to most countries around the world, except for the then-Soviet Union and East European states. The international community reacted in varying ways to Peking's reactionary convulsion.

Officially, the Soviet Union considered the suppression "an internal matter," and Soviet officials said nothing that would undermine the recent normalization of relations sealed by Mikhail Gorbachev and Teng Hsiao-p'ing. Unofficially, however, there was considerable criticism of Peking in the Congress of People's Deputies and other forums.[9] The Soviet government, though, calculated that its national interests were much better served by silence than sanctions. Since the collapse of the Soviet Union, the Yeltsin government has continued the accommodating policy of peaceful coexistence begun by Gorbachev and has expanded trade and military sales to the PRC.

The reaction in Eastern Europe was varied. The Polish, Hungarian, and Yugoslavian governments made public statements condemning the use of

---

[9]See Alexander Lukin, "The Initial Soviet Reaction to the Events in China in 1989 and the Prospects for Sino-Soviet Relations," *China Quarterly*, no. 125 (March 1991): 119-36.

force but did not join international sanctions against the PRC. In contrast, Bulgaria, Czechoslovakia, East Germany, and Romania made their approval of the crackdown known to the Peking government and stifled news of the massacre domestically. These were the first governments to exchange high-level visits with the PRC following the massacre.[10] Ironically, several of these reactionary governments were themselves confronted with "people power" only a few months after the Tienanmen suppression. Erich Honecker in East Germany and Romania's Nicolae Ceausescu opted for "the Chinese solution," only to have their security services revolt and fail to follow orders. The collapse of Communist rule in these nations—particularly the Ceausescu execution—reverberated sharply in the Chungnanhai (Peking's leadership compound), causing the leadership to put the PLA on high alert and tighten control over domestic security for fear of a repeat performance in the Chinese capital. Following the collapse of these Communist regimes, Peking moved quickly to reaffirm diplomatic ties with their successors throughout Eastern Europe. The same was true in the former Soviet republics following the disintegration of the Soviet Union in 1991, when the PRC promptly set up embassies and signed trade accords with the new republics.[11]

Nations of the developing world reacted in a generally muted manner to the massacre. None suspended trade, cultural, military, or diplomatic ties. The PRC capitalized on the silence from the Third World to step up diplomatic contacts with these countries and, in some cases, to repair strained ties. To a real extent, this was a policy of necessity as the PRC faced a closed door from the West. The priority on strengthening ties with the developing world reaped diplomatic and commercial benefits for Peking. Israel, Saudi Arabia, the Republic of Korea, Singapore, and Indonesia all established diplomatic relations with the PRC following Tienanmen, while South Africa opened a pseudo-embassy in Peking. Taiwan moved aggressively to expand its trade and other ties with the mainland. In lieu of Western emissaries, a steady stream of Third World dignitaries visited mainland China and Chinese leaders were dispatched to a large number of Asian, African, and Latin American countries.

The G-7 industrialized nations responded to the events in Peking individually and collectively. All vigorously condemned the atrocities. Each instituted a range of punitive sanctions, paralleling those announced by the United States one day after the massacre, and further actions were coordinated

---

[10]See the discussion in David Shambaugh, "China and Europe," *The Annals of the American Academy of Political and Social Science* 519 (January 1992): 112-13.

[11]These efforts were largely successful, except in Latvia where Peking closed its embassy after the Latvian government permitted the Republic of China to open a consulate. Taipei's aggressive "aid diplomacy" in the former Soviet republics and East European states may still result in such further reversals for the PRC. For its part, the Russian Republic opened unofficial relations and liaison offices with Taipei in August 1992.

at the summit meetings of the G-7 and the European Community later that month. These measures included the suspension of high-level consultations and exchanges between government officials; the suspension of all weapons sales and transfers of technologies with military applications; the suspension of all collaborative programs and meetings between Western militaries and the PLA; the freezing of all government-guaranteed loans; and the extension of visas for mainland Chinese students, scholars, and others resident abroad who had reason to fear persecution if they returned home. The United States went beyond these common sanctions in a number of areas, but in the immediate aftermath of the massacre there existed considerable consensus among the G-7 nations. Several Western nations (particularly France, Canada, and the United States, as well as Australia) provided refuge and political asylum for exiled Chinese dissidents.

One year later, at the G-7 summit in Houston, evidence of splits in the Western coalition became apparent. Under pressure from Japan and Europe, President Bush conceded that the United States "would not oppose" the allies' lifting of sanctions (although the Bush administration was under tremendous pressure from Congress to leave U.S. sanctions in place). Japanese and European businessmen were anxious to resume trading with and investing in mainland China, and their governments consciously adopted a policy of not isolating the PRC. The Tienanmen atrocities had begun to fade from memory in European capitals as the parliaments, politicians, and publics in Europe did not, on the whole, debate Peking's human rights violations or aggressive arms sales policies. Japan's suspended loan of US$6.25 billion to finance projects during the Eighth Five-Year Plan (1991-95) was reinstated after the Houston summit. This opened the way to the signing of several other loan agreements and commercial projects. For their part, West European governments resumed high-level exchanges during the autumn of 1990, although the ban on weapons sales and military contacts was left in place (the latter was quietly lifted during 1992).[12] Great Britain, in particular, felt the necessity to resume high-level dialogue with PRC leaders because of several pressing problems associated with the reversion of Hong Kong to PRC sovereignty in 1997. Japan was also particularly keen to resume normal relations with Peking. President Bush's decision to permit the other G-7 nations to pursue their own China policies also freed blocked lending from the World Bank (especially its soft-loan window, the International Development Association), the IMF, and the ADB (the ADB had frozen US$490 million in allocated funds).

---

[12]For further detail on the PRC's relations with the G-7 nations and the world in the aftermath of Tienanmen, see the excellent set of essays in *The Annals of the American Academy of Political and Social Science* 519 (January 1992) (special editor: Allen S. Whiting). Also see John Garver, "Chinese Foreign Policy: The Diplomacy of Damage Control," *Current History* 90, no. 557 (September 1991): 241-46; and Samuel S. Kim, "Chinese Foreign Policy After Tiananmen," ibid. 89, no. 548 (September 1990): 248.

While West European nations and Japan generally shared America's sense of outrage over the killings in Peking, they calculated their national interests with respect to mainland China, and hence their China policies, very differently from the United States. Japanese and European statesmen, politicians, and governments hold differing views from their American counterparts on how hard to press the Peking government, the potential for external influence on Chinese policies, on the PRC's role in the world, and on its future. Indeed, it is not just Japan and Western Europe that hold differing perspectives from the United States; the United States stands virtually alone in the world by maintaining a tough and punitive policy toward Peking. Herein lies the essence of the PRC's dichotomous relations with the world since 1989.

Different Nations, Different Missions, Different Relations

For all practical purposes, since 1990, when the G-7 coalition on mainland China came apart and sanctions were progressively lifted by Japan and European states, the PRC has been able to pursue "normal" bilateral relations with virtually every nation on earth except the United States. Why? To oversimplify (but also to capture the thrust of my argument), America's policy toward the PRC is premised on fostering internal political and economic change in mainland China rather than simply pursuing mutually beneficial bilateral relations. **America's agenda is to change mainland China.** This is principally an ideologically motivated agenda that derives both from the superpower status of the United States, its democratic tradition, as well as the continuing century-long effort to transform China in America's image.[13] Other nations do not pursue this interventionist agenda in mainland China, but rather are content to engage in the full range of commercial, cultural, and diplomatic interchange as ends in themselves. As a superpower with a self-righteous belief in the efficacy and appeal of its own political, economic, and social systems, the United States has stood alone among Western nations as a fashioner of an interventionist foreign policy in the postwar and post-colonial eras. Thus, America's policy toward the PRC must be viewed against the backdrop of the broader Cold War environment and America's super-power status in the world.

Since at least the Carter administration, the U.S. government has adopted policies aimed at increasing the role of the market in the PRC's domestic economy, integrating (and entrapping) Peking into a range of Western

---

[13]See Warren I. Cohen, *America's Response to China* (New York: Wiley, 1971); Michael Hunt, *The Making of a Special Relationship: The United States and China to 1914* (New York: Columbia University Press, 1983); James C. Thomson, Jr., Peter W. Stanley, and John Curtis Perry, *Sentimental Imperialists: The American Experience in East Asia* (New York: Harper & Row, 1981).

(and U.S.) dominated international institutional mechanisms and regimes, promoting human rights and the liberalization of the mainland Chinese polity, and—until 1989—augmenting the PRC's national security. In addition to government policies which promote these goals, a variety of private sector actors have developed programs in mainland China which have supported these broader government goals. In this observer's opinion, the PRC government is therefore not incorrect to charge the United States with pursuing a policy of "peaceful evolution," as this has been the underlying premise—if not the active policy guide—for America's China policy since 1979. To be sure, the PRC's strategic importance and the common threat from the Soviet Union also served to glue the Washington-Peking relationship together from 1971 to 1989, but a bipartisan belief in the United States that fostering greater political pluralism and economic expansion in mainland China was in America's national interest also underpinned the U.S. approach to the PRC.

Any full examination of the United States' China policy (and this is not the place for one[14]) will reveal cleavages of opinion over China policy in the U.S. body politic, but these have been more a matter of degree than substance. That is, debates have existed largely over the proper mix of policy instruments to bring about change in mainland China rather than about the desirability of doing so. This has been particularly apparent since Tiananmen as an annual, heated debate over China policy has taken place in Washington under the rubric of renewing MFN trade status for the PRC. A wide variety of issues have been subsumed under this debate, only a few of which have to do with trade. Peking's human rights abuses, conventional arms transfers, and suspected nuclear proliferation have joined a host of complaints about unfair and unethical trading practices, the export of goods made by prison labor, a ballooning trade deficit with the United States (an estimated US$19 billion in 1992), intellectual property rights infringements, and other issues in the annual MFN debate.[15]

As a forum for discussion of China policy, the annual MFN debates have illuminated two distinct constituencies in the United States. These may be described as the "open door" and "closed door" constituencies. The former, epitomized by President Bush, a minority of senators, and some China specialists, advocate a policy of "constructive engagement" with the

---

[14]See, for example, Harry Harding, *A Fragile Relationship* (Washington, D.C.: Brookings Institution Press, 1992); David Shambaugh, "Patterns of Interaction in U.S.-China Relations," in *Chinese Foreign Policy: Theory and Practice*, ed. Thomas W. Robinson and David Shambaugh (Oxford: Oxford University Press, forthcoming).

[15]For fine surveys of this period in Washington-Peking relations, see David Zweig, "The Downward Spiral: Sino-American Relations Since Tiananmen," in *China Briefing, 1991*, ed. William Joseph (Boulder, Colo.: Westview Press, 1991), 119-142; and Robert G. Sutter, "Tiananmen's Lingering Fallout on Sino-American Relations," *Current History* 90, no. 557 (September 1991): 247-50.

PRC. They argue that to penalize and isolate mainland China would be counterproductive to bringing about eventual political and economic change there. In order to change the PRC, the "open door" constituency argues, the United States must have leverage. And to have leverage, the argument goes, America must have a presence in mainland China. By withdrawing MFN status, the U.S. presence declines and along with it channels of communication and leverage. Moreover, they argue, the progressive sectors of mainland Chinese society would be penalized and U.S. business interests would be hurt by a withdrawal of MFN status. The second constituency, represented by the majority of Congress and a host of special interest concerns in the American body politic, take the opposite position. They argue that the PRC must be ostracized and penalized in every conceivable way; only by doing so will sufficient pressure be brought to bear on the Communist regime in Peking. Further, the "closed door" constituency argues that to do business with the "butchers of Peking" sends precisely the wrong message to mainland China's aspiring democrats and serves to affirm in the minds of the regime that the United States supports their rule.

The important point about these two positions is that they are in agreement on the goals of America's China policy. Both constituencies share the goal of hastening the demise of the Communist system in mainland China; they only disagree about the tactics of facilitating that eventuality. Both positions—it is important to note—remain locked in the Cold War struggle against Chinese Communism. Their cause is essentially ideological, and has been fueled by the demise of Communism around the globe in the three years since a group of students sparked the whole process by audaciously challenging the Chinese state in Tienanmen Square. I do not mean to suggest that America's China policy has been directed by a cabal of conspirators who control various governmental and private sector programs aimed at destabilizing the Chinese Communist regime, as that has definitely not been the case, but I do suggest that there has existed more of an unspoken consensus about the desired direction and end result of change in mainland China. I think it fair to say that all parties in the United States involved in making the government's China policy and facilitating exchange programs with the PRC share the view that American and Chinese national interests are best served by:

* a more liberal political climate, leading ultimately to the demise of the CCP's political hegemony;
* a market-led economy;
* a more free social environment that tolerates and facilitates the freedoms of choice, religious belief, ethnic identity, and respect for fundamental human rights;
* a peaceful and secure mainland China free from any pressing external threat, and posing no military threat to the United States, its Asian allies, or other neighboring countries.

These are the goals and underlying premises that have guided the American approach to the PRC since 1979. This is largely an agenda for change, not the status quo. Nor, as is the case in many European countries, is it an agenda for neutral, mutually beneficial exchange programs. Embedded in this agenda for change is a strong American paternalism toward China, a characteristic that has been present in the American approach to China since at least the 1920s.

Why is it that Chinese behavior is of such great concern and debate in the United States Congress but not in the British Parliament, the Japanese Diet, the German Bundestag, or other parliaments and government offices around the world? Is this solely America's vendetta? Apparently so. Aside from some debate and articulated concern by the French, Australian, and Canadian governments, the world has been content to restore and repair relations with Peking. The reasons for this vary by country. In the case of the United Kingdom, America's closest ally, the overriding British preoccupation with issues related to the reversion of Hong Kong to PRC sovereignty has emasculated and dominated Britain's China policy. That is, the House of Commons has failed to debate, and Whitehall has failed to press, Peking on its arms sales and nuclear proliferation policies, trade and investment practices, and human rights record (although British diplomats maintain that these concerns are pursued through private diplomatic channels). White House officials have expressed dismay over Britain's failure to support the U.S. administration's criticisms of Peking and disgust over what they perceive to be a policy of appeasing the PRC over Hong Kong.[16]

In Asia, concerns about the PRC are different than in the West. It can be said that all Asian governments believe that the maintenance of social and political stability in mainland China is in their national interests. This is particularly the case for Japan. The potential refugee exodus and general disruption caused by internal tumult in mainland China would impact quickly upon most Asian nations. A September 1992 public opinion survey conducted by *Yomiuri Shimbun* revealed that instability in mainland China and the potential refugee exodus was the issue of greatest concern to the Japanese public, scoring considerably higher than concerns about human rights abuses there, Peking's arms sales, military buildup, or other issues.[17] Most Asian nations therefore view political stability in mainland China—even of the hardline Communist variety—as preferable to uncertain alternatives. Moreover, since democracies are few in Asia, concerns about human rights abuses in the PRC are also limited. Some Asian nations find themselves on the same State Department human rights blacklist as Peking.

In Asia, the threat from the PRC is a commercial and increasingly

---

[16]Personal communication with U.S. official, November 1991.

[17]*Yomiuri Shimbun* (Tokyo), September 12, 1992, 3.

military one. The rapid growth of mainland China's export sector directly threatens the market share that the "four dragons" previously held in the Western light industrial export markets. To some extent this competition is offset by growing intraregional trade, the opening of new markets in Asia, and the retooling of domestic industries among Asian newly industrialized countries (NICs), but there is no doubt that the Chinese economic behemoth is cutting into long-established trade patterns.

More pressing than commercial concerns, however, is the rising "threat" from the Chinese military. Since 1989, Peking's defense budget has grown in real terms by nearly 50 percent. The aggregate increases are a source of great concern to mainland China's neighbors, but more threatening has been the development—since the late 1980s—of a blue water navy, rapid deployment units, long-range reconnaissance, mid-air refueling, and other capabilities to sustain low-intensity conflicts around mainland China's periphery. Peking is clearly developing the capacity to press its territorial claims in the East and South China seas. These force and doctrinal changes also threaten Taiwan.

Thus, approaches to the PRC vary considerably among nations, and particularly among the G-7 industrialized countries where one would expect to find greater consensus, unanimity, and policy coordination. The reason for the variance lies in an iron law of international relations: shared national interests are temporal and situation-specific. Even the United States and the United Kingdom, which possess broad bonds of shared culture, have demonstrated distinctly different China policies since the immediate aftermath of the Tienanmen tragedy.

Conclusion

The import of the above discussion is that there has been a dichotomy in the world's policies toward the PRC and in the PRC's foreign relations since Tienanmen, which I have distinguished as "peaceful coexistence" versus (anti-) "peaceful evolution" policy strains. I have traced how the PRC rather rapidly and assiduously overcame the international sanctions and ostracism it experienced in the wake of Tienanmen. Having regained acceptance from the world community, the PRC enjoys peaceful coexistence with almost all nations. However, the PRC has had a distinctly different experience with the United States since 1989. The Sino-American relationship over the last three years has been contentious and often acrimonious. It must be recognized that there has always been a contentious dimension to the Washington-Peking relationship (largely over Taiwan), and many of the strains that have come to the forefront since Tienanmen actually began to appear before Tienanmen (Peking's arms sales, nuclear proliferation, human rights abuses, trade disputes), but since 1989, Washington-Peking relations have reached a low ebb unseen since before the rapprochement of the early 1970s.

In other words, Peking has pursued two foreign policies since Tienanmen—one for the United States and one for the rest of the world. It is also clear that the United States has pursued a China policy at variance with the rest of the world. This is not to overlook the fact that the United States and the PRC have found some common ground and cooperated on regional security issues (Cambodia and Korea), have hammered out agreements on intellectual property rights and prison labor exports, and have negotiated over structural impediments in the mainland Chinese economy that inhibit American investment in and exports to the PRC, but contention has far outweighed cooperation between the two countries since 1989. Such contention is rooted very clearly in the American agenda for bringing about political, economic, and social change in mainland China. These changes—if followed to their logical conclusion—imply the erosion and/or downfall of the Chinese Communist political system (and all of its attendant features), the socialist command economy, and the repressive intellectual and social environment. Therefore, it is no wonder that the Peking government is resisting American efforts to undermine its power and rule.

What are the prospects for this state of affairs to continue? In the near future, following Bill Clinton's election as president, one should expect an even tougher American China policy. MFN trading status will, in all probability, be explicitly linked to the PRC's human rights record, trade practices, and arms sales abroad, as there would no longer be a Republican president to veto the Congressional resolutions to make conditional or revoke MFN. Such a potential reversal of Bush's policy toward the PRC is of concern to other G-7 nations. Japanese officials are deeply concerned by the atmosphere of "China bashing" in the United States and continue to argue for a policy of not isolating the PRC.[18] British Foreign Secretary Douglas Hurd expressed Britain's concern over Clinton's intentions toward the PRC to Clinton's advisors during a visit to the United States on the eve of the American election, and warned them that a tougher U.S. policy on mainland China trade "would have a disastrous impact on Hong Kong and, by extension, British business interests."[19]

In the longer term, American relations with mainland China will be partially determined by how the United States reformulates its foreign policy and adjusts to a different role in the world after the Cold War. For some American policymakers the Cold War will not be over until the four remaining socialist states (mainland China, Vietnam, North Korea, Cuba) cease to be run by Communist parties, and this cohort believes that all

---

[18]Interviews with Japanese Diet members and Foreign Ministry officials, Tokyo, September 1992.

[19]"British Concerns over Clinton's Election Pledges," *The Independent* (London), October 5, 1992, 1.

possible pressure should be brought to bear on these regimes until they fall from power. Others, though, believe that they will implode and collapse under their own authoritarian weight—as was the case in Eastern Europe and the Soviet Union. This second cohort consequently argues that America's policy toward the PRC should be a tough but distant one.

If history is any guide, the United States will not abandon its attempts to remold mainland China in its image. The American missionary impulse to change China has well-developed roots. It is questionable that even a retreat from empire and decline in superpower status would diminish this long-standing national impulse, and only a democratic-capitalist revolution in mainland China would satisfy it. During the spring of 1989, Americans believed they were witnessing just such a revolution. Chinese students in Tienanmen Square quoted Jefferson, Paine, Nathan Hale, and other American revolutionaries. A reincarnation of the American system seemed in the offing, only to be crushed by the tanks of the authoritarian state. Many in the United States will not be satisfied until the Chinese Communist Party follows its erstwhile comrades into the dustbin of history. The democratic revolution which has swept Latin America, Europe, Africa, and Asia in recent years has only emboldened Americans' belief in their national mission. Bilateral disputes over trade, human rights, security issues, and so on, are serious in their own right, but also tend to mask the real American problem in Sino-American relations—two antithetical political, economic, and social systems.

The American mission to change China is not shared by the European powers, Japan, the NICs, or the developing world. Even those European nations with a long social-democratic tradition do not share America's missionary impulse and righteous conviction in the Western form of governance. Their beliefs in democracy no doubt run just as deep, but the urge to proselytize and convert has not been nearly as strong since the end of the colonial era. No doubt most European governments would welcome the demise of Communism in mainland China, but are prepared to do little to contribute to the process. Even if they felt the need to do so, they do not believe that they possess the influence and leverage to make a difference. Japanese officials are of the view that political change in mainland China would create instability which, in turn, would have damaging implications for Japanese investments and security concerns. In the short term, Japan favors the status quo in mainland China. In the long term, as Cold War alignments in Asia become more fluid, there exists the further possibility that a Sino-Japanese economic and military rivalry may reignite, and there is considerable concern in both Japan and the PRC about the other's military capabilities and aspirations.[20]

---

[20]For further analysis of this possibility and the PRC's redefined security policy, see David Shambaugh, "China's Security Policy in the Post-Cold War Era," *Survival* 34, no. 2 (Summer 1992): 88-106.

The dichotomy witnessed in the PRC's foreign policy since Tienanmen—and particularly the tension with the United States—can thus be expected to continue until either the Chinese Communist Party falls from power or the United States abandons its century-long attempt to remold China in its image. History will prove which has greater staying power. In the meantime, the PRC will continue to build its ties with all countries which do not seek to subvert its government or threaten its national security interests. In the final analysis, Peking's foreign policy conundrum will be more of a problem for Washington than Peking, as America's China policy varies from that of its allies and other nations.

CHAPTER 17

Peking's Diplomatic Strategies in a Changing World, 1989-92

Tzong-Ho Bau

The period from June 1989 to June 1992 was of great importance to mainland China. Numerous events occurred which pushed the Peking (Beijing) government to reevaluate its policy toward other countries. The post-Cold War era brought about a redistribution of power among nations, and the resulting change in the world order has had considerable impact on the mainland Chinese leadership.

First, there was true détente between the United States and the Soviet Union. Washington and Moscow successfully achieved a basic consensus that they should reduce the numbers of strategic nuclear weapons such as ICBMs and IRBMs.[1] One immediate impact of the Washington-Moscow rapprochement was that Peking's strategic standing inevitably declined. The Washington-Moscow-Peking triangle is no longer in mainland China's favor since the "China card" is not as meaningful as it was in the Cold War era.

Second, between June 1989 and June 1990, elections were held in Poland, East Germany, Hungary, Romania, Czechoslovakia, and Bulgaria, and all of these elections, except in Poland, were free and open. As a result, the Communist parties lost power in most of these countries, and in Poland and Bulgaria the Communists had to share power with other parties under the framework of a coalition government.[2] In October 1990, Germany was reunified when East Germany yielded its sovereignty and ruling power to West Germany through a democratic process. In December 1991, the Soviet Union was formally broken up into many independent states. The virtual collapse of the Communist community of nations, along with the end of the Cold War, further contributed to the marginalization of mainland China in world affairs.

---

[1] Henry Trofimenko, "The End of the Cold War, Not History," *The Washington Quarterly* 13, no. 2 (Spring 1990): 21.

[2] Mao-hsiung Hung, "Political Changes in Eastern Europe: Characteristics and Impact," *Issues & Studies* 26, no. 10 (October 1990): 122.

Third, national interests instead of ideology emerged as a dominant factor in foreign policy decision-making. The end of East-West confrontation provided countries with more opportunities to develop their foreign relations. The bipolar system gave way to a multipolar system under which the United States, the world's only superpower, has to share its power and obligations with more and more countries, no matter whether they are its allies or not. This decentralization of power among nations is offering new challenges and opportunities for many countries.

Fourth, improved cooperation between the United States and the Soviet Union (Russia since 1992) in the post-Cold War era has enhanced the standing of the United Nations. The Group of 77, with its majority of votes in the U.N. General Assembly, plays an increasingly important role in that organization. The lack of foreign aid from the Soviet Union over the past few years has given other countries, such as mainland China, a chance to intensify their connections with the Third World.[3]

Fifth, the political disintegration of the Eastern and Western blocs has encouraged regional integration in terms of economic and geopolitical cooperation among nations. Regional organizations, such as the European Community (EC), the European Political Cooperation (EPC), the Independent European Program Group (IEPG), the Pacific Economic Cooperation Conference (PECC), the Pacific Basin Economic Council (PBEC), the Asia-Pacific Economic Cooperation (APEC) forum, and the South Pacific Forum, have evolved into more active and dynamic groups over the past few years. The development of these organizations would mean that further regional integration might occur in the future.

Finally, with the easing of ideological conflicts in the post-Cold War era, human rights have been transformed from a political issue into a moral one. All countries, Communist or otherwise, are liable to be criticized for human rights violations. That is to say, idealism prevails over realism when political leaders bring the issue of human rights into account.

The Pressure on Mainland China

This changing environment imposed great pressure on the Peking government. Mainland China's image was seriously damaged by the Tienanmen (Tiananmen) massacre of June 4, 1989. The world deeply questioned the legitimacy and morality of the Peking government, and mainland China became isolated, particularly from the West.

The collapse of the Communist bloc intensified the negative impact of

---

[3]For the decline in Moscow's assistance to the Third World, see Charles H. Fairbanks, Jr., "Gorbachev's Global Doughnut: The Empire with a Hole in the Middle," *The National Interest*, Spring 1990, 21.

the Tienanmen incident on Peking's foreign relations. Mainland China can no longer take advantage of a superpower rivalry to expand its interests, and the West can attach much more importance to issues such as arms sales and human rights, where Peking's record is poor. Moreover, the disintegration of the Soviet Union encouraged the West to choose Peking as the next target of so-called peaceful evolution. The promotion of peace by the West through economic and technological cooperation among nations is, according to the hardline leadership in Peking, an effort by developed countries to "integrate mainland China into the community of capitalism and democracy."[4]

The rise of the United States as the only superpower in the wake of the Gulf War and the demise of the Soviet Union meant that the Peking government had to deal with American hegemony and, particularly, American values that are definitely detrimental to the survival of mainland China.[5] Consequently, the Western mass media have been regarded as capable of undermining the socialist order. The Peace Corps, the Fulbright program, and other "nongovernmental" academic and cultural exchange programs are classified as forms of Western ideological and cultural infiltration into socialist countries.[6]

In addition, the pragmatic and aggressive diplomacy of the Republic of China (ROC) on Taiwan has also made it more difficult for Peking to maintain and develop its foreign relations. In 1989, Peking severed diplomatic relations with three Third World nations—Grenada, Belize, and Liberia, because they established formal ties with the ROC. The diplomatic pressure exerted on Peking by the ROC is the result, first of all, of Taipei's success in employing its economic resources to attract some Third World nations; it is also a consequence of the zero-sum game Peking is engaged in with the ROC in the international community.

In response to its isolation after the Tienanmen crackdown and the downfall of the Soviet Union, Peking had to transform its role in international relations from that of the pursued to that of a pursuer.[7]

Peking's Diplomatic Strategies

Peking's foreign policy objective is to survive in a changing world. Its first goal is to achieve the modernization of the Chinese mainland, and its

---

[4]"Larger World Role Forces China to Moderate Policies at Home," *Christian Science Monitor*, February 26, 1992, 11.

[5]Samuel S. Kim, "Mainland China and a New World Order," *Issues & Studies* 27, no. 11 (November 1991): 31-32.

[6]Samuel S. Kim, "Chinese Foreign Policy After Tiananmen," *Current History* 89, no. 548 (September 1990): 247.

[7]See note 4 above.

second is to resist "peaceful evolution" which might occur during the process of modernization. There is an apparent contradiction between these two goals. The third goal is to diplomatically isolate the ROC on Taiwan so that Peking can coerce Taipei to accept the "one country, two systems" model of reunification. The fourth goal is to create a friendly and safe international environment, despite inevitable differences among nations.[8]

To achieve these goals, the Peking government has chosen a defensive strategy to maintain its existing interests. Tactically, Peking has been particularly aggressive in competing for regional and global influence.

A Defensive Foreign Policy Guideline

The Peking leadership fully understood that it would find it very difficult to resist "peaceful evolution" after the collapse of the Communist community. In dealing with this issue, the Peking government exploited the Five Principles of Peaceful Coexistence to defend its international standing. The Five Principles, which were embodied in the Sino-Indian Treaty of 1954, involve mutual respect among nations for territorial integrity and sovereignty, nonintervention, noninterference with the internal affairs of other countries, equal and mutual benefits, and peaceful coexistence. Some of Peking's diplomatic positions have developed from these five principles.

The first of these is opposition to "hegemonism" which inevitably means interference in the domestic politics of other countries. This refusal to give way to hegemonic powers is the basis of Peking's "independent" foreign policy. The second aspect of Peking's foreign policy that derives from the Five Principles is the insistence that every country has the right to choose its own political, economic, and social system. Therefore, no other country is allowed to criticize Chinese internal affairs. Third, since all countries are equal regardless of their size, cooperation rather than confrontation is seen as the guideline for international interaction. Fourth, Peking holds that international disputes should be settled peacefully. Fifth, it believes that world affairs should be settled through the participation of all countries.[9] Sixth, national self-determination means that no country should impose its will on other countries. The Five Principles of Peaceful Coexistence and the spirit of the U.N. Charter would otherwise be infringed upon.[10]

Peking has frequently mentioned the Five Principles since 1989. The main purpose is to resist the infiltration of the West, and hence possible "peaceful evolution" on the Chinese mainland. The Peking government

[8]Pi Ying-hsien, "Peking's Foreign Relations in the New International Situation," *Issues & Studies* 28, no. 5 (May 1992): 14-18.

[9]See the speech of Ch'ien Ch'i-ch'en delivered at the 45th General Assembly of the United Nations, *People's Daily*, September 29, 1990, 6.

[10]*People's Daily*, October 16, 1989, 3.

has tried to minimize the costs of modernization by the use of an old code of conduct in foreign policy.

Pragmatism

According to the Five Principles, countries with different ideologies, political systems, and values can still coexist peacefully. Thus mainland China endeavors to improve its relations with all other countries, regardless of their ideology. National interests rather than ideology are the main principles for developing foreign relations.[11] For example, Peking held that the transition from Communism to capitalism in Eastern Europe was an internal affair of the countries concerned, and mainland China, though still socialist, would continue its friendly relations with them. Moreover, Peking has improved its relations with South Korea and intensified its contacts with South Africa. This growing pragmatism in foreign policy is part of the general easing of ideological conflicts that characterizes the post-Cold War era. The number of countries that share the same ideology with mainland China was significantly reduced after the demise of the Soviet Union, and the Peking government now has to make a choice between isolation and ideology when dealing with foreign affairs.

Bilateral Diplomacy

During 1990-91, mainland China was very active in its attempts to rehabilitate its international image by means of a program of official visits. In 1990, people such as Party leader Chiang Tse-min (Jiang Zemin), Premier Li P'eng (Li Peng), Foreign Minister Ch'ien Ch'i-ch'en (Qian Qichen), and Wan Li, chairman of the National People's Congress Standing Committee, visited nine countries in Asia, fourteen in the Middle East, nine in Latin America, and three in Africa. Li P'eng also visited the Soviet Union and Ch'ien Ch'i-ch'en toured the United States.[12] During the same year, leaders from nine Asian countries, eight Middle Eastern countries, seven African countries, two South Pacific island countries, three Latin American countries, the Soviet Union, and Spain visited Peking.[13]

These visits continued during 1991 and early 1992. Ch'ien Ch'i-ch'en visited seven West European countries in February 1991; in May, Chiang Tse-min visited the Soviet Union and signed an agreement on the eastern section of their border; in July, Li P'eng traveled to six countries in the Middle East; and state President Yang Shang-k'un (Yang Shangkun) paid visits to Indonesia, Thailand, Mongolia, Pakistan, and Iran. In December, Li P'eng visited India, thus achieving a diplomatic breakthrough with that

---

[11]*Chung-yang jih-pao* (Central Daily News) (Taipei), November 18, 1990, 7.
[12]*Wen Wei Po* (Hong Kong), January 6, 1991, 2.
[13]Ibid., January 7, 1991, 2.

country.[14] During the same year, the leaders of more than thirty countries visited mainland China.[15] In January 1992, Li P'eng made a six-nation tour of Western Europe, while Ch'ien Ch'i-ch'en called on seven West African countries. Yang Shang-k'un also visited Singapore and Malaysia in mid-January. Clearly, bilateral diplomacy through mutual visits has been an important strategy in Peking's effort to reenter international society.

Multilateral Diplomacy

Peking considers multilateral diplomacy to be another valuable approach to enhancing its international standing. In both 1990 and 1991, Foreign Minister Ch'ien Ch'i-ch'en delivered speeches at the U.N. General Assembly which were characterized by calls for peace and cooperation. On January 31, 1992, Premier Li P'eng took an opportunity to rehabilitate mainland China's image when he attended the Security Council "summit." The summit gave Li a good chance to communicate with the leaders of the major powers and also allowed mainland China to demonstrate its goodwill and cooperative attitude toward international organizations. Finally, it symbolized mainland China's acceptance by the international community as an arbiter of world affairs.

In addition to participating actively in U.N. meetings, mainland China never missed an opportunity to side with the United Nations on important issues. For example, on the Middle East, mainland China formally joined the U.N. Special Committee on the Peacekeeping Operation and sent five military observers to the region in 1990.[16] During the Gulf Crisis, Peking supported all the U.S.-led resolutions in the U.N. Security Council. The Gulf Crisis offered Peking a good chance to improve its international image, especially in comparison to Iraq, by always complying with U.N. decisions.[17]

Moreover, Peking cooperated fully with the United Nations in its handling of the Cambodia issue. It also allowed both North and South Korea to enter the United Nations. Using the United Nations as a bridge, mainland China now participates in more than five hundred international organizations,[18] demonstrating the success of its aggressive multilateral diplomacy.

---

[14]See David Shambaugh, "China in 1991: Living Cautiously," *Asian Survey* 32, no. 1 (January 1992): 28-30. Also see *Kuo-chi chi Chung-kuo ta-lu ch'ing-shih fa-chan yü p'ing-ku: Min-kuo pa-shih nien* (An evaluation of international and Chinese mainland development: 1991) (Taipei: Institute of International Relations, December 1991), 67, and *Chung-kuo shih-pao* (China Times) (Taipei), January 5, 1992, 10.

[15]*People's Daily*, December 31, 1991, 6.

[16]*Ming Pao* (Hong Kong), April 20, 1990, 8.

[17]Lena H. Sun, "China Hopes Its Cooperation Will Reap Benefits," *Washington Post*, September 15, 1990, A13-14.

[18]*Lien-ho pao* (United Daily News) (Taipei), December 27, 1991, 9.

Attracting the First World

Peking's Foreign Minister Ch'ien Ch'i-ch'en frequently claimed that mainland China would continue to maintain its "open-door" policy toward the "first world," in particular the United States. Peking, according to Ch'ien, was not only eager to carry out economic reforms, but was also ready to start an incremental process of political reform.[19] The purpose of these statements is very clear. First, Peking's "open-door" policy is the bottom line as far as the West is concerned if mainland China is to be accepted as an active member of international society. Second, it provides Peking with a good excuse to ask for economic and technological assistance from the West. Third, this policy could be used as a bargaining chip in Peking's effort to force the United States to continue mainland China's most-favored-nation (MFN) status. The Peking leaders were anxious to convince the West that they were reasonable and could negotiate.

Maintaining Friendship with the Former Second World[20]

The decline of Communism in Eastern Europe and the Soviet Union put mainland China under great pressure. As part of its process of readjustment, the Peking leadership decided to adopt a pragmatic policy toward its old allies. In 1990, mainland China worked out five methods for improving its relations with Moscow: (1) to continue the improvement of economic and trade relations; (2) to settle border disputes through negotiation; (3) to create mutual trust; (4) to resume military ties and cooperation; and (5) to resume party-to-party relations.[21] The Moscow-Peking relationship was further improved by Chiang Tse-min's visit to the Soviet Union in May 1991. The achievements of the Moscow summit included closer economic and technological cooperation between the two sides, an agreement on the sale of ten Su-27 fighter jets to Peking, and the stabilization of bilateral relations. Ideological differences between the Soviet Union and mainland China were put aside.[22] Peking's pragmatic policy toward Moscow did not change after the fall of the Soviet Union.

In 1990, Li P'eng claimed that although Peking was concerned about the radical changes in Eastern Europe, the Chinese did not wish to interfere

---

[19]Ch'ien Ch'i-ch'en, "The Changing International Conditions and Chinese Diplomacy," *Kwang-ming Daily* (Peking), December 14, 1990, 1. Also see Ch'ien's speech at the 46th General Assembly of the United Nations, *People's Daily*, September 26, 1991, 7.

[20]The Second World is defined as the Communist states during the Cold War era. See Charles W. Kegley, Jr. and Eugene R. Wittkopf, *World Politics: Trend and Transformation* (New York: St. Martin's Press, 1981), 36.

[21]*Kuo-chi chi Chung-kuo ta-lu ch'ing-shih yü fa-chan p'ing-ku: Min-kuo ch'i-shih-chiu nien* (An evaluation of international and Chinese mainland development: 1990) (Taipei: Institute of International Relations, December 1990), 113-15.

[22]Pi Ying-hsien, "Chiang Tse-min's Visit to Moscow and Peking-Moscow Relations," *Issues & Studies* 27, no. 12 (December 1991): 109-10.

with the internal affairs of these countries and hoped to maintain friendly relations with them. Li also supported the reunification of Germany because this was consistent with the wishes of the German people and conducive to world peace and stability.[23] All in all, Peking seemed to respond to the changing circumstances in Eastern Europe with flexibility and restraint.

Mainland China is now the sole large socialist country in the world. No matter how successful Peking's diplomatic efforts are, it is still isolated from most other countries ideologically. Mainland China has therefore been very anxious to maintain close ties with the remaining socialist countries, and has attempted to improve its relations with the hardline Communist states of Cuba, North Korea, and Vietnam. Relations between mainland China and Vietnam were normalized by the end of 1991. Peking-Havana ties were furthered in September 1991 after a mainland Chinese delegation visited Cuba to seek the expansion of bilateral trade. The Peking leadership also tried to coax the North Korean leader Kim Il-sung to pay a visit to the Chinese mainland in the same year.[24]

Siding with the Third World

Peking was eager to reconstruct its ties with the Third World in the wake of the Tienanmen massacre and the collapse of Communism in Eastern Europe. Peking has always considered the Third World to be its traditional sphere of influence, and particularly in the years before 1979, it claimed leadership of the Third World. In common with the Third World countries, mainland China's level of economic development lags far behind the developed countries. Mainland China was also more acceptable to the Third World because, as the Norwegian defense minister, Johan Joergen Holst, put it, "it has less a legacy of imperialism than any of the other great powers."[25]

Mainland China could even argue that it shared the same past as the Third World countries, since all of them had been victims of Western imperialism and colonialism. Besides, the Third World countries, unlike countries in the West, were not so serious about criticizing Peking for its crackdown in Tienanmen Square. Some of them were even indifferent to this event because their own human rights records were as poor as that of mainland China.

By rallying support in the Third World, Peking has been able to secure its international standing, but since most Third World countries are very poor, foreign aid is a critical factor. The Republic of China on Taiwan, with its strong economy, is particularly attractive to the Third World, and

---

[23]*Sing Tao Jih Pao* (Hong Kong), March 21, 1990, 2.

[24]*Kuo-chi chi Chung-kuo ta-lu ch'ing-shih* (1991), 67. Also see *Christian Science Monitor*, October 8, 1991, 3.

[25]*Christian Science Monitor*, June 21, 1989, 4.

the Peking leadership is worried that Taiwan might win the friendship of many countries in the Third World if mainland China is not so active diplomatically.

Mainland China has sought to win over the Third World first by a program of official visits, as discussed previously. Peking has also taken advantage of its permanent membership of the U.N. Security Council to stand up for the rights of the Third World, and the mainland Chinese have furthered their cooperation with these countries by means of a close relationship with the Group of 77. In 1992, Peking was allowed to sit in at the conference of nonaligned states held in Indonesia. In another move to strengthen mainland China's position among the Third World countries, Peking's delegation to the United Nations in 1990 proposed a six-point solution to the loan issue which had troubled the Third World for a long time. This involved (1) reducing the total costs of the loans; (2) encouraging the transfer of funds from developed countries to developing countries; (3) developing the foreign aid programs of developed countries; (4) easing the financial burden on recipient countries; (5) assisting the Third World through multilateral channels; and (6) creating a fairer international economic environment.[26] In 1991, Peking asked the developed countries to open up their markets to the developing world during the Bangkok convention of the International Monetary Fund (IMF) and the World Bank.[27] Peking has also proposed the establishment of a new international economic order which would guarantee the full participation of the developing countries in the process of world economic development. Regional cooperation among developing countries would also be encouraged.[28]

Mainland China successfully employed North-South issues to compete for the friendship of the Third World. Behaving as an agent of the underdeveloped and developing countries, Peking found a short cut to enhance its international standing.

Good-Neighbor Policy

During 1990, Premier Li P'eng visited the Soviet Union, Indonesia, Singapore, Thailand, and the Philippines. In 1991, he visited North Korea. The following year, Chiang Tse-min visited Moscow, Yang Shang-k'un visited Pakistan and Iran, and Li P'eng visited India, while relations between mainland China and Vietnam were normalized by the end of November.[29] Moreover, mainland China successfully developed its relations with Laos, Japan,

---

[26]*People's Daily*, July 8, 1990, 6.

[27]Ibid., December 16, 1991, 7.

[28]Ibid., December 13, 1991, 7.

[29]*Kuo-chi chi Chung-kuo ta-lu ch'ing-shih* (1990), 110; *Kuo-chi chi Chung-kuo ta-lu ch'ing-shih* (1991), 67.

and eleven states of the former Soviet Union during early 1992.

Peking's good-neighbor policy is based on the realization that it is almost impossible for a country to enhance its international standing without good relations with its neighbors. Peking could not afford to face the criticism of Asian states while its ties with the West were already strained by Tienanmen. Peking's sense of insecurity was so strong after 1989 that it was anxious to foster, at the very least, a safe environment in Asia. The Peking leadership believed that Asia could be stabilized and the modernization of the Chinese mainland would be achieved if its good-neighbor policy took effect.[30] According to the *People's Daily*, by April 1992, economic and technological cooperation contracts with neighboring states accounted for one-third of the total value of all mainland China's economic and technological cooperation projects with foreign countries.[31]

Besides, the active participation of mainland China in Asia-Pacific economic organizations such as PECC and APEC reminded the Asian states that Peking was an indispensable member of the new post-Cold War order in Asia.

Image Rehabilitation

The collapse of Peking's moral image was the biggest problem the regime faced as it tried to reenter the international community. In order to burnish its image, Peking has tried to utilize a number of moral issues. First, mainland China has frequently claimed that it supports arms control. In 1989, Peking's representative at the United Nations argued that the process of arms reduction must be accelerated, and that a country's military capability should not exceed the minimum required to guarantee its national security. The superpowers, he said, were particularly responsible for the success or failure of arms control.[32]

In 1990, Peking's Foreign Minister Ch'ien Ch'i-ch'en asserted at the Geneva Arms Control Convention that the superpowers should not only stop the quantitative arms race, but also stop qualitative competition. They should disengage themselves militarily throughout the world. He argued that all the countries concerned were entitled to participate in the arms control talks.[33] The same position was repeated by Ch'ien when he went to the United Nations in 1990 and 1991, and he called for a ban on both nuclear and chemical weapons. Moreover, Peking claimed that it supported the non-militarization of space and the negotiation of a Nuclear Non-Proliferation Treaty.

---

[30]*Sing Tao Jih Pao*, December 26, 1991, 2.

[31]*People's Daily*, April 7, 1992, 2.

[32]Ibid., November 30, 1989, 4.

[33]Ibid., March 1, 1990, 4.

Second, Peking said that it fully supported the concept of regional peace. For example, the Peking government stood up for the creation of a nuclear-free zone of peace in the Indian Ocean.[34] The peaceful reunification of Korea, stability and cooperation among the countries of Indochina, the Middle East peace talks, and the easing of nationalist conflicts in Eastern Europe have all been frequently advocated by the Peking government in recent years.

Third, Peking did not forget to denounce colonialism. Peking's representative at the United Nations, Liu Sha, argued in 1991 that the collapse of colonialism was out of the question; the end of colonialism was still dependent on whether or not hegemonism could be eventually destroyed.[35]

Peking also embraced anti-terrorism in an effort to convince other countries of its moral rectitude. In 1991, Peking's deputy representative at the United Nations, Chin Yün-chien (Jin Yunjian), indicated mainland China's willingness to cooperate in the fight against terrorism by means of domestic and international legislation to ensure punishment for terrorists. Nevertheless, Chin argued that these efforts should be undertaken peacefully, and the meaning of terrorism should be defined.[36]

Peking also paid attention to environmental issues, and in particular blamed the developed countries for their indifference to the environment. Clearly, Peking chose this topic to demonstrate its long-term claim to the leadership of the Third World.

In a word, Peking was attempting to persuade other countries that it always stood up for international morality. At the same time, it blamed the developed countries, who were themselves Peking's strongest critics, for their colonialism and hegemonism. Peking's philosophy is that even if it has its faults, it is at least better than those Western countries who pretend to be moral.

Peking's Interpretation of Human Rights

In response to criticism of its poor human rights record, mainland China lifted martial law in Peking and Tibet and permitted Fang Li-chih (Fang Lizhi) and his wife to leave the U.S. ambassador's residence, where they had taken refuge after Tienanmen, for exile in the West. Defending the regime's policy toward its own people, Ch'ien Ch'i-ch'en argued at the 46th U.N. General Assembly that human rights should not be employed as a political tool by the major powers, nor should it be used as an excuse to interfere in the domestic affairs of other countries. He blamed mainland China's critics for having double standards, arguing that racial discrimination,

---

[34]Ibid., April 19, 1991, 6.
[35]Ibid., October 20, 1991, 6.
[36]Ibid., October 10, 1991, 6.

apartheid, colonialism, and hegemonism were all serious violations of human rights. He said that human rights involves not only civil and political rights, but also a better economic, social, and cultural life.

Ch'ien pointed out that mainland China is a developing country with a population of 1.15 billion, and it must feed 22 percent of the world's population with only 7 percent of the world's arable land. In doing so, he said, mainland China had made its utmost contribution to the protection of mankind's right to subsistence.[37] Clearly, the Peking government was trying to put aside the political aspects of human rights and emphasize instead their economic aspects. If this interpretation of human rights were generally accepted by other countries, Peking's reputation in this respect would naturally be much better.

People-to-People Diplomacy

In 1990, mainland China began to employ people-to-people diplomacy as part of its drive to improve its international image. During that year, a large number of goodwill missions were exchanged, more than ten sister-city agreements were signed, and quite a few congressmen, former government leaders, and ambassadors were invited to visit the Chinese mainland. Cultural exchange between mainland China and Japan, including academic conferences, visits, exhibitions, and sports fixtures, also flourished.[38] The Peking government was able to reap benefits from people-to-people diplomacy because this approach is normally associated with friendship and co-operation rather than politics.

In sum, Peking's strategy to enhance its international standing included a pragmatic, non-ideological approach to international relations, competing for friendship in the Third World, a slight relaxation of political control over dissidents, a reinterpretation of human rights, support for some moral issues, a good-neighbor policy, and people-to-people diplomacy. Furthermore, Peking kept up an active bilateral and multilateral diplomatic program during the three years in question. A low-key attitude toward other countries was basically the principle of Peking's diplomacy after 1989, although its concept of human rights showed little room for modification.

Diplomatic Achievements

Peking's diplomatic achievements were quite substantial during 1990-92. In 1990, it established diplomatic relations with Indonesia, Saudi Arabia, and Singapore. On May 29, 1990, the World Bank slightly relaxed its sanctions against mainland China by allowing a US$300 million loan for a re-

---

[37]Ibid., September 26, 1991, 7.
[38]Ibid., December 26, 1990, 7.

forestation project.[39] At the Houston summit of the Group of Seven in July, U.S. President George Bush passed on a message to Japan and the EC nations that the United States would not prevent them from lifting the sanctions against Peking and expanding diplomatic contacts with mainland China. Japan subsequently allowed new credits totaling 810 billion yen for 1990-95. The EC nations also resumed ministerial-level contacts and cultural and scientific ties with Peking.[40]

In 1991, Peking's relations with Japan, Great Britain, and the United States were normalized after visits to mainland China by the British and Japanese prime ministers and the U.S. secretary of state. In September, Peking established diplomatic relations with the three Baltic states. Moreover, normal relations with Canada, Australia, and New Zealand were resumed during the same year, as were relations with Vietnam.[41]

By the end of January 1992, Peking had already established ambassadorial-level relations with some of the former Soviet republics such as Uzbekistan, Kazakhstan, Tajikistan, Kirghizstan, Turkmenistan, and Belarus. Li P'eng's participation in the U.N. Security Council summit in New York at the end of January symbolized mainland China's return to the international community, despite the fact that Li's personal reputation remains poor. Peking also established diplomatic relations with Israel in January 1992.

Mainland China clearly benefitted from its chosen diplomatic strategy. First, it maintained its open-door policy, which convinced the West that it would be unwise to isolate the Chinese mainland. At least, the Western nations hoped that the door would remain open in the future. Second, the Gulf Crisis of 1990-91 gave Peking a very good chance to rehabilitate its international image. Its cooperative attitude in the United Nations pleased Western countries and to some extent gave them a new impression of the Peking regime. Third, mainland Chinese leaders were very successful in resuming their relations with other countries through an intensive program of official visits.

Issues and Limitations

Although Peking's foreign policy achievements were quite impressive after 1989, some problems remained. The most important of these is mainland China's poor human rights record. No matter how active Peking's foreign policy may be, the shadow of Tienanmen still hangs over mainland

---

[39]Kim, "Chinese Foreign Policy After Tiananmen," 282.
[40]David Shambaugh, "China in 1990: The Year of Damage Control," *Asian Survey* 31, no. 1 (January 1991): 39.
[41]See note 8 above.

China in the eyes of many foreign leaders, especially when leaders such as Li P'eng remain in power. This is one reason why the U.S. Congress has threatened to revoke mainland China's MFN status.

Peking's reputation for repression looks even worse now, after the collapse of Communism in Eastern Europe and the Soviet Union. The demise of the Soviet Union reminded people that mainland China is the only major nation that still embraces a totalitarian ideology. Consequently, countries might question Peking's sincerity when it tries to improve its foreign relations. After all, Communism, like Fascism, has long been considered expansionist.

Another problem results from Peking's unyielding position toward the ROC on Taiwan. Peking has always played a zero-sum game with Taipei in the international arena. However, the ROC has abandoned its long-standing position that Taipei and Peking cannot coexist, and it no longer demands that Peking be expelled from international organizations. Taipei's pragmatic diplomacy has persuaded quite a few countries that the ROC is friendly, reasonable, and considerate. This gives Taipei more room to develop its foreign relations. Peking's unyielding attitude on this issue is regarded as arrogant and irrational by many countries. Ironically, most of the countries which are interested in resuming relations with Taipei are Third World nations.

It seems sound to conclude that mainland China will be successful in its struggle to survive in the changing world in the short term, but could lose in the long run if it does not attempt to improve its record on human rights. Moreover, it may encounter some diplomatic frustration unless it agrees to play a non-zero-sum game with Taipei in the international arena.

Part Seven

Integration in America, Asia, and Europe and Their Prospects

CHAPTER 18

Toward a Regional "Block" in East Asia: Implications for Europe

Philippe Régnier,
Niu Yuanming, and Zhang Ruijun

Derived from customs union and functional integration theories, the concept of regional cooperation seemed to hold great promise in the 1960s, but was followed by about twenty years of relative decline or stagnation of both the idea and most concrete experiences observed worldwide. Since the early 1990s the concept has been on the move again, especially in Europe and North America, but within the new context of the necessity to reconcile globalization and regionalization.

Chiefly as a reaction to the European Community (EC) 1992 and the North American Free Trade Agreement (NAFTA), but also to some extent due to a dynamic redistribution of geopolitical and economic power in the region, East Asia (namely Japan, mainland China, the newly industrialized economies [NIEs], North Korea, Mongolia, the Russian Far East, the Association of Southeast Asian Nations [ASEAN], Indochina, and Burma) could become a third major actor on the intraregional and interregional scenes in the coming decade. This chapter argues that a de facto economic integration is strongly emerging in this part of the world, but that several unclear scenarios of regional or subregional economic (if not political) groupings have to be considered. East Asian regionalism may be expected to have some impact on Europe—being a cause for much skepticism in the short or medium term, but with enormous scope for mutual attraction and cooperation between the two regions in the long run.

Toward Economic "Integration" in East Asia

Regional "Integration" of Commerce

During the 1980s and early 1990s, East Asian countries maintained a high growth rate despite the worldwide recession. Their annual growth rate averaged 7 to 8 percent, more than twice the world average. According

Table 18.1
Selected Leading World Exporters and Importers (1990)

Country	Rank	Exporters Value	Share	Rank	Importers Value	Share
		(US$b.)	(%)		(US$b.)	(%)
Germany	1	421	12.1	2	356	9.9
United States	2	394	11.3	1	517	14.3
Japan	3	288	8.3	3	235	6.5
Hong Kong	11	82	2.4	12	82	2.3
Taiwan	12	67	1.9	16	55	1.5
South Korea	13	65	1.9	14	70	1.9
Mainland China	15	61	1.8	18	52	1.5
Singapore	18	53	1.5	15	61	1.7
World		3,480	100		3,610	100
East Asia*		693.9	20		639.9	17.7

Source: General Agreement on Tariffs and Trade (GATT) Annual Report, 1990-91.
*Japan, mainland China, Taiwan, South Korea, Hong Kong, Singapore, Malaysia, Indonesia, and Thailand.

to the World Bank, the region already accounts for approximately 20 percent of world gross domestic product (GDP), and this share will certainly rise further. One of the generally accepted predictions is that by the year 2000, the whole GDP of East Asia will exceed that of the EC and the European Free Trade Association (EFTA).

The increasing weight of the region's economy is undoubtedly the result of its export performance in manufacturing. For the period 1980-90, the real growth rate of world trade was 5.5 percent, while it was as high as 9 percent in East Asia. According to the last General Agreement on Tariffs and Trade (GATT) Annual Report, East Asia's contribution as a major manufacturing exporter was so great that it was the only region which increased its share of world manufacturing exports. The four Asian NIEs (South Korea, Taiwan, Hong Kong, and Singapore) supplied nearly as large a portion of world exports as Japan, with a share of 7.7 percent in 1990. In 1990, the total trade of Japan, the Asian NIEs, and ASEAN accounted for 20 percent of world trade, a figure close to the total share of U.S. and German trade (see table 18.1).

Most significant is the growth of intra-East Asian trade. Since 1986, a profound shift has occurred in the geographic pattern of East Asian exports, with trade within the region itself becoming the most important and rapidly expanding sector of East Asian commerce. This change is the result of several factors, such as currency realignments following the Plaza Accord in 1985, various commercial pressures, mainly from the United States and

Table 18.2
Developments in Major Interregional and Intraregional Merchandise
Export Flows (1985-90)

	% of World Exports 1990	Average 1985-90	Annual 1989	Change 1990
Intra-Asia	10.3	16.5	14	10
Western Europe to Asia	3.4	19	11	18
Asia to Western Europe	4.3	21	3	15
North America to Asia	3.8	15	12	6
Asia to North America	6.0	9.5	6	1
Intra-Western Europe	33.4	18	7	22
Intra-North America	5.1	8	7	9

Source: GATT Annual Report, 1990-91.

Western Europe, related to worldwide payment imbalances, and shifting comparative advantages in the region. Consequently, intra-East Asian exports grew at a stunning annual rate of 40 percent in 1986-90, reaching US$330 billion, accounting for 10 percent of total world trade (US$3,480 billion in 1990), compared with East Asia's exports of US$220 billion to North America and US$198 billion to Western Europe (see table 18.2). Intra-East Asian exports accounted for 45 percent of total East Asian exports worldwide in 1990.

Regional "Integration" in Terms
of Labor Division and Technology Diffusion

East Asia includes a wide range of countries at different stages of economic development. Japan stands at the top of the list, the NIEs come next, some of them already knocking at the door of the Organization for Economic Cooperation and Development (OECD), followed by the ASEAN subregion. Mainland China is now rapidly entering the world economic scene, and Vietnam/Indochina may follow in the not too distant future. A gradual division of labor is emerging in East Asia, mirroring that in Europe, including horizontal divisions and vertical specializations among industries in different countries.

The regional changes in labor patterns have reflected two characteristics: division of labor and migration of labor. First, labor-intensive production is being gradually relocated to countries or areas where labor conditions and costs are more attractive. This pattern of division of labor is closely correlated to the pattern of foreign direct investment and technology transfer, especially among countries of the region. Second, labor mobility occurs within the region itself: the recipient countries include Japan, Taiwan, Hong Kong, Singapore, and Brunei (see table 18.3), while labor exporting countries

Table 18.3
East Asian Migrant Workers (1989)
(in 1,000)

To \ From	Indonesia	Philippines	Malaysia	Thailand	Mainland China	Total
Japan	0	60	11	10	4	85
Taiwan	4.8	9	18	6.3	—	38.1
Hong Kong	—	75	—	2	25	102
Singapore	20	30	50	20	—	120
Malaysia	350	60	—	10	—	420

Source: *Far Eastern Economic Review*, April 2, 1992, 21.

include the Philippines, Indonesia, Thailand, and mainland China. The likely emergence of intraregional transfers of technology can be based on several existing conditions: (1) the coexistence in a region of economies at different technological levels; (2) the existence and further building up of local technological capability and innovation; and (3) the existence or possibility of technological cooperation, if not partnership, among the countries of the region concerned.

Such conditions are obviously materializing in East Asia. While foreign direct investment is indeed one of the most important sources of technology transfers, other sources are also available such as licensing contracts, technical tie-ups, patent transfers, etc. Japan is of course the single largest source of new technology for most of the NIEs and ASEAN countries (see table 18.4). However, the NIEs are not only the recipients of high-technology supplied by Japan and other industrialized countries, but they are also exporters of their own technology and know-how. The NIEs are keenly aware of the importance of research and development (R&D) and expend considerable human and financial efforts to bridge the technological gap and upgrade their economies to OECD levels. The other East Asian latecomers, such as mainland China, are absorbing more and more technology, know-how, and managerial skills originating from the region, though they are not yet exporting it themselves.

When discussing such scientific and technological issues, the role of high standards of education and training in East Asia should also be kept in mind. This factor could be a major catalyst for the region (and not exclusively in Japan), which is competing more and more on world technology markets.

Regional "Integration" of Finance

Continuous intraregional economic expansion calls for corresponding intraregional investment and financial flows. Although the savings rates

Table 18.4
ASEAN and NIE Technology Imports by Origin
(Number of Transfers)

From \ To	Malaysia	Philippines	Singapore	S. Korea	Taiwan	Thailand
Japan	106	31	135	1,856	1,226	141
United States	51	69	132	789	401	73
Britain	47	10	51	129	—	30
West Germany	—	—	32	182	—	—
Others	144	40	191	441	244	144
Total	348	150	541	3,397	1,871	388
% of Japan	30.5	20.7	25	54.6	65.6	36.5

Source: Toru Nakakita, "The Takeoff of the East Asian Economic Sphere," *Japan Review of International Affairs*, Spring-Summer 1991, 77.
Note: Malaysia, 1960-81; Philippines, 1978-79; Singapore, up to 1983; South Korea, 1969-85; Taiwan, 1952-83; Thailand, 1981.

in East Asia are among the highest in the world, this relatively high degree of financial self-sustainability does not make redundant the additional external sources of finance, which can be categorized as public financial assistance (official development assistance, ODA), direct foreign investment (DFI), and portfolio investment.

Traditionally, Japan is not only the number one banker to the region (much smaller East Asian bankers are located in Hong Kong, Singapore, and Bangkok), but also the biggest contributor of public financial assistance, while Indonesia, mainland China, and the Philippines are the principal recipients (see table 18.5). Approximately 60 to 70 percent of bilateral ODA flows come from Japan. Recently, Taiwan and Singapore have shifted from net debtors to net donors, and their public aid will go primarily to the region (ASEAN, mainland China, and possibly Indochina). South Korea is now considering similar moves.

Table 18.5
Shares of ODA to Selected East Asian Countries by Origin of Donor (1987-88)

From \ To	Malaysia '87	'88	Indonesia '87	'88	Philippines '87	'88	Thailand '87	'88	M. China '87	'88
Japan	76	73	57	58	49	44	60	56	38	42
United States	3	4	9	7	9	11	15	16	15	17
Multilateral	0	2	3	6	30	32	5	8	22	25

Source: Organization for Economic Cooperation and Development (OECD), *Geographical Distribution of Financial Flows to Developing Countries, 1985-88* (Paris: OECD, 1991).

Table 18.6
Foreign Direct Investment Approvals, Cumulative Total (1980-88)
(US$ million)

From \ To	S. Korea	Taiwan	Indonesia	Malaysia	Philippines	Thailand
Japan	2,070.3	1,837.6	1,209.8	512.6	302.7	1,245.3
Hong Kong	155.2	400.5	932.9	123.1	81.7	359.7
South Korea	—	—	212.3	19.8	4.4	14.4
Singapore	—	67.9	410.5	250.8	13.7	170.3
Taiwan	—	—	117.5	75.4	122.0	49.8
Asia	2,264.6	2,320.7	3,759.4	918.7	630.3	1,999.2
World	4,108.2	5,464.8	9,374.0	2,213.7	2,095.4	3,313.7

Source: James Riedel, "Intra-Asian Trade and Foreign Direct Investment," *Asian Development Review* 9, no. 1 (1991).

East Asia secures a growing share of worldwide flows of DFI, and there has been a phenomenal increase in intra-East Asian flows of DFI in recent years. Traditionally, Japan has been the main source of DFI within the region, with a contribution of 15 to 40 percent of total DFI received by the different countries concerned (see table 18.6). The second major source of intra-East Asian investment is constituted by the NIEs, which have so far invested slightly less than Japan. DFI flows from the NIEs are mainly concentrated in ASEAN, while Hong Kong and Taiwan are also playing a significant investment role in mainland China. Of course, because of limited and unreliable data on DFI in this particular region, and the rest of the world as well, the observation of general trends in DFI tends to make more sense than the analysis of tentative statistics country by country.

Portfolio investment is another form of private financing, although the amount is still relatively small for East Asian developing countries. The emergence of portfolio finance derives from the gradual liberalization of cross-border capital flows and it has contributed to the rise of significant capital markets in the region. Far behind Tokyo, Hong Kong and Singapore are the two significant financial markets in the region. In terms of market capitalization, three of the five largest emerging markets in developing countries are also located in the region (Taipei, Seoul, and Kuala Lumpur). The rising density of regional commercial banking networks and regional financial service centers offers various facilities for commercial credit, public and private bond issues, foreign exchange management, offshore banking, and insurance activities.

Some Characteristics of
East Asian Economic Cooperation

Apart from limited regional or trans-Pacific experiences (see the following section), no in-depth economic dialogue has been opened so far among all the East Asian countries, especially when compared to the EC-EFTA in Europe or NAFTA in North America.

The chief characteristic of the regional economy is the prominent leading role of Japan. This leadership is reflected in the size of its economy (its gross national product [GNP] almost equals the sum of the GNPs of the NIEs, ASEAN, and mainland China), the volume of its external trade (including that with the region), its dominant financial power (including the international role of the yen as a reserve currency), and its highly advanced level of technology and know-how. Projects for further East Asian economic cooperation will depend on Japan's macroeconomic policy, namely its monetary and trade policies. But actually, Japan is already the most active, though not the only, de facto player in East Asia's economic integration. The Asian NIEs and coastal mainland China definitely come next.

The second characteristic is the existence of subregional economic groupings. The most formal and advanced structure (de jure) of economic cooperation is ASEAN (since 1976, and especially since early 1992 with the ASEAN Free Trade Area [AFTA] Project), and within ASEAN there is the recently proposed "Growth Triangle" concept involving Johore (Malaysia), Singapore, and the Rhiau Islands (Indonesia). A second (de facto) economic grouping is southern coastal mainland China plus Hong Kong, Macao, and Taiwan. A third de facto grouping is that of Japan, South Korea, and Taiwan, with growing ramifications in the whole of Northeast Asia.

The third and more traditional, if not permanent, characteristic of East Asian economic cooperation is its reliance on old and/or more recent trading and financial networks, often related to ethnicity (especially the so-called Overseas Chinese) and regional/subregional centers such as Singapore, Hong Kong, Bangkok, and Shanghai.

Globally, it can be said that most indicators plead for an already existing and de facto economic "integration" of most parts of East Asia (with the semi- and temporary exceptions of Indochina, North Korea, Mongolia, and the Russian Far East). If this is to develop further, or even to become de jure (though East Asians might prefer to keep it informal and flexible), the regional political context would play a role at some point.

The Difficult Construction of Political Regionalism in East Asia

The high rate of growth in East Asia since the 1970s has provided a rather strong base for the economic "integration" of the region, but political trends have made it difficult so far to catch up with the North Americans or Europeans. The end of the Cold War and the collapse of Communism in the Soviet Union and Eastern Europe have not yet had a drastic impact on the traditional political and social divisions in East Asia.

Trends for Regional Cooperation

Up until now, one regional grouping and one subregional grouping have been the most influential in the process of East Asian regional cooperation: the Asia-Pacific Economic Cooperation (APEC) forum and ASEAN. The origins of both groupings can be traced to the early 1960s.

APEC: The 1960s and 1970s witnessed a series of regional economic integration programs, followed by the establishment of the EC, EFTA, the Latin American Free Trade Association (LAFTA), the Central American Common Market (CACM), the Andean Group in South America, and other similar groupings in South Asia, Southeast Asia, and Africa. Fearing that East Asia would be left out of the game, a Japanese economist, Kiyoshi Kojima, took the lead in suggesting the formation of a regional economic block, known as the Pacific Free Trade Area (PAFTA), including the industrialized countries of the Pacific: Japan, the United States, Canada, Australia, and New Zealand. In the late 1960s, the Pacific Basin Economic Council (PBEC) was established for businessmen and scholars to discuss trade and investment matters.

In the late 1970s, the idea of establishing an Asian-Pacific economic grouping was once again considered, first in Japan, and then in other Pacific countries. In 1980, the first Pacific Economic Cooperation Conference (PECC) was held in Canberra. Similar meetings were held in the following years among scholars, businessmen, and officials to discuss economic cooperation in the region.

The idea of APEC was put forward by the Australian prime minister in Seoul in 1989, and it was regarded as a major step forward because the conference would meet regularly at the ministerial level. The first ministerial meeting of APEC was held in Canberra in November 1989, attended by twelve countries: Japan, the United States, Canada, Australia, New Zealand, South Korea, and the ASEAN countries. At the third ministerial meeting held in Seoul in 1991, mainland China, Taiwan, and Hong Kong participated for the first time.

APEC does provide a chance for East Asian countries to discuss and promote political and economic cooperation, but its weakness is that the participating countries are different not only in terms of economic development and geostrategic location, but also in terms of political and social regimes. After the 1992 ministerial meeting, a permanent APEC secretariat was set up in Singapore.

ASEAN: It appears, at least for the moment, that a subregional grouping like ASEAN has a better chance of success. ASEAN was formed in the 1960s, and was further strengthened in the mid-1970s, mainly for internal and external political reasons. More recently, the six member countries have started to promote economic cooperation among themselves, with rather limited success so far despite the announcement in early 1992 of an ASEAN Free Trade Area (AFTA) for the year 2015. With or without the Indochinese states (and Burma?), ASEAN remains "relatively small" in terms of economic capability, and it has a limited capacity to bargain either with the outside world to counterbalance regionalism in Europe and in North America, or even to influence, in a decisive manner, the destiny of East Asian cooperation as a whole.

In December 1990, Prime Minister Datuk Seri Mahathir Mohamad of Malaysia proposed the establishment of an East Asian Economic Grouping (EAEG), a regional block that would exclude the United States, Canada, Australia, and New Zealand. Due to the hostile reaction of the United States and the cautious response of the APEC countries, the EAEG (or EAEC, East Asian Economic Caucus) has not been formalized so far. However, the proposal has opened lively debates taking into consideration the ongoing economic "integration" of East Asia and a certain necessity to counterbalance rising regionalism in America and Europe.

From Confrontation to Cooperation in East Asia

Why was the EAEG proposal put forward so late? The absence of a united regional economic grouping in East Asia can be explained by various regional conflicts which have restricted the possibility of cooperation. During the Cold War, there were three major points of conflict in the region: Northeast Asia, the Taiwan Strait, and Indochina. Military tensions, caused by ideological and geopolitical disputes, have prevented any form of dialogue, and economic gains through regional cooperation have been ignored till very recently.

During the 1980s, however, with the development of global détente and the economic reforms in some socialist countries, especially mainland China, the whole situation in East Asia started to change. Conflicts among the major regional powers and superpowers have begun to decline and have been gradually replaced by bilateral and regional economic cooperation initiatives.

Northeast Asia: The divisions in Northeast Asia, the result of the Korean War and Soviet-Japanese and Sino-Soviet territorial tensions, remain today, and this despite recent moves for gradual changes. The normalization of relations between mainland China and the Soviet Union in the mid-1980s, which culminated in the bilateral summit of May 1989, paved the way for more economic interaction, though this was limited again after the collapse of the Soviet Union. Due to drastic changes in Russian foreign policy and a certain moderation in mainland China, the Korean Peninsula is slowly moving toward more stability. Political contacts have intensified between North and South Korea though the final outcome is still difficult to predict. Commercial relations have also been established between mainland China and South Korea, and this led to the establishment of diplomatic relations in August 1992. Finally, Japan and Russia have now started to work seriously toward normalization.

The Taiwan Strait: One of the most important changes in East Asia in the 1980s was the change in the relationship between mainland China and Taiwan. Only a decade ago, the two political rivals were mobilizing resources for military defense and were struggling for their security. Due to international and domestic changes on both sides, Peking (Beijing) and Taipei have been moving toward smoother mutual accommodation. One important initiative was Taipei's decision to allow its citizens to visit the mainland and, more recently, to permit scholars, scientists, and journalists from the mainland to visit the island. Intensive contacts and unofficial diplomacy have flourished in combination with a boom in trade and investment from the island, especially to southern coastal China. The fast growing interdependence between the two sides of the Strait could lead to further political compromise: Peking and Taipei are now repeating that unification can be achieved only by peaceful means, and direct trade and air transportation could be agreed upon in the near future.

Indochina: The long series of wars and chronic instability in Indochina have created security problems for both the ASEAN countries and Vietnam, with the involvement of the big powers—the United States, the Soviet Union, and mainland China.

The collapse of Communism in the Soviet Union, the tentative attempt to achieve a political solution for Cambodia, and the new economic priorities in both mainland China and Vietnam have led ASEAN and Indochina to envisage for the first time sustainable peace in Southeast Asia. This new trend has positively affected the course of regional diplomacy in the early 1990s, not only between ASEAN and Indochina, but also between mainland China and Russia, and ASEAN/Indochina and Japan. In July 1992, Vietnam and Laos signed the Bali Treaty of Amity and Cooperation in Southeast Asia, one of the cornerstones of ASEAN cooperation. This event might be the first sign of possible associate or full membership in ASEAN for Vietnam and Laos by the turn of the century. There is little doubt that the renewed but cautious Malaysian proposal for an East Asian economic grouping or caucus is also a strong bet, given this new diplomatic climate in the region.

The Emergence of Regionalism in East Asia

While the change in the political situation within the region is important in determining the options for economic cooperation, some external factors also play a crucial role in reshaping the form of global East Asian cooperation. The possible acceleration of regional "integration" in East Asia could also be regarded as the result of both changes in the world community and their direct and indirect impacts on regional affairs.

The end of a world order and its impact on East Asia: During the Cold War period, the whole region was dominated by the two superpowers, and to a lesser extent by mainland China. The sudden decline of world Communism in the early 1990s has led to a drastic reappraisal of American, Japanese, and Russian strategic interests in East Asia.

The continuity (but probably not sustainability) of Communist regimes in mainland China, North Korea, Vietnam, and Mongolia and various traditional suspicions between Japan and the rest of East Asia (including the Russian Far East) have prevented any multilateral approach in the region so far. However, mounting pressures for increased economic cooperation (even between the two Koreas) could pave the way for a more permanent geopolitical dialogue between all East Asian nations, with the strong backing of Europe and North America.

EEC and NAFTA: Challenges for East Asia: The EC single market of 1993 and NAFTA have also been a major source of concern in East Asia. Most industrialized or newly industrialized countries of the region fear that they could be left behind in both economic and political terms, considering the possible integration of Europe (including EFTA and Eastern Europe) and of North and Central America (including Mexico).

The difficult issue to decide is whether or not East Asia should form its own regional block in response to possible American and European "fortresses." In other words, the major question is whether three-tier regionalism and globalization could be reconciled worldwide, and the economic and political answers do not automatically coincide.

Patterns of Regional "Integration" in East Asia

Beyond the de facto economic integration of East Asia and the timid attempts at economic dialogue by APEC (which includes non-East Asian nations, especially the United States), there is still little evidence of East Asia's global integration being on the move. Up until now, there have been only three subregional spheres of economic, if not political, cooperation.

ASEAN moving ahead? ASEAN is the only formal grouping. It has experienced twenty-five years of subregional cooperation from political coordination to economic matters since the 1980s. In addition, the organization has proved to be rather good at reacting to external challenges or threats and at tackling some (if not all) sensitive internal issues in both the economic and political fields. As the only relatively successful grouping in the Third World, the ASEAN member states remain skeptical of any enlarged organization including the whole of East Asia and most of them have reacted with caution to Prime Minister Mahathir's recent proposals for an EAEC.

In contrast to the EC functional approach to regionalism, the ASEAN countries have recently adopted a more pragmatic and flexible approach, as evinced by the "Growth Triangle" program. This approach is not only derived from many historical, economic, and political factors, but also from rather refined cultural perceptions and networks among the six member states. The AFTA Agreement of January 1992 goes more in the direction of the EC/EFTA experience, but should not materialize before 2010 or 2015.

Toward a "Greater China"? With ASEAN, governments made the first move, but the de facto integration of coastal China, Hong Kong-Macao, and Taiwan is primarily led by booming private economic activities and interlinkages. It does not mean that central or local governments do not play an important role as facilitators, but the major actors are businessmen, technicians, scholars, and scientists, and various types of nongovernmental organizations. In the event of any removal of political barriers in the future, this subregion could become a single market, tentatively paving the way for Chinese reunification.

Northeast Asia: Division or cooperation? Northeast Asia remains a very difficult story of love and hate between big regional powers (mainland China, Russia, and Japan), an external superpower (the United States), and small powers (North and South Korea, Mongolia, and more distant Taiwan). Several subregional spheres may be distinguished in both economic and political terms. The very dense interlinkages among Japan, South Korea, and Taiwan are probably the most convincing. Newly emerging economic interaction can also be observed among South Korea, North China, and North Korea (and Mongolia), and among Japan, South Korea, and the Russian Far East.

Finally, in 1990-91, the United Nations Development Program (UNDP) suggested a new concept of regional economic cooperation among mainland China, Russia, North Korea, South Korea, and Mongolia (with some backing from Japan), which should materialize as the Tumen River Development Program. Preliminary studies have been carried out but the early euphoric publicity surrounding the project seems to have died down somewhat.

Toward regional "integration" in East Asia: The future. If regional cooperation, if not "integration," seems quite inevitable in East Asia, the next question is what kind of regional scheme will emerge in this part of the world? Are the East Asian countries likely to follow the EC or NAFTA model or would they prefer to do things their own way?

Just a few preliminary scenarios can be envisaged at this stage:

1. There is overwhelming evidence that economic "integration" would definitely progress faster than any political initiative;
2. Informal economic and political networking (through APEC, for instance), rather than the Western functional type of regional cooperation, is more likely to emerge in East Asia and would probably prove to be flexible, pragmatic, and efficient;
3. The de facto economic "integration" of East Asia—the biggest potential market in the world—is on the move, and it could be strengthened further by more in-depth economic and political arrangements at various subregional levels in Southeast Asia, southern China, and Northeast Asia;
4. Instead of forming a de jure organization (which might be very difficult anyway) as a reaction to the formation of the EC and North American blocks, East Asian countries could create an informal grouping;

5. East Asia could remain, in a very oriental way, somewhere in between regionalism and globalism, making one of the most significant
economic (if not political) contributions to the world in the twenty-
first century.

East Asian Regionalism:
Implications for Europe

Despite numerous articles dealing with the implications of EC 1992
for Japan, the NIEs, and the other developing nations of East Asia, very
little has been produced so far on the implications of East Asian regionalism
or subregionalism for Europe. Let us hope that this is not a first indication
that Europeans have, despite their rhetoric, less interest in the regional construction of East Asia than East Asians have in Europe. This section presents a few initial ideas and suggestions for a very open debate.

Precarious Definitions of Regionalism
in East Asia and Europe

If evidence argues in favor of an ongoing and de facto economic
integration in East Asia, both the format and content of regionalism remain uncertain in this part of the world, depending on the countries and
variables to be considered. Of course, this lack of a clear definition is a
major obstacle to assessing the possible implications for Europe. But, it
might also be assumed that the informal and nonwritten dimensions of the
increasing cooperation on all fronts in East Asia are misunderstood or completely underestimated by excessively Cartesian or legalist European observers
who are used to customs union and functional integration theories, mainly
the EC model.

On the other hand, the difficulty of identifying a possible regional
scenario does not exclusively apply to efforts in East Asia, it also applies
to Europe. Until the late 1980s, the construction process of the EC and
its 1993 single market was rather clear, and NAFTA, APEC, and the EAEC
were initiated partly as a reaction to it. However, since the collapse of
Communism in the Soviet Union and Eastern Europe, and the multiplication
of local conflicts and instability in Southern and Eastern Europe, the very
concept of Europe has changed radically. What kind of Europe do we
envisage on the eve of the twenty-first century? Should we talk of the
existing EC, which is facing various difficulties in moving forward at the
moment, or should we assume that the EC and EFTA will have merged by
1996 and that a few East European countries will have negotiated associate
membership? Or is it possible to predict that some kind of European confederation from the British Isles to the Urals will emerge by the turn of the
century? East Asian regionalism could have quite different impacts on each
of these scenarios.

Whatever the definitions and possible scenarios for the two regions, it is likely that most European decision-makers will continue, for better or for worse, to analyze regional developments in East Asia more from their own cultural, psychological, if not emotional, perceptions, than from an objective viewpoint or from an East Asian perspective.

Economic Implications for Europe

During the three decades after World War II, Europe lost most of its historical ties with East Asia, including its economic ties. Europe has also allowed the Americans and then the Japanese to seize most of the opportunities in the region. A change emerged only in the late 1970s, with the increasing penetration of East Asian products into the European market, and from the mid-1980s the EC nations started to give East Asia a higher priority. However, the new objective of EC 1992, the sudden collapse of Communism in Eastern Europe, and the Gulf Crisis seem to have restored some degree of economic confidence within Europe, and these events have certainly distracted the old continent (with the exception of a few European multinational firms) from looking to far distant markets and booming East Asia in particular. Several European observers have argued that the momentum of the 1980s for strengthening Euro-East Asian economic relations has been lost.

However, two major factors could continue to act in favor of more active economic cooperation between the two regions:

1. Within both East Asia and Europe, intraindustry and intraservice trade among mature or semimature economies will remain buoyant, and this leaves some promising scope for the multiplication of diversified interlinkages between the two regions as well. In the near future, the Asian markets will become as competitive as, if not more competitive than, the European and North American markets.

2. As long-term growth potential is greater outside Europe (including Eastern Europe), notably in the Asia-Pacific region, Europe will only be permitted to participate in the expanding East Asian markets if it guarantees relatively free access to its own markets and R&D facilities: this should be an encouraging signal for active economic and scientific cooperation among the two regions (rather than a resort to trade conflicts in a very limited number of sectors) and for protecting the world economy from fragmenting into three protectionist blocks. Both Japan and the Asian NIEs and Western Europe should play a leading role here considering their high dependency on external markets.

There is also no reason to believe that the formation of regional trading areas should be automatically detrimental to other regions or to the world economy as a whole. The limited experience of the EC/EFTA seems to indicate that such areas can be a faster track to freer trade within a specific region and with the rest of the world as well. Therefore, Europe should give East Asia every encouragement to go down the road of economic integration, which should include mainland China, Indochina, and North Korea, in order to counterbalance their political insecurity. Whether Japan and the NIEs should follow that path or not (like the original six members of the EC did in Europe in the 1950s) is, of course, up to them to decide. Both the French and the Germans could testify that deeply rooted suspicions and conflicts can be replaced by sustainable peace and cooperation.

Political Implications for Europe

In contrast to Europe, East Asia has not yet been greatly affected by the change of the late 1980s, and though highly desirable, region-wide political integration is still out of sight.

As expressed by Brian Bridges during the Eighth Sino-European Conference (Geneva, 1991, see bibliographical references), Europe has a general interest in East Asian peace and stability (as a major regional pole of world economic growth), but it no longer has vital interests in East Asia, in the sense of interests that, if threatened, would directly and immediately affect Europe's own survival, or those which Europeans would defend or promote by force of arms if necessary. It is also doubtful that Europeans would be ready in the near future to share the U.S. military burden in East Asia, considering that they are already having to share it more and more in Europe (including the periphery). They would probably prefer the Japanese to play a more active role, at least in a regional context (after the model of the Conference on Security and Cooperation in Europe [CSCE], for instance) or in a United Nations multilateral context. There is no doubt that East Asians and Europeans should consult each other on such important matters, not only because of their respective alliances with the United States (with the exception of mainland China, North Korea, Mongolia, and Indochina), but also because of their common interest in dealing with Russia and the other states of the former Soviet Union.

However, up to the present, Europe has maintained a low profile in its diplomatic relations with East Asian countries. The existing instruments of economic, political, and strategic dialogue remain on both sides fragmented, uncoordinated, and largely bilateral among individual countries, despite the rhetoric of the EC or the Council of Europe in favor of regionalism worldwide. Considering the lack of an East Asian counterpart organization open to a permanent dialogue with Europe, the EC-ASEAN cooperation agreements or the EC-Japan, EC-mainland China, and EC-Korea economic dialogues are the only existing attempts at intensified political contacts between the two regions.

Future political dialogue between Europe and East Asia should explore two different directions:

1. There should be an attempt to share common experiences and explore tentative solutions to conflicts at the subregional and local levels within Europe and East Asia. This is necessary, considering the post-Cold War multiplication of local conflicts derived from old enmities, and simultaneous attempts at cooperation between neighboring countries or transfrontier regions interested in looking after their own interests.

2. There should be an attempt to broaden the agenda of mutual consultations and negotiations on the multitude of interregional and global issues which individual governments find it difficult or impossible to address effectively on their own.

Conclusion

The East Asian House is still very far from construction and the building of the West European or European House is proving to be far more difficult and much slower than expected. But neither East Asians nor Europeans should be prevented from attempting such projects. The long and solid tradition of cultural attraction and fascination between Europe and East Asia could pave the way for intensive and harmonious bilateral relations beyond immediate economic and political interests. In a multilateral context, the two regions could also make a major contribution to a more balanced and peaceful world. They have decisive roles to play in promoting a combination of regionalization and globalization.

References

ADIPA (Association of Development Research and Training Institutes of Asia and the Pacific). Eighth Biennial General Meeting, "Asian and Pacific Region in the 1990s: Challenges and Responses," Manila, October 23-26, 1989, various papers.

Awanohara, Susumu. "Japan and East Asia: Towards a New Division of Labor." *The Pacific Review* 2, no. 3 (1989): 198-208.

Bridges, Brian. "The Western European and East Asian Political Agenda." In *Asia and Europe: A Comparison of Developmental Experiences*, edited by Bih-jaw Lin, 56-69. Taipei: Institute of International Relations, 1993.

Drobnick, Richard. "American Involvement in the Economic Integration of the East Asia Pacific Region: Current Situation and Scenarios." Paper delivered at the INSEAD (Institut Européen de l'Administration des Affaires) Conference on "Europe, U.S. and Japan in the Asia Pacific Region: Current Situation and Perspectives," Fontainebleau. 1992.

Grosser, Kate, and Brian Bridges. "Economic Interdependence in East Asia: The Global Context." *The Pacific Review* 3, no. 1 (1990): 1-14.

Huang, Deng-shing, and J. H. Tu. "On the Feasibility of Economic Cooperation in East Asia." Paper delivered at the ADIPA Ninth General Meeting, Macao, 1991.

Kiss, Judit. "Hungary's New Strategy towards the Developing World: The Special Role of the Asia-Pacific Region." Paper delivered at the Korean Management Seminar, Budapest, 1992.

Lee, Hsien Loong. "Future of the World Trading System." Asia Society

Conference on "The Asian Regional Economy: Growing Linkages, Global Implications," Taipei, 1992.

Low, Linda. "The East Asian Economic Grouping." *The Pacific Review* 4, no. 4 (1991): 375-82.

Maurer, Jean-Luc, and Philippe Régnier, eds. *Investment Flows between Asia and Europe: What Strategies for the Future?* Geneva: Modern Asia Research Center, 1990.

Nakakita, Toru. "The Takeoff of the East Asian Economic Sphere." *Japan Review of International Affairs*, Spring/Summer 1991, 62-80.

Rana, Pradumna B., and J. Malcolm Dowling. "Foreign Capital and Asian Economic Growth." *Asian Development Review* 8, no. 2 (1990): 77-102.

Rao, D. C. "International Economic Prospects and Implications on the Growing Process of Integration of Countries in the Asia-Pacific Region." Paper delivered at the ADIPA Ninth General Meeting, Macao, 1991.

Riedel, James. "Intra-Asian Trade and Foreign Direct Investment." *Asian Development Review* 9, no. 1 (1991): 111-46.

Rieger, Hans C. "Regional Economic Cooperation in the Asian-Pacific Region." *Asian-Pacific Economic Literature* 3, no. 2 (1989): 5-33.

Scalapino, Robert A. "Northeast Asia: Prospects for Cooperation." *The Pacific Review* 5, no. 2 (1992): 101-11.

Schiavone, Giuseppe, ed. *Western Europe and South-East Asia.* London: Macmillan, 1989.

Shibusawa, Masahide, et al. *Pacific Asia in the 1990s.* London: Royal Institute of International Affairs, 1992.

Steele, Mark. "Recent Developments of Asia-Pacific and European Trade Policies." In Lin, *Asia and Europe*, 38-55.

Von Kirchbach, Friedrich, and A. Bushaev. "Recent Patterns and Perspectives in Euro-Asian Trade." Paper delivered at the INSEAD Conference on "Europe, U.S. and Japan in the Asia-Pacific Region: Current Situation and Perspectives," Fontainebleau, 1992.

CHAPTER 19

Circling the Wagons: The Trend Toward Economic Regionalism and Its Consequences for Asia

Karl J. Fields*

> The Asian economic zone will outdo the North American economic zone and European zone at the beginning of the twenty-first century and assume a very crucial role.
>
> **Kiichi Miyazawa (June 1991)[1]**

Over a hundred years ago, settlers trekked across the great expanse of the American heartland in covered wagons and handcarts. In a situation of virtual anarchy, and in the absence of other forms of security, it became common practice on these Westward journeys to "circle up" the wagons at night as a means of protection against outside threats.

Although the end of the Cold War has perhaps eased the threat of global war, the decline of American hegemony and the uncertainty of a new world order remind us that anarchy is as much a part of the international system as it was of the American West. Vulnerable nation-states in the great expanse of this global anarchy are also inclined to protect their interests by circling up.

Economic regionalism and trading blocs—its institutional manifestation—are born of fear and uncertainty. Western Europeans formed the European Community (EC)—the oldest, largest, and most successful trading bloc—in the wake of World War II because they feared the consequences of a third. Since the 1980s, the driving force behind their renewed efforts to further economic integration was European fear of Soviet military might and Japanese economic prowess. More recently, Germany's reunification has proved a

---

*The author wishes to acknowledge the helpful comments of Michael Veseth on an earlier draft of this article.
[1]As quoted in Kenneth Pyle, "How Japan Sees Itself," *The American Enterprise*, November-December 1991, 33.

further "catalyst" for European integration as "the only way to provide neighbors with leverage over the new German colossus."[2] Like the American West of a century ago, the anarchical global arena prompts those outside the circle to seek others with shared interests with whom to counter-consolidate. The result is the creation of additional groups designed to compete with or withstand the initial grouping.

In short, blocs tend to beget blocs; ample evidence of this tendency can be found in the growing economic regional integration and the formation of regional trading blocs in the world today.[3] One recent study found thirty-two trading blocs in the current international system.[4] Another places the number of preferential trading arrangements at twenty-three, involving 119 countries and more than 80 percent of the world's international trade in goods.[5] Capturing more headlines (though less empirical confirmation), observers now point to the emergence of three "super" regions of economic integration, Europe, North America, and Asia. While there is general consensus on this trend, defining these regions and determining the consequences of their integration are subject to very wide interpretation.

In spite of (or perhaps even because of) the Danish "no" vote in June and the feeble French "oui" in September to the Maastricht accords on economic and political union,[6] the economic integration of (at least) Western Europe would seem inevitable. If the original twelve members of the EC are able to merge with members of the European Free Trade Area (EFTA), they would combine to create a market of 380 million people, accounting for nearly 50 percent of world trade.[7] If central (what used to be eastern) European countries join this common market, there will be over 850 million

---

[2]Elizabeth Pond, "Germany in the New Europe," *Foreign Affairs* 71, no. 2 (Spring 1992): 114.

[3]The analysis of this trend has blossomed into a growth industry in the social sciences. See, for example, Jagdish Bhagwati, "Departures from Multilateralism: Regionalism and Aggressive Unilateralism," *The Economic Journal* 100 (December 1990): 1304-17; Norman S. Fieleke, "One Trading World, or Many: The Issue of Regional Trading Blocs," *New England Economic Review*, May-June 1992, 3-20; Chalmers A. Johnson, "Mainland China's Place in the New World Regional Groupings," in *Forces for Change in Contemporary China*, ed. Bih-jaw Lin and James T. Myers (Taipei: Institute of International Relations, 1992), 47-59. Kazuo Nukazawa, "Interdependence and Regionalism," *Journal of International Affairs* 42 (Fall 1988): 43-51; Lester C. Thurow, *Head to Head: The Coming Economic Battle Among Japan, Europe, and America* (New York: William Morrow and Company, 1992).

[4]Joseph L. Brand, "The New World Order," *Vital Speeches of the Day* 58 (December 15, 1992): 155-60.

[5]Fieleke, "One Trading World, or Many," 3-20.

[6]European Community (EC) "spin doctors" argued the defeat of EC92 in the Danish referendum would in fact galvanize support among the other eleven members of the community for further integration. See *Christian Science Monitor*, June 10, 1992. In the wake of the narrow margin of French support and further grumbling within the community, these spin doctors are less sanguine.

[7]Fieleke, "One Trading World, or Many," 14; George F. Treverton, "The New Europe," *Foreign Affairs* 71, no. 1 (1992): 94.

relatively well-educated and prosperous producers and consumers capable of virtual self-sufficiency.[8]

Faced with this prospect, the two countries with the largest bilateral trading relationship in the world—the United States and Canada—implemented a free trade agreement in 1989. One year later, formal negotiations began which—if ratified—would link these two countries with Mexico in a North American Free Trade Area (NAFTA) of 360 million people from the Yukon to the Yucatan, with a combined gross national product (GNP) of over US$6 trillion and nearly one-fourth of total world trade.[9] President George Bush has offered to extend NAFTA to include Latin American countries in what could conceivably become a free trade area embracing the entire Western Hemisphere (WHFTA).[10]

What does this mean for East Asia?[11] More than any other region in the world, the countries of East Asia have blossomed under the aegis of the U.S.-sponsored General Agreement on Tariffs and Trade (GATT) with its mandate of expanding unfettered world commerce. In the face of this "head-to-head" competition with two other institutionalized and potentially self-sufficient trading blocs,[12] will the Asia-Pacific region be compelled to circle up as well? If so, what would or should such a bloc look like? If not, what other options are available to this dynamic region of export-led capitalist development?

Trends toward economic regionalism in Europe and America will continue, and perhaps even accelerate, pressuring an increasing number of East Asian countries to integrate in a similar way. However, for a variety of reasons, the degree, and in fact the type of integration likely to occur in East Asia in this last decade of the twentieth century will be very different from its American and European counterparts. In short, historical legacies

---

[8]A *Beijing Review* article notes that of the three regions, the European Community is already the most self-reliant, with member countries absorbing 58 percent of EC exports in 1987. The comparable figures for North America were 39 percent and for East Asia 44 percent in the same year. Wang Juyi, "An Analysis of the Three Economic Rims," *Beijing Review* 32, no. 11 (March 20-26, 1989): 17.

[9]Earl H. Fry, "A Continent of Free Trade: Negotiations Toward a North American Free Trade Agreement," *Journal of State Government* 64 (October-December 1991): 128; Fieleke, "One Trading World, or Many," 15.

[10]Bhagwati, "Departures from Multilateralism," 1311.

[11]For the purposes of this chapter, East Asia refers to Japan; the four East Asian newly industrializing economies (EANIEs) of South Korea, Taiwan, Hong Kong, and Singapore; and the four member states of the Association of Southeast Asian Nations (ASEAN)—Thailand, Indonesia, Malaysia, and the Philippines. In certain specified contexts it will include Russia and the Leninist command economies of North Korea, mainland China, and Indochina. Australasia includes, in addition to all the countries noted above, Australia and New Zealand. The Pacific Basin adds to these the countries of North America (Canada, the United States, and Mexico) and in certain specified contexts the countries of Central and South America bordering the Pacific.

[12]The term "head-to-head" is taken from Thurow, *The Coming Economic Battle.*

(distrust of Japanese hegemony outside Japan and reluctance within Japan to bear hegemonic public goods), situational imperatives (disparities among the various countries), and heterogeneous economic ties (dependencies on markets external to the region) will lead to a hybrid regional integration in East Asia characterized by overlapping subregional (and supraregional) bilateral and multilateral arrangements.

The Gathering Storm

Trading Blocs and Their Consequences

A trading bloc is a broadly-based preferential economic relationship among a group of countries. While economic integration can, and does, often flow naturally from open market transactions, the presence of a bloc implies the concentration is the consequence of government policy or other intentional noneconomic factors such as common language or culture.[13]

Brand distinguishes five degrees of trade integration that—in ascending order of integration—include: *preferential trade arrangements* (extending members freer access to markets); *free trade areas* (eliminating tariffs among members, but maintaining original tariffs against nonmembers); *customs unions* (freeing trade among members and erecting a common tariff wall against all nonmembers); *common markets* (removing restrictions on the internal movement of the means of production); and *economic unions* (unifying fiscal, monetary, and social policies within the common market).[14] The NAFTA arrangement among the United States, Canada, and Mexico, if approved, would be a free trade area, as the U.S.-Canada pact already is. The twelve-member EC, as now constituted, approaches a common market and aspires to become a genuine economic union.

The phrase "trading bloc," particularly in liberal trade circles, carries with it the negative connotation of zero-sum protectionism. Much of this infamy stems from the association of the term with the protectionist blocs formed in the wake of the financial crashes and global Great Depression in the late 1920s and early 1930s. Adopting trade policies of economic nationalism, the dominant powers of the day circled their wagons (Japanese Greater East Asian Co-Prosperity Sphere, the British Empire, the French Union, Germany and central Europe, and the United States with a revived Monroe Doctrine) in an effort to minimize imports and preserve jobs. The blocs were so effective in achieving the former goal they brought exports to a virtual standstill, exacerbating the economic consequences of the depression.

---

[13] Jeffrey A. Frankel, "Is Japan Creating a Yen Bloc in East Asia and the Pacific?" *NBER Working Paper Series* (National Bureau of Economic Research, Cambridge, Mass.), no. 4050 (April 1992): 1.

[14] Brand, "The New World Order," 156.

Ultimately, these economic blocs gave way to the formation of military alliances and the outbreak of World War II.[15]

It was in this context that technocrats and visionaries met at Bretton Woods after the war to create a system that would prevent a recurrence of these events. Armed with a religious sense of mission and the liberal canons of comparative advantage and nondiscrimination, the unchallenged American hegemon imposed a system of "unilateral global Keynesianism" and institutionalized it under GATT.[16] Based on the principles of most-favored-nation (MFN) and mutual reciprocity, GATT's objective of expanding global trade through reducing tariffs and other trade barriers was remarkably successful. Tariffs on manufactured goods were cut from a global average of 40 percent in 1947 to less than 5 percent in 1990.[17]

During the 1980s, events conspired to spell the doom of GATT and its liberal trading order. The relative and absolute decline of the United States as the global economic hegemon has meant that while it may still be capable of "imperial overreach" in a military sense,[18] GATT's hegemonic sponsor can no longer fulfill its roles of promoting free trade by carrying free riders or pulling the world out of recession on the strength of its import market. In addition, it became increasingly obvious that multilateral GATT proceedings were ill-prepared to resolve the issue of nontariff barriers. With no one country able or willing to impose a universal system, narrow self-interest dictated bilateral trade negotiations and regional economic integration. This regionalism further stymied the functioning of GATT as internal commitments deemed necessary to bloc cohesion became more imperative than the promotion of global trade efficiency. The recent foundering of "yet another round" of the Uruguay Round of GATT negotiations prompted one observer to rename this hallowed postwar institution the "General Agreement to Talk and Talk."[19]

From the outset, GATT provisions have tolerated the formation of free trade areas and customs unions when the ultimate objective of these blocs is a complete political union.[20] Thurow argues, however, that a common market as large as the EC violates the spirit of GATT and the planned inclusion of associate members to the EC violates the letter of GATT law.

---

[15]Robert Gilpin, *The Political Economy of International Relations* (Princeton, N.J.: Princeton University Press, 1987): 190; Thurow, *The Coming Economic Battle*, 55-56.

[16]Thurow, *The Coming Economic Battle*, 56.

[17]Susan Lee, "Are We Building New Berlin Walls?" *Forbes*, January 7, 1991, 88.

[18]Paul Kennedy, *The Rise and Fall of the Great Powers: Economic Change and Military Conflict from 1550-2000* (New York: Random House, 1987).

[19]Brand, "The New World Order," 157.

[20]See Thurow, *The Coming Economic Battle*, 59. Bhagwati notes this escape clause was included to allow and facilitate European integration because the United States felt it could tolerate an imperfect economic union "in the cause of what it saw as a politically beneficial union." Bhagwati, "Departures from Multilateralism," 1304.

North Americans, he points out, have not even bothered with this "legal fig leaf" as they negotiate NAFTA and as the United States pushes its bilateral Structural Impediment talks with the Japanese.[21]

This economic regionalism will likely endure and gain in strength. What does this circling of wagons mean for global economic efficiency and political stability? The classic danger of trading blocs is that trade will be diverted from efficient nonmembers to less efficient bloc members leading to a net decline in global trade efficiency.[22] Further, as blocs form they tend to adopt the policies of the most protectionist members as the path of least resistance. Also, regional integration, particularly of the tripolar variety anticipated, would operate most perniciously against the world's poorest and most dependent nations, those in most desperate need of trade.[23] Finally, and most dangerously, history has demonstrated economic blocs can provide justification for countervailing blocs, destroying liberal trade institutions and feeding the escalating fires of protectionism and trade wars, with potentially disastrous economic, social, and ultimately international political consequences.

If properly managed, however, it is argued that the potential costs of trading blocs can be minimized while the potential benefits in an imperfect post-GATT world can be substantial. Most observers believe that while a certain amount of trade diversion is probably unavoidable, regional free trade areas cannot afford to cease trading with other regions. Thurow contends that three regional trade arrangements will form in the 1990s, around Europe, North America, and Japan, but refers to them as "quasi-trading blocs" in order to "distinguish them from the trading blocs of the 1930s." These quasi-blocs of the 1990s, he argues, "will attempt to manage trade, but they will not attempt to reduce or eliminate it as the trading blocs of the 1930s did."[24] Johnson argues competition among and within these three regions may in fact be as great a stimulus to growth as the liberal trade regime that preceded it.[25]

Moreover, there is no question that preferential trade arrangements generate huge increases in trade among participants. A 1988 study commissioned by the European Community estimated that EC92 would create 2 million jobs, boost corporate profits by nearly 2 percent and gross domestic product by 5 percent, and cut consumer prices by 6 percent and industrial production costs by 7 percent. Similarly, it is estimated that by 1999 the Canada-U.S. free trade pact will have raised the U.S. GNP by 1 percent and the Canadian GNP by 5 percent and have created a total of nearly one and

---

[21]Thurow, *The Coming Economic Battle*, 59, 76.
[22]Lee, "Are We Building New Berlin Walls?" 87.
[23]Brand, "The New World Order," 159.
[24]Thurow, *The Coming Economic Battle*, 66.
[25]Johnson, "Mainland China's Place in the New World Regional Groupings," 58.

a half million jobs in both countries.[26]

Trading blocs are particularly useful in eliminating import quotas and other nontariff barriers among member countries, and as such may in fact offer "a supplemental, practical route to the universal free trade that GATT favored as the ultimate goal."[27] Free trade within regions and managed trade between them may prove to be a necessary and workable intermediate step between national economies and a single world economy, cementing pro-liberal sentiment at national and regional levels.[28]

A final justification that may prove more compelling than all others is political. Whatever the economic costs or gains, European unity makes good political sense and, despite the trepidations of Margaret Thatcher and now many other Europeans, is "one of the most encouraging developments in Western history."[29] The greater amity among the United States and its Latin American neighbors that could result from voluntary economic integration in the Western Hemisphere is also long overdue.

Further economic integration into some form of regional blocs over the course of the next decade is inevitable, but not inimicable to the expansion of global welfare if managed properly.

European and North American Blocs

The EC is the oldest, largest, and most effective of all trading blocs. Its origins lie in the European Coal and Steel Community established in 1951, and the European Economic Community and European Atomic Energy Community created under the 1957 Treaties of Rome. The fundamental objectives of these regimes—binding German industry to the rest of Europe and restarting economic growth in the region—were largely accomplished without achieving the degree of economic and political integration that some hoped would naturally flow from interdependence.[30]

Since the mid-1980s, however, the regional integration of Europe has taken on new life and new urgency. Under the standard of "European Community 1992," the EC initiated a series of measures designed to remove all barriers to the movement of capital, goods, and people and the creation of a genuine common market. In December 1991, EC representatives (if not their national constituencies) agreed in treaties on a European monetary union (EMU) and political union (EPU) to form a new federation anchored by a single currency (ECU) and central bank by the end of this century.[31]

---

[26]As cited by Wang, "An Analysis of the Three Economic Rims," 17.

[27]Bhagwati, "Departures from Multilateralism," 1308.

[28]Gilpin, *The Political Economy,* 190; Thurow, *The Coming Economic Battle,* 82.

[29]Bhagwati, "Departures from Multilateralism," 1308.

[30]Wayne Sandholtz et al., *The Highest Stakes: The Economic Foundations of the New Security System* (New York: Oxford University Press, 1992), 75.

[31]Treverton, "The New Europe," 94.

The decline of the United States, the rise of Japan, the disintegration of the Soviet empire, and the reunification of Germany spurred the Community to redouble its efforts to circle the wagons in a way that was deemed neither possible nor necessary under the bipolar "old world order."

These efforts, since 1985, it is argued, are,

> a disjunction, a dramatic new start, rather than the fulfillment of the original effort to construct Europe. . . . Nineteen ninety-two is a vision as much as a program—a vision of Europe's place in the world. The vision is already producing a new awareness of European strengths and a seemingly sudden assertion of the will to exploit those strengths in competition with the United States and Japan.[32]

And a formidable competitor it is. With a GNP exceeding US$4 trillion and total world trade valued at nearly US$2.8 trillion, this is the largest "common" market in the world.[33] With European Free Trade Area members now candidates for merger and central European and North African countries also knocking at the door, this region's economic clout can only expand.

While initial fears of "Fortress Europe" have diminished somewhat, concern in the United States, Asia, and elsewhere about protectionism within the bloc is well-founded. "Economic gains not shared with outsiders," Thurow argues, are "the glue necessary to politically weld together" these disparate European nations.[34] If integration brings no special privileges, why participate? While EC demands of reciprocity will certainly discriminate against outsiders unwilling to conform to European standards, the strongest glue binding the EC together has been the subsidy programs under the Common Agriculture Policy (CAP). Arguing that Italy and France would not have joined the Community without them, Brand notes that these subsidies for production and export eat up 60 percent of the EC budget and persist as the EC's single most difficult international problem.[35]

Responding to both the rise of Japan and a resurgent Europe as economic competitors, the Reagan and Bush administrations have sought to play midwife to a trading bloc larger than the EC in size, population, and wealth. Reagan first proposed the idea of a North American common market during his 1980 election campaign, envisioning it to include the United States, Canada, Mexico, and the Caribbean nations.[36] President Reagan launched the Caribbean Basin Initiative (CBI) in 1983, extending trade preferences and access to U.S. markets to the 50 million people in the Caribbean and Central America. Discussions for a Canadian-U.S. Free Trade Area (FTA) began in 1986, and the FTA went into effect on January 1, 1989. The agreement

---

[32]Sandholtz et al., *The Highest Stakes*, 73.
[33]Brand, "The New World Order," 156; Fieleke, "One Trading World, or Many," 12.
[34]Thurow, *The Coming Economic Battle*, 68.
[35]Brand, "The New World Order," 156.
[36]Wang, "An Analysis of the Three Economic Rims," 15.

calls for the gradual reduction of tariffs in three stages over the course of the decade until all commodities and ultimately capital and labor would be free flowing.[37]

In June 1990, Presidents Carlos Salinas and Bush committed to negotiate a bilateral free trade agreement between Mexico and the United States. Canada joined the discussions three months later, and the three nations have been working toward the creation of a North American Free Trade Area (NAFTA). Formal talks began in June 1991, and trilateral negotiations were completed in August. If the accord can meet the approval of legislative bodies in all three countries, implementation could come as early as 1993.[38] In May 1992, the Bush administration announced that it would begin to negotiate a free trade pact with Chile as soon as NAFTA is enacted as "a first step toward setting up a free trade bloc with all of South America."[39]

The United States and Canada comprise the world's largest and eighth largest economies and are ranked first and second in the world in terms of purchasing power. They have a combined population of 270 million and combined world trade valued at nearly US$1.2 trillion. The Canadian province of Ontario alone received more U.S. exports than all of Japan during the 1980s.[40] A combined NAFTA would have 360 million people creating more than US$6 trillion in economic activity, more than one-and-a-half times that of the EC.[41] Merging the remainder of the Caribbean and Latin America could create an Americas bloc of 600 million people and would give the region, like a European bloc, near self-sufficiency in both markets and means of production.

While NAFTA negotiators have claimed that any free trade arrangement will not be protectionist, outsiders—particularly East Asian nations dependent on the North American market—are concerned that higher local content requirements or preferential trade and investment policies will restrict their access to the North American market. U.S. trade officials have offered little evidence to allay these concerns, and America's willingness to pursue aggressive unilateralism in trade negotiations with Japan and other East Asian countries gives Asian nations both reason for apprehension and motivation to respond.

The East Asian Response

East Asia has been alarmed by the regional integration of the economies of Europe and the Americas. While calls to circle up the wagons in Asia

---

[37]Ibid.; Brand, "The New World Order," 158.

[38]Fry, "A Continent of Free Trade," 128.

[39]*New York Times*, May 14, 1992.

[40]Fieleke, "One Trading World, or Many," 15; Fry, "A Continent of Free Trade," 128.

[41]Blayne Cutler, "North American Demographics," *American Demographics*, March 1992, 38.

have increased, the particular nature of the Asian political economy is producing different consequences.

Natural Integration

East Asia lacks the geopolitical circumstances and shared economic and cultural interests integrating the regions of Europe and North America. Despite the absence of these factors or any formal trading bloc, intraregional trade, investment, and financial ties are nonetheless increasing rapidly in the region, regardless of how the area is defined geographically.[42] Pacific Basin trade surpassed transatlantic trade for the first time in 1983, and trade among East Asian countries will surpass trans-Pacific trade during this decade. Since 1989, Japan's trade with Asia has been greater than its trade with North America, though the United States is still Japan's single largest market.[43]

This pattern of integration also holds true for the East Asian newly industrializing economies (EANIEs) and the Association of Southeast Asian Nations (ASEAN). From 1970 through 1987, Japan's trade with ASEAN grew eight-fold, trade between Japan and North America grew tenfold, between the EANIEs and ASEAN fifteenfold, between Japan and the EANIEs eighteenfold, and between the EANIEs and North America forty-eight-fold.[44] This increase in intra-Asian trade has cut the EANIEs' dependence on the U.S. market from one-half to one-third of total exports. But like Japan, the United States remains the largest market for the EANIEs.

While the pace of East Asian intraregional trade and investment has accelerated more rapidly than trans-Pacific trade since 1985, the North American market still looms largest. Frankel finds that while East Asian intraregional trade grew from 33 percent of these countries' total trade in 1980 to 37 percent in 1989, the "bias" of this trade (measured in terms of ratio of the proportion of intraregional trade to the region's share of world trade) actually declined over the course of the decade and the intensification of trade bias during this period was actually much greater in the EC and NAFTA regions.[45] Frankel concludes that in terms of trade, the United States and Canada should be considered full partners in any Pacific bloc

---

[42]See note 13 above.

[43]Chalmers A. Johnson, "Japan in Search of a 'Normal' Role" (Unpublished manuscript, May 1992), 30.

[44]Saburo Okita, "Japan's Role in Asia-Pacific Cooperation," *Annals of the American Academy of Political and Social Science* 513 (January 1991): 26.

[45]It is worth noting, however, that the intraregional trade bias in East Asia was higher in 1980 than it was in the other two regions and, despite a decline in this bias over the decade, remained higher than that of the EC even by 1989 (1.85 for East Asia compared to 1.77 for the EC). Frankel attributes this higher figure to the networks of overseas Chinese and the role of Japanese capital in the region. Frankel, "Is Japan Creating a Yen Bloc?" 10; *Far Eastern Economic Review*, December 19, 1991, 69.

and that this broader Pacific bloc has the strongest trade bias of any region.[46] When North America is included, the percentage of intraregional trade practically doubles, to over two-thirds of total trade.[47] The same holds true of investment, with Okita finding that fully 80 percent of foreign investment within this Pacific region comes from other countries within the region.[48]

Despite the continued importance of North America, and particularly the United States, to East Asian trade and investment patterns, there is no question that "Japan, rather than the U.S., is now the dominant economic player in Asia. Japan is the region's technology leader, its primary supplier of capital goods, its dominant exporter, its largest annual foreign direct investor and foreign aid supplier, and increasingly a vital market for imports."[49] Without deliberate governmental efforts to link the region through institutional means, these trade, aid, and investment ties are serving to naturally integrate the economies of East Asia vertically and horizontally with Japan at the core.

This process of Japanese-led regional integration has its origins in the nineteenth century and reached its first crest under Imperial Japan's Greater East Asian Co-Prosperity Sphere in the 1930s.[50] The most recent integration boom, however, may be dated not from some Japanese imperial plot, but rather the 1985 Plaza Accord that revalued the Japanese yen against the U.S. dollar by some 60 percent. This revaluation of the Japanese currency combined with rising domestic labor and land prices and increased foreign pressure to expand imports and liberalize capital markets pushed Japanese transnationals to penetrate regional markets and seek cheaper offshore production sites in the region for reimport as well as export to third countries.

Japanese government and businesses have worked in tandem, integrating Japan's neighbors into an informal grouping by proffering aid, loans, technology transfers, direct investment, and preferential access to the Japanese market.[51] From 1984 to 1989, Japanese investment in the EANIEs grew by roughly 50 percent per year, and by roughly 100 percent per year in the ASEAN

---

[46]Frankel, "Is Japan Creating a Yen Bloc?" 4, 11.

[47]Kym Anderson, "Is an Asian-Pacific Trade Bloc Next?" *Journal of World Trade* 25 (August 1991): 31.

[48]As cited by Anderson in ibid.

[49]Sandholtz et al., *The Highest Stakes*, 27.

[50]Cumings notes "in this decade what we might call the 'natural economy' of the [Northeast Asian] region was created; although it was not natural, its rational division of labor and set of possibilities have skewed East Asian development ever since." Bruce Cumings, "The Origins and Development of the Northeast Asian Political Economy: Industrial Sectors, Product Cycles and Political Consequences," in *The Political Economy of the New Asian Industrialism*, ed. Frederic Deyo (Ithaca, N.Y.: Cornell University Press, 1987), 55.

[51]See note 1 above.

economies.[52] In 1991, a new Japanese factory opened every three days in Thailand.[53]

Many now speak of the region as a multi-tiered division of labor or "flying geese" pattern (to use the Japanese term) with Japan on top trailed by the EANIEs, the lower income ASEAN countries, and the Leninist laggards.[54] Though this division of labor has been predominantly vertical in the past, increasingly Taiwan and South Korea—facing the same external and internal pressures as the lead goose—are also moving production offshore through direct investment in Southeast Asia and the mainland Chinese seaboard. In 1988, Taiwan led all other investors in Thailand in terms of number of investments, and was the largest investor in the Philippines and second largest investor in Indonesia in terms of total value.[55] In 1991, Indonesia received over US$1 billion in foreign investment each month with other Asian countries as its top three investors.[56] The EANIEs· and ASEAN economies, while remaining dependent on the Japanese for capital goods, have also been able to increase their exports of finished manufactured products to the Japanese market.

While Japan's economic clout and "long experience in creating institutions and formulating policies" may make it seem "the ideal motive force for directing an Asian regional division of labor,"[57] not all (or even many) of Japan's Asian neighbors concur. Aware of these concerns, Japan traditionally deferred to the wishes and concerns of other regional actors and assumed the role of low-key advocate for some form of "soft" regionalism. Stirred by the fears of the EC and NAFTA as potentially discriminatory trading blocs, Japan since the late 1980s has begun to assume a station concomitant with its economic status in the region. Japan's Ministry of International Trade and Industry (MITI), Ministry of Finance, and Economic Planning Agency all created committees and commissioned reports during the period 1987-88 aimed at enhancing Asian economic integration.[58]

The consequence of these growing regional ties is the emergence of an informal yen bloc of comparable proportions (if not equal institutionalization) to the European and North American trade blocs. It has a GNP of over

---

[52]Sandholtz et al., *The Highest Stakes*, 27.

[53]See note 1 above.

[54]See, for example, Okita, "Japan's Role in Asia-Pacific Cooperation"; Johnson, "Mainland China's Place in the New World Regional Groupings"; and Christopher Howe, "China, Japan and Economic Interdependence in the Asia Pacific Region," *China Quarterly*, no. 124 (December 1990): 662-93.

[55]Karl Fields, "DFI Diplomacy: The Politics of Taiwan's Outward Investment" (Unpublished manuscript, November 1991), 8.

[56]Brand, "The New World Order," 159.

[57]See note 1 above.

[58]John Greenwood, "Potential for an Asian Free Trade Area," *Business Economics*, January 1990, 33.

US$4 trillion compared to US$4.6 trillion for the EC and roughly US$6 trillion for NAFTA.[59] Led by the sophisticated prongs of Japanese trading companies and the subtle undertows of overseas Chinese investors, this dynamic East Asian region will continue to integrate, and as Kiichi Miyazawa predicted in June 1991, will likely "outdo the North American economic zone and European zone at the beginning of the twenty-first century and assume a very crucial role."[60]

Intentional Integration

Asian government officials, business leaders, and futurists have struggled to keep pace with events in attempting to chart and manage the course of this regional integration. True certainly of efforts in the other regions as well, formal efforts to institutionalize the Asian regional economy have faced particularly daunting obstacles in the form of historical legacies, economic and ideological differences, and ambiguous geographical boundaries. Before turning to these obstacles, it is worthwhile examining the formal efforts of institutionalizing the integration process in East Asia both for what these efforts tell about the difficulty of overcoming these impediments and the ultimate and divergent course of East Asian integration.

Concrete proposals for some form of "Pacific OECD" have been tossed around the Pacific region for nearly three decades with the Australians, Japanese, and (sometimes) Americans as major promoters.[61] These efforts have resulted in the formation of at least three formal regional institutions and the proposed formation of a fourth. The oldest and least official of these institutions is the Pacific Basin Economic Council (PBEC), founded in 1968 by regional industrialists. A decade later, Japanese Prime Minister Ohira put forth a Pacific Basin Economic Cooperation Initiative that served as the basis for the creation of the Pacific Economic Cooperation Conference (PECC) in 1980. Indonesian opposition to Ohira's original initiative forced the Japanese and Australian organizers to create a much looser and less official organization than originally planned. Government officials, industrialists, and academics participate in PECC only in a private, unofficial capacity. PECC has formed various task forces and forums to deal with regional cooperation on a wide range of issues. It includes members from Japan, the United States, Canada, South Korea, Taiwan, mainland China, Australia, New Zealand, the Pacific island nations, and all six ASEAN countries.

Since 1989, PBEC and PECC have been overshadowed by the creation of the Asia-Pacific Economic Cooperation (APEC) forum. The idea was

---

[59]*Free China Journal* (Taipei), 9, no. 34 (May 15, 1992): 8; Fry, "A Continent of Free Trade," 128.

[60]See note 1 above.

[61]*Far Eastern Economic Review*, June 8, 1989, 51, 56.

first broached by Australian Prime Minister Bob Hawke in January 1989, in a surprise announcement during a speech to South Korean businessmen in Seoul. Concerned about growing regionalism in Europe and North America and the prospects of Australia being excluded from a yen-dominated East Asian bloc, Hawke (with Malaysian Prime Minister Mahathir) called for a strictly regional grouping excluding the United States and Canada.[62] Fearing U.S. reaction to the formation of an exclusive Australasian group, Japan successfully lobbied to include the United States in the core group of founders. APEC's inaugural meetings were held in Canberra in November 1989.

APEC brings together ministerial-level delegations acting in their official capacities. The organization has commissioned a number of significant studies on regional issues. In the 1991 annual meeting held in Seoul, APEC expanded its membership to include Taiwan (under the name of Chinese Taipei), mainland China, and Hong Kong and issued a "Seoul Declaration" endorsing GATT and multilateralism. Countering the trend toward separate blocs in North America and Asia, APEC seems to be "taking root as a supraregional organization" embracing both sides of the Pacific. Several Latin American countries have applied for membership, as have Russia, Mongolia, and India.[63]

Malaysia's reluctance to include non-Asians in an Asian-Pacific trade grouping resurfaced in December 1990, when Mahathir proposed the formation of an East Asian Economic Grouping (EAEG) that would exclude the non-Asian countries of Australia, New Zealand, and North America. The announcement came in the wake of the collapse of the four-year-long Uruguay Round of the GATT talks and the feared consequences of growing protectionism in the form of European and North American blocs.[64] Initial reactions to the idea of an exclusive Asian bloc were strongly negative both inside and outside the region.

In consultation with ASEAN, Mahathir subsequently repackaged the EAEG as the East Asian Economic Caucus (EAEC) and argued it would serve only as an informal consultative grouping of Asian nations, not a trading bloc, and that it would enhance APEC and not harm those nations excluded. Both Japan and mainland China were initially unsympathetic to the idea, but have recently expressed more interest as leverage against potential protectionism in the European and American trading blocs.[65]

This ambivalence toward an exclusive East Asian club reflects the debate over two very different alternatives of regional integration in Asia. The

---

[62]*Far Eastern Economic Review*, November 16, 1989, 10; Brand, "The New World Order," 159.

[63]*Far Eastern Economic Review*, November 14, 1991, 27.

[64]*Asian Finance*, March 15, 1991, 4.

[65]Johnson, "Mainland China's Place in the New World Regional Groupings," 57; *Far Eastern Economic Review*, November 28, 1991, and April 16, 1992, 26.

first, with APEC as its institutional manifestation, calls for a broad, almost open-ended regionalism including the United States and Canada, and conceivably the entire Pacific Basin. Some have speculated there may be only two trading blocs in the twenty-first century: one European, the other Pacific.[66] Such a Pacific bloc would have a GNP of well over US$10 trillion and would account for nearly half of the global volume of trade.[67]

The second option, with EAEC as its formal expression, would be smaller and more exclusive, but with Japan and the EANIEs at its center and ASEAN, Indochina, and the Chinese seaboard at the perimeter, it would be a very formidable contender. The uncertainty of the new world order combined with the inevitability of increased integration of some form in Asia, render either of these alternatives distinct possibilities. But a third, hybrid outcome is much more likely in the short run, and is much healthier for both East Asia and the global economy.

The Ties That Bind

The continued economic integration of the Asian region is inevitable. But for at least three reasons, the nature of this integrative process will likely be very different from the deliberate, self-contained, and more nearly homogeneous integration taking place in Europe and North America.

The first obstacle to the formation of a regional trading bloc is the great diversity among the nations involved, particularly when the region is defined broadly. While the cultural and ideological differences are certainly greater than either a European or any version of an Americas bloc,[68] it is the economic disparity within the region that will prove the most difficult to overcome. Income levels in the region vary sharply, with GNP per capita in 1991 ranging from over US$25,000 in Japan to barely US$400 in mainland China,[69] and with wages roughly 27 times higher in Japan.[70] As one observer noted, "If one of the tests of regional integration is the free movement of labor, and approximate equality of working conditions in different countries, then the Asia-Pacific region must be decades, if not centuries, away from achieving such integration."[71]

In a recent conference on Asian regionalism held in Taipei, Valery Giscard d'Estaing argued that this disparity made an EC type of regionalism in Asia highly unlikely. He noted in the EC, dominant Germany is respon-

---

[66]Johnson, "Mainland China's Place in the New World Regional Groupings," 58.

[67]*Far Eastern Economic Review*, November 14, 1991, 27.

[68]Nukazawa, "Interdependence and Regionalism," 48.

[69]I am indebted to Harmon Zeigler and his "PC Globe" database for these numbers.

[70]*Far Eastern Economic Review*, April 25, 1991, 54.

[71]Ibid., June 8, 1989, 76.

sible for less than 30 percent of the EC's total GNP, whereas Japan is responsible for fully 80 percent of Asia's GNP.[72] The vertical nature of the "flying geese" complementarity between resource-rich and resource-poor nations in the region also makes it politically very difficult to create a trading bloc. Unlike the EC, where economic gains are made in intraindustry trade specialization, integration in Asia threatens a division of labor much less profitable to those on the bottom.[73]

The solution some have offered to this problem of diversity is to shrink the perimeters of the region to embrace only Asia or even capitalist East Asia. But the leader of such a bloc would certainly be Japan, and this is a prospect that stirs fear (or at least reluctance) in the hearts of many Asians, both inside and outside Japan, for several reasons.

Most Asians have bitter memories of Japan's military domination of Asia in the 1930s and 1940s. While regional groupings work best with a leader (Germany in the EC, the United States in NAFTA), there is no enthusiasm anywhere in Asia for a militarily strong Japan and little more interest in Japanese political leadership.[74] In a *Nihon Keizai* poll conducted in February and March 1992, some 449 scholars and businessmen in eleven Asian countries and Australia were asked a number of questions concerning Japan's role in Asia. Nearly 80 percent of those questioned were in favor of a regional economic bloc with Japan participating and over 90 percent of those surveyed in Indonesia, Thailand, and the Philippines indicated they would welcome Japanese leadership of such a bloc. However, 78 percent of mainland Chinese and 54 percent of South Koreans rejected Japanese leadership. Some 90 percent of all respondents said they would like their country to strengthen economic ties with Japan, but only 10 percent wanted stronger political ties and none wanted military ties.[75]

This reluctance for Japanese leadership seems just as strong within Japan, as one observer notes:

> The absence of a supranational guiding hand [in Asia] has not come about by accident. The difficulty in setting up any form of Asian economic grouping is that Japan would have to play the leading role and nobody wants that, least of all, it seems, the Japanese. The economic leviathan is a political pygmy. And this inversion affects every aspect of integration—political, economic, financial, and military.[76]

Despite its economic dominance of the region, Japan is not even prepared economically to pilot an Asian bloc with the relatively free flow of

---

[72]*Free China Journal* 9, no. 36 (May 22, 1992): 7.

[73]Anderson, "Is an Asian-Pacific Trade Bloc Next?" 39.

[74]Howard H. Baker, Jr. and Ellen L. Frost, "Rescuing the U.S.-Japan Alliance," *Foreign Affairs* 71, no. 2 (Spring 1992): 104.

[75]As cited by Johnson, "Japan in Search of a 'Normal' Role," 32.

[76]*Far Eastern Economic Review*, June 8, 1989, 88.

labor and trade such a bloc would entail. To do so, Japan would have to be prepared (economically and culturally) to digest foreign labor on an unprecedented scale as well as replace the United States as the primary market for East Asian exports and investments. While only Japan among the Asian countries has the necessary wealth to support a persistent trade deficit, this would require it to shift from a strategy of producer-oriented capitalism to one of consumer-oriented capitalism, a change that will be some time in coming.[77]

Japan's share of world imports actually declined during the 1980s, and its per capita imports in 1988 were only US$752, compared to US$3,076 for West Germany, US$2,651 for the United Kingdom, US$2,572 for France, and US$1,484 for the United States.[78] Although EANIE and ASEAN manufactured exports have been making inroads into the Japanese market, most of these transactions involve Japanese companies at both ends.[79] Moreover, EANIE and ASEAN dependence on Japanese industrial goods is actually widening their bilateral trade gaps. A MITI white paper recently concluded that the EANIEs will continue to post larger trade deficits with Japan through the 1990s, and that the ASEAN economies will soon be in deficit as well.[80]

This is closely related to a final reason why Asia is not likely to experience self-contained economic regionalism in the near future. Even if the fear and loathing of Japanese regional hegemony could be overcome, the very nature of East Asian dynamism precludes this kind of inward-looking strategy. The East Asian developmental miracles have been predicated on export-oriented growth, and the consumer markets of North America and Europe have ingested the overwhelming majority of these exports. During the 1980s, U.S. imports from the EANIEs, ASEAN, and mainland China were 50 percent more than those of neighboring Japan, and Asian dependence on the U.S. market actually grew over the course of the decade.[81] While the American twin deficits guarantee this trend cannot continue for long, the North American and European markets remain vital to Asia. Even Malaysia, the country most actively pushing for an exclusive East Asian bloc, still has its major markets in the West, with 30 percent of its total trade in 1991 conducted with the United States and the EC.[82]

---

[77]Thurow, *The Coming Economic Battle*, 250-51.

[78]Okita, "Japan's Role in Asia-Pacific Cooperation," 30; *Far Eastern Economic Review*, June 15, 1989, 59.

[79]A 1990 study concluded that 70 percent of Japan's worldwide trade involves a Japanese company at each end of the transaction, typically an overseas Japanese subsidiary exporting finished goods back to its domestic parent. In the EC, the corresponding figure is less than 50 percent and in the United States only 20 percent. (*Far Eastern Economic Review*, October 11, 1990, 72).

[80]*Far Eastern Economic Review*, May 21, 1992, 38.

[81]Ibid., October 11, 1990, 73.

[82]Ibid., April 16, 1992, 50.

For these (and other) reasons, both the intentional efforts and natural tendencies toward the integration of the Asian economies have begun, and will continue, to create a hybrid regional integration characterized by overlapping subregional (and supraregional) bilateral and multilateral arrangements. These miniregions, or what the *Nihon Keizai* refers to as "spontaneous economic spheres" and Singapore ambassador-at-large Tommy Koh describes as "expanding and intersecting circles," may best be labeled (at the risk of yet another acronym) subregional free trade areas (SRFTA). While an extensive discussion of their emergence and development is beyond the scope of this chapter, it is useful to note some of the more important of these blossoming SRFTAs.

Japan Sea Rim: Starting north and working south, the first of these miniregions is the basin formed by Asiatic Russia, Japan, the two Koreas, mainland China's Kirin (Jilin) Province, and by extension, Mongolia. Greatest interest is now focused on the Tumen (Yimen) River delta area where industrialists, academics, government officials, and now the United Nations Development Program are promoting the creation of a free trade zone embracing portions of North Korea, Russia, and mainland China. The ambitious plans call for the joint creation of a US$30 billion trade and transport complex that would ultimately rival Rotterdam or Hong Kong. The Tumen project would be the centerpiece of a broader scheme for regional economic cooperation.[83]

Yellow Sea Rim: This SRFTA would also involve the two Koreas, Japan, and mainland China (in this case, the Po Hai [Bohai] provinces of Hopei [Hebei], Liaoning, and Shantung [Shandong]) in a regional division of labor capitalizing on the comparative advantages of each of the participants. The creation of a free trade area would reduce the transaction costs and other inefficiencies currently associated with the indirect trade conducted in the region, and like the Japan Sea cooperation, could have even more significant positive externalities in reducing political tensions in the region.[84]

Nichibei Bloc: Reflecting their dominance of the Pacific region and the remarkable interdependence of their economies, there have been calls for the creation of a Japan-U.S. free trade area. Arguing that either economy could now destroy the other, Nukazawa claims these two Pacific super-

---

[83]Sueo Sekiguchi, "Trade, Investment and Technology Transfer in Northeast Asia: A Japanese View on Future Development" (Unpublished paper presented at the Conference on Regional Development in the Yellow Sea Rimland, East-West Center, Honolulu, Hawaii, January 1990); *Far Eastern Economic Review*, October 24, 1991, 22, and January 16, 1992, 16-20.

[84]Chung H. Lee and Keun Lee, "Trade between Bohai of China and Korea: Present and Future," and Xiangwei He, Yan Zhuang, and Ying Huang, "The Foreign Investment, Technology Import and Regional Economic Development in the Yellow Sea Rimlands" (Unpublished papers presented at the Conference on Regional Development in the Yellow Sea Rimland, East-West Center, Honolulu, Hawaii, January 1990).

powers exist in a situation of economic MAD (mutual assured destruction) with more calculable consequences than its nuclear namesake.[85] One way to manage this relationship and the tensions arising from conflicts in trade, investment and monetary policies would be to negotiate a bilateral free trade agreement similar to that between the United States and Canada or the United States and Israel. Other variations of this proposal link Japan and other East Asian economies with the Pacific west coastal areas of Cascadia (British Columbia, Washington, and Oregon), California, and Mexico.[86]

South China Zone: Mainland China's participation in these SRFTAs is a consequence of its "coastal development" strategy, emulating the developmental strategies of the EANIEs.[87] The most successful of these efforts have been the southern seaboard provinces of Fukien (Fujian) and Kwangtung (Guangdong) because of their proximity to Taiwan and Hong Kong. The remarkable entrepreneurial activities of Chinese industrialists in this region have outpaced any official efforts to promote (or more often impede) the economic integration of this miniregion. A tidy division of labor has emerged with Taiwan and Hong Kong providing investment capital, technology, and management expertise, and the mainland provinces providing cheap and abundant labor. Mainland China recently announced the opening of a special port designed exclusively for Taiwan trade to be built on Fukien's Meichow island, south of Foochow (Fuzhou), north of Amoy (Xiamen), and less than 100 nautical miles from Taiwan. The geographical, cultural, and linguistic affinities of this region assure it a promising future, despite obvious political obstacles.[88]

ASEAN Free Trade Area: ASEAN was formed in 1967, as much for strategic and security reasons as for motives of economic cooperation. Despite efforts over the past twenty-five years to enhance the latter, the ASEAN nations have largely failed to acquire a truly regional perspective. Intraregional trade and other forms of cooperation are much less common than head-to-head competition for the same markets and resources. In an effort to overcome this, ASEAN leaders agreed in January 1992, to form a free trade area among ASEAN members (AFTA) to be implemented over the next fifteen years. Even more promising (and attainable in the short run) is the Singapore-led effort to knit the economies of Johor in Malaysia, Batam (Riau) in Indonesia, and Singapore into what it calls the "Growth Triangle"

---

[85]Nukazawa, "Interdependence and Regionalism," 45.

[86]*Far Eastern Economic Review*, September 13, 1990, 52; March 7, 1991, 48; and June 6, 1991, 48; Howe, "China, Japan and Economic Interdependence," 667.

[87]Howe, "China, Japan and Economic Interdependence," 689.

[88]Pamela Baldinger, "The Birth of Greater China," *The China Business Review*, May-June 1992, 13-17; Howe, "China, Japan and Economic Interdependence," 683-89; Harry Harding, "The US and Greater China," *The China Business Review*, May-June 1992, 18.

project, capitalizing on the comparative advantages of each participant.[89] These SRFTAs promise much good and little ill for East Asia. As one observer of the Japan Sea Rim concluded:

> Seen from the perspective of attempts to organize an open trading system for the entire Asia Pacific region these events may still appear peripheral. However, attempts to organize economic cooperation among the Japan Sea rim countries illustrate a broader regional theme. How to open up the shorelines of formally hostile states and to use the waters dividing them as means of bringing local communities closer should be regarded as a central issue for the post-Cold War regional order in East Asia.[90]

Conclusion

The possibilities for this kind of regionalism are practically endless and many additional combinations have been contemplated, involving Indochina, South Asia, and even Latin America. The formation of these SRFTAs will have positive consequences both inside and outside the region. Internally, these diverse ties and subregional free trade zones will reap economic, and often times more important political benefits. Externally, the dynamism and wealth of a region advocating multilateralism will temper any trend toward global protectionism of the severity of the 1930s, with its disastrous economic and political consequences.[91]

The result of regional economic integration in East Asia and worldwide will be an international trade regime characterized by relatively free trade within the regions and "managed" but at least manageable trade without. The wagons will inevitably circle, but like their predecessors in the American Far West, these protective rings may only be temporary gatherings as a prelude to greener and more open climes.

---

[89]Anderson, "Is an Asian-Pacific Trade Bloc Next?" 28; *Asian Finance*, March 15, 1991, 5; *Far Eastern Economic Review*, January 31, 1991, 33, and April 16, 1992, 48.

[90]*Far Eastern Economic Review*, October 24, 1991, 22.

[91]In fact, there is evidence that this notion of subregional cooperation is also appealing to Europeans wary of the confines of a United States of Europe. *The Economist* proposes an ECA (Europe of Consenting Adults) in which European states would be free to "pick and choose" when and where they want to cooperate, through intertwined spheres of alliances and agreements (*The Economist*, June 24, 1992, 60). *Die Zeit* also endorses subregionalism with a metaphor of a spacious cathedral housing many chapels (as cited in *World Press Review*, November 1991).

368   Karl J. Fields

Other References

Jacquemin, Alexis, and Andre Sapir. "Europe Post-1992: Internal and External Liberalization." *AEA Papers and Proceedings* 81 (May 1991): 166-70.

Kellas, James G. "European Integration and the Regions." *Parliamentary Affairs* 44 (April 1991): 226-39.

McCracken, Paul W. "Will the Third Great Wave Continue?" *The American Enterprise,* March-April 1991, 52-57.

Scalapino, Robert A. "Regionalism in the Pacific: Prospects and Problems for the Pacific Basin." *The Atlantic Community Quarterly* 26 (Summer 1988): 174-88.

Taira, Koji. "Japan, an Imminent Hegemon?" *Annals of the American Academy of Political and Social Science* 513 (January 1991): 151-63.

CHAPTER 20

Are East Asian Models Relevant to the Baltic?

Walter C. Clemens, Jr.

Asia's four "Tigers"—Singapore, Hong Kong, South Korea, and the Republic of China (ROC)—have set the pace for the world's newly industrializing countries (NICs). At least two of them, South Korea and the ROC, have become more democratic. Their experience may hold lessons for all developing countries, but this essay focuses on the possible significance of East Asian development for Estonia, Latvia, and Lithuania—the first three republics to establish their independence from the Soviet Union. Of all ex-Soviet republics, the three Baltic states are most like the Asian Tigers in size and setting. Unlike the Tigers, Russia and many of the other ex-Soviet republics are huge and many are cut off from access to the sea.

Can the Baltics hope to replicate the East Asian experience? If so, what lessons can they derive from East Asia?[1]

From Rags to Riches

A visitor to the Baltic republics in the early 1990s would be more impressed by the problems they face than by their potential for prosperity. But the fact is that they appear better off than did any of the four Tigers just one generation ago.

In 1970, none of these four resembled a "tiger." Hong Kong then struggled with waves of refugees from mainland China's Cultural Revolution. Taiwan was still a police state under martial law. Next to major hotels in

---

[1] Shenzhen and Canton (Guangzhou) have learned something from Hong Kong; now inland provinces such as Hunan are trying to emulate the special economic zones close to the Chinese coast. Perhaps mainland China as a whole has learned something from Japan and the Tigers. The PRC gross domestic product grew two and one-half times in 1980-81. If so, *scale* may not be a vital factor. Perhaps a large state such as Russia could also learn something from the Tigers—or even from mainland China. See Alexander Nicoll, "Winds of Reform Blow in from a Prosperous Coast," *Financial Times*, June 19, 1992, 15; Martin Wolf, "Rise and Rise of the East Asian Trading Economies," ibid., June 15, 1992, 6.

Taipei whole families camped on sidewalks under improvised awnings. South Korea and Singapore were also politically tense and far from being economically developed. Thousands lived in caves and huts on a hillside close to downtown Seoul. In one such cave a father told me how he had brought his family to the city so his children could obtain education. Unfortunately, the state provided only a few years of free education. Therefore the older sons, like their father, dug ditches the few days a week they could get work. In Korea's countryside a chicken farmer showed me how he had rationalized production and found a way to deliver eggs to the city each morning. But his innovations and wealth had a price. He was ostracized by his neighbors, who preferred traditional ways. Korea's urban and country poor in 1970 were not yet part of a modernizing, participant society.[2]

In the 1970s, the four Tigers advanced from low-income to low-medium-income ratings. As incomes mounted, infant mortality declined. By the end of the 1980s, South Korea's per capita income had reached US$4,400. The other three ranked as high-income countries: Taiwan at US$7,500; Hong Kong at US$10,350; and Singapore at US$10,450 per capita.[3]

Taiwan's average annual rate of gross national product (GNP) growth from 1952 to 1989 was nearly 9 percent—about twice the highest protracted rate ever achieved in the United States (after the Civil War). Taiwan's growth was led by exports, which made up 9.7 percent of GNP in 1952, but 50.7 percent in 1987.[4] Infant mortality declined from 24.11 per thousand in 1965 to 5.71 per thousand in 1989.[5]

By 1980, Singapore placed third worldwide in microelectronics exports; Hong Kong, seventh; and South Korea, ninth. By 1990, South Korea advanced to fourth; Taiwan, to sixth; Singapore slipped to seventh; and Hong Kong disappeared from the top ten. In 1990, Singapore, South Korea, and Taiwan were among the world's top ten exporters of computers and/or telecommunications equipment. They did not place among the top ten exporters of aerospace equipment, scientific equipment, medicine, or organic chemicals. Taiwan, however, rose to tenth place among exporters of machine tools and robotics.[6]

Each Tiger based its wealth on exports. In the years from 1970 to 1990, South Korea increased its exports by 78 times; Taiwan, by 47 times;

---

[2]These concepts are analyzed in Daniel Lerner, *The Passing of Traditional Society: Modernizing the Middle East* (New York: Free Press, 1958).

[3]Taiwan's per capita income was under US$2,000 in 1980. See *Republic of China Yearbook 1990-91* (Taipei: Kwang Hwa, 1990), 253. Other statistics are from World Bank, *World Development Report 1991* (New York: Oxford University Press, 1991), 205.

[4]*Republic of China Yearbook 1990-91*, 252-54.

[5]Ibid., 428.

[6]*Handbook of Economic Statistics, 1991: A Reference Aid* (Washington, D.C.: Central Intelligence Agency, 1991), 144.

and Singapore and Hong Kong by 34 and 33 times respectively. In the same twenty-year period Japan multiplied the value of its exports by only 15; West Germany, by 12; and the United States, by 9. Oil exporters such as Iraq and Indonesia increased the value of their exports by about 19 times and Saudi Arabia by 11 times. Europe's most prosperous small states, Switzerland and Sweden, by 13 and 9 times respectively.[7]

From the 1970s through 1990, tiny Hong Kong exported more than any of the other Tigers. The United States led the world in exports, but these were only 4.8 times more than Hong Kong's in 1990; Japan exported 3.5 times more than Hong Kong at that time, and 4.3 times more than Taiwan. Like Japan, each Tiger exported far more than it imported.[8] The Tigers' exports consisted almost entirely of manufactured goods.

Manufacturing as a share of Taiwan's GNP climbed from 17 percent in 1961 to 40 percent in 1986, after which it declined to about one-third in the early 1990s, as services became more important and some industries searched for cheaper facilities offshore.[9]

By 1992, Taiwan's Central Bank possessed foreign exchange reserves of nearly US$90 billion, more than any other country in the world. Taipei is now embarking on a US$303 billion Six-Year National Development Plan (1991-96) to renovate its infrastructure and the environment and promote science and technology.

Each of the Asian Tigers has its own specific characteristics, but all shared certain liabilities and assets for development.

Tiger Liabilities

—Poor resource base: few minerals or cash crops; heavy dependence on imported energy[10]
—Vulnerability to destructive rains
—Dense population relative to area under cultivation
—Small domestic market
—Political tension and little democracy
—Severe external threats to stability and independence
—The burden of large armies and heavy military spending (except in Hong Kong)

---

[7]Ibid., 130-31.

[8]Ibid., 134-35.

[9]Schive Chi, an economist at National Taiwan University, observed that in other industrialized countries the manufacturing sector's weight declined after national incomes reached US$5,000. See Ko Liang-yi, "Manufacturing Firms Drop Reins," *Free China Journal* (Taipei) 8, no. 91 (November 29, 1991): 3.

[10]Taiwan's development in the 1950s was fired by domestically produced coal, but there was a shift to imported oil, gas, and coal in the 1960s and 1970s. Nuclear power supplied 8 percent of Taiwan's energy by 1981 and 13 percent in 1989. See *Republic of China Yearbook 1990-91*, 305.

Tiger Assets

Tangibles:
—For several decades, substantial economic aid from the United States for Taiwan and Korea; support for Singapore and Hong Kong from the United Kingdom
—Inducements to foreign capital, including the physical infrastructure, tax holidays, cheap energy, and low operational costs
—Investment capital available from expatriates and the United States, United Kingdom, Germany, and Japan
—Financing by bank loans rather than stocks and bonds, which was conducive to long-term investment horizons

The Tigers benefitted from Cold War priorities that led Washington to cultivate dependable allies regardless of their potential as economic competitors. The NICs moved in a "flying geese formation," pursuing Japanese innovations and filling economic niches evacuated by Japan. The Tigers took advantage of low labor costs but gradually moved toward products requiring high technology.

Intangibles:
—New societies starting afresh
—Strong work ethic
—High rates of saving and investment[11]
—Cheap labor relative to advanced industrial countries[12]
—Considerable autonomy for the economic sphere regardless of politics
—Entrepreneurial spirit linked to long-term horizons
—Little resistance to potentially useful innovations; quick assimilation and improvement of Western technology
—Wide support for education on all levels—elementary to postgraduate
—Many family-owned enterprises with decision-making flexibility and high employee loyalty
—A pliant and willing labor force, fostered by paternalistic company policies and profit-sharing bonuses; weak trade unions
—Ethnic homogeneity or, if ethnic differences existed, their suppression

---

[11]Rich data on these patterns is cited in chapter 4 of this volume: Gee San, "The ROC's Economic Development and Its International Cooperation Program." But none of these assets is etched in stone. Savings in Taiwan declined from 38.4 percent of GNP in 1986 to 29.6 percent in 1990. Saving and investment funds will also be curtailed by pressures to spend more for the growing elderly population and by the pluralization of stock market listings. Still, Taiwan's rate of saving and investment in the early 1990s was much higher than in the United States (about 15 percent). See report by Jung Chuen-wen summarized in "Savings Drop Worries Economist," *Free China Journal* 8, no. 91 (November 29, 1991): 8.
[12]High labor costs and land rents pressed Taiwanese manufacturers to relocate some manufacturing facilities offshore in the early 1990s.

—Land reform in Korea and Taiwan[13]
—A strong government able to enforce rules and collect taxes (except in Hong Kong)
—An industrial and strategic trade policy that nursed infant industries while obtaining foreign capital and technology (except in Hong Kong)
—Political-military support from the United States and/or United Kingdom
—A global environment in the 1970s-80s favorable to expansion and free trade
—The Japanese model, which each of the four latecomers emulated in some, but not all, respects

Most of the Tigers' assets were intangible and few depended on government intervention. Rather, government policies reinforced and harmonized with long-established habits of saving, hard work, and study. No doubt many of the Tigers' citizens would have preferred to consume more and save less, but most understood and respected government policies that deliberately delayed consumer gratification.

Three of the Tigers, like Japan, may have profited from neo-mercantilism, compelling liberal economists to reconsider the merits of free trade. But Hong Kong prospered under laissez faire without any help from government industrial policy. The other three Tiger governments steered a middle course between doing too little and too much. They promoted industrialization and exports without neglecting the impulses of the free market. They pressed for reinvestment of profits, but they also collected taxes.

Except for Hong Kong, each of the Tigers developed safeguards against foreign ownership of vital national enterprises, such as banking and steel. Each welcomed useful foreign capital and marketing expertise while discouraging foreign ownership and control.

The Tigers proved that less developed countries could break from structural dependency. Each of the Tigers began with an import substitution policy and gradually developed a strong export-led growth. Each acquired a dynamic conception of competitive advantage, shifting from cheap labor to rapid accommodation to foreign market demands. Each captured specialty niches in Western markets by satisfying consumer demand while maintaining competitive prices.

Korea and Taiwan had large conglomerates, as in Japan, but these firms showed little disposition to give up production in favor of parasitic "rent-collecting." Unlike powerful special interests in Britain and the United

---

[13]Asked what lessons the ROC experience held for the Baltics, President Lee Teng-hui immediately cited Taiwan's land reforms (in which he played a major role). Meeting with Sino-American-European Conference participants, August 21, 1992.

States, the Korean and Taiwanese firms did not seek to fix prices, restrict supply, or curtail competition by political action. They did not claim social and economic output for themselves at society's expense.

The big picture is clear: Those countries that bucked the First World trading system—much of the Third World as well as mainland China—did worse than those that joined it. Despite structural impediments, a late start, and other disadvantages, four low-income countries, Hong Kong, Singapore, South Korea, and the ROC, became medium- and even high-income countries within decades. Their growth benefitted from foreign aid and favorable circumstances, but depended ultimately on their own efforts.

The Baltic Balance Sheet

How do the liabilities and assets of the Baltic states in the 1990s compare with those of the Asian Tigers a generation before?[14]

Living Standards

The Baltic states are poor compared to their northern and western neighbors, but they long had the highest living standards in the ex-Soviet Union. Infant mortality for the entire Soviet Union in 1989 was at least 24.7 per thousand. The highest reported infant mortality rate was in Tajikistan—49 per thousand. But in Latvia the infant mortality rate was only 11 per thousand; in Lithuania, 11.5 per thousand; in Estonia, 12.4 per thousand; and in Russia, 18.9 per thousand.[15]

Location

Each of the Tigers benefitted from its location which was made more important by the Korean and Vietnam wars. But the Baltic lands and ports are also major factors in geopolitics, and have been for millennia. They stand at a crossroads where northern, western, and eastern Europe meet Russia, Belarus, and Ukraine. Riga, Tallinn (Reval), and Klaipeda (Memel) were major participants in the Hanseatic trade. In the 1920s, Russia paid a pretty coin to assure access to these ports. Today they are even more important if Russian oil and Ukrainian grain are to make their way to the West.

---

[14]For background, see John Hiden and Patrick Salmon, *The Baltic Nations and Europe: Estonia, Latvia and Lithuania in the Twentieth Century* (London: Longman, 1991); Walter C. Clemens, Jr., *Baltic Independence and Russian Empire* (New York: St. Martin's, 1991); Toivo U. Raun, *Estonia and the Estonians*, 2d ed. (Stanford, Calif.: Hoover Institution, 1991). For updates, see essays by Clemens and others in *Nationality Papers* in 1990-1992; *Journal of Baltic Studies; Journal of Soviet Nationalities*; Radio Free Europe/Radio Liberty *Research Report*; and *Berichte des Bundesinstituts für ostwissenschaftliche und internationale Studien.*
[15]Clemens, *Baltic Independence*, 66-67.

Natural Resources

The Baltics possess good farming land, minerals, and energy that made them net exporters to the other Soviet republics for two generations. Population density is not a serious problem. The region has not been subject to natural catastrophes such as earthquakes or typhoons.

But environmental degradation in the Baltic region may equal or surpass that in East Asia. Communist managers have proved even more rapacious than capitalist. Water, air, and soil have been badly polluted across the entire Soviet Union. The Baltics' problems are acute because the region was highly industrialized and militarized under Soviet rule. Military units often drained their left-over fuel rations each month into the soil or water.

Nuclear radiation has left its mark on the Baltic region as on other lands close to Chernobyl. Balts want to sell their produce to Europe for hard currency, but Europeans demur. They are faced with mountains of butter and other foods, but fear products may be tinged with radioactive poison.

Enormous capital is needed to restore some measure of environmental quality to the Baltics. Rich neighbors such as Sweden and Finland could help, but so far have done little. To date there has been much more talk than action. The temptation—even in the richer countries—is to wait for others to do the job.[16] Norwegians are offering Balts scrubbers and other environmental technology but at steep prices.

Today the ecological situation in all of the ex-Soviet republics looks almost hopeless. But it did not look bright in Japan or Taiwan a generation ago either. Conditions in Japan have improved considerably since the 1970s, when traffic police often took refuge in artificial oxygen. Taiwan's environment has gotten worse as its material condition has improved. But in 1991-92, the ROC government planned a huge investment to help clean the environment.

Imperial Legacies

British imperialists took the lead in building the infrastructure of Singapore and Hong Kong; Imperial Japan did the same for Taiwan and, to some extent, for Korea. Similarly, Tsarist Russia and the Soviet Union developed the infrastructure and industry of the Baltics. Indeed, railroads set down by Tsarist Russia facilitated the growth of Estonian, Latvian, and Lithuanian national consciousness. What had been isolated country parishes began to meet one another in the mid-nineteenth century and sing national songs together in regular festivals.

---

[16]On the temptation to "ride free," see Mancur Olson, *The Logic of Collective Action* (Cambridge, Mass.: Harvard University Press, 1965). For analyses of this theory and Soviet-type economies, see *Journal of Soviet Nationalities* 1, no. 2 (Summer 1990): 1-65.

But Soviet imperial rule was much more onerous to the Baltics than was foreign rule over Singapore, Hong Kong, Taiwan, and perhaps even Korea. The Soviets made to disappear—in camps, graves, or by emigration—a large portion of the Baltic population, especially the local elites. After 1945, huge numbers of Russian and other Soviet migrants poured into the Baltic republics, taking the jobs and quarters of Balts killed, or simply not born, due to Soviet genocide. The indigenous people make up just over half of Latvia's population, about 62 percent of Estonia's, and about 80 percent of Lithuania's.

Besides suffering ecocide and genocide, the Baltic peoples have seen their cultures undermined by Russification and Sovietization. Generations of Japanese rule weighed heavy on South Korea and Taiwan, but Koreans and the Chinese of Taiwan may have kept their own languages and traditions more intact than have the Balts under Soviet rule.[17] Chinese language and tradition have lost ground in Singapore and Hong Kong, but the reason for this has been local choice and the impact of modernization more than British policy.[18] In the Baltic states the erosion of Baltic culture has been caused more by Soviet imperialism than by a freely made decision to modernize.

There may have been positive as well as negative consequences for the Tigers' development from the many decades of severe tensions with Peking (Beijing) and other neighbors. Political insecurity probably diminished confidence in the future, but it also helped to unify each country against external threats.[19] The retreat of the Japanese, and then the British empire, left the peoples of Singapore, Korea, and Taiwan hopeful but unsure about their respective futures. The expected transfer of Hong Kong from British administration to rule by the People's Republic of China (PRC) in 1997 is what worries Hong Kong residents. Many flee or seek a second passport, but the shadow of Communism has not stopped investment or hard work in Hong Kong.

Most native Balts welcomed independence, formally achieved in September 1991, but they may be less sanguine about their future than were the East

---

[17]But an editorial in *Free China Review* 3, no. 11 (November 1989) lamented the impact of nouveaux riches in Taiwan: "a loss of traditional values . . . based upon thousands of years of extended family life in rural settings." The editorialist hoped that, with time and experience, traditional Chinese values would adapt and reemerge to fit the demands of new conditions.
    While Chinese culture is comparatively strong in Taiwan, the culture and physical well-being of aboriginals on the island are under intense stress—as in the Americas and elsewhere.

[18]Korea under Japanese rule bore a greater resemblance to the Baltics. Japanese forced many Koreans to take Japanese names. Japanese rule in Taiwan was less harsh and is remembered as having positive as well as negative features. In the 1990s some professors at Taiwan universities—age 60 and up—still tell jokes among themselves in Japanese. Balts might curse but never joke in Russian.

[19]Foreign threats are not a panacea. Malaysia was under greater threat than Singapore but suffered greater domestic turmoil. Still, it seems likely that Singapore's success in welding together four disparate cultures has been aided by several foreign bogies.

Asian peoples when Japan and Britain withdrew. Baltic anxieties arise from many sources, but one results from the anomaly that Russian troops remain on their soil even after Moscow has recognized Baltic independence. It is as though Japanese troops remained in South Korea or Taiwan after 1945, pleading that they and their families had no place to live back home!

The Baltics have demanded the complete withdrawal of foreign troops by the end of 1992. Russian spokesmen replied that this goal could not be realized for several years, but President Boris Yeltsin hinted in mid-1992 that all Russian troops might leave by the end of 1993. Russian authorities say the main problem is to find alternative housing for the ex-Soviet army back in Russia. But this answer does not placate the Balts who want the land, housing, and equipment now used by alien occupiers. Balts object to troop movements, maneuvers, and even the deployment of reinforcements conducted without their permission. An Estonian official worries that a Russian controlled directional finding station near Tallinn can monitor cellular telephones and all radio broadcasts including those of Estonian security forces and police.[20] A customs agent complains that armed Russian troops bully their way through Estonian customs transporting mini-submarines labeled as "industrial products."[21] Ex-KGB workers allege that Soviet secret agents have been absorbed into the security apparatus of President Yeltsin's Russia. These agents still operate in the Baltic region, their organizational structures intact.[22]

To be sure, the Kremlin's will to reannex the Baltics seems to have almost disappeared. But the presence of large Russian forces on Baltic soil gives Moscow a huge bargaining chip in negotiations over borders, debts, and all other unresolved issues between Russia and the newly independent states. The fact that the Balts are still occupied and almost unarmed puts them at a serious disadvantage in all negotiations with Moscow—especially as Europe shifts its attention to active crises in Yugoslavia and elsewhere. Meanwhile, Balts worry that the Russian forces might actively interfere in local affairs, siding with Russian settlers against the local authorities, as in Moldova.

At the outset of the 1990s, the danger of Russian imperialism is probably less for the Baltics than the PRC or North Korea is a threat to the East Asian Tigers.

Domestic Strains

The four Asian Tigers face fewer internal ethnic problems than do the Baltic republics. The only one of the Tigers with significant ethnic divisions

---

[20]Jüri Pihl, Director of Kaitsepolitsei [Protection Service], interviewed in *Postimees*, June 22, 1992.

[21]Open letter from customs agent Ilmar Vananurm, "This Misty Estonian Border," *Rahva Hääl*, July 1, 1992.

[22]Interviews by Toomas Kümmel in *Eesti Aeg*, July 1, 1992.

is Singapore, which has used carrots, sticks, and an imposed language—English—to repress ethnic strife. Neighboring Malaysia and Sri Lanka, however, have been rent by ethnic hatred and official discrimination. Will the Balts follow the Malay or Sri Lankan rather than the Singapore model?

The ex-Soviet empire is engulfed by waves of chauvinism and national intolerance. The Baltics have to date been spared the large-scale violence that has claimed many lives in the Caucasus, Central Asia, and Moldova. Still, tensions within the Baltic republics between natives and settlers have risen, fallen, and risen again since political controls loosened in the late 1980s. The feelings of native Balts have resembled those of Algerians toward French *colons*. Many Balts have worked for mutual understanding with non-Baltic settlers, but many are impatient—understandably so. Burning issues remain unresolved: Who may be a citizen of the new republics? Who may vote? Who may continue to live there, work, and receive welfare benefits—citizen or not? Language and citizenship requirements that seem reasonable to a Balt may be treated as "racial discrimination" and a "violation of human rights" by a Slav, particularly if he or she moved to the Baltic region decades ago.

A worst-case scenario sees the Soviet troops still stationed in the Baltics coming to the aid of Russian settlers who claim human rights abuses. Thousands of Russian demonstrators—some workers, some military—in Tallinn in March 1990 carried banners inscribed, "The Army and People Are One." These signs supplanted an earlier version reading "The Party and People Are One."

Work Ethic

The most important of the Tigers' assets may be a propensity to work hard, save, and invest. Balts have been noted for their work ethic, especially Latvians and Estonians, dominated for centuries by Scandinavians and Germans and heavily influenced by Lutheran pastors. Lithuanian Catholics, Max Weber might predict, would be less hard-working and self-effacing than their Protestant neighbors, but there is little evidence of such differences among Balts after fifty years of Sovietization.

What has been the impact on this work ethic of Soviet rule?

—Large numbers of the most energetic Baltic citizenry have been killed or driven into exile, where their offspring now live.

—Private trade, farming, business, and banking have been extinguished for half a century, so that the know-how has disappeared from living memory.

—Capital that could now be invested has disappeared or migrated.

—Communist propaganda has denounced private property and praised egalitarianism.

—Communist institutions extolled hard work and self-sacrifice but offered few incentives for such behavior.

—Large numbers of Russians, already numbed by even longer years of Soviet rule, came to make up a large part of the work force in Estonia, Latvia, and Lithuania.

The combined effects of Soviet rule have kept the Baltics backward compared to Scandinavia and Finland. In the 1930s, living standards in Estonia and Latvia were about like in Finland—if anything, a bit higher. Some sixty years later, however, gleaming Finland is like another world compared to the drab Baltic states. How will the Balts respond to this gap? Will they be willing to work diligently and defer consumption for decades when payoffs do not come quickly? Will they think in optimistic terms— "If Finland can do it, so can we"; or pessimistic terms—"We'll never catch up"?

Despite Soviet rule and despite the modern advances, many Balts do not despise agriculture. There was a considerable back-to-the-land movement in the 1980s. As collective farms are replaced by private ones, Balts will increase their food surpluses.[23] It is unclear whether Baltic products can penetrate West European markets, but the demand for Baltic foods—and light industry products—should remain strong in Russia.

Russia and other ex-Soviet republics will continue to seek food and other exports from the Baltics. Barter deals can surely be worked out (for example, oil for food), but as the ruble and other currencies become convertible, Baltic trade to the east and southeast will become even easier.

Comparing East Asian and Baltic Liabilities and Assets

Let us review the Tigers' assets and liabilities as they were in the 1970s and 1980s, and compare them with the Baltic region's conditions in the 1990s. A plus sign (+) means the Baltics are better off than the Tigers were in a certain respect; a minus (−) they are worse off; and an equal sign (=) means that they are about the same as the Tigers were. In many places, we must use a question mark (?), because sufficient data for comparison is not yet available.

1970s	1990s
The Tigers' Liabilities	*The Baltics*
—Poor resource base	+ (Better resources but more pollution)

---

[23]The first U.S. Peace Corps volunteers reached the Baltics in 1992. Among them were business experts who hoped to share U.S. farm cooperative, accounting, and credit experiences to help restore private agriculture.

—Vulnerability to weather   + (Less vulnerability)
—Dense population   + (Not so dense)
—Small domestic market   − (Much smaller—the Baltic region's
                                      population is only slightly larger
                                      than Hong Kong's)
—External threats (which may also − (Alien occupation backed by a
  stimulate cohesion)   potential Fifth Column of alien
                                      settlers)
—Little democracy (which also may + (More democracy but less
  imply social stability and strong   cohesion)
  leadership)
—Heavy defense burdens   + (Little defense burden but almost
                                      no defensive capacity)

The Tigers' Assets   *The Baltics*

Tangibles

—Location/ports   = (Equally good)
—Economic support from outside   − (As yet, little)
—Inducements to foreign capital   − (Few—laws in flux)
—Investment from outside   − (Many investors bypass the Baltics
                                      for Russia)
—Financing by bank loans   − (Little)

Intangibles

—Fresh start   = (Similar)
—Strong work ethic   ? (Untested)
—High saving and investment   − (Not yet)
—Cheap labor   = (Relative to EC)
—Autonomy for the economic   = (In flux)
  sphere
—Entrepreneurial spirit   ? (Untested)
—Ability to assimilate and innovate ? (Untested)
—Support for education   = (Similar)
—Family-owned enterprises   − (Not yet)
—A pliant and willing labor force − (Spoiled)
—Ethnic homogeneity   − (Native vs. settlers)
—Land reform   ? (In flux)
—Strong government   − (Not yet)
—Industrial/strategic trade policy − (Not yet)
—External political-military   − (Weak)
  support
—Global free trade environment   − (Not in the 1990s)
—A successful local model   − (Not yet but one may emerge in
  (such as Japan) to follow   Eastern Europe)

Lessons

What lessons can the Baltics derive from the East Asian Tigers?

General

Small states can achieve political independence in the face of global anarchy and international conflict. They can improve living standards for large segments of the population despite great obstacles and liabilities. They can strengthen their cultural autonomy despite world trends toward homogenization.

Economic and Social Policy

The essential ingredients for growth are a strong work ethic, high rates of saving and investment, and a commitment to education. These ingredients may not be sufficient in themselves, but they are essential to long-term growth.

Neither East Asian genes nor Confucian traditions are a sufficient or necessary condition for development. If they were sufficient, mainland China would not have remained such a poor country. If they were necessary, the West would not have become rich before Asia.

Devotion to learning and work may be rooted in Calvinism, Confucianism, or other world views. Such habits have been crucial to the rapid advance of Japan and the four Tiger dynamos. But they have also helped Jewish, Chinese, Indian, Farsi, and other migrants globally. Liberated from the restrictions of their own societies, they have flourished in other countries in science and commerce. Like Dr. An Wang in Boston, they prospered with no special protection from their new government. This is a message of hope for the Baltics and other ex-Soviet republics. With a fresh start, hard work could transform their lives.[24]

There is no easy formula by which poor countries with modest resources can become materially rich. But a good starting point is to expand public health and education. The statistical achievements of the Baltics in these areas are eroding, because the necessary infrastructure and basic investments were neglected for decades in the entire Soviet Union. Public health and all areas of education need large injections of enthusiasm, capital, technology, and fresh thinking. Such services are urgent, and not expensive compared to road building and electric grids.

Politics

The optimum role for government in development is not clear. Surely

---

[24]An Wang traveled from China to take up graduate studies at Harvard after World War II. Some twenty-five years later he had become Boston's leading philanthropist. Success was not genetic, however. Wang Computer later crashed under his son's leadership.

government must maintain order, collect taxes, build a modern infrastructure, support education, and create a climate hospitable to domestic and foreign investors. The jury is still out on whether industrial and strategic trade policies are useful or necessary. Laissez faire may have served Hong Kong better than neo-mercantilism did the other Tigers.

It is also undecided what is the ideal blending of economic development and democratic institutions. In East Asia prosperity preceded democracy, but this may not be the ideal formula, especially for European countries still smarting from a long foreign rule.

What is more obvious is the need for prolonged social peace—whether the result of a paternalistic regime as in Singapore, or a democracy based on two or more parties—and to avoid a civil war as in Sri Lanka, Georgia, or Bosnia. With this in mind, the Baltic governments would be wise to conciliate rather than alienate the Russian and other settlers in their midst. Still, Baltic cultural survival is far more tenuous than Chinese or Korean, and warrants stronger measures for protection.

Defense

The Balts need border patrols and forces adequate to maintain internal security. But does it follow that just because three of the Tigers have had large military expenditures, the Baltic states should also spend heavily on defense? Because the Baltic republics are so small, they are unlikely ever to be able to resist larger neighbors such as a resurgent Russia, Germany, or Poland.[25] The Baltics should count instead on diplomacy, collective security, and—if necessary—nonviolent modes of defense such as they used in fending off the Kremlin's Black Berets in 1990-91.

International Law and Order in the 1990s

The international system in the 1990s offers the Baltic region some advantages unknown to the Tigers in the 1970s. Only one of the Tigers was then seated in the United Nations and the ROC's security links with the United States were eroding. In the 1990s, all three Baltic republics belong to the United Nations, to the Conference on Security and Cooperation in Europe, and to a host of European Community working groups (for example, meetings of ministers of transportation). The Baltics benefit from a growing awareness in the West, and even in Moscow, that international institutions must be strengthened to "make peace" as well as "keep peace." Erstwhile threats to the Baltics—Russia, Germany, and perhaps Poland—now appear more interested in business than in aggressive expansion.

---

[25]Estonia and Latvia border Russia directly. They do not benefit from a natural barrier such as the Taiwan Strait, or the U.S. forces that back South Korea at the 38th parallel. The Balts could not have stopped the Red Army in 1919-20 except that Soviet Russia then was harassed from within and without by multiple enemies.

The U.N. Gulf War coalition gave some hope that no state will be permitted to devour another. International institutions operate on the premise that every state is equal and independent. This gives some protection to the Baltics even though they have no formal alliances with friendly powers.

The ascendancy of international institutions and a lessening of great power bullying permitted Latvia in 1992 to pursue opening official relations with the Republic of China as well as the PRC.[26]

Both the four Tigers and the Baltic states profit from a climate in which resorting to force is less thinkable as a way to solve international conflicts. A large portion of the Tigers' ability to maneuver in the world scene is built upon their demonstrated economic prowess as well as shrewd diplomacy. The Baltics are materially weak but they profit, as do all U.N. members, from the legal fiction of sovereign equality.

Value-Creating: The Wealth of Nations

Realists hold that material wealth is the key to state power and influence in world affairs. They advise a kind of neo-mercantilism: government should pursue industrial and strategic trade policies that enhance the state's material bounty. Some idealists call for sharing the wealth; a redistribution between the North's haves and the South's have-nots. Other idealists trust in the natural harmony of global interests: free trade will enable each sector and nation to optimize its interests based on complementarity of resources and needs.

Each of these approaches may have merit in certain times and places. None works as a blanket prescription for humanity. None is guaranteed to fit the Baltic region's needs in the 1990s.

In economics, no less than in politics, it is wiser to pursue value-creation than value-claiming; to search for strategies for mutual gain over the long haul rather than short-term profits.[27] Within each country and between countries internationally, cooperation can net more than zero-sum competition. Secrecy, like exploitative policies, may serve immediate needs but obstruct wealth-creation in the long run. A global perspective is needed to prosper in an interdependent world. Even for large countries such as the United States, no sector of the economy can count merely on dominating the national market. An international outlook is needed, one that asks how best to compete and cooperate with buyers and suppliers around the world.[28]

The major lesson that East Asia offers to other nations is not the

---

[26]Peking suspended its relations with Latvia but left open its ultimate response. Meanwhile, Estonia and Lithuania agreed to establish trade and other relations with Taipei just short of official ties.

[27]David A. Lax and James K. Sebenius, *The Manager as Negotiator: Bargaining for Cooperation and Competitive Gain* (New York: Free Press, 1986).

[28]Michael E. Porter, *The Competitive Advantage of Nations* (New York: Free Press, 1990).

utility of industrial policy but of cooperation: strong ties between suppliers and the marketplace; loyalty by and toward the work force; and loyalty to and by consumers. Such practices and attitudes are virtually unknown anywhere in the ex-Soviet Union.

East Asia's prosperity also confirms the utility of investing for the long term and of seeking out niches in the global market—also alien concepts in the ex-Soviet realm.

The Baltic region teeters between civil peace and civil war. For the moment there is little cooperation among the three Baltic states or within them. Even among native Estonians and native Latvians, suspicion and jealousy overshadow efforts to build a new life as ex-gulag prisoners accuse ex-Communists of greed and betrayal. One legacy of Communism is to trust almost no one and to share ideas only with a handful of friends.

Trust and openness cost almost nothing, but they entail risks that few Balts are ready to take. Like other ex-Soviets, Balts have been schooled too long in Lenin's view that all life is a question of *"kto kovo*—who [will destroy] whom?'' Caution is necessary lest one become a sucker or martyr; but excessive cynicism makes mutual gain impossible. It condemns each party to the inevitable losses suffered by the diffident players in a Prisoner's Dilemma.

The Outlook

Differences of time and place make comparisons between East Asia and the Baltic states precarious. Serendipity and synergy—positive and negative—can upset all predictions. Still, this is a world in which mice *can* roar—especially if they believe they can drown out the dragons and bears.

About the Contributors

Tzong-Ho Bau is Professor of Political Science at National Taiwan University and President of the Chinese Political Science Association. He is the author of *Chung-hua-min-kuo Chung-tung cheng-ts'e san-shih-nien hui-ku* (The ROC's policy toward the Middle East: 1956-86) and *T'ai-hai liang-an hu-tung te li-lun yü cheng-ts'e mien-hsiang: 1950-89* (Interaction between the two sides of the Taiwan Strait: Theory and policy, 1950-89).

Maria Hsia Chang is an Associate Professor of Political Science at the University of Nevada, Reno. She is the author of *The Chinese Blue Shirt Society: Fascism and Developmental Nationalism* and co-author of a number of other works on the ROC and mainland China affairs.

Chu-yuan Cheng, Professor of Economics and Chairman of the Asian Studies Committee at Ball State University, Muncie, Indiana, is the author of more than twenty books, including *Behind the Tiananmen Massacre: Social, Political, and Economic Ferment in China*.

Tuan Y. Cheng is an Associate Research Fellow at the Institute of International Relations, National Chengchi University, Taipei.

Hungdah Chiu is Professor of Law at the University of Maryland. He is the author of *The Capacity of International Organizations to Conclude Treaties* and *The People's Republic of China and the Law of Treaties*, and co-author of *People's China and International Law: A Documentary Study* and *Criminal Justice in Post-Mao China: Analysis and Documents*. He edited *China and the Question of Taiwan, China and the Taiwan Issue*, and *Agreements of the People's Republic of China, 1966-1980: A Calendar of Events*, and co-edited *Agreements of the People's Republic of China, 1949-1967: A Calendar, Law in Chinese Foreign Policy*, and *China: Seventy Years After the 1911 Hsin-hai Revolution*. He has also contributed numerous articles to various academic journals.

Walter C. Clemens, Jr., Professor of Political Science at Boston University, is the author of *Baltic Independence and Russian Empire*.

Ralph N. Clough is a Professorial Lecturer at the School of Advanced International Studies, Johns Hopkins University, Washington, D.C. He is a retired foreign service officer who served in Taiwan, Hong Kong, and mainland China. His publications include *Island China, Embattled Korea,* and *Reaching Across the Taiwan Strait* (1993).

Jyh-Pin Fa is Professor of Law at National Chengchi University.

Karl J. Fields is an Assistant Professor in the Department of Politics and Government, the University of Puget Sound, Tacoma, Washington, and author of several articles on East Asian political economy.

Gerrit W. Gong is Director of Asian Studies at the Center for Strategic and International Studies (CSIS), Washington, D.C.

Gottfried-Karl Kindermann is Professor and Director of the Center for International Politics, University of Munich. He is the author of, among others, *Sun Yat-sen: Founder and Symbol of China's Revolutionary Nation-Building* and *Grundelemente der Weltpolitik* (Basic elements of world politics).

Kenneth Lieberthal, Professor of Political Science at the University of Michigan, is the author of *Sino-Soviet Conflict in the 1970s,* and co-author of *Research Guide to Central Party and Government Meetings in China, 1949-1987* (with Bruce Dickson) and *Policy Making in China: Leaders, Structures, and Process* (with Michel Oksenberg).

Françoise Mengin is a doctoral candidate at the Fondation Nationale des Sciences Politiques, Paris.

Niu Yuanming is a research intern at the Modern Asia Research Center, Geneva.

Jan S. Prybyla, Professor of Economics at the Pennsylvania State University, is the author of *The Chinese Economy: Problems and Policies, Market and Plan Under Socialism: The Bird in the Cage,* and *Reform in China and Other Socialist Economies.*

Philippe Régnier, Director of the Modern Asia Research Center, Geneva, is co-editor of *Investment Flows between Asia and Europe: What Strategies for the Future?*

Gee San is a Professor in the Department of Economics and Graduate Institute of Industrial Economics, National Central University. He is co-author of *In-Service Training in Taiwan, ROC* and has contributed many articles to various professional journals.

David Shambaugh is Senior Lecturer in Chinese Politics at the School of

Oriental and African Studies, University of London, and Editor of *The China Quarterly*.

Wen-hui Tsai is Professor of Sociology at Indiana University-Purdue University at Fort Wayne, Indiana.

An-chia Wu is a Research Fellow at the Institute of International Relations, National Chengchi University, Taipei. He is the author of numerous articles and books on mainland Chinese politics.

Jaushieh Joseph Wu is an Associate Research Fellow at the Institute of International Relations, National Chengchi University, Taipei.

Zhang Ruijun is a research intern at the Modern Asia Research Center, Geneva.

INDEX